Rafael Hirschfeld (Ed.)

Financial Cryptography

Second International Conference, FC '98
Anguilla, British West Indies
February 23-25, 1998
Proceedings

 Springer

Series Editors

Gerhard Goos, Karlsruhe University, Germany
Juris Hartmanis, Cornell University, NY, USA
Jan van Leeuwen, Utrecht University, The Netherlands

Volume Editor

Rafael Hirschfeld
Unipay Technologies
Prinsengracht 748, 1017 LC Amsterdam, The Netherlands
E-mail: unipay@xs4all.nl

Cataloging-in-Publication data applied for

Die Deutsche Bibliothek - CIP-Einheitsaufnahme

Financial cryptography : second international conference ; proceedings / FC
'98, Anguilla, British West Indies, February 23 - 25, 1998. Rafael Hirschfeld
(ed.). - Berlin ; Heidelberg ; New York ; Barcelona ; Budapest ; Hong Kong ;
London ; Milan ; Paris ; Singapore ; Tokyo : Springer, 1998
  (Lecture notes in computer science ; Vol. 1465)
  ISBN 3-540-64951-4

CR Subject Classification (1991): E.3, D.4.6, K.6.5, J.1, C.2

ISSN 0302-9743
ISBN 3-540-64951-4 Springer-Verlag Berlin Heidelberg New York

© Springer-Verlag Berlin Heidelberg 1998
Printed in Germany

Typesetting: Camera-ready by author
SPIN 10638499   06/3142 – 5 4 3 2 1 0   Printed on acid-free paper

Preface

Following the success of the first Financial Cryptography conference in 1997, a second meeting was held in February 1998, again on the Caribbean island of Anguilla, and drew an even larger group of attendees. The conference struck a chord among participants with a broad range of backgrounds who share a common concern with the security of digital commerce, and it provided a forum for the fertile exchange of ideas among this diverse group.

Submissions to this year's conference, and hence the resulting program, were quite strong. Compared to the previous year, however, they tended to focus more on technical issues and less on policy. Policy issues were covered in panel and roundtable discussions scheduled in separate sessions. One panel discussion, moderated by Barbara Fox on the topic of certificate revocation, was included in the scientific program, and the panelists have provided summaries of their remarks for the printed proceedings.

An informal rump session provided an opportunity for presentation of the latest results and work in progress. One of these was an attack on a cipher presented at FC97. A brief summary of this result is included at the end of this volume; a fuller version has been submitted for presentation elsewhere. With this exception, the papers appear in the order in which they were presented at the conference. These are revised versions of the accepted submissions. Revisions were not checked on their scientific aspects, and the authors bear full responsibility for the contents of their papers.

Many people deserve thanks for their contributions to the success of FC98. Robert Hettinga and Vincent Cate were responsible for the general arrangements, and the smooth operation of the conference was due to them. Ian Goldberg led the post-conference workshop, and Blanc Weber was responsible for the exhibition and sponsorship and also took on a variety of other tasks. Thanks are due to the members of the program committee for their efforts in evaluating the submissions and selecting the program, and of course to the authors, without whose contributions there could be no conference. I am especially grateful to Matthew Franklin, whose assistance as Co-Chair, particularly in helping to resolve crises when they arose, was invaluable.

June 1998

Rafael Hirschfeld
FC98 Program Chair

Financial Cryptography '98
Anguilla, BWI
23–25 February 1998

Program Committee

Matt Blaze, AT&T Laboratories, Florham Park, NJ, USA
Antoon Bosselaers, Katholieke Universiteit Leuven, Leuven, Belgium
Yves Carlier, Bank for International Settlements, Basel, Switzerland
Walter Effross, Washington College of Law, American U., Washington DC, USA
Matthew Franklin (Co-Chair), AT&T Laboratories, Florham Park, NJ, USA
Michael Froomkin, U. Miami School of Law, Coral Gables, FL, USA
Rafael Hirschfeld (Chair), Unipay Technologies, Amsterdam, The Netherlands
Alain Mayer, Bell Laboratories/Lucent Technologies, Murray Hill, NJ, USA
Moni Naor, Weizmann Institute of Science, Rehovot, Israel
Frank Trotter, Mark Twain Ecash/Mercantile Bank, St. Louis, MO, USA
Doug Tygar, Carnegie Mellon University, Pittsburgh, PA, USA
Moti Yung, CertCo LLC, New York, NY, USA

General Chairs

Robert Hettinga, Shipwright, Boston, MA, USA
Vincent Cate, Offshore Information Services, Anguilla, BWI

Exhibits and Sponsorship Manager

Blanc Weber, Seattle, WA, USA

Workshop Leader

Ian Goldberg, Berkeley, CA, USA

Financial Cryptography '98 was held in cooperation with the International Association for Cryptologic Research and was sponsored by RSA Data Security, C2NET, Hansa Bank & Trust Company, Sicherheit und Privat- International Bank, Offshore Information Services, and e$.

Table of Contents

Micro-Payments via Efficient Coin-Flipping
(EXTENDED ABSTRACT)

Richard J. Lipton[1]   Rafail Ostrovsky[2]

[1] Department of Computer Science, Princeton University, Princeton, NJ and
Bellcore, USA Email: `rjlv@cs.princeton.edu`.
[2] Bell Communications Research, 445 South St., MCC 1C-365B, Morristown, NJ
07960-6438, USA. Email: `rafail@bellcore.com`.

Abstract. We present an authenticated coin-flipping protocol and its
proof of security. We demonstrate the applicability of our scheme for on-
line randomized micro-payment protocols. We also review some essential aspects of other micro-payment proposals (including SET, PayWord
and MicroMint, PayTree, NetCheque, NetCash, Agora, NetCard, CAFE,
Pederson's proposal, micro-iKP, Milicent, proposal of Jarecki-Odlyzko,
proposal of Yacobi, SVP, DigiCash, Rivest's "Lottery tickets as Micro-
Cash" and Wheeler's proposal) and compare it with our scheme.

1   Design Principles and Parameters

This paper presents another micro-payment scheme, designed for world-wide web
applications. It avoids many shortcomings of previous schemes. In particular,
our scheme can support tiny transactions (like buying individual web-pages)
at (amortized) cost of a fraction of a cent per web-page. We give an overview
of other existing proposals and compare it with our scheme. In the heart of
our construction is a new, on-line, fair and authenticated coin-flipping protocol,
which is of independent interest and could be used in other settings as well. We
start by surveying the setting and parameters considered.

THE PARTICIPANTS: As in all the payment schemes, the main participants are
the User $\mathcal{U}$ who wishes to get some information (i.e., a web page) from some
Vendor $\mathcal{V}$ (i.e. from some web site, like on-line Encyclopedia Britannica). Vendor
$\mathcal{V}$ wants to get paid for the provided information, while the User $\mathcal{U}$ wishes to pay
only for the information that she gets. We operate in the setting where neither
Vendors nor Users trust each other, hence, Vendors wish to make sure that they
get paid for the provided information, while Users wish to make sure that they
are not "over-charged" for the services that they did not get. Additionally, there
is the third party, a Broker (or a Bank) $\mathcal{B}$ which assists in various ways for
fund transfer between users and vendors and tries to detect/prevent various
fraud of dishonest Users and Vendors. In the simplest setting, the Broker (or a
Bank) is assumed to be trusted. More generally, some schemes do not assume
that Brokers/Banks are trusted, and then introduce one or two more additional
participants, such as central authority and/or one or several arbiters in order to
resolve disputes and provide checks on other participants.

DESIGN OBJECTIVES: One of our goals is to minimize the computational requirements of our scheme. For micro-payments, this means minimizing public-key

cryptography in favor of faster private-key— and hash-function— based schemes. For example, as [27] point out: "as a rough guide, hash functions are about 100 times faster than RSA signature verification, and about 10,000 times faster then RSA signature generation: on a typical workstation, one can sign two messages per second, verify 200 signatures per second and compute 20,000 hash function values per second." (We remark that cryptographic hash-functions are in many of the above applications used solely as one-way functions which are one-way on their iterates – technically a weaker property then collision-resistance.) We also remark that private-key cryptography (for example, pseudo-random generators) is often even more efficient. Summarizing, one of our design objectives is to make use of efficient one-way functions (like MD5 [26]) and/or private-key cryptography and to minimize the use of digital signatures. Additionally, we wish to minimize the communication (both the number of rounds and the number of bits transmitted) per transaction, between all the parties, as well as computational requirements of our scheme and memory requirements for all the participants. We also wish to minimize potential fraud, which we elaborate upon further after reviewing previous proposals. To summarize, we wish to optimize the following parameters:

- minimize the number of rounds of interaction per transaction between users and vendors and between the bank/broker and users and vendors;
- minimize the number of total bits transmitted per transaction between users, vendors and the bank/broker;
- minimize the computational demands needed per transaction for all the participants (i.e. minimizing the use of digital signatures in favor of less-expensive means — see above);
- minimize hardware requirements for all the participants (i.e. eliminate and/or minimize the use of large databases of revocation lists or other "per-transaction" lists; and/or the need of smart-cards; and/or expensive hardware for pre-processing);
- minimize fraud (to be discussed in below after surveying other schemes.)

Additionally, we discuss the issue of anonymity, which plays a role in some micro-payment schemes, such as DigiCash [8]. Informally, the goal of anonymity is to minimize the user identification (both to the vendor and to the bank) when purchases are made. We remark that our schemes can be made anonymous as well.

OUR RESULT: In the heart of our construction is an authenticated coin-flipping protocol. The protocol requires evaluation (and transmission) of only two hash functions per coin-flip after the initial setup. The *authentication* in our protocols guarantees (among other things) that the vendor can request a third party (such as bank/arbiter) to verify what the outcome of the coin-flip should be, and if the protocol is aborted in the middle, to prove (to arbiter/bank) what the outcome is and insist on the resumption from the right point in the protocol execution.

We show how our protocols can be utilized to efficiently implement a coin flipping protocol of [31] where with some small probability (say, $\frac{1}{200}$) the user pays a larger (say, 1$ dollar) amount. Notice that the *expected* cost per transaction in the above example is half a cent, while the *expected* overhead of handling the payment is now two hundred times smaller, thus allowing us to use (in the event of the "payment"-outcome coin-flip) an alternative, slow but secure payment mechanism. Our scheme is related to that of [24, 25], but with some important differences, especially in the setup stage. We discuss these differences and why they seem to be essential for the proof of security. In summary, the main technical contribution of this paper is the design of *fair* and *authenticated* coin-flipping protocol together with its proof of security.

2 Previous Schemes and Techniques

CREDIT-CARD SETTING AND ON-LINE SCHEMES: In the current credit-card setting, every transaction is on-line, where whenever some customer wishes to pay a vendor, the Bank is always contacted. In particular, the Bank gets a request to transfer money from user's account to vendor's account. In order to do so, the bank first verifies that the customer's account is in good standing (which requires a database lookup) and then gives to the vendor a validation number for the transaction. If Vendor's account is with a different Bank, this contact is also made at some point in time, different for different schemes. The cost per such transaction is about 10 cents, and hence is not financially viable for tiny-cost transactions. Moreover, since the Bank must maintain 99.99% availability, even during peak traffic time (Anderson at. all. [1] mention that typically 1pm on the Saturday before Christmas is such a peak-time) this requires additional cost in order to maintain capability for additional throughput and backup systems.

The main source of fraud in the current credit-card practice is from stolen [credit-card number, expiration-date] information, which can (and is) used to impersonate users.

SET: Recently, Visa and Master-card developed a SET on-line analog of the credit-card setting, where digital signatures are used to authenticate all three parties (i.e. users, vendors and banks), so that an adversary who wire-taps all the communications, still can not impersonate users, since he can not forge signatures (for further details and features, see [30]). However, since signature generation and verification is required for all the parties, and since the Bank must be present on-line for every transaction, SET is clearly not suitable for tiny web-related transactions.

NetBill: NetBill [6] is another on-line protocol (it has additional features like atomicity – i.e. customer pays only for messages that he gets; and anonymity via pseudonyms). It requires eight messages for each transaction and on-line communication with the intermediary NetBill server for each transaction.

Electronic currency: DigiCash; NetCash. In electronic currency schemes, a user deposits some amount of money into the bank, that in return gives some digital data representing "Electronic currency" (also called an electronic "coin"). In its simplest form, electronic currency is an authenticated (by the bank) serial number. Of course, the danger with any such scheme is double-spending (i.e. where a user or someone else "spends" the same "coin" more the once). There are several ways to combat this: one is to insist on the on-line check (with the

Bank) to verify if the coin have been already spent; the second is for the Bank to pay for each coin only once [27]; the third is to incorporate the identity of the user (who bought an electronic coin) into the coin itself, so that if it is spent twice, the known user will be prosecuted. A twist proposed by Chaum is to also have anonymity, where again Bank keeps track which "coins" have been spent, but where DigiCash [8] in case of double-spending reveals the identity of the User (for later prosecution – see also [9]). The issue, of course, is when to check for double-spending. One possibility (which *is* what Chaum's [8] current implementation does) is to do the check on-line, the other possibility is to check off-line, running the risk that the user will spend huge sums of money and then disappear, when discovering fraudulent activity is too late. Another "electronic currency" scheme is that of Medvinsky and Newman "NetCash" scheme [19]. The twist there is that they keep track only of the outstanding "tokens" (i.e. those that have been issued but have not been deposited), compared to Chaum's scheme where comparison with all tokens ever issued must be made. Never-the-less, all these schemes must either be on-line, or stand the risk of "huge-spending-with-quick-gateway" attack.

NetCheque: University of Southern California NetCheque (TM) project [21] is another on-line scheme, where users issue checks for vendors using (as a cer-tificates of the validity of a check) a private-key cryptography (shared between a user and a bank.) This scheme is more efficient then public-key signatures, but requires registration of users at the banks and then subsequent clearance (i.e. checking by the bank of the validity of the private-key authentication) of checks by the bank to verify both correctness of the check and the availability of funds in user's account. Neuman and Medvinsky [21] argue that such on-line verification can be in some cases done off-line, but then the fraud (of bad checks) becomes as issue.

HARDWARE-BASED SCHEMES In hardware-based schemes, one assumes the ex-istence of temper-resistant smart-cards, which contain private-keys, but such that this private-keys can not be extracted from the card without destroying its contents. This, in principle, allows to use faster private-key cryptographic means. One such example is the proposal of Stern and Vaudeny [29]. They of-fer a scheme where every smart card contains a master private key for MAC (i.e., private-key Message Authentication Codes). Every Vendor is given such a tamper-resistant smart card. Users buy from the bank "tokens" which are authenticated with banks private-key authentication mechanism. When a user wishes to make a payment, it gives the token that was provided by the bank to the Vendor's tamper-resistant devise which then verifies that it is a valid pay-ment, and then gets paid from the bank. The idea is that the private key is known only by the bank, yet all vendors can verify that users provide correct private-key authentication tags, since they all have smart-cards with the banks private key. Again, clearance of this payments can be done either on-line (to prevent double-spending) or off-line (with black-listing double-spending users) as before. The drawback of this scheme is that if the unique bank's key on each of the vendors smart cards is recovered by an adversary, the security is lost. That is, the single private-key of the bank is distributed to every device, hence break-ing even a single tamper-resistant device completely compromises the scheme. They suggest an extension which uses logarithmic (in the number of users) keys, and authenticating with all of them, but this, while it prevents the above threat makes the proposal less efficient.

Various "electronic-wallet" hardware-based solutions are proposed by Mondex [18] and others, such as Yacobi e-war [32]. There are basically two different approaches. The first approach is to keep the actual counter on the card – which increases/decreases during transactions, where the counter denotes the actual cash value (up to a certain limit). Since the counter is on the tamper-proof device it can not be increased. Of course, if one can artificially increase the counter, this leads to money forgery. Another approach, is to keep digitally signed (by the bank) coins, where the only goal of the tamper-resistant device is to prevent double-spending [32] (where various methods (either on-line or off-line and/or probabilistic) are made to detect if some coin is spent twice and by what smart-card – the scheme requires revocation lists and if not done on-line has some over-spending threat.)

Rivest and Shamir's Micro-Mint [27] propose to run (using huge off-line computations) schemes which find collisions of (properly tuned, only somewhat hard to find) collisions of collision-free hash-functions, to be used instead of signatures. This guarantees that forging is hard (basically using birthday-paradox type argument) but still duplication easy. They argue that duplication is not an issue since every coin will be paid only once (which requires storage of all the coins as well).

SUBSCRIPTION SCHEMES: Many large vendors, sell *subscriptions* for certain websites. Examples include $ 40 year-based subscription to on-line Wall-Street journal and $ 150 year-based subscription to Encyclopedia Britannica. The subscription payment is performed only once a year (by various means). Clearly, one of the drawbacks is that infrequent customers are not willing to pay a relatively high subscription cost. Moreover, the subscription-method is not suitable for "infrequently used" vendors of specialized information (like consumer reports information on how to purchase a new car). Besides, there is only so many subscriptions any user will sign-on, even if the cost of subscription is falling. In summary, while subscription-based approaches are and will be in use, an additional micro-payment approaches are needed as well.

Another variant on the subscription scheme is a *registration scheme* where first, customers *register* with the Vendor and prove its identity and then Vendors regularly *charge* them for transactions made. One such scheme is the "Chrg-http' protocol [7]. The drawback is the cost of registration, and, of subsequent unpaid charges.

In light of the above, the development for tiny "per-use" payments schemes received considerable attention in the last two years. Below, we review various proposals.

COUPON-BASED SCHEMES DIGITAL's *Milicent* [11] is basically a private-key solution, where there is a "broker" which sells "vendor-specific" coins. Vendor-specific coin can only be authenticated by this vendor using vendor's private key (recall that the private-key authentication is much cheaper than public-key). Of course this solution requires "brokers" who must be trusted, and who should have agreements with vendors.

Another coupon-based family of (similar to each other) solutions is Rivest and Shamir's *PayWord*, [27], Anderson's *NetCard* [1], Pederson's at. al. scheme [23], Jutla and Yung *PayTree* [22] and Hauser at. al *micro-iKP* [15]. The top-level idea of all this schemes is basically one of Lamport's [17] (also used for S/key [14]), and it is as follows: take a one-way permutation f (or a hash-function or a one-way function which is one-way on its iterates), pick a random input x, and iterate it some sufficiently large number of times (say a 1000) (i.e. compute $y = f(f(f \ldots (f(x)))))$, then authenticate y (i.e. sign y and perhaps user's ID with banks public key signature). Now we have a *chain* of values of the form $f^{-1}(y), f^{-1}(f^{-1}(y)) \ldots x$ with the property that given any prefix of this chain, it is hard to compute the next pre-image (since it involves inverting a one-way permutation) but easy to verify that this chain leads back to an authenticated y. The idea is for the bank to issue such $(x, y, bank's\ signature(y))$ triple to the user (for the appropriate fee), where every inverse is a single micro-payment. The user, when he wishes to make a payment to the Vendor, gives y (with appropriate banks public-key authentication of y – this is a one-time setup operation) to the Vendor, but then for each subsequent payment just gives the next inverse in the above chain. Jutla and Yung [22] generalize this chains to trees in a natural way. The drawback of all this schemes is double-spending, where to combat this the two approaches being taken are either to check on-line (which is expensive) or to black-list users (which is somewhat expensive too, and may not be sufficient if user's identity can be easily changed/forged).

PROBABILISTIC SCHEMES The probabilistic schemes can be divided into two categories: probabilistic checking and probabilistic payment. We first outline the probabilistic checking schemes and then describe the two previous probabilistic payment schemes.

The first two probabilistic checking protocols are **probabilistic audit** Agora protocol of Gabber and Silberschatz [10], and Jareski and Odlyzko probabilistic polling [16]. The idea there is basically as follows: the user gives (signed) promisory notes to the vendor, which the vendor later "cashes" to the bank, but when exactly this happens is done probabilistically, in order to limit the amount of over-spending. This approach combines (expensive) on-line approach of always verifying that the user has the money in his account (witch is communication-expensive) and the off-line credit-based solution (which leads to over-spending/black-listing solution.) Here the over-spending (by tuning the rate with which vendor talks to the bank to be a probabilistic function depending of the transaction size) can be limited. The drawback is similar to coupon-based schemes, namely the requirement that in case of detected over-spending the vendors/banks must "black-list" users (and, hence keep such databases) and to inform all vendors of bad users [16], as well as keeping, by each Vendor the list of revoked users [10].

The combination of software-based and **hardware-based solution with probabilistic audit** was suggested by Yacobi's e-war [32] project at Microsoft. In [32] Yacobi proposes smart-card id-based wallets that keep signed by the bank coins. Notice that the new coins can not be forged since only bank can sign, and the duplication is controlled using hardware where probabilistic checking is used to prevent double-spending. This solution requires both software and hardware, and can still take some amount of over-spending, though the amount can (as in the previous scheme) be made limited. The drawback is the need to black-list users/smart-cards and keep this databases around as above.

The final category of the probabilistic schemes is the so-called **probabilistic payment** category. Our scheme belongs in this category as well. The two other scheme in this category is Rivest's "lottery tickets as Micro-Cash" [24, 25] and Wheeler's "Transactions Using Bets" [31].

The [24] and [25] differ, and we review both. The idea of [24] scheme is for the bank to issue for each user a book of "lottery tickets" as follows: As in coupon-based schemes, the bank, picks a random x, computes $y = f(f(f \ldots (f(x))))$ for f a one-way permutation or a cryptographically-strong hash function, then authenticates y (i.e. signs y and perhaps user's ID with banks public key signature). Now we have a *chain* of values of the form $f^{-1}(y), f^{-1}(f^{-1}(y)) \ldots x$ which is a "lottery book" of tickets (for each user and each vendor that the user wishes to talk to), where for each micro-payment transaction, the user pays with the next pre-image from this book (just like the coupon-based scheme.) The twist here is that the bank, later on announces one of the tickets from each book as a "winning ticket". If the user did not give this winning ticket to a Vendor (since it stopped early and did not use the entire book), it does not have to pay anything, if it did, it is responsible for the winning ticket (i.e. the bank will pay the amount to the Vendor upon Vendor's presentation of the winning ticket and will subtract it from user's account). It is important to note that the "lottery" is held *after* the book in question (say for this day) is no longer in use, otherwise the user could always avoid giving out the winning ticket. The advantage of the scheme is that if, say, half of the lottery tickets from a book have been used, then with probability one-half the user will not have to pay, thus making the amortized cost of transactions less costly. The drawback is the Bank's overhead of holding lotteries and having to check the results as well as the issue of timing (since the payments to the Vendor can be made only after the lottery is announced, at which time the user may not have sufficient funds in its account.) In cite [25] (independently of our work) Rivest extends [24] suggestion using [31] approach and two chains, similar to our approach, but with some important differences. We first describe Wheeler's suggestion [31]:

The second probabilistic micro-payment scheme is the protocol of Wheeler "Transactions Using Bets" [31], where he suggests, similar to our scheme to decide probabilistically whether the payment should be made. In particular, he suggests for the user and vendor to execute a standard coin-flipping protocol [2] (vendor commits a random number to the user, then user sends a guess of this number to the vendor, then vendor de-commits) in order for the user and vendor to decide if the user should pay. One of the aspects not addressed by the paper, is that the user should not be able to deny that the coin-flip protocol execution took place, and hence that he has to pay the agreed-upon amount in case of an unfavorable coin-flip. A natural way of dealing with this problem is to introduce digital signatures into the protocol, so that the vendor can prove (to a bank/arbiter) that this interaction took place. However the use of signatures makes the protocol inefficient. Another drawback of the [31] protocol is the danger that the protocol is aborted in the middle of the execution. Indeed this is a serious problem, since if the seller/user are allowed to abort the coin-flipping protocols and re-try again, the probabilities can be altered. This problem is indeed mentioned in the [31] paper, but no solution how to resolve this problem is given. In the current paper, we show how both problems can be resolved in an efficient manner.

The most related (to our scheme) is the work of Rivest [25], which suggests for the user and vendor to exchange roots of two chains, and show inverses in order to define coin-flips. However, there are several crucial differences in the two approaches, especially in the setup stage. We discuss specific differences in two schemes (and why they seem to be essential for the proof of security) after we preset our scheme.

3 Our Scheme

Our scheme is a probabilistic payment scheme. It involves probabilistic polynomial-time user, vendor and the bank. It is probabilistic in the same sense as [31] and [25]: User and Vendor are going to flip (appropriately biased) coin flips, so that with small probability (for example, with probability $\frac{1}{200}$ the user will have to pay a larger amount (for example, 1$ dollar charge) and the rest of the time it has a free access. Notice that the expected price per page in above example is thus half a cent.

Now, we need to define the properties needed from our coin-flipping protocol. Of course, one of the properties is efficiency (i.e. we should try to avoid costly digital signatures as much as possible.) Additionally, we need *fairness* and *authentication* properties.

Our coin-flip protocol mainly involves two probabilistic polynomially bounded players (i.e. algorithms) – a Vendor and a User (both polynomially bounded by a security parameter). We operate in the public-key setting, where both User and Vendor have public/private signature key pairs [12] (authenticated by the trusted third party, such as a Bank). The protocol proceeds in rounds. The rounds are divided into a pre-processing stage and polynomially-bounded subsequent on-line "coin-flip" rounds. After the initial pre-processing stage, if the Vendor and the User do not abort during this pre-processing stage, the sequence of future output "coin-flips" is uniquely defined. More specifically, every additional round reveals one (or several) coin-flips which was defined in the pre-processing stage (where a round consists of two messages one from User to Vendor and another from Vendor to User). Of course, within each round, one of the players (who already received a message of this round but did not yet send his message of this round) can efficiently compute the outcome of this round coin-flip before the other player. We are not trying to prevent this asymmetry, but rather we require that all the coin-flips associated with *future* rounds are pseudo-random for both players (for definitions of pseudo-randomness, see [3, 33].) More specifically, we say that the coin-flipping protocol is *fair* if the following three conditions are satisfied:

- If both players follow the protocol then there are no aborts.
- For all probabilistic polynomial-time Adversary-User algorithms, if the Vendor follows the protocol and does not abort in the pre-processing stage, then all the coin-flips are uniquely defined and for any non-aborting prefix of the protocol execution, the coin-flips of future rounds are pseudo-random for the Adversary-User.

– For all probabilistic polynomial-time Adversary-Vendor algorithms, if the User follows the protocol and does not abort in the pre-processing stage, then all the coin-flips are uniquely defined and for any non-aborting prefix of the protocol execution, the coin-flips of future rounds are pseudo-random for the Adversary-Vendor.

Additionally, we say that the coin-flipping protocol is Vendor-*authenticated* if it allows the Vendor to convince a third party what the outcome of the coin-flip is, given the transcript of the protocol execution (and an authenticated public key).

We satisfy these properties in the following protocol. First, the bank issues to the user certified public/private key pair for digital signatures. Then every time the user wishes to start making micro-payments to some Vendor, User and Vendor participate in the following two-stage coin-flipping process, assuming the existence of a one-way permutation f:

– SETUP
First, user and vendor run the following setup protocol:

s1. Vendor: The Vendor picks a random x and computes a *chain* of values (just as in coupon-based scheme) to produce a $y = f(f(f \ldots (x)))$. The Vendor sends y to the User.
After y is sent, the Vendor gives to the User a zero-knowledge proof of knowledge of x (using standard cut-and-choose methods – for definitions and further references see [5]).

s2. User: The User checks a zero-knowledge proof of knowledge of the Vendor (and if rejecting, aborts.) If the proof is accepting, then the User picks a random x' and computes a *chain* of values $y' = f(f(f \ldots (x')))$. The User signs and sends (y, y') (together with it's signature) to the Vendor.
After (y, y') is sent, the User gives to the Vendor a zero-knowledge proof of knowledge of x'.

s3. Vendor: The Vendor verifies user's proof of knowledge, user's signature and user's public key (if incorrect aborts.)

– COIN-FLIP
Now we are ready for the efficient coin-flip stage. Recall that both y and y' define roots of the two chains. To make the next coin-flip the user and the vendor execute the following protocol round:

c1. User: The User reveals to the Vendor its next pre-image in the y' chain.

c2. Vendor: the Vendor reveals to the user its next pre-image of the y chain. For both chains, one can associate hard-core bits with each pre-image (in fact up to logarithmically-many hard-core bits [13]) The xor of hard-core bits from y and y' chains define the coin-flip output for this round.

Before we proceed to describe the properties of the protocol, let us answer several frequently asked questions regarding our protocol:

REMARKS:

- One of the frequently asked questions regarding the design of the above protocol is: why is it necessary for both the user and the vendor to give zero-knowledge proofs of knowledge? (In fact, Rivest's scheme [25] omits the proofs of knowledge and does not use the hard-core bits [13].) The actual reason comes from a formal proof, but let us briefly mention the technical problem: in order to show that the scheme is fair for the User/Vendor, we must show that if the User/Vendor can predict future coin-flips (and, say, abort the protocol if the coin-flips are extremely unfavorable), then we can use such a predicting User/Vendor to invert a one-way function, thus reaching a contradiction. Now, the problem of using such an algorithm is that the prediction of the future coin-flips *does not* directly give us information regarding hard-core bits of the individual chains, but rather of the xor of two hard-core bits of both chains. Since one of this two hard-core bits does in fact belong to the predicting User/Vendor (and he does not need to disclose this hard-core bit) the prediction of the future coin-flips does not seem to help in predicting the corresponding hard-core bits in the other chain.
- Another problem of eliminating proofs of knowledge is that the user can set $y' = y$, which will certainly not make the future coin-flips pseudo-random. One can try to play with definitions, and say that only *revealed* coin-flips should be pseudo-random, but since the proofs of knowledge seem to be needed for the security proof anyway, we do not see any advantage of working with this less natural definition.
- One possible criticism of our scheme is that while the on-line stage is extremely efficient, a pre-processing stage is somewhat expensive. Indeed, zero-knowledge proofs of knowledge are the main source of inefficiency in our scheme. Yet, we do not know how to make the proof of security go through without such a pre-processing stage due to the reasons indicated above.
- We should also compare our coin-flipping protocol and the coupon-based schemes, such as PayWord [27]. The main advantage of our scheme is that the actual payments can be done very infrequently. Hence, in the (infrequent) case that the user has to pay, we can afford expensive on-line processing, including the on-line secure payment and receipts, thus eliminating the need for black-lists of credit-based approaches that were needed to prevent double-spending. Note that if the user refuses to pay the necessary amount the Vendor has a proof that the user has to pay which it can take to the bank/arbiter (since it has signed by the user (y, y') pair as well as the necessary inverses for both chains with the right properties.) Thus, we stress that in our scheme the (infrequent) payment can be done on-line, avoiding drawbacks of credit-based approaches and double-spending. We should point out that our proposal also differs from [25] in this regard, namely the scheme of [25] is proposed to be used as a credit-based scheme. In contrast, we suggest that in case of the Vendor-favorable coin-flip the payment will be made on-line, thus avoiding the drawbacks of credit-based approach. Since the payment is very infrequent we can in this case afford to do expensive on-line processing.

- There is another asymmetry in our protocol, namely that the user signs the value (y, y') while the vendor does not sign anything. The reason is that the Vendor in any event has a lot of control which information to provide to the user (and in fact can always provide bad, incomplete or incorrect information) and the way this is combatted in the business world is that the vendor gets bad publicity, loses customers, etc. (In particular, if the customer does not get the desired "free" information, it will simply stop interacting with the current Vendor.) We stress, though, that in our scheme, even a cheating vendor can not influence the outcome of the coin-flip and make the customer pay more "frequently".

- Notice that in the coin-flipping stage, the Vendor learns the value of the coin first. This is important, since otherwise, the user can stop the interaction if he discovers that he has to pay. Additionally, note that it is strait-forward to make biased coin-flips by combining several unbiased bits. Further, note that each iteration of the permutation can produce many (in fact, up to logarithmically many) hard-core bits [13] leading to further savings.

- Analogous to coupon-based PayTree scheme of Jutla and Yung [22], our scheme can be made more efficient by using tree-based construction for coin-flips.

We now list some of the properties of our protocol.

Claim 1 *If both players did not abort in the setup stage, then the coin-flips are uniquely defined.*

Proof: Since f is a one-way permutation, and y, y' are fixed, their pre-images and hard-core bits are uniquely defined. ∎

Claim 2 *Assume that one-way permutations exist and that the Vendor follows the protocol. Then, for any polynomially-bounded Adversary-User if the pre-processing stage is not aborted by the Vendor then for any prefix of the protocol execution the coin-flips of subsequent rounds are pseudo-random for the Adversary-User.*

Proof: Assume not. Then there exists probabilistic polynomial-time Adversary-User algorithm which after the (non-aborting) pre-processing stage and some prefix of the protocol execution can distinguish future coin-flips from a random sequence. The distinguishability implies that there is some the next-bit test that is not passed [3, 33]. Thus, there exists some future coin-flip which a probabilistic polynomial-time Adversary-User algorithm can predict with non-negligible probability. Now, we will show how this prediction can be used to invert a one-way permutation f on a random input z. Given a z for which we wish to find $f^{-1}(z)$, we put z in a random place in the Vendor's chain, and compute (by iterating f) the corresponding y, then run a zero-knowledge *simulator* to simulate the proof of knowledge of x (if the adversary can distinguish a simulation and the actual proof we reach a contradiction of zero-knowledge). Then, after the Adversary-User provides its y' and gives a zero-knowledge proof of knowledge of x' we use a *knowledge extractor* to get from the Adversary-User x'. Now, since we assume that the adversary can predict a coin of some future round with non-negligible probability, and since we know x', we can now compute all hard-core bits associated with y' chain and predict with polynomial probability the hard-core bit of $f^{-1}(z)$. Using [13] this leads to inversion of f — a contradiction. ∎

Now, the proof of the claim in the opposite direction mimics the previous proof:

Claim 3 *Assume that one-way permutations exist and that the User follows the protocol. Then, for any polynomially-bounded Adversary-Vendor if the pre-processing stage is not aborted by the User then for any prefix of the protocol execution the coin-flips of subsequent rounds are pseudo-random for the Adversary-Vendor.*

Proof: Similar to the previous claim, where we now use *knowledge extractor* for the Adversary-Vendor's proof of knowledge and *zero-knowledge simulator* for the User's proof of knowledge. ∎

Thus, we have

Theorem 4 *In section 3, we presented* fair, authenticated *coin-flipping protocol.*

Finally it it worth-while to point out some of the the advantages of our scheme:

- Unlike the lottery solution [24], the bank does not have to participate in the coin-flip, and the number of bank-related transactions (which can be done using any other, more expensive payment scheme) is greatly reduced.
- Unlike the coin-flipping solution for [25], for which we do not know how to prove its security, our scheme is secure according to a strong pseudo-random definition for all the future rounds.
- After the setup stage, if the coin-flip is favorable to the Vendor, than it has the proof that the user must pay certain amount, which it can show to the bank/arbiter in case of dispute/nonpayment.
- If some site is used infrequently by some user, our coin-flip solution can be viewed as offering a "free-trial" service, where if tuned appropriately it can attract additional customers.
- Our solution can (and should) be combined with other more expensive schemes when the coin-flip is for payment, thus providing overall high security of the system.

4   Conclusions

The initial setup price involves checking one signature during connection to a new site and two proofs of knowledge, which can be done using standard cut and choose methods. After the setup stage, our solution is similar (up to a factor of two) in efficiency to the coupon-based schemes, but our scheme avoids "over-spending" issue and the need to black-list users. Moreover,

- after the pre-processing stage is done, the subsequent number of rounds is minimized – our scheme does not add *any* additional rounds when there is no payment necessary (since we can "piggy-back" our coin-flip messages with standard "get-page/here-it-is" interaction), and bank it not involved at all, thus saving the overall round complexity between users, vendors and banks.
- we minimize the (amortized) number of total bits transmitted per transaction between users, vendors and the bank/broker, since most of the time the "for-free" coin-flip avoids expensive payment protocol, and the on-line coin-flip price is similar to coupon-based solutions.
- we minimize (amortized) computational demands needed per transaction for all the participants (i.e. both users and vendors as well as banks);
- we eliminate tamper-proof hardware requirements for all the participants (i.e. we do not need smart-cards) or other "per-transaction" lists or expensive hardware for pre-processing);
- we minimize fraud since this is not credit-based solution and the payment (if the coin-flip is favorable) must be made immediately, avoiding the problems of over-charging the accounts, having to wait for bank-sponsored lotteries, and risking non-payments.

Additionally, our scheme can be made anonymous, with the use of *pseudonyms*, similar to Chaum's scheme. We postpone this discussion to the full version of the paper.

A possible criticism of our scheme (as well as Wheeler's [31] and Rivest's [24, 25]) is that probabilistic payments is some weak form of *gambling* which is forbidden by U.S. laws. We do not address this issue here, but rather, say that in our view this may not constitute gambling since the expected profit of the Vendor is very close (by the law of large numbers) to a deterministic (but more expensive) schemes. Of course, the legal ramifications of the proposed scheme are beyond the scope of this paper.

Acknowledgements

The authors are grateful to William Aiello, Sanjoy Dasgupta, Stuart Haber, Ashwin Nyack, Ron Rivest and Victor Shoup for several valuable discussions regarding coin-flipping protocols. We also wish to thank an anonymous referee of the FC98 conference for some useful remarks.

References

1. R. ANDERSON, C. MANIFAVAS, C. SUTHERLAND "Netcard - a practical electronic cash system" In Fourth Cambridge Workshop on Security Protocols. Springer Verlag, Lecture Notes in Computer Science, April 1996.
   available online URL http://www.cl.cam.ac.uk/users/rja14/
2. Blum, M., "Coin Flipping over the Telephone," IEEE COMPCON 1982, pp. 133-137.
3. M. Blum, and S. Micali "How to Generate Cryptographically Strong Sequences Of Pseudo-Random Bits" *SIAM J. on Computing,* Vol 13, 1984, pp. 850-864, FOCS 82.

4. J.P. BOLY, A. BOSSELAERS, R. CRAMER, R. MICHELSEN, S. MJØLSNES, F. MULLER, T. PEDERSEN, B. PFITZMANN, P. DE ROOIJ, B. SCHOENMAKERS, L. VALLÉE, AND M. WAIDNER.

5. M. BELLARE AND O. GOLDREICH. "On defining proofs of knowledge." Extended abstract in Advances in Cryptology - Crypto 92 Proceedings, Lecture Notes in Computer Science Vol. 740, E. Brickell ed, Springer-Verlag, 1993.

6. B. COX, D. TYGAR, M. SIRBU "NetBill security and transaction proptocol" First USENIX Workshop on Electronic Commerce, New York, July 1995.
   available online URL http://www.ini.cmu/NETBILL/home.html

7. L. Tang and S. Low "Chrg-http: A Tool for Micropayments on the World Wide Web" 6th USENIX Security Symposium, San Jose, CA July 1996.

8. D. Chaum "Achieving Electronic Privacy" Scientific American, pp. 96-101, August 1992.

9. D. CHAUM, A. FIAT, M. NAOR "Untracable electronic Cash" Crypto-89.

10. E. GABBER AND A. SILBERSCHATZ "Agora: A Minimal Distributed Protocol for Electronic Commerce" USENIX Workshop on E-Commerce, Oakland CA Nov. 1996.

11. S. GLASSMAN, M. MANASSE, M. ABADAI, P. GAUTHIER, AND P. SOBALVARRO "The milicent protocol for inexpensive electronic commerce" In Proc. of the forth International World Wide Web Conference", 1995.
    available online URL http://www.research.digital.com/SRC/milicent

12. S. GOLDWASSER, S. MICALI, AND R. RIVEST "A Digital Signature Scheme Secure Against Adaptive Chosen-Message Attacks". *SIAM Journal of Computing* vol 17, No 2, (April 1988), pp. 281-308.

13. O. GOLDREICH, L. LEVIN "A hard-core predicate for all one-way functions." In Porc. of 21st STOC, pp. 25-32 ACM 1989.

14. N. M. HALLER "The S/KEY one-time password system. In ISOC 94.

15. R. HAUSER, M. STEINER, M. WAIDNER "Micro-payments based on ikp" In 14th Worldwide Congress on Computer and Communication Security Protection, CNIT Paris -La defense France, June 1996.
    available online URL http://www.zurich.ibm.com./Technology/ Security/publications/1996/HSW96-new.ps.gz

16. S. JARECKI, A. ADLYZKO "An efficient micropayment system based on probabilistic polling" Conference proceedings of *Financial Cryptography'97*, February 1997, Anguilla, BWI.

17. L. LAMPORT "Password authentication with insecure communication" Communications of the ACVM, 24(11):770-771, November 1981.

18. MONDEX USA
    available online URL http://www2.mondexusa.com/

19. G. MEDVINSKY, C. NEUMAN NetCash: A design for practical electronic currency on the internet. In *Proceeding sof the Second ACM Conference on Computer and Communcation Security* Novemeber 1994.

20. M. NAOR "Bit Commitment using Pseudo-Ranomness" Proc. CRYPTO 89.

21. C. NEUMAN, G. MEDVINSKY Requirements for network payment: The Netcheque prospective. In Proc. of IEEE COMCON, March 95.
    available online FTP ftp://prospero.isi/edu/pub/papers/security/

22. C. JUTLA AND M. YUNG "Paytree: amortized signature for flexible micropayments" In Second USENIX workshop on Electronic Commerce, November 1996.

23. T. PEDERSEN "Electronic payments of small amounts" Technical Report DAIMI PB-495, Aarhus University, Computer Science Department, Århus, Denmark, August 1995.

24. R. RIVEST "Lottery tickets as Micro-Cash" rump session talk at *Financial Cryptography'97*, February 1997, Anguilla, BWI.

25. R. RIVEST "Electronic Lottery tickets as Micropayments" Proceedings of *Financial Cryptography'97*, LNCS series 1318, pp. 306-314.

26. R. RIVEST "The MD5 message-digest algorithm" Internet Request for Comments, April 1992. RFC 1321.
available online URL http://theory.lcs.mit.edu/rivest/publications.html

27. R. RIVEST AND A. SHAMIR "Payword and micromint: Two simple micropayment schemes" In fourth Cambridge workshop on security protocols. Springer Verlag, lecture Notes in Computer Science, April 1996.
available online URL http://theory.lcs.mit.edu/rivest/publications.html

28. V. SHOUP "On Fast and Provaaably Secure Message Authentication Based On Universal Hashing" CRYPTO-96.

29. J. STERN, S. VAUDENAY "Small-Value-Payment: a Flexible Micropayment Scheme" Conference proceedings of *Financial Cryptography'97*, February 1997, Anguilla, BWI.

30. VISA AND MASTERCARD "Secure Electronic Transactions (SET) specification, *available online* URL http://www.mastercard.com/set

31. D. WHEELER "Transactions using bets" in security protocols Int. Workshop, cambridge, UK April 1996. In LNCS 1189 pp. 89-92
available *online* URL
http://www.cl.cam.ac.uk/users/cm213/Project/project_publ.html

32. Y. YACOBI "On the continuum between on-line and off-line e-cash systems - I" Conference proceedings of *Financial Cryptography'97*, February 1997, Anguilla,

33. A.C. Yao "Theory and Applications of Trapdoor Functions" *FOCS 82*.

X-Cash: Executable Digital Cash

(Extended Abstract)

Markus Jakobsson[1] Ari Juels[2]

[1] Information Sciences Research Center, Bell Laboratories
Murray Hill, NJ 07974
markusj@research.bell-labs.com
[2] RSA Laboratories
Bedford, MA 01730
ari@rsa.com

Abstract. In this paper, we propose a new financial instrument known as *executable digital cash*, or *X-cash*. X-cash is a means of binding an offer to the accompanying goods or payment, enabling the processes of searching and paying to be unified. The result is a mechanism by which electronic trades can occur in a highly distributed setting with strong security guarantees. When a party receives an X-cash offer, he or she can verify that it is *bona fide* and can initiate a trade immediately, without contacting the originator directly. X-cash may therefore be used, among other things, to enable mobile agents to carry funds and make payments on-site without running the risk of "pick-pocketing". In this paper, we introduce X-cash, describe some variants, and sketch proofs of its security properties.

1   Introduction

The growth of the Internet and the increasing sophistication and availability of cryptographic tools have promised to bring commerce to new heights of efficiency and international breadth. Efficiency suggests a number of things, including minimized human involvement, improved distribution of goods and information, and more rapid processing of transactions. Ideally, prospective traders should be able to locate one another in a highly automated fashion and then execute trades with strong security guarantees. Until now, two trends in the research area of electronic commerce have been visible. Starting with the introduction of payment schemes to the field of cryptography by Chaum, Fiat and Naor ([7], also see [9],) research contributions have tended either to introduce new features into existing payment paradigms or to address stronger attack models. Among the new features recently introduced are off-line payments [2, 3, 14], divisibility [27, 20], and micro-payments [17, 18, 23, 25, 28, 33]. Examples of stronger attack models or improved protection against attacks include tamper-resistance [10], provable security against forgery [24], fairness [19], probabilistic on-line verification [23, 37], and revocable anonymity [4, 5, 6, 12, 15, 16, 20, 21, 22, 26, 30, 31, 32, 34, 36]. In all of these schemes, however, it has been assumed that we start at a point where we have two parties who are aware of each other's existence and where-abouts and wish to perform a transfer of funds and merchandise. Whereas this is true for a conventional commercial setting, it is not necessarily true for the type of setting which is the main driving force of electronic commerce-namely one in which there is a large number of uncoordinated and distributed partici-pants potentially willing to engage in barters, but unaware of each other's trade goals. It is possible in such a setting to let prospective trading partners seek each other out and then initiate peer-to-peer transactions. This, however, increases the risk of communications bottlenecks, as communicating with the originator of an offer may require costly traversals of a network. In addition, if the issuer of an offer receives many bids but has limited computational power, this means of commerce could overtax his or her resources. In order to obtain a realistic and efficient solution, we must consider alternative methods of establishing first contact between traders, and develop methods to perform a transaction with-out peer-to-peer contact when a desirable match is found. To do this, we may consider the *mobile agent* paradigm that has recently become the focus of much attention in the AI and distributed systems communities. Mobile agents are pro-gram segments sent across a network which execute on host machines (very much like a friendly virus). Their aim is to perform some task on behalf of the user with a certain degree of autonomy (see [29] for an overview). Proposed uses include bartering, negotiating, entertainment, monitoring, data selection and filtration, searching, and distributed processing. Current suggestions for payment schemes are not well adapted to use with mobile agents: if an agent carries digital cash, for instance, it is vulnerable to "pick-pocketing" [35]. On the other hand, not allowing agents to carry funds to perform commerce requires a reduction to the peer-to-peer setting with its attendant bottlenecks. Our aim is to avoid these two types of problems, and to supply an efficient and practical payment scheme which may be based upon any type of broadcast mechanism, including mobile agents. To this end, we propose a new financial instrument known as *executable digital cash*, or *X-cash*. X-cash is a means of binding an offer to the accompa-nying goods or payment, enabling the processes of searching and payment to be unified. The result is a mechanism by which electronic trades can occur in a highly distributed setting with strong security guarantees. When a party re-ceives an X-cash offer, he or she can verify that it is *bona fide* and can initiate a trade immediately, without contacting the originator directly. The basic idea is as follows. Alice obtains from her bank a signed certificate bearing her public key PK_A and authorizing her to make payments using a corresponding secret key SK_A. Alice signs a program ω using SK_A. This program ω acts like an agent for Alice (in the usual sense of the word not related to mobile agents). It takes as input some item (e.g., a program, a news article, or frequent flier miles), and outputs the amount which Alice is willing to pay for that item. The program ω along with the certificate constitute a piece of X-cash. If Bob wishes to sell an item Q to Alice, he can take the X-cash and the item Q to Alice's bank. By running the program ω on Q, Alice's bank can determine how much to pay Bob. Alice's bank may then hold the item Q for Alice or otherwise arrange to send it to her. The trade is thus completed in a secure fashion without any direct contact between Alice and Bob. X-cash may be regarded as an extension of the recently introduced concept of *challenge semantics* [20]. This concept uses the challenge of a payment to indicate the conditions of the barter. In its original version, it only allowed a designation of the payment to be specified. We extend the concept and the use of it by allowing any executable program to be used instead, which enables a solution to the problem of agent-based trade. Our method can be applied to any payment scheme with revocable anonymity controlled by a set of trustees, to certificate-based payment schemes without anonymity (such as [11]), and to payment schemes with on-line redemption (such as [13]).

Organization of Paper

The remainder of this paper is organized as follows. Section 2 gives the definitions and notation used in the paper, describes our trust model, and formalizes the goals we are seeking to achieve. Section 3 describes how we achieve these goals using X-cash. We sketch some proofs on the security of our X-cash scheme in section 4. In section 5, we describe some extensions and improvements to the basic X-cash scheme.

2   Definitions, Model, and Goals

Definitions

Informally, an *offer* is a proposal to trade some collection of goods, moneys, or services for another collection of goods, moneys, or services according to a set of well defined terms. An offer may involve either buying and selling: the term in our usage eliminates the distinction between these two activities. Alice might, for instance, make an offer to sell 500 French francs at 5 francs per \$1, or she might make an offer to buy up to 500 French francs at \$1 per 5 francs. A *bid* is a response to an offer. If Alice is selling French francs, and Bob tenders her \$5, then Bob is making a bid. We refer generically to any entity making an offer or a bid as a *trader*. We may describe these ideas more formally in terms of an *offer function*, defined as a function $\omega : S \to T$. Here $S = \{0,1\}^*$ is the space of possible bids and $T = \{0,1\}^* \cup \phi$ is the space of possible goods, moneys, or services proposed in response to these bids. The symbol ϕ indicates a null response, i.e., the bid is deemed unacceptable. We shall use ω interchangably to indicate an offer function and the code implementing an offer function. We denote by $\omega(Q)$ the output of ω on a bid Q. Observe that ω is stateless. It does not compute, for example, based on the current time or on a history of bids. In advanced protocols which we shall touch on only briefly in this paper, S may be defined to include parameters like the current time and a lists of all bids made in response to an offer. We define an *X-cash coin* Ω to be an expression of an offer ω (as a program or a text description, or in any other form) along with all accompanying signatures, certificates, programs, and instructions. Alice will transmit or broadcast Ω in order to initiate a trade (by means, e.g., of a mobile agent.) The aim of this paper will be to determine what form the X-cash coin must assume to achieve the flexibility and security guarantees desired in our model for electronic commerce. The system we propose will make extensive use of what we refer to as *negotiable certificates*. A negotiable certificate is an authorization, issued by a financial or other institution, for a trader to make offers using some quantity of assets held by the institution. Let (SK_A, PK_A) denote a secret/public signature key pair held by a trader Alice, and let (SK_F, PK_F) denote a secret/public signature key pair held by Alice's financial institution. A negotiable certificate C assumes the form $\sigma_{SK_F}(PK_A)$, where σ_{SK_F} denotes a signature using the secret key SK_F. (Note that the units of value of the certificate may either be left implicit, or may be specified in an extra field.) If Alice wishes to sign over a quantity m of assets to Bob, she creates the signature $\sigma_{SK_A}(Bob, m)$, and gives it to Bob along with the negotiable certificate C to be redeemed by her financial institution. Thus a negotiable certificate may be loosely regarded as a license to write checks up to a certain amount.

Trust Model

Let us now present the trust model in which we seek to conduct trades. We then give a formal statement of the goals, regarding both security and flexibility, which we are trying to achieve in this model.

Network Alice will broadcast her X-cash coin in an open network (by means, e.g., of a mobile agent which may spawn). We assume the following about this network.

1. An adversary may inject X-cash coins of her own construction into the network (such as a coin Ω' purporting to come from Alice).
2. The X-cash coin Ω may be freely read and executed by any party.
3. An adversary cannot significantly impede normal delivery of an X-cash coin. In particular, let $\mathcal{D}$ denote the total set of delivery points potentially reachable by an X-cash coin Ω. Let $p_t(D)$ be the probability that Ω reaches a delivery point $D \in \mathcal{D}$ after broadcast in a non-adversarial network in time t. Let $p'_t(D)$ be the probability that Ω reaches delivery point D in time t in a setting where at least a constant c-fraction of network servers are honest, but the rest may refuse to deliver any message. Suppose that t is such that $p_t(D) > (1 - \epsilon) \lim_{t \to \infty} p_t(D)$ for all $D \in \mathcal{D}$ and for some constant ϵ s.t. $0 < \epsilon < 1$. In other words, t represents a long enough time for almost all of the broadcast to be accomplished under normal circumstances. We require that the probability distributions p_t and p'_t be polynomial time indistinguishable over coin flips of the entities in the network.
4. All parties have unimpeded access to financial institutions.

Parties We assume the following about the parties in our model.

1. Financial institutions may be trusted to act on behalf of their patrons, but not necessarily of other parties.
2. Financial institutions trust one another.[3]
3. Parties other than financial institutions are not necessarily trustworthy.

Computational assumptions We make the following computational assumptions.

1. All parties have conventionally limited computational resources (polynomial in an appropriate security parameter).
2. A digital signature scheme is employed in which it is infeasible to commit existentially forgery of signatures.

Goals of this paper Our goal is to achieve realize electronic commerce with the following properties within the trust model described above:

1. *Entitlement authentication.* Any party considering an offer ω issued by Alice must be able to determine from the X-cash coin Ω whether Alice has been issued the goods, services, or moneys being offered. This should be achievable off-line. Note that this property is different from authentication in the usual sense in that Alice's identity is not of concern (and may not even be known). Note also that entitlement authentication is a guarantee that Alice has been issued, but not necessarily that she *currently* possesses the funds or rights in question: these funds or rights may already have been spent.
2. *Fairness.* No one should be able to engage in any exchange not defined by ω. Moreover, Alice should be able to specify (in her X-cash coin) how many such exchanges she wishes to engage in.
3. *Perfect matchmaking.* Any party that receives the X-cash coin Ω should be able to engage in a fair exchange with Alice. No information beyond publicly available information and that provided by Ω is required.
4. *Integrity.* Any party must be able to verify that the X-cash coin Ω has not been tampered with.
5. *Efficiency.* The X-cash coin Ω should be compact, and offers and bids should be capable of being processed efficiently.

3 Solution

In this section, we provide details of the X-cash protocols used to achieve the goals described above. Before presenting these protocols formally, let us take a brief look at the intuition behind them. Recall that before making an offer, Alice obtains a negotiable certificate C granting her rights to the funds or rights

---

[3] Note that this assumption is not necessary if we make use of a fair exchange protocol, such as that proposed in, e.g., [1].

she wishes to offer, and enabling her to transfer those rights to another party. The key idea behind X-cash is the following. Alice constructs her X-cash coin Ω in such a way that the transfer of rights using C is conditional on having a suitable bid R as input to a piece of code ω. In other words, instead of signing over funds or rights to an individual, Alice signs them over based on a piece of code ω which evaluates the worth of a bid R. To make a bid, Bob creates a suitable, signed representation R of his bid, and submits it to Alice's financial institution along with Ω. This financial institution verifies that Alice's negotiable certificate still retains sufficient value for the transaction with Bob, and contacts Bob's financial institution to ensure that Bob too has sufficient funds available. The two financial institutions then process the exchange. The formal details of the protocols are given below. Note that for simplicity of notation, we assume that all signatures have full message recovery.

X-Cash Protocols

Initiation of Trade

1. Alice has a negotiable certificate C from her financial institution F_A, attributing to her rights to all goods or moneys in T, the range of the offer function ω to be used in her X-cash. This certificate is issued against public key PK_A for which Alice holds the corresponding private key SK_A.
2. Alice decides what offer she wishes to make, and constructs an offer function $\omega : S \to T$. Again, $S = \{0,1\}^*$ is the space of possible bids and $T = \{0,1\}^* \cup \phi$ is the space of possible responses to these bids. Alice creates a piece of executable code for her offer function ω.
3. Alice decides what policy she wishes to use in accepting bids. For the sake of simplicity, we might allow three possible policies: (1) She accepts all bids until all rights attributed by C are exhausted; (2) She accepts the first j valid bids; or (3) She accepts the best bid received before date d. Alice encodes her policy choice in a field P.
4. Alice constructs the X-cash coin Ω containing $[\sigma_{SK_A}(\omega, P), C]$.
5. Alice transmits Ω.

Initiation of Bid

1. On receiving Alice's offer, Bob verifies the correctness of $\sigma_{SK_A}(\omega, P)$.
2. Bob evaluates Alice's offer ω. (This may involve reading or automatically processing an attached prose description of the offer and/or executing ω on possible bids.)
3. Bob executes ω on input Q, which is his matching bid. He verifies that the output indicates acceptance of the bid, i.e., that $\omega(Q) \neq \phi$ and that the corresponding offer is as desired.
4. Bob obtains from the financial institution F_B a certificate C' bound to a public key PK_B for which Bob holds the corresponding secret key SK_B. (Note that Bob may have to perform this step earlier if ω checks certificates.)

5. Bob creates[4] a bid capsule $R = [\sigma_{SK_B}(\Omega, Q, \omega(Q)), C']$.
6. Bob sends R to financial institution F_A.

Clearing Process

1. On receiving the first bid capsule with the X-cash coin Ω, the financial institution F_A reads the policy P in Ω, verifies that Ω is correctly formed (that all signatures and certificates are valid), and then stores Ω.
2. In accordance with the policy P in Ω, the financial institution F_A collects all valid bid capsules $R_1, R_2, \ldots, R_m$ (containing bids $Q_1, Q_2, \ldots, Q_m$).
3. For each R_i in $\{R_1, R_2, \ldots, R_m\}$, the financial institution F_A does the following:
   (a) F_A checks that R_i is correctly formed.
   (b) F_A then runs ω on the bid Q_i contained in capsule R_i.
   (c) If $\omega(Q_i) \neq \phi$, then F_A checks that Alice has funds worth at least $\omega(Q_i)$ remaining against the negotiable certificate C. If not, F_A does not process R_i.
   (d) F_A checks with the appropriate financial institution F_B that there are funds to back the bid Q_i. If not, then F_A does not process R_i.
4. If Alice has sufficient funds, and there are sufficient funds remaining to support the bid Q_i, then F_A and F_B perform the exchange specified by offer and bid, as explained below.

Performing the Exchange

When the two financial institutions, F_A and F_B, have agreed on an exchange as specified by Ω and some bid capsule R_i, the ownership rights need to be exchanged correspondingly. This can be done in a variety of ways, out of which we suggest two: (1) If the same public key is to be used for the newly acquired merchandise, the financial institutions simply re-issue certificates on the public keys corresponding to the new owners of the merchandise. These certificates can then be forwarded by either financial institution to the acquirers, or "picked up" by the same. (2) If a new public key is to be employed, the financial institutions may enter the old public keys of the parties acquiring the merchandise that they certify in a database, and the new owners have to supply a new public key to be certified, and prove knowledge of the secret key corresponding to the old public key in order for the exchange to occur.

4 Proofs

We claim that our basic scheme implements *entitlement authentication* (Theorem 1), *fairness* (Theorem 2), *perfect matchmaking* (Theorem 3), and *integrity* (Theorem 4).

---

[4] Note that the expected output of ω on Q is included in the bid in order to avoid bait-and-switch attacks in which an offer appears one way when first inspected by Bob, and in another way when redeemed by the bank.

Theorem 1: The basic scheme implements entitlement authentication, i.e., it is possible for a party examining an offer to determine that the party making the offer has been issued the rights to the goods of the offer.

Proof of Theorem 1: *(Sketch)*
Recall that Alice signs the offer using the key associated with the negotiable certificate C. The public key in C is signed by a financial institution, meaning that this institution is responsible for redeeming the value implicitly specified by the public key and certificate. Thus, by examining the signatures, Bob can ascertain that the certifying entity will redeem this value in the case of a transaction if there are funds remaining. It is not possible to forge either of these signatures, by the assumption of existential unforgeability of the corresponding signature schemes. $\square$

Theorem 2: The basic scheme implements fairness, i.e., no one should be able to engage in an exchange not defined by the corresponding offer and bid.

Proof of Theorem 2: *(Sketch)*
First, a bid is made with respect to an offer in a binding way: a matching offer constitutes a pair of offer and bid. In particular, Bob signs both offer and bid together, so that they may not be dissociated without forgery or alteration of his signature. Likewise, Alice protected the integrity of the offer by signing it. Therefore, the scheme implements fairness under the assumption that the financial entities will not steal resources. $\square$

Theorem 3: The basic scheme implements perfect matchmaking.[5] In other words, any party with a strategy for producing valid bids and appropriate access to broadcasts of an offer Ω should be allowed a fair exchange based on Ω.

Proof of Theorem 3: *(Sketch)*
By assumption 3 about the broadcast network, it is not possible for an adversary to impede the broadcast of an X-cash coin Ω significantly. In particular, any party which has access to a distribution point $D \in \mathcal{D}$ such that $p_t(D)$ is significantly large for suitable t will obtain Ω with high probability even in the face of an adversarial attack. By assumption 4 about the broadcast network, bids will arrive at the appropriate financial institution unimpeded. Having collected bids in accordance with the policy P specified in Ω, the financial institution backing the offer will process all matching bids. Selected offers and bids will then be resolved atomically by the financial institutions backing the funds of the offer and the selected bids. By Theorem 2, the resulting trade will be fair. $\square$

Theorem 4: The basic scheme implements integrity, i.e., any party must be able to verify that a given offer capsule has not been tampered with.

---

[5] We note that if the selection strategies governing how matches are made are very complex, then the computational task of finding the "best fit" is significant. We can only hope for heuristic matchmaking schemes to be "almost perfect". The work of matching received offers and bids, however, is outside the scope of this paper. We assume that there is a mechanism for selection of offers and bids in place, and for simplicity, that this mechanism effects perfect matches.

This follows automatically from the use of digital signatures to authenticate offers; if it is possible to tamper with an offer capsule, this breaks the assumption that the corresponding signature scheme is existentially unforgeable.

5 Extensions

There are a number of possible ways of extending the functionality of X-cash. We will touch briefly on some of these in this section.

5.1 Anonymity

The ability to perform financial transactions anonymously has been of major concern to proponents of digital cash since its inception. Anonymity is of equal or greater importance in X-cash transactions, particularly as a single coin may be viewed openly by many parties. X-cash may be rendered anonymous by essentially the same means as traditional e-cash. Many off-line anonymous cash schemes, however, have mechanisms for protecting against overspending by the use of thresholds. Since redemption of X-cash occurs on-line, these mechanisms are not relevant here. On the other hand, schemes with perfect privacy and on-line redemption (e.g. [8]) are quite suitable for use with X-cash, as are many of the schemes with anonymity controlled by trustees.

5.2 Stateful Offers and Bids

In the body of this paper, we consider only stateless offers, i.e., offers ω which take as input a single bid. In some situations, though, the party making an offer may wish to take into account the value of multiple bids or other information simultaneously. For this reason, it may be desirable to extend the scope of the offer function ω to allow for a range of possible inputs and outputs, and also to change the policy field P. We sketch a couple of examples here:

- Alice has 50,000 frequent flier miles to sell. She is willing to sell them piecemeal, but wishes to dispose of as many as possible in the next month. Alice therefore indicates in her policy description P that the Bank should collect all bids $Q_1, Q_2, ..., Q_n$ over the next month and then run ω on them, processing all bids output by ω. Alice constructs an offer program ω which finds and outputs the subset of bids among $Q_1, Q_2, ..., Q_n$ whose sum is as close as possible to but not greater than 50,000.
- Alice wishes to sell a 6 ounce gold bar for its market price on the day of sale. She obtains from her Bank a negotiable certificate of entitlement to the gold and constructs an offer program ω. When given a bid Q, the program ω goes out onto the Web, checks the current price per ounce d of gold bullion, and outputs "yes" if $Q \geq 6d$, and "no" otherwise. Alice indicates in P that her Bank should redeem any bid Q which yields a "yes" output. (Note that the state in ω is external in this example.)

5.3 Secret Strategies

We have just demonstrated how it is possible to enhance the offer program to make X-cash more flexible. It is equally possible to make enhancements to the policy statement P. This may be particularly useful if Alice wishes to pursue what we refer to as a *secret strategy*, i.e., if she wishes for her method for selecting among bids to remain concealed from potential trading partners. She may be accomplish this by constructing a piece of X-cash of the form $\Omega = \sigma_{SK_A}(\omega, E_{PK_F}[P], C)$, where PK_F is the public key of Alice's issuing financial institution. Consider the following scenario. Alice wishes to sell one million shares of Mata Hari Crypto Corp., Inc.-a controlling interest-at the price of \$100/share. She does not want anyone to know how large a block of stock is being sold, and wants to avoid having any one individual accumulate too many shares from the offering. Alice may accomplish this by constructing an offer program ω which takes as input a bid \$Q and outputs "Q/100 shares". She constructs a policy P stating that any bid for more than 10,000 shares should be rejected. Alice includes an encryption of P in her X-cash coin as described above. Note that if complex policy statements are permitted, then it may be beneficial for P to take the form of a program whose inputs are bids and timestamps associated with these bids and whose outputs are accepted bids.

6 Acknowledgments

The authors wish to express thanks to Burt Kaliski and Marty Wattenberg for their many helpful suggestions on this paper.

References

1. N. Asokan and Victor Shoup, "Optimistic fair exchange of digital signatures (to appear)," In Kaisa Nyberg, editor, Advances in Cryptology - EUROCRYPT '98, number to be assigned in Lecture Notes in Computer Science. Springer-Verlag, Berlin Germany, 1998.
2. S. Brands, "Untraceable Off-line Cash in Wallets with Observers," Advances in Cryptology - Proceedings of Crypto '93, pp. 302–318.
3. S. Brands, "An Efficient Off-line Electronic Cash Systems Based on the Representation Problem," C.W.I. Technical Report CS-T9323, The Netherlands.
4. E. Brickell, P. Gemmell and D. Kravitz, "Trustee-based Tracing Extensions to Anonymous Cash and the Making of Anonymous Change," Proc. 6th Annual ACM-SIAM Symposium on Discrete Algorithms (SODA), 1995, pp. 457–466.
5. J. Camenisch, U. Maurer and M. Stadler, "Digital Payment Systems with Passive Anonymity-Revoking Trustees," Computer Security - ESORICS 96, volume 1146, pp. 33–43.
6. J. Camenisch, J-M. Piveteau and M. Stadler, "An Efficient Fair Payment System," Proceedings of the 3rd ACM Conference on Computer and Communications Security, 1996, pp. 88–94.
7. D. Chaum, A. Fiat and M. Naor, "Untraceable Electronic Cash," Advances in Cryptology - Proceedings of Crypto '88, pp. 319–327.

8. D. Chaum, "Blind Signatures for Untraceable Payments," Advances in Cryptology - Proceedings of Crypto '82, pp. 199-203.

9. D. Chaum, "Achieving Electronic Privacy," Scientific American, August 1992, pp. 96–101.

10. D. Chaum and T. Pedersen, "Wallet databases with observers," Advances in Cryptology - Proceedings of Crypto '92, pp. 89–105.

11. CitiBank and S. S. Rosen, "Electronic-Monetary System," International Publication Number WO 93/10503; May 27 1993.

12. G.I. Davida, Y. Frankel, Y. Tsiounis, and M. Yung, "Anonymity Control in E-Cash Systems," Financial Cryptography 97, pp. 1–16.

13. DigiCash' payment scheme; http://www.digicash.com

14. N. Ferguson, "Extensions of Single-term Coins," Advances in Cryptology - Proceedings of Crypto '93, pp. 292–301.

15. Y. Frankel, Y. Tsiounis, and M. Yung, "Indirect Discourse Proofs: Achieving Efficient Fair Off-Line E-Cash," Advances in Cryptology - Proceedings of Asiacrypt 96, pp. 286–300.

16. E. Fujisaki, T. Okamoto, "Practical Escrow Cash System", LNCS 1189, Proceedings of 1996 Cambridge Workshop on Security Protocols, Springer Verlag, pp. 33 – 48.

17. S. Glassman, M. Manasse, M. Abadi, P. Gauthier and P. Sobalvarro, "The Millicent Protocol for Inexpensive Electronic Commerce," In World Wide Web Journal, Fourth International World Wide Web Conference Proceedings, O'Reilly, December 1995, pp. 603–618.

18. R. Hauser, M. Steiner and M. Waidner, "Micropayments Based on iKP," 14th Worldwide Congress on Computer and Communications Security Protection, 1996, pp. 67–84.

19. M. Jakobsson, "Ripping Coins for a Fair Exchange," Advances in Cryptology - Proceedings of Eurocrypt '95, pp. 220–230.

20. M. Jakobsson and M. Yung, "Revokable and Versatile Electronic Money," 3rd ACM Conference on Computer and Communications Security, 1996, pp. 76–87.

21. M. Jakobsson and M. Yung, "Distributed 'Magic Ink' Signatures," Advances in Cryptology - Proceedings of Eurocrypt '97, pp. 450–464.

22. M. Jakobsson and M. Yung, "Applying Anti-Trust Policies to Increase Trust in a Versatile E-Money System," Advances in Cryptology - Proceedings of Financial Cryptography '97, pp. 217–238.

23. S. Jarecki and A. Odlyzko, "An Efficient Micropayment System Based on Probabilistic Polling," Advances in Cryptology - Proceedings of Financial Cryptography '97, pp. 173–191.

24. A. Juels, M. Luby and R. Ostrovsky, "Security of Blind Digital Signatures," Advances in Cryptology - Proceedings of Crypto '97, pp. 150-164.

25. C. Jutla and M. Yung, "Paytree: 'Amortized Signature' for Flexible Micropayments," 2nd USENIX Workshop on Electronic Commerce, November 1996.

26. D. M'Raïhi, "Cost-Effective Payment Schemes with Privacy Regulation," Advances in Cryptology - Proceedings of Asiacrypt '96.

27. T. Okamoto, "An Efficient Divisible Electronic Cash Scheme," Advances in Cryptology - Proceedings of Crypto '95, pp. 438–451.

28. R. Rivest and A. Shamir, "PayWord and MicroMint: Two Simple Micropayment Schemes," Cryptobytes, vol. 2, num. 1, 1996, pp. 7–11.

29. D. Rus, R. Gray and D. Kotz, "Transportable Information Agents", 1st Intl. Conf. Autonomous Agents, 1997.

30. S. von Solms and D. Naccache, "On Blind Signatures and Perfect Crimes," Computers and Security, 11 (1992) pp. 581–583.
31. M. Stadler, "Cryptographic Protocols for Revokable Privacy," PhD Thesis, ETH No. 11651, Swiss Federal Institute of Technology, Zürich, 1996.
32. M. Stadler, J-M. Piveteau and J. Camenisch, "Fair Blind Signatures," Advances in Cryptology - Proceedings of Eurocrypt '95, pp. 209–219.
33. J. Stern and S. Vaudenay, "SVP: a Flexible Micropayment Scheme," Advances in Cryptology - Proceedings of Financial Cryptography '97, pp. 161–171.
34. Y. Tsiounis, "Efficient Electronic Cash: New Notions and Techniques," PhD Thesis, College of Computer Science, Northeastern University, 1997. http://www.ccs.neu.edu/home/yiannis
35. B. Venners, "Solve Real Problems with Aglets, a Type of Mobile Agent," Javaworld, May 1997.
36. B. Witter, "The Dark Side of Digital Cash," Legal Times, January 30, 1995.
37. Y. Yacobi, "On the Continuum Between On-line and Off-line E-cash Systems - I," Advances in Cryptology - Proceedings of Financial Cryptography '97, pp. 193–201.

Distributed Trustees and Revocability:
A Framework for Internet Payment

David M'Raïhi* and David Pointcheval**

Abstract. From von Solms and Naccache's standpoint, constructing a practical and secure e-money system implies a proper regulation of its privacy level. Furthermore, when the system benefits from a widely connected communication network, tuning precisely this control for achieving efficiency without endangering security is a hard task. In order to solve this specific problem, we propose an e-cash scheme based on the usage of provably secure primitives, where trustee quora are in charge of privacy control. Moreover, Trustees remain off-line throughout the e-coin's life to reduce the communication flow and improve the resulting scheme performance.

1   Introduction

Reaching the end of the twentieth century, our society is deeply engaged in a vast technologic revolution. The huge growth of digital communications and mobile technologies reflects this transformation, a paper-based society changing to an electronic media world. The introduction of public-key cryptography [9] opened the door for capital additions to this construction of a technological-oriented society. Digital signature [22, 12, 24] is obviously one of the most significant examples of this major contribution.

Electronic cash, originally based on a variation of the digital signature paradigm, blind signatures [7], is a practical aspect of the continuous mutation we are living now. The core idea is to mimic metal coins, by delivering electronic coins that users could also spend anonymously. Another important goal consists in avoiding calling the bank at payment time to prevent double-spending. In Chaum's original proposal, the bank had to check every deposited coin against the list of spent coins. Shop's guarantee that a coin received is a valid coin therefore required the bank to support a real-time payment architecture, at a huge investment cost in terms of computation and communication capacities.

Chaum, Fiat and Naor [8] proposed to add detection mechanisms to solve this particular issue. They introduce the first off-line electronic cash scheme, based on zero-knowledge proofs and cut-and-choose techniques. Hence, the first *practical* electronic cash system [8] would provide privacy and security, but at a huge computational cost.

* GEMPLUS, Cryptography Department, 34 rue Guynemer, 92447 Issy-les-Moulineaux, France. E-mail: David.Mraihi@ccmail.edt.fr.
** GREYC, Université de Caen, 14032 Caen Cedex, France and LIENS, École Normale Supérieure, 75230 Paris Cedex 05, France. E-mail: David.Pointcheval@info.unicaen.fr.

Nevertheless, digital age is not the perfect age and as digital technologies were growing on, Evil found its path through a new mutation: digital crime. Thus, anonymity granted by blind signatures could lead to various criminal activities [26, 2, 4]. Considering potential attacks from large-scale criminal organizations, introducing the concept of revocability is a natural approach. Basically, the idea is to give the control of all privacy issues to a trusted entity, being any combination of different parties such as judges, users' associations or governmental representatives.

Related work: Escrowed cash introduced in [2] as schemes [5] based on the fair blind signature primitive [4] give a good flavor of the concept but required the presence of Trustee during withdrawals thereby decreasing drastically overall performance of the scheme. A new model [13], solving the bank robbery attack by implementing a secret channel between the bank and the trustee and introducing the concept of challenge semantic, leads to reconsider security, scalability and flexibility topics of revocable e-cash schemes. A very interesting technique based on a modification of DSS [14] proposed a distributed architecture for the trustees; this paper mainly concentrate on the protocol aspect as a basic block for scheme construction. The attack model and the impact on security are analyzed in [15]. Recent works introduce the first revocable off-line (with respect to the Trustees) e-cash schemes, based on proofs of knowledge and equality of discrete logarithms [3] or on indirect discourse proofs [11]. In this setting, the idea is to reduce the communication burden while preventing most of the possible attacks. Trustees never participate in protocols related to the normal usage of coins: they are only involved in tracing operations.

Our solution is smart-card oriented, taking into account the main advances in this field, namely the possibility to achieve public-key operations efficiently. We also wanted to emphasize the impact of the network structure in terms of communication and security; using only provably secure primitives is eventually a new contribution to the promotion of prudently designed e-cash schemes.

Achievements: In this paper, we extend [17] introducing revocability over a distributed communication network, *i.e.* where trustees are distributed over a network as Internet. Such a structure provides both high resistance to attacks and faults as well as various trade-offs in terms of computation, communication cost and memory requirements. Our main concern is to focus on the user's side and limit its technical requirements, specifically computational and communication requirements. The second objective was to reduce the level of trust implied by [17] while respecting our primary purpose. We concentrate therefore on the network topology and security aspects, investigating several solutions. In particular, the primitives [23, 24, 21] considered in our scheme are provably secure in order to enhance security analysis.

The main principles are:

1. Usage of Pseudonyms [6]: users are able to communicate anonymously with Trustees and Payees. Using [17] techniques, Pseudonyms (in short Ps) are

derived from public user IDs I only a Trustee (in short TTP) subset knows the link between I and Ps. Furthermore, those pseudonyms offer the possibility to exchange coins (received from other users) and have the bank refresh coins (when validity date expires) without revealing any user ID-related. Obviously, by revealing a couple (I, Ps), Trustees enable payment tracing.

2. Combined certification of Ps (by TTP) and e-coins (by the bank): such a double certification enables TTPs to remain off-line during all coins-life related actions: withdrawal, payment, deposit, transfer and refreshment. TTPs interact with users only at the account opening stage[1].

3. Distribution of the Trustees: a collaboration of k trustees is required for any operation related to Ps certification. Privacy control is ruled by a quorum of trustees and as long as k trustees remain honest, user and transaction tracings are possible. Finally, the presence of any subset of k trustees is required to prove that a coin is related to a transaction, giving honest users an additive protection against a malevolent trustee.

2 Communication Models

Different constructions are possible (see figure 1):

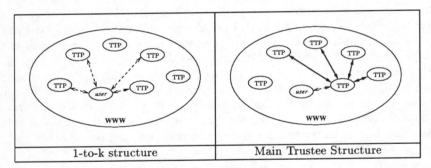

| 1-to-k structure | Main Trustee Structure |

Fig. 1. Communication Model

- Basic 1-to-k Structure: a user contacts all trustees and engages protocols with them; a clear bottleneck of this solution is the transmission rate between the user and TTPs, since we can assume that the user's communication routines run on low-cost devices. On the other hand, user's control is simplified since he initiates all communications.
- Main Trustee Structure: a user initiates communication with a trustee T_i (chosen at random among the k trustees) and delegates all the other tasks to T_i. In this setting, T_i is used as a gate to the global network of trustees; communication speed is therefore improved due to the usage of T_i fast transmission facilities.

---

[1] which is not the case in [3] and [11] schemes where Trustees collaboration is only required in case of disputes or overspending detection

3 The Basic Scheme

3.1 Primitives

The proposed scheme uses various primitives for authentication of users, issuing and verification of credentials, signature of transaction transcripts and encryption of privacy related information. These basic blocks are (where p and q are large prime integers such that $q \mid p - 1$, and g is an element of $\mathbb{Z}_p$ of order q):

1. User's Identification (protocol initiation): Schnorr identification scheme [23] whose security has been proven to be equivalent to the discrete logarithm problem (even against active attacks [25]);

$$A \begin{array}{|c|} \hline k \in_R \mathbb{Z}_q, \, r = g^k \bmod p \quad \xrightarrow{\quad r \quad} \\ \xleftarrow{\quad e \quad} \qquad e \in_R \mathbb{Z}_q \\ t = k - es \bmod q \quad \xrightarrow{\quad t \quad} r \stackrel{?}{=} g^t P^e \bmod p \\ \hline \mathsf{DL}(g, P) = (r, e, t) \\ \hline \end{array} \, B$$

   $\mathsf{DL}(g, P)$ proves to B that A knows s such that $P = g^s \bmod p$.

2. Signature (transaction and I certification) – Signature: the signature [24] derived from Schnorr's identification protocol. An existential forgery under an adaptive attack is equivalent to solving the underlying discrete logarithm problem [20];

3. Verifiable Secret Sharing (distributed trustees): let s be a secret key and $P = g^s \bmod p$ the associated public key. We want to distribute s among n participants in such a way that only a collusion of k of them might retreive, or at least use, s. Let Q be a random polynomial of degree $k - 1$ over $\mathbb{Z}_q$ such that $Q(0) = s$: $Q(x) = a_{k-1}x^{k-1} + \ldots, a_1 x + s$. The secret s can then be shared among the n participants secretly distributing $s_i = Q(i)$ to the ith one and broadcasting $P_i = g^{s_i} \bmod p$ for $i = 1, \ldots, n$. For any subset E of $\{1, \ldots, n\}$, and any $j \in E$, let us denote by $L_{E,j}$ the Lagrange's polynomial:

$$L_{E,j}(x) = \prod_{i \in E \backslash \{j\}} \frac{i - x}{i - j} \text{ so that } L_{E,j}(i) = 0 \ (\forall i \in E \backslash \{j\}) \text{ and } L_{E,j}(j) = 1.$$

Therefore, for any subset E of $\{1, \ldots, n\}$ with at least k elements,

$$Q(x) = \sum_{j \in E} s_j L_{E,j}(x), \text{ and so } s = \sum_{j \in E} \alpha(E, j) s_j \text{ where } \alpha(E, j) = L_{E,j}(0).$$

Furthermore, each participant can verify that his share is correctly related to $P_j = g^{s_j} \bmod p$, and that the secret can be properly rebuilt from the shares:

$$P = g^s = \prod_{j \in E} (g^{s_j})^{\alpha(E,j)} = \prod_{j \in E} P_j^{\alpha(E,j)} \bmod p.$$

Then $\mathsf{VSS}(s) = (s_1, \ldots, s_n)$.

4. Distributed Computation (Ps computation) – Dist-Comp: let us denote by X and s_j, for $j = 1, \ldots, n$, respectively, the secret key and shares VSS(X). Let E be a subset of k trustees who want to secretly compute $J = I^X \bmod p$. By broadcasting their shares $J_j = I^{s_j} \bmod p$ they get:

$$J = \prod J_j^{\alpha(E,j)} \bmod p = \text{Dist-Comp}(X, I).$$

5. Shared Signatures (Ps certification): let us denote by X, $Y = g^X \bmod p$ and s_j, for $j = 1, \ldots, n$, respectively, the secret key, the public key and shares VSS(X). Let E be a subset of k trustees. They each choose a random element $k_j \in_R \mathbb{Z}_q$ and broadcast $r_j = g^{k_j} \bmod p$ and all compute:

$$r = \prod r_j^{\alpha(E,j)} = g^{\sum k_j \alpha(E,j)} = g^k \bmod p, \text{ where } k = \sum k_j \alpha(E,j) \bmod q.$$

They can compute the challenge $e = H(m, r)$, where m is the message to be signed. Then they compute their part of the signature: $t_j = k_j - e s_j \bmod q$. The signature of m is the triple (r, e, t) where $t = \sum \alpha(E,j) t_j \bmod q$:

$$g^t Y^e = \prod g^{\alpha(E,j)t_j} g^{e\alpha(E,j)s_j} = \prod g^{\alpha(E,j)(t_j+es_j)} = \prod g^{\alpha(E,j)k_j} = r \bmod p.$$

This protocol Sh-Sig(X, m) provides a Schnorr signature (r, e, t) in such a way that no participant learns anything about others participants' secrets.

6. Blind Signature (coin certification) – Bl-Sig: the Okamoto-Schnorr blind scheme [18, 21]. If the secret key is denoted by $S = (x, z)$ and the public one by $P = y = g_1^x g_2^z \bmod p$, the signature the user gets is a tuple $(\varepsilon, \rho, \sigma)$ such that $\varepsilon = H(g_1^\rho g_2^\sigma y^\varepsilon, m)$, where m is the message to be blindly signed. This protocol offers a nice property for e-cash scheme construction: one-more forgery (i.e. generating one more signature) is infeasible;

7. Encryption (private channel between bank and users) – Cipher: El Gamal encryption scheme [12] which security is equivalent to the Diffie-Hellman problem, proven [9] equivalent in almost all cases to the discrete logarithm problem [16].

8. Shared Proof of Equality of Discrete Logarithms (privacy revocation) – SEqDL(I, J, g, Y): The n trustees share a secret X into s_j (for $j = 1, \ldots, n$) as described above and $Y = g^X \bmod p$. The user possesses a secret key s and $I = g^s \bmod p$. Furthermore, $J = Y^s = I^X \bmod p$. The trustees want to prove that $\log_I J = \log_g Y$. In order to achieve this goal, they randomly choose a secret $k_j \in \mathbb{Z}_q$, broadcast $u_j = I^{k_j} \bmod p$ and $v_j = g^{k_j} \bmod p$. They can compute $u = \prod u_j^{\alpha(E,j)}$ and $v = \prod v_j^{\alpha(E,j)}$ as well as the challenge $e = H(u, v)$. Then, they broadcast $t_j = k_j - e s_j \bmod q$. Finally, if we compute $t = \sum t_j \alpha(E,j) \bmod q$, it satisfies

$$u = I^t J^e \bmod p \text{ and } v = g^t Y^e \bmod p.$$

The triple SEqDL(I, J, g, Y) = (u, v, t) provides a proof of equality of the discrete logarithms $\log_I J = \log_g Y$, without revealing anything.

3.2 Protocols

In this section, the different protocols involved in the scheme are presented: registration (where a user obtains a set of Pseudonyms for protecting his privacy) and the different actions related to a financial transaction, namely withdrawal of coins, payment of purchases and deposit of transaction transcripts.

Registration Opening an account consists in two distinct phases (see figure 5) where a user interacts with the bank and a subset of k trustees:

1. Bank: the user proves his identity by exhibiting a "physical" proof such as a passport or any official document. He generates and sends his public identity $I = g^s$, where I represents an El Gamal-like public key. The bank stores I and the user's real identity ID and sends back the related certificate $Sig = \mathsf{Signature}_B(I)$.
2. TTPs: the user interacts with k TTPs to get his pseudonyms. The TTPs share the knowledge of:
   - a master secret key X splitted into n sub-keys $(s_1, \ldots, s_n) = \mathsf{VSS}(X)$.
   - π keys X_j, each distributed in n sub-keys $(s_{j,1}, \ldots, s_{j,n}) = \mathsf{VSS}(X_j)$ for $j = 1, \ldots, \pi$.

   We denote by E the subset of the k TTPs contacted by the user.
   The user first proves his knowledge of the secret information s related to I. Every TTP delivering his share of the pseudonyms $J_{j,i} = I^{s_{j,i}} \bmod p$, they can compute the pseudonyms $J_j = \prod_i J_{j,i}^{\alpha(E,i)} = I^{X_j} = Y_j^s \bmod p$, and produce a shared signature of J_j. The triple (J_j, e_j, t_j) corresponds to a certified pseudonym Ps_j and satisfies $e_j = H(g^{t_j} Y^{e_j}, J_j)$. Eventually, TTPs store in the registration log file the set $(I, \{Ps_j\}_{j \leq \pi})$ to be able to revoke privacy when required.

   Observation: Any TTP, merely reading the registration log file, could link I to a specific transaction since the user must "pseudo-signs" (using Ps_j) to spend coins. However, only a quorum of any k trustees can prove this link, as we will see below.

Withdrawal In order to withdraw coins (see figure 2) the user first sends I and proves his knowledge of s such that $I = g^s \bmod p$ [23]. Then, the bank blindly signs a coin in which the user embeds the public part of one of his pseudonyms J_j. Obviously, such a coin is not traceable by the bank but the different spendings related to this coin are linkable. The value of each coin is represented by a counter which must be controlled before any payment (to avoid overspending).

Observation: Data required to rebuild the coin signature are encrypted by the bank, using I as an El Gamal public key. This additional protection certifies that only a user knowing s can recover J_j signature and improves the protocol's robustness.

Payment During payment (see figure 3), the payer sends Ps_j and a coin C, after verification of the associated counter, to the payee who checks Ps_j certificate and C validity. The payer generates the transaction signature, proving that he knows s such that $J_j = g^{X_j s} = Y_j^{\,s}$, with a challenge depending on the amount, the pseudonym, the coin and the "name" of the payee.

Observation: The payee can decide whether he prefers to deposit the coin or transfer it: if he declares $Name$ to be his public identity I, he must deposit the coin at the bank on his non-anonymous account; if he defines it to be one of his Pseudonyms, he can transfer transactions, with the help of the bank, into a new anonymous coin.

Deposit A user must deposit a transaction which field $Name = I$ (see figure 4). Basically, the user sends a transaction τ then the bank checks data validity, performs overspending verification and credits the corresponding account.

Transfer If a payee has associated one of his Pseudonyms to several transactions, he must transfer them with the help of the bank to obtain a coin corresponding to the total transaction amount:

1. the user sends the transactions associated to his Pseudonym J'_j
2. the bank checks their validity
3. the bank checks that the user knows the associated secret key
4. the bank generates a new coin C' linked to the transfered transactions The link with the transactions is necessary to enable the bank to prove a possible overspending.

Observation: This protocol is a straightforward concatenation of the deposit and withdrawal protocols in order to minimize computations.

Refreshment A refreshment protocol is possible in order to enable a user to exchange coins whose validity date is near expiration. The new coin cumulates the corresponding amounts and is associated to the previous ones by using the same random value, in order to guarantee correct overspending verification. As above, this protocol is simply the combination of a deposit and a withdrawal.

Privacy Revocation

- *Payment-based Tracing*: Upon overspending detection, the bank issues the list of transactions and sends them to the TTPs center. After verifying the bank's claim, the TTPs return the identity I associated to the J_j included in the transactions together with the proof that $\log_I J_j = \log_g Y_j \; (= X_j)$.
- *Withdrawal-based Tracing*: In this situation, the user requiring protection against abuse (such as a criminal forcing him to withdraw anonymously e-coins and reveal the Ps related to the secret key s) will give the Ps corresponding to the withdrawal session and prove that he knows s (in order to avoid false accusations by a malevolent user knowing a certain Ps). The pseudonym is blacklisted to identify related-coins on-the-fly and block the transaction.

4 Security Analysis:

In this section, we sketch the different security rationale of our scheme.

4.1 Forgery

A money forgery attack consists in a coalition of payers, payees and trustees making extra-money from the original pool of electronic coins certified by the bank or modifying coin values. Consider two possibilities:

1. transform a bank signature on a coin with value a into a signature on a coin with value a' where $a' > a$: we assume that the bank's secret keys have been properly generated (i.e. randomly) to avoid any correlation between keys. Any other manipulation is equivalent to possibility 2;
2. build a new certified coin from the public view of the protocols: this is equivalent to generate more coins than what allowed. The usage of a blind signature based on the witness indistinguishability guarantees the bank against such a forgery [21].

4.2 Bank Robbery

We consider that the attack can either consist in simply forcing the bank to deliver blindly certified coins or even stealing the bank's keys by any mean (a physical attack of the bank system or kidnapping the bank manager). In order to prevent such an attack, two kinds of techniques can be applied:

– the bank stores any withdrawal [19] she properly completes, until their expiration date, and TTPS to periodically blind-certify the list. If a robbery occurs, the bank replaces its keys, and asks everybody to refresh their coins. The refreshment is performed with the help of TTPs who control, in the previous list, whether the coins have been fairly withdrawn. The logical consequence is that the thief cannot spend his coins, otherwise he will be discovered.
– after any withdrawal, the user asks TTPs to perform a shared signature of his new coin. Next, this certificate will be required for any transaction. In case of bank robbery, TTPs stop certifying coins which contain stolen keys of the Bank.

4.3 Privacy

Obviously, privacy protection provided by our scheme is only conditional, since users' untraceability is revocable and relies on the difficulty of the Diffie-Hellman problem [9]. Nevertheless, this problem has been proven to be equivalent in almost all instances to the discrete logarithm problem [16]. One may also observe that privacy is restricted by the number of Ps since transactions related to a certain J_j are linkable; but the bank cannot link these transactions to I anyway.

Private Channel The very nature of I and Ps enables the bank to communicate securely with a user by El Gamal encryption (with $I = g^s$ during withdrawal and $Y_j = J_j^s$ during transfer) to prevent other users (I' or Y_j') from eavesdropping and mounting a very basic active attack: ask the question e' instead of the e from I or Y_j. A similar mechanism at registration time protects the user from the bank trying to discover a link between user's identity and his pseudonyms when the user sends I to the TTPs: since I is probabilistically encrypted, the bank cannot correlate $\{Ps_j\}$ to any known I.

Privacy Revocation

Theorem 1. *The scheme achieves overspending robustness.*

Proof. A user has to sign a transaction in order to spend a coin; given that the user's signature is existentially unforgeable, it is infeasible for an attacker to generate a different signature for a given transaction. $\square$

Theorem 2. *The scheme achieves revocable privacy: only the bank and at least k TTPs can prove that a transaction was issued by a user whose identity is ID.*

Proof. First, observe that at withdrawal time, the user sends his public identity I but obtains a blind signature on J_j, that will be associated with further transactions performed by the user. Therefore, any coin related to J_j is spent anonymously. The bank can neither link any transaction to a specific I (since a transaction is linked to J_j that the bank blindly signs during withdrawal) nor trace a coin. On the contrary, the bank and any TTP can easily link a transaction to user's identity:
- assuming that the bank detects overspending of coin C, she presents the related transaction τ to any TTP who extracts J_j and looks-up the corresponding I in the database. This TTP reveals I to the bank who can identify the user responsible of the fraud. However, only k TTPs can prove together the link between I and J_j with $\log_I J_j = \log_g Y_j$, since this link is protected by the Diffie-Hellman decisional problem[2];
- assuming that the user's secret key have been stolen; the user asks the TTPs to reveal the set $\{J_j\}_{j \leq \pi}$ corresponding to I; TTPs add them to the coin blacklist. $\square$

4.4 Impersonation

Theorem 3. *The scheme achieves framing freeness:*
1. *neither the bank nor TTP can falsely prove that a user performed a transaction,*
2. *neither the bank nor TTP can spend a coin withdrawn by a user.*

---

[2] given Y_j, $g = Y_j^{1/X_j}$ and $J_j = Y_j^s$, for any T, it is computationally impossible to decide whether $T \stackrel{?}{=} Y_j^{s/X_j} = g^s = I \bmod p$

Proof. Again, consider the two possible attacks:

1. Assuming that the bank wants to prove that a user overspent coin C; the bank has to deliver to TTPs the corresponding set of transactions τ_i and the signatures corresponding to (J_j, Y_j) public key which is equivalent to knowing the secret key s since user's signature scheme is existentially unforgeable. Assuming now that TTPs want to hide the identity I of a malevolent user and reveal I'; TTPs must prove that: $\log_{I'} J_j = \log_g Y_j = X_j = \log_I J_j$. Therefore, $J_j = I^{X_j} = I'^{X_j}$ which is equivalent to $I' = I$, implying that TTPs must send $I' = I$.

2. User's signature implies that spending a coin required to know user's secret key s due to the existentially unforgeability property; therefore neither the bank nor TTP can spend users' coins.

$\square$

4.5 Usage of Keys

A careful analysis of the scheme leads to the following observation: secret keys s and X are used for El Gamal encryption and Schnorr signature. This feature, introduced for the sake of efficiency (see next section), could open the door to some attacks in case information related to the keys leaks during protocols exchange.

Assuming that signing with a key k reveals enough information for breaking El Gamal: it could be possible to break the related Diffie-Hellman problem with the same key k. Since this problem has been proven to be equivalent in almost all instances to the discrete logarithm problem [16], it means that one could eventually break Schnorr protocol using these information. Thus, the usage of k in our setting does not give any extra advantage over a direct attack on the signature scheme (which means breaking discrete logarithm).

5 Efficiency

The scheme presented is generic in the sense that implementations could rely on different cryptographic primitives. Nevertheless, choosing DLP-based primitives is well-suited to our construction since discrete logarithm provides several provably secure schemes [23, 24, 20, 21]. Furthermore, Ps security and efficiency rely on the exponentiation properties (in the sense of Diffie-Hellman's key-exchange protocol [9]). These properties are therefore closely related to our scheme's overall performance. Finally, the scheme is computationally efficient and offers protection (conditional privacy for users, revocable privacy for the bank) to all participants.

Computations: From the user's standpoint, the maximal number of cumbersome computations, *i.e.* exponentiations in a finite field, is four at registration and six at withdrawal time whereas the user has to perform only one exponentiation to spend a coin. Now, we must consider that the registration at the TTPs will be performed once for all, *i.e.* once the user stored the $\{Ps_j\}$ list, he will only withdraw coins from time to time. The extra cost of three exponentiations for obtaining a $\{Ps_j\}$ set is therefore merely marginal. Furthermore, a user may decide to store coins received from other users in order to transfer them to the bank and obtain a coin which value is equivalent to the total value of collected coins. This may result in reducing computations for subsequent payments since the user may exchange a lot of coins at the cost of about one exponentiation only.

The average time for computing an exponentiation on a station or Pentium-like PC is around 40 ms, mainly depending on the exponent size and techniques used for reduction; this is roughly equivalent to performance obtained with a portable device (e.g a smart card) with a cryptographic accelerator. Such timings clearly clamp the total time for a transaction under 1 s, even assuming a low-rate communication link between users and TTPs.

Communications: An important property of this scheme is to allow the trustees to be off-line during payment and withdrawal. A structure where communication between users and trustees is minimized increases overall performance (e.g Main Trustee Structure presented in section 2). The transfer protocol may also reduce global communication in the system by enabling users to avoid several payment interactions (for spending many coins).

Memory Requirements: Considering usual size of parameters, Ps_j is 104-byte long since this is a Schnorr's public key J_j (64 bytes) with its certificate (40 bytes). A coin requires only 64 bytes to be stored with:
Public Information: Ps reference j (1 byte),
                            date (1 byte) and amount (2 bytes);
Coin Signature: digest (20 bytes) and blind signature (40 bytes).
Observe that this is significantly less than most previously proposed schemes [1, 10, 13] even considering that coins grow in size after transfer operations. Actually, a coin corresponding to n coins is $(64+8n)$-byte long since the list of coin-related randoms is appended to the new coin. Nevertheless, since the user transfered n coins, he saves $n \times (64 - 8)$ bytes of storage.

The other advantage granted by pseudonym usage is that the cost for Ps storage is divided by the total number of related coins. Since payments performed with a Ps are linkable, this amortization of the memory requirement is clearly associated to the privacy level a user wants to achieve.

Overall Performance: The scheme efficiency thereby compares favorably with recently proposed schemes [3, 11] at a double cost:

- scalable restriction of payment anonymity at the exact appreciation of users,
- presence of Trustees at the account opening, which is not a serious drawback considering that registration is performed only once.

6   Conclusion

We exhibited an efficient electronic cash scheme providing a high level of performance and security. The structure of the public-key architecture combined with Diffie-Hellman's paradigm leads to an efficient construction, resistant to various attacks [13]. The scheme offers also coin semi-transferability and refreshment in order to achieve an user-friendly electronic money system. Finally, the distribution of trustees through a communication network allows several implementation choices, in order to precisely balance security and efficiency.

References

1. S. A. Brands. Untraceable Off-line Cash in Wallets with Observers. In *Crypto '93*, LNCS 773, pages 302–318. Springer-Verlag, 1994.
2. E. Brickell, P. Gemmell, and D. Kravitz. Trustee-based Tracing Extensions to Anonymous Cash and Making of Anonymous Change. In *SODA '95*, pages 457–466, 1995.
3. J. Camenisch, U. Maurer, and M. Stadler. Digital Payment Systems with Passive Anonymity-Revoking Trustees. In *ESORICS '96*, LNCS 1146. Springer-Verlag, 1996.
4. J. Camenisch, J.-M. Piveteau, and M. Stadler. Fair Blind Signatures. In *Eurocrypt '95*, LNCS 921, pages 209–219. Springer-Verlag, 1995.
5. J. Camenisch, J.-M. Piveteau, and M. Stadler. An Efficient Fair Payment System. In *Proc. of the 3rd CCCS*, pages 88–94. ACM press, 1996.
6. D. Chaum. Untraceable Electronic Mail, Return Addresses, and Digital Pseudonyms. *Communications of the ACM*, 24(2):84–88, February 1981.
7. D. Chaum. Blind Signatures for Untraceable Payments. In *Crypto '82*, pages 199–203. Plenum, NY, 1983.
8. D. Chaum, A. Fiat, and M. Naor. Untraceable Electronic Cash. In *Crypto '88*, LNCS 403, pages 319–327. Springer-Verlag, 1989.
9. W. Diffie and M. E. Hellman. New Directions in Cryptography. In *IEEE Transactions on Information Theory*, volume IT–22, no. 6, pages 644–654, november 1976.
10. N. Ferguson. Extensions of Single Term Coins. In *Crypto '93*, LNCS 773, pages 292–301. Springer-Verlag, 1994.
11. Y. Frankel, Y. Tsiounis, and M. Yung. "Indirect Disclosure Proof": Achieving Efficient Fair Off-Line E-Cash. In *Asiacrypt '96*, LNCS 1163, pages 286–300. Springer-Verlag, 1996.
12. T. El Gamal. A Public Key Cryptosystem and a Signature Scheme Based on Discrete Logarithms. In *IEEE Transactions on Information Theory*, volume IT–31, no. 4, pages 469–472, july 1985.
13. M. Jakobsson and M. Yung. Revokable and Versatile Electronic Money. In *Proc. of the 3rd CCCS*, pages 76–87. ACM press, 1996.
14. M. Jakobsson and M. Yung. Distributed "Magic Ink" Signatures. In *Eurocrypt '97*, LNCS 1233, pages 450–464. Springer-Verlag, 1997.
15. M. Jakobsson and M. Yung. Applying Anti-Trust Policies to Increase Trust in a Versatile e-money System. In *Financial Cryptography '97*, LNCS 1318. Springer-Verlag, 1998.

40

16. U. M. Maurer. Diffie Hellman Oracles. In *Crypto '96*, LNCS 1109, pages 268–282. Springer-Verlag, 1996.

17. D. M'Raïhi. Cost-Effective Payment Schemes with Privacy Regulation. In *Asiacrypt '96*, LNCS 1163, pages 266–275. Springer-Verlag, 1996.

18. T. Okamoto. Provably Secure and Practical Identification Schemes and Corresponding Signature Schemes. In *Crypto '92*, LNCS 740, pages 31–53. Springer-Verlag, 1992.

19. H. Petersen and G. Poupard. Efficient Scalable Fair Cash with Off-line Extortion Prevention. In *Proc. of ICICS'97*, LNCS 1334, pages 463–477. Springer-Verlag, 1997.

20. D. Pointcheval and J. Stern. Security Proofs for Signature Schemes. In *Eurocrypt '96*, LNCS 1070, pages 387–398. Springer-Verlag, 1996.

21. D. Pointcheval and J. Stern. Provably Secure Blind Signature Schemes. In *Asiacrypt '96*, LNCS 1163, pages 252–265. Springer-Verlag, 1996.

22. R. Rivest, A. Shamir, and L. Adleman. A Method for Obtaining Digital Signatures and Public Key Cryptosystems. *Communications of the ACM*, 21(2):120–126, february 1978.

23. C. P. Schnorr. Efficient Identification and Signatures for Smart Cards. In *Crypto '89*, LNCS 435, pages 235–251. Springer-Verlag, 1990.

24. C. P. Schnorr. Efficient Signature Generation by Smart Cards. *Journal of Cryptology*, 4(3):161–174, 1991.

25. V. Shoup. Lower Bounds for Discrete Logarithms and Related Problems. In *Eurocrypt '97*, LNCS 1233, pages 256–266. Springer-Verlag, 1997.

26. S. von Solms and D. Naccache. On Blind Signatures and Perfect Crimes. *Computers & Security*, 11:581–583, 1992.

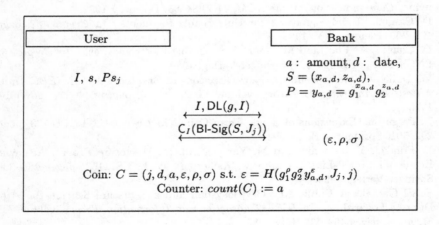

Fig. 2. Withdrawal

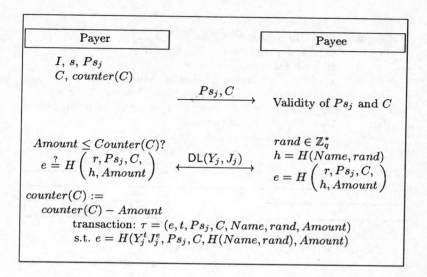

Fig. 3. Payment

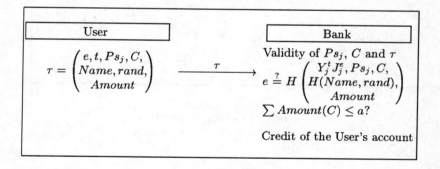

Fig. 4. Deposit ($Name = I$)

Common: p, q large primes such that $q|p-1$.
 g, g_1 and g_2 elements of $\mathbb{Z}_p^*$ of order q.
 H, hash function.
 π, integer, maximum number of pseudonyms.

TTP: Global keys X (secret), $Y = g^X \bmod p$ (public)
 for $j = 1, \ldots, \pi$ X_j (secret), $Y_j = g^{X_j} \bmod p$ (public)

Bank: Global key B (public)
 amount a, date d $x_{a,d}, z_{a,d}$ (secret)
 $y_{a,d} = g_1^{x_{a,d}} g_2^{z_{a,d}} \bmod p$ (public)

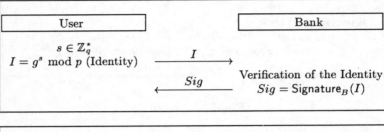

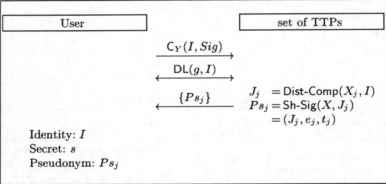

Fig. 5. Opening account

A Platform for Privately Defined Currencies, Loyalty Credits, and Play Money

David P. Maher

AT&T Labs Research
Room B245
180 Park Avenue
Florham Park, NJ 07932-0971
dpm@research.att.com

Abstract. We use techniques from financial cryptography to define new electronic currencies that are suitable for many applications. We use a platform approach to allow a single, world-wide infrastructure to support a practically unlimited number of new currencies. The platform permits new currencies to be defined with little effort, and allows an individual to effectively manage and use perhaps a few dozen of those currencies that he finds personally useful. We describe the structures and mechanisms of the platform, various applications, and the risks associated with its use.

1 Introduction

We have designed a system that allows individuals to use an efficient, publicly available infrastructure to define and dispense private currencies and other types of value such as loyalty credits and play money. We want to make it straightforward for a corner sandwich shop owner to set up a loyalty system or for an airline to enhance its frequent flyer program. We want to allow a corporation to easily set up a private scrip system to simplify internal account transfers, and to make it easy for children to issue and exchange play money for games they might play over a network. Likewise, we want to make it very easy for people to use multiple currencies and value systems by using a single simple device. The platform, which uses smart cards, could in the future allow new currencies to be instantly defined with as little effort as it takes to visit a web site and complete a form. The platform is extremely scaleable, easily supporting millions of currencies, and allows individuals to practically use as many currencies or value systems as one can imagine. In the long run, we believe that the marginal cost of defining and supporting a new currency that can be used world wide can approach zero.

An interesting aspect of the system is that it can be used to conveniently exchange value of different types, depending on their rules of use. Thus, an individual could exchange frequent flier points for free haircuts or meals. We briefly discuss the implications of such possibilities, and claim that firm conclusions regarding effects on various micro-economies can be obtained only through experimentation. Fortunately, the platform described here should make it easy to experiment with various rules of value exchange.

The platform that enables this free use of new currencies is based on a cryptographic key management system that was designed to be simple yet very effective. The art here is in finding a minimal system that is broadly useful.

Before discussing some of the technical details, we explain how someone might use the system. Then we describe the platform components, how they work, some of the security risks, and some of the risk mitigation possibilities. Then we return to a discussion of applications of the platform.

2 Definition

We define *currency* as any medium of exchange. Currency is not necessarily legal tender, and in the context of this paper, it usually is not. The platform that we describe allows a person to define either *directed* or *undirected* systems of currency. In directed systems, currency follows a directed path among classes of users and is not normally *negotiable* within the system. In undirected systems, currency follows undirected paths and the currency is negotiable by peers in the system much as US Federal Reserve Notes are today.

3 End-User's View of the Platform

We suppose that smart cards with certain properties defined below are universally distributed and accessible to anyone. For simplicity, assume that there is one distributor of smart cards that are called Xcards who maintains a web-site where new forms of currency that can be carried on the card may be defined. Let's say that a grocery store chain wants to set up a loyalty point system. A representative who will originate the points visits the card distributor's web-site and completes a form that includes

- a name for the currency (e.g. "Shop and Save Green Points")
- properties (such as whether the point system is directed or undirected)
- An initial value sum to be distributed to this originator

At the web-site, a script is executed whereby the entries on the form are checked for consistency, and the name given to the points is ensured to be unique. If all goes well, a multi-layer secure protocol is executed between the web-site and the grocery chain representative's client whereby the representative's smart card is initialized with the specified number of Green points.

Now, the grocery chain can use electronic means to distribute the Green Points internally for further distribution at grocery store point-of-sale terminals. Points are distributed from the originator's Xcard to intermediate Xcards held by store managers, and then to Xcards at Point-Of-Sale terminals. When a consumer pays for groceries at such a terminal, he can insert his Xcard and receive a certain number of points through a simple value transfer protocol. If the consumer is receiving Shop and Save Green Points for the first time, the consumer's Xcard is automatically initialized, without disturbing any of the other currencies this consumer may be using. If Green Points constitute a directed currency system, the consumer can redeem the points only at a Shop and Save grocery. If the system is undirected, the consumer can exchange the points with any other holder of an Xcard, in person or over the Internet, for any value he can negotiate. These Green Points have some initial value as soon as Shop and Save declares a redemption schedule which may consist of prizes, discounts, or any number of other goods or services. The Grocery chain might easily specify that Green Points could be officially exchanged for a variety of other types of currency such as frequent flyer points or credits for compact disks, or whatever.

4 System Goals

We endeavor to make the platform as simple as possible, with as little overhead as possible. We want currencies to:

1. *Be very easy to define:* We want the platform to allow an infrastructure to be shared by perhaps millions of merchants and other individuals worldwide who may want to define a value system that captures everything from loyalty to discounts to hypothetical or imaginary value in instructional or recreational games.
2. *Be very easy to use:* Many people get dozens of opportunities to participate in various currency and loyalty systems. However, they are often a hassle to use, people need to carry around various cards that often get lost, and people often forget that they are participating.
3. *Have a simple, low overhead infrastructure:* We would like a certain uniformity of procedure and a sharing of costs. We would like the marginal cost of supporting a new currency to be negligible. From the point of view of the user, one or two cards may allow participation in a large number of currency schemes in a number of domains, including mercantile, corporate and recreational domains.
4. *Have enough flexibility to allow schemes to be suited to a number of purposes and environments*: We want to allow currency systems to interact, and strengthen one another, and to provide a viable means of trade that can operate at grass-roots levels.

5 The Platform Components

The platform consists of a number of specifications that we describe here at a very high level. The tangible components are smart cards (or some other trusted computing base), their associated interface devices, and pages on card issuer web-sites. A full set of detailed specifications has not yet been completed. Omitted here is a description of the card issuer's Key Management System. However, one may infer the functional requirements of the Key Management System from the descriptions of the other parts of the platform. The intangible elements of the platform consist of various data structures, cryptographic schema, process descriptions, and interface specifications.

5.1 Smart Cards

For currency management, we suppose the availability of single chip smart cards (as specified in ISO Standard 7816). In principle, other types of devices can substitute for smart cards. In general, we need something that is portable and has some computing capability with some tamper resistance. Smart Cards are the paradigm that we have chosen, although in reality they typically do not presently have a great deal of tamper resistance. We believe that today, for many applications, their security capabilities will suffice, and there are prospects for improvements to their security design in the future.

We presume that each smart card chip that complies with the platform specification has the following:

- A processor that supports cryptographic functions
- Permanent program memory (ROM)
- A small amount of protected nonvolatile memory (PNVM) that is used for chip-specific cryptographic keys
- A card unique secret symmetric key (CSK) stored in PNVM
- A unique ID vector
- Non-volatile RAM (NVM) for additional programs and data
- A number of card issuer's public keys (CIPKs)
- A random number generator
- A card-unique asymmetric (public, private) key pair
- A certificate for the public key signed by the card issuer

During the final stages of manufacturing, a program on the chip generates the CSK for use with symmetric ciphers. This key never leaves the chip but is stored in protected non-volatile memory. The chip[1] also generates a private and public key pair for an asymmetric cipher system such as RSA. The private key is stored, encrypted, in non-volatile memory and the public key and chip ID are exported for certification by the manufacturer. The chip then receives and stores a unique chip certificate for use with the asymmetric key pair, signed by the issuer using one of the RSA secret keys whose public counterpart is stored in the card as a CIPK. In general we presume that the PNVM resists tampering, and that the CSK stored there is used to ensure the integrity and confidentiality of the rest of the key information that is stored in regular NVM.

The set of CIPKs on the chip includes at least two RSA public keys. One is used for signing card credentials, and one is used for signing messages generated in the currency definition process described below. The card may also include a Diffie-

---

[1] For chips with weak cryptographic function capabilities, it may be more reasonable to simply inject the keys and the accompanying certificate.

Hellman public key for use in generating symmetric keys that are shared between the card issuer and the card to support some optional data backup protocols.

5.2 Card Interface Devices

Users and networks interact with smart cards through interface devices. Consumers will use two types of devices: The first is a hand-held device resembling a calculator with a small keypad and display and one or two slots slot in which cards are inserted. This device will usually have its own processor, and may have non-volatile memory that stores currency information that can be managed by the user in conjunction with the capabilities of the card. Such a device can inexpensively include enough memory to support hundreds of currencies. With an Interface Device that has two slots, value can be exchanged between two cards using just that device. The second type of interface device is a PC or other computer terminal that includes a smart card reader. This device may be connected to a network. The non-volatile memory in the PC as well as in the network can store currency information that can be managed by an individual using her card. For both types of interface devices, the keyboard and display support the command interface between the user and the card. We expect standards to emerge that will support the definition of the interfaces between cards and interface devices and the processes that run on those devices. Microsoft, for example has proposed such a standard, called PCSC, for use with their operating systems.

Merchants can use similar interface devices, but they will be optimized for point of sale or network applications.

5.3 Card Issuer Web Sites

We speculate that major banks, telecommunications companies, and other organizations will be issuing smart cards to their customers. Although we do not believe that a given consumer will maintain all of their applications on one card, we do believe that multiple applications will be bundled on cards. Multiple applications can be used to increase the likelihood that a consumer will carry and use a given card. So, it will be in the card issuer's interest to maintain a web-site that will support the use of their cards. Pages on the site will be used to allow the definition of new currencies that can be available for use by anyone. Pages will contain forms that can be completed by anyone wishing to define a new currency. Java programs interact with the user's card, and CGI scripts interact with card issuer's databases. The process of defining a new currency is discussed below.

We also expect that the card-issuer web-site will provide customer support for cards. In particular, a card memory backup and error recovery service can be provided.

5.4 Currency Trees

Programs on the smart card chip can construct binary signature trees similar to those suggested by Merkle [1]. We call these currency trees. Here, each leaf of the tree will contain data for a particular currency, as described below. Interior nodes will contain the result of the keyed CBC MAC [2] of the data in its two child nodes. The root of the tree will be stored in the chip card's non-volatile memory. Typically the key used for this MAC will be the smart card chip's own secret key or CSK. In some cases, it will be a key shared with the card issuer by use of one of the issuer's public Diffie-Hellman keys (CIPKs) stored in the chip.

In general, programs on the chip card will manipulate a number of currency trees. Note that the chip need only store the root value of a given tree. The details of some currencies that are most frequently used will be kept in a currency tree stored on the chip itself. The details of other currencies that are less often used are kept in trees stored in smart card interface devices the size of small calculators, or on Personal Computers or network appliances.

The reader may note that a non-keyed hash function could be used here in place of the keyed MAC, since we are storing the root of the hash tree in a secured place on the smart card chip. However, we believe that the keyed MAC can be more efficient, and supports some features that we will discuss later.

5.5 Currency Tree Entries

A currency tree entry is a record that contains a small amount of information:

1. Name of the currency
2. Currency type
3. Role played by this user (originator, redeemer, consumer, etc, see below)
4. Transaction sequence number
5. An integer amount corresponding to the value in this currency owned by the bearer
6. Special permissions

The currency name must be globally unique. The currency type is a designator that determines the rules of use of the currency. For example is currency flow undirected, allowing full negotiability, or directed, requiring the designation of cards that have special permissions allowing the redemption of currency? In this latter case, it is necessary to store the designated role in the currency tree record. So, a user may play the role of originator of new currency, or redeemer, whereby the user in a directed system can accept payment using the currency. The user's transaction serial number is required to defend against replays of messages used to transfer value. Special permissions are required to mint more currency, or to designate user-roles.

5.6 Card API.

There is a card API that describes the formal command set that is used to interact with the card currency application. This API allows applications running on various interface devices such as PCs, workstations, and personal electronic wallets to interact with the currency applications on the card.

5.7 Processes

We describe the most fundamental processes supported by the platform at a very high level. We have endeavored to minimize the complexity of the processes. We observe, however, that as we attempt to mitigate risks, provide for robust recovery from errors, and allow for renewability of security schemes and parameters, the complexity of the system grows. For the moment we favor a minimal approach until we can determine what additional processes are truly useful and clearly pay their way in exchange for the added complexity.

Defining currencies and originating value. As mentioned above, the card issuer will maintain a web-site that will include scripts that allow the definition of new currencies in an automated fashion. Any visitor to the site can define a new currency. There is no need to identify the visitor. A Java program can carry out the currency definition protocol on the visitor's client. The visitor completes a form, supplying the currency name (which is checked at the server for uniqueness), and then the currency type value (directed or undirected) and the initial amount to be originated are entered. The visitor will also specify whether he, as the originator, wants the privilege of generating more of the same currency in the future, without interacting with the issuer's server. The server computes a new currency data structure, signs it using the secret key associated with one of the RSA CIPKs stored in the visitor's card, and sends it to the visitor's client. The client issues a card API command to accept the new currency structure. The visitor's card verifies the authenticity of the currency structure using the CIPK, and then adds the new currency to its local currency tree using the MAC key (usually the card's CSK) associated with that tree. At this point, the new currency is defined, and an initial amount has been minted.

The integrity of this process is highly dependent on the uniqueness of the currency name, and the integrity of the CIPK. If an impostor who knows just the CIPK public key carries out this protocol with an issuer, a new currency may still be defined, however, the currency will not be useable, as the value transfer protocol described below requires use of the issuer certified asymmetric key pair. To prevent impostors from using this service, we may want to require the visitor card to use its certified cryptographic keys, binding them into the currency definition protocol.

Creating more value. The originator of a currency may, if the currency rules allow, create more value. A simple request is sent to the originator's card, naming the currency and the new amount to be put on that card. The card complies if the data in the currency tree affirms the privilege to create more value. Note, below it is stated that the originator may grant currency creation privileges to others. Cards with this ability need to be carefully managed. In many circumstances, this privilege is not needed or can be limited to a very few cards.

Transferring value. Currency value can be sent from one card to another by use of a value transfer protocol such as one of those specified in CEN standard 1546, part 2 [3]. In these protocols, payer and payee cards first exchange transaction details including the certificates of their respective cards and the amount to be transferred. Recall these certificates bind a card ID to a public key. In CEN 1546, the payer and payee exchange signed messages to complete the transfer.

In our case, we follow a similar arrangement, except that we need to deal with selection of currency. In the initialization phase, the name of the currency to be used is included in the transaction preamble, when the card certificates are exchanged. In our protocol, it is not necessary for the payee card to initially recognize the currency name, as the card may not be initialized with that currency. After transaction initialization, the payee's card then sends a formal signed message, requesting payment. Many of the payment details are repeated in this message, including the currency name, amount, and transaction sequence numbers used to foil replay attacks. The payer then debits the currency amount, recomputes the currency tree values from this leaf to the root, stores the new root value, and sends a signed message to the payee asserting that the debit has been made. The payee, upon receiving the message and verifying its authenticity, increments its currency value amount. If the currency name is unknown to the payee's card, a new leaf is automatically created for it in a currency tree. In either case, tree values are then recomputed along the path from this leaf to the root, and the new root is stored on the card. In some variations of the protocol, the payee then sends a signed acknowledgement message back to the payer.

Of course, the actual payee and payer are oblivious to the details carried out by their cards. They do interact with their cards through an interface device that typically has a small display and keypad. For value transfer, the payer need only specify the amount to be paid (though it is the payee's card that formally requests it), and the payee signifies acceptance.

Granting special permissions. Special permissions that can be recorded in a currency leaf's data structure include:

- bearer is an originator (and can therefore grant special permissions in a directed system)
- bearer can mint more currency
- bearer can grant permission to mint more currency
- bearer may dispense this currency to consumers in a directed system
- bearer is authorized to redeem value in a directed system
- bearer can grant special permissions in a directed system

Special permissions are necessary in a directed currency system, as the currency is non-negotiable by consumers, but there needs to be special classes of cards that can dispense the currency and redeem it. An originator can set up those classes by using the permission granting protocol.

For a given currency, a user may have special permissions. Those permissions are exercised through a protocol that involves commands in the API. Permissions are granted using signed messages between grantee and grantor, similar to the value transfer protocol described above.

Whether the system is directed or not, we may want to increase the amount of currency in circulation. This could be done with the cooperation of a card issuer (by reserving the right for the currency originator to go back to the card issuer to create more currency, or it can be done with cards specifically designated to increase the currency supply.

Maintaining currency trees. Merkle hash trees are ideal for this platform, as they are very efficient when there is a relatively large amount of data that needs to be selectively verified and updated. The use of a symmetric key MAC makes transactions even more efficient. Very little data needs to be stored within the smart card, and only a small number of MAC operations (log n, where n is the number of currencies in the tree) need to be called.

We believe that once alternate currencies are made easy to use, then people will use dozens of currencies from different loyalty programs, corporate scrip, and other applications.

The trees maintain the integrity of the various currency amounts, and permit the backup and off-loading of the details from each user's card. We envision currency systems to be just one of many applications that may be included on a given smart card. There is usually very little room for applications on a card in any case, as current cards typically have very little memory, perhaps 16K bytes of ROM and 2K to 8K bytes of NVRAM. We want to minimize the latter, as the amount of NVRAM significantly contributes to the expense of the card. Thus, having a single platform for multiple currencies is very useful, and having the ability to store details of the applications off-chip with integrity is another bonus. We also want to have provisions in case cards are lost, since we are concentrating a lot of value. In some cases, the amount of value can be real and significant such as in the application of a corporate scrip system.

A user's card interface device (hand-held device or PC or workstation) can maintain card currency trees and even archive them redundantly on public servers. The card only need keep the value of the root of the tree in the card chip's memory. The interface device can run programs to exchange segments of trees that are stored on-chip with trees that are stored off-chip. The card can always verify tree integrity and recalculate tree values when trees are reconfigured in order to allow often used currencies to be stored on-chip, and less-often used currencies to be stored in trees on the PC. Copies of trees can be stored off-chip including the transaction sequence numbers included in the authenticated data. When a card is lost or becomes corrupted, one can appeal to the archived versions. One method for verifying integrity includes a simple escrow method using the card issuer. If the tree is stored with a MAC key and a backup vector constructed from the card issuer's public key stored on the chip, then the escrow method described in [4] can be used to allow the issuer to verify the integrity of the given currency tree. Of course, an unscrupulous user may execute several transactions in his favor after having claimed to have lost his card. This is risky in directed currency systems where the redeemer of currency may have records that can be reconciled with the values in the old trees. A currency transaction serial number could be a give-away. Even in the case of negotiable currencies, the archived values can be useful in decisions as to whether to restore value.

6 Risk Analysis

A number of risks must be analyzed with this platform. In general, risks need to be analyzed in the context of a specific application. However, there are common aspects of the platform that will impute risks across all applications. The most glaring risks for each currency involve dependence on a third party, namely the card issuer who is in a position to mint any currency. Such risks can easily be mitigated to an extent, and the risks will obviously be acceptable in some cases, but will clearly not be acceptable in others. One could use this technology in stock exchanges, where dependence on another third party would be a major issue. Specific risk mitigation for such cases can be added to the platform whereby the role of the card issuer in the definition of the currency can be diluted through redundancy techniques as described in Mike Reiter's Rampart System [5], but that is beyond the scope of this paper.

A second obvious class of risks has to do with the integrity of smart cards. We implicitly depend on the assumption that it is non-trivial to make modifications to the card that will cause keys to be revealed, and computations to be in error. This set of risks is mainly beyond the scope of this paper, however a reference that attempts to put some of these risks in perspective can be found in [6].

The risk of using a common platform is itself interesting, as diversity of approach will in general reduce risk. However, there are some advantages to the common platform in that the cost of risk mitigation can be spread across many applications. A number of diversification methods can be used within the platform itself. In general, we have favored the risk reduction approach of simplicity, while allowing the additional complexity of some mitigation measures to be applied when the benefits can be more clearly accrued.

6.1 Risks associated with the card issuer

The card issuer has the responsibility for providing cards with system credentials, signing those credentials on a per card basis. The card issuer manages the secret key(s) that correspond to the CIPKs that are stored in the cards. We advocate using different keys for signing credentials from keys used to sign messages that initiate currencies. The credential keys typically need to be managed at the point of card origination, while the message signing keys need to be used at a web-site. If either type of key is compromised, however, the scheme is severely affected.

When a credential-signing key is compromised, that key along with other information can be used to create a practically unlimited number of counterfeit card emulators running on personal computers. Such emulators can produce arbitrarily large currency value sums and can behave outwardly in a way that is indistinguishable from an authentic card, except in ways that may be evident only to the user. For example, emulators can be used to initiate currency and to exchange value with legitimate cards.

When a currency initiation message-signing key is compromised, counterfeit currency that is indistinguishable from legitimate currency can be injected into the supply. Such events can be just as devastating as the production of counterfeit card emulators. Thus, we need some effective risk mitigation measures.

Instead of using traditional certificate revocation measures to mitigate the risks associated with possible key compromise, and depending on protocols for replaacing compromised keys, we favor an approach that is better matched to the mixed on-line and off-line use that we expect of the cards. In particular, we generate several extra CIPKs and store them on each card. The extra private keys are stored in a highly secure place (perhaps split among several places) until they need to be used. Individual CIPKs can be activated and de-activated using an authenticated system message that acts like a virus that is passed from card to card whenever two cards interact. The virus can be seeded from the issuer's web-site, as well as through merchants. Known on-line users can be actively contacted. Only a few users will need to be called, as the virus will propagate efficiently if it is transferred during every transaction. The card lifecycle needs to be taken into account here. We expect a given card to be in the field for 2 to 4 years. New cards can include new keys that get activated as old cards are retired.

6.2 Risks associated with card integrity

If the tamper resistance mechanisms of a given card fail in certain ways, then the card may give up its secrets, providing the possibility that clones of that card may be created. Such clones may not be expected to follow rules of use, and can be allowed to have forge arbitrarily large currency sums. There are a number of ways to violate the physical and logical integrity of the card. Classes of attacks include bus probing, memory imaging, fault induction, and the observation of channels that leak cryptographic information. Examples of the latter include timing attacks and observation of dynamic microprocessor characteristics such RF emissions and power consumption. A complete description of these is beyond the scope of this paper.

Although CIPKs are "public keys", in this system, there is no need to make them public. They could just as well be kept secret. However, in the case where they are revealed, there are more possibilities for a cryptographic attack. Therefore, appropriate key sizes must be chosen. However, for keys used during value transfer, there is a trade-off with transaction times. For mass transit payment systems, toll roads, and the like, the transaction time is severely constrained, and we will want to minimize the time required for all operations including public key cryptographic operations.

6.3 Risks associated with currency management

Currency originators bear a responsibility for managing the currency supply and the currency flow. There are a number of risks associated with mismanagement. In general, the currency management risks are independent from one currency to another, in contrast to the system level risks associated with key management. In our platform, originators of currency can authorize new currency issues, and grant privileges to people to dispense or to issue more of a given currency. There is a risk that these privileges can be abused.

6.4 Risks associated with user behavior

A major risk is loss of a card. There are a number of data recovery techniques that are reasonable to use in the case when the card is used exclusively on-line. For example, we can implement a service and a protocol that backs up the card information and currency trees to the issuer's web site, and locks the card so that it cannot be used. The card issuer site knows the lock state, and if the card is lost when in the locked state, a new card can be issued, with the card currency trees fully restored. To exit the locked state in order to use the card, the user would have to participate in a simple unlocking protocol with the issuer's site. These protocols can be very straightforward, and the user interface would be a simple toggle switch on the on-line interface device GUI. Cards that are used off-line, or are lost while in the unlocked state present a much harder problem. A backup process can still be used, but the backup data must be presumed to be incomplete. In general, we do not know who the currency originators are, but individual originators could register with the card issuer, and provide a policy for dealing with lost cards.

6.5 Risk mitigation concerns

In considering risk mitigation measures, there are tradeoffs to be made among challenges to simplicity, cost of risk mitigation, and the comfort obtained from the mitigation schemes. We will claim that for most applications the simplest approach, consistent with what has been described here will suffice, and that over time, as the infrastructure scales up, the cost of more elaborate procedures to protect keys will fall within the range of reason. The system design is modular enough that strengthening the security of certain procedures will often not require massive system redesign.

7 Applications and Negotiability

We have mentioned the number of loyalty programs that seem to spring up everywhere. We believe that this platform can make such programs much easier to use, and that we can thereby enhance the value of these programs. With a common platform, we can make it much more feasible for people to trade value of different types. This itself can enhance the value of a given loyalty program. Frequent Flyer Points that are highly negotiable can be much more valuable, and can therefore be more effective in promoting loyalty. Of course, there are downsides to negotiability to the airline. It would be interesting to see how the tradeoffs evolve. There are some psychological aspects of these currencies that need to be better understood. Will people value them against a single standard such as some legal tender? Or will people continue to put these currencies in a special class? One could always transfer undirected currency value in return for cash, and one might imagine a broker system arising to aid this. Loyalty programs are supported by two main economic principles: First, the consumer of loyalty points values the points more than the redeemer or issuer. Second, the consumer is reinforced for the use of the issuer's products or services. Loyalty points that are negotiable still operate within these principles.

One can imagine two-way transfers that involve different currencies, such as in this anecdote: Parent: "Johnny! You mean that you traded your school good-behavior points for some 'Quake IV' ammunition credits?" Johnny: "Ted was grounded until he got enough points at school, so I got a good deal." Johnny, who may not have cared about the good-behavior points before, now finds value in them, as he can impress his friends with his prowess at a popular Internet game. He is now motivated to collect more points. Of course, Ted is another story. This example illustrates the idea that value is variable and can be enhanced by opportunity. We often don't capture this in most alternative currency systems.

Applications of this platform over the Internet abound. The value transfer protocol described above needs to be encapsulated in an Internet value transfer protocol that solves the problem of payee spoofing. Such protocols can be constructed, and generally depend on certification of the payee. This is beyond the scope of this paper, as well.

We have already mentioned the idea that in large corporations, internal accounting might be simplified if there were a very easy to administer scrip system. Large corporations are micro-economies wherein commerce is often thwarted by the need to make deals using account transfer techniques involving expensive bookkeeping. We conjecture that a scrip system such as can be constructed using this platform, can be much more efficient both by saving bookkeeping costs, and by promoting more spontaneity of transactions. It can change a planned economy into a more efficient market-based economy.

The final application type that we consider is the area of games. The use of currencies in Internet-based Multi-User-Dimensions (MUDs) and related applications can provide a very significant new strategic dimension. The platform that we describe here can allow this dimension to persist over time and allow the currency to be more portable. These properties can allow serious game playing to include fascinating economic aspects, and can be extended to experiments in commodities trading and stock transactions over the Internet.

8 Notes

We note that for some low-security applications, the use of a smart card is not necessary, or at least the need is less obvious. However, we find it difficult to assess the intensity of the motivation to cheat, and therefore we always presume the use of smart cards or a similar device that provides some non-trivial barrier to cheating.

In some parts of the world, smart cards are becoming very commonplace. In the US, they are arriving slowly. However, the credit card associations seem now to be determined to issue them worldwide over the next few years. There are at least two approaches to smart cards that will promote the use of multiple applications and that might accommodate this platform for privately defined currencies as just one application to co-exist with others such as credit and debit applications and general digital signature apps. These two approaches are Multos from Mondex International and JavaCard from Sun Microsystems. Both of these approaches will illustrate the need to pay strict attention to efficiency concerns, as both systems currently leave little room for individual applications once their respective virtual machines are installed on a smart card. Multos is an operating system for smart cards that features cryptographic services. It is designed to allow multiple applications while addressing the risk that one application might attack or interfere with another. Multos has a virtual machine that interprets a language called MEL. Alternatively, MULTOS can use the JavaCard VM with its API. There are some advantages to this, as JavaCard is a subset of Java, designed to run on smart cards. Unfortunately, many of the security features of Java are absent in the JavaCard specs, and therefore many of the security features of MULTOS or some other operating system are required. MULTOS features aspirations of ITSEC level E6 security. This is the highest security rating in the ITSEC (Information Technology Security Evaluation Criteria) process.

In this paper we have presumed, for simplicity, that there is a single card issuer. In general, we expect that there will be multiple issuers using a common, interoperable infrastructure. This could be accomplished in a number of ways. By forming an association, and offering a service that operates as if there were in fact, one issuer, we can avoid adding complexity to the key management system.

9 Conclusion

The private currency systems that can be constructed using the platform are very easy to use. Consumers need only possess a card to collect currency value, and they can begin to use new currencies without pre-arrangement. Thus, it is very easy for a new customer to begin using a loyalty program. It is also easy for anyone to initiate a currency for almost any application.

The system should be useful for relatively low valued currencies, local loyalty systems, corporate scrip, and games. As we examine and solve various security issues, it may be possible to use a platform like this for major loyalty schemes and even for systems such as stock exchanges.

10 References

1 R.C. Merkle, "A certified Digital Signature", *Advances in Cryptology*, Crypto '89 Proceedings, LNCS# 435, G. Brassard (Ed.), Springer, NY, 1990, p. 218.

2 G.J. Simmons, "A survey of Information Authentication", Chapter 7 of *Contemporary Cryptology*, Edited by G.J. Simmons, IEEE Press, New York, 1992.

3 CEN standard 1546-2, "Identification Card Systems – Inter-sector electronic purse Part 2: Security Architecture ", European Committee for Standardization, Central Secretariat: rue de Stassart 36, B-1050 Brussels, 1995.

4 D. P. Maher, "Crypto Backup and Key Escrow", CACM, March 1996.

5 M. K. Reiter, "Secure Agreement Protocols: Reliable and Atomic Group Multicast in Rampart". In Proceedings of the 2nd ACM Conference on Computer and Communications Security, pages 68-80, November 1994.

6 D. P. Maher, "Fault Induction Attacks, Tamper Resistance, and Hostile Reverse Engineering in Perspective", Proceedings of the1997 Financial Cryptography Conference, LNCS# 1318, R. Hirschfeld (Ed.), Springer, New York, 1997.

Assessment of Threats for
Smart Card Based Electronic Cash

Kazuo J. Ezawa
Gregory Napiorkowski

Mondex International Limited
Atlantic Technology Center
Suite 109
100 Campus Drive
P.O. Box 972
Florham Park, New Jersey, 07932-0972
USA

Abstract. The security of smart card based electronic cash have been receiving significant attention recently. However, there has been little systematic analysis or quantification of the impact of the security break on the smart card based electronic cash economy. This paper discusses the assessment of threats in two phases using two different methodologies. The first is the assessment of overall threat using the business system analysis model called "value chain" - the methodology to evaluate the activities necessary to achieve the final objectives of the counterfeiting organization. It is a qualitative method. The second is the quantification of such a threat using micro dynamic simulation.

1   Introduction

There have been many technical discussions of the security of smart card based electronic cash. However, there has been little attention paid to the systematic analysis of the way to achieve objectives of counterfeiting (e.g., economic gain, sabotage, blackmail, etc.), nor the subsequent quantification of the impact of the security break on the smart card based electronic cash economy. Clearly, one has to perform these analyses before one claims the demise of the smart card based electronic cash. This paper discusses the assessment of threats in two phases using two different methodologies. The first phase is the assessment of overall threat using the business system analysis model called "value chain" [5] - the methodology to evaluate the activities necessary to achieve the final objectives of the counterfeiting organization. It is a qualitative method. The second phase is the quantification of such a threat using micro dynamic simulation.

The counterfeiter's challenges are both strictly technical as well as of organizational and behavioral nature, and go well beyond the security break, a formidable barrier itself, but only the first barrier to be broken. This paper discusses how a global smart card based electronic cash product (such as Mondex electronic cash) using various security, risk management capability, and taking advantages of other natural human and organizational behaviors prevents counterfeiters from achieving their ultimate goal.

The paper is organized as follows. Section 1 describes the qualitative assessment using the counterfeiter's value chain model. It discusses using two illustrative examples overall challenges that are faced by the counterfeiters. Section 2 discusses the quantification of impact of counterfeiter's threat scenarios using micro dynamic simulator. Section 3 summarizes the discussion.

2   Qualitative Overall Assessment of Threats Using Business System Analysis Methodology

There are many possible motivations for counterfeiting smart card based electronic cash application; from the economic gain, to fame, to sabotage, and to the international blackmail. Whatever the motive of the counterfeiter, it is beneficial to analyze the counterfeiter's *"value chain"*[1] from the business perspective, since the principal motivation for setting up a counterfeiting operation is to achieve an "objective." Clearly, depending on the objectives, types of the target product for the counterfeiting, and types of exploitation strategies (threat scenarios), the value chain model will look different.

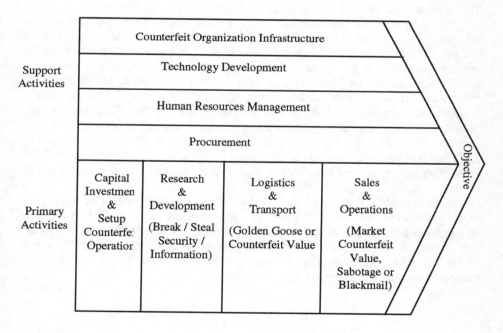

Figure 1. Generic Counterfeiter's Value Chain

---

[1] The business system concept of value chain captures the idea that a firm or, in our case, a counterfeit organization has a series of functions to perform, and each of them needs to accomplish some specific goals in order to produce a profit.

The value chain model explicitly and visually describes the requirement for the supporting infrastructure and the primary activities of the organization to accomplish the mission. The model is a *qualitative model*, and has been extensively used in the business to evaluate the effectiveness of the firm and the competitive position in the industry that it serves. In this paper, we explore the value chain models that assume one of the possible motivations - "profit generation" as the primary objective of the organization to counterfeit smart card based electronic cash application[2]. Each threat scenario has its unique resource, organizational and primary activities requirement. Therefore the value chain model and its associated analysis is different for each threat scenario.

Once the model identifies strength and weakness of the firm, further *quantitative analysis* is conducted to gain additional insights and recommendations to improve the firm's competitive position in the industry. The use of micro dynamic simulation for the quantification of counterfeit threat scenarios is discussed in the section 2.

The counterfeit organization requires a good "business case" before it commits the substantial up-front investment, large organizational resources and time to a "project". It is logical for such an organization to evaluate its counterfeiting business, as one of many business opportunities, in terms of return on investment. The business case for counterfeiting has to be superior to its alternatives.

Figure 1 shows the generic counterfeiter's value chain. There are two types of activities: support and primary. The support activities include the organization's infrastructure (e.g., network of agents, offices, etc.), technology development (e.g., technology to break the security barriers), human resource management (i.e., assembling various technical skilled and operational skilled personnel), and procurement (i.e., hardware, software, and others). The primary activities show a chain of tasks required to achieve an objective of the organization. They include, the capital investment and setting up of the counterfeit operations, the research and development (i.e., breaking the security or stealing security information), the logistics and transportation of counterfeited application (i.e., golden goose) or counterfeit values, and the sales and operations (i.e., marketing of counterfeit value or blackmail.)

In the following section, we discuss the global smart card based electronic cash product features. Some of the features are designed so that they make the counterfeiter's challenges to be formidable. After the discussion of product features, two counterfeit scenarios are examined using value chain models. One is the street corner counterfeit value distribution scenario, and the other is the case when a member (bank) is the catalyst for the counterfeit activities.

---

[2] There are many other non-profit oriented attack scenarios with objectives such as "just for fun" (e.g., by university students), fame, or political blackmail by foreign government. They constitute important threat scenarios not to be ignored, but for this paper, we discuss only the two specific scenarios with "profit" motivation.

2.1 Global Smart Card Based Electronic Cash Product

The global smart card based electronic cash product such as Mondex electronic cash has the security and the risk management to prevent, detect, contain, and recover from potential counterfeit activities. It is designed to make counterfeiter's "chain" of tasks as difficult as possible in every step of the way.

The product is designed for the efficient electronic cash payment transactions. It performs purse (chip) to purse (chip) transactions without central authorization. It has many on-chip capability and features such as physical security, cryptographic security, purse class structure (i.e., it restrict the interactions of different type of purses), purse limit, on-chip risk management capability (e.g., credit turnover limit), and migration[3]. Security issues related to Mondex electronic cash application are discussed in [4]. Purse class structure, purse limit, credit turnover limit will be revisited in the following section.

Figure 2 shows the Mondex transactions among the different classes of purses. Solid line indicates transactions currently allowed, and dotted line indicates the transactions severely restricted (or disallowed) at this stage of product evolution.

Ideally, an advanced smart card based electronic cash scheme, as a substitute for "real" money, should parallel the existing money supply and banking system. Therefore such a scheme would include a currency "originator" (equivalent of central bank), and "members" (commercial banks and other financial institutions with their branches). There are merchants who transact with consumers and members, and consumers transacting with other consumers, merchants, and members.

In the following we discuss non-security related features:

Chip to Chip: The value (electronic cash) is transferred from payer purse (chip) to payee purse (chip) without third party authorization. Even if a counterfeiter succeeds in creating a "golden goose", it has to transact with other legitimate purses to actually transfer counterfeit value. The transacting purse has on-chip risk management capability to monitor "unusual" behavior of the purse transaction pattern.

Purse Class Structure: It classifies purses into different types of purses and determines what types of purses can transact with each other. Each purse can transact only with predetermined list of purse classes. For example, a consumer purse which is linked to the purse holder's direct deposit account of the member can transact with other consumer purses, two types of member purses, and three types of merchant purses.

Purse limits: High value limit purses (such as originator, and member purses) are monitored on line. All transactions to and from these purses are recorded and monitored (e.g., merchants and consumer deposit transactions.) Consumer purses are expected to have relatively low purse limits (e.g., up to $1000.)

---

[3] It involves switching of one public key scheme to the other.

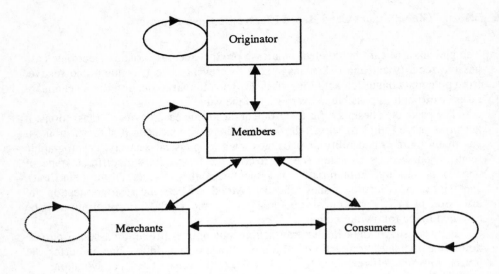

Figure 2. Transactions among different class of purses

Credit turnover limit: An on-chip risk management capability to monitor amount of value being received by a consumer purse from non-member purses such as consumer to consumer, and merchant refund transactions. If the transaction causes the credit turnover limit to be exceeded, this on-chip logic suspends a part or whole features of the purse. The credit turnover limit is customized by members to fit for the purse holder's normal needs.

One of the critical elements and advantages of the on-chip risk management capability (such as credit turnover limit) is that it continuously functions on the legitimate purses and constrain the flow of counterfeit value, even under complete physical security breakdown of the attacked purses. The fact that the risk management functionality of the compromised chip will be disabled doesn't directly benefit the counterfeiters. They need to interact with legitimate purses (cards) which still have active and functioning on-chip risk management capability. It is unlikely to be able to transfer all the counterfeit value to legitimate purses without triggering some actions by this on-chip risk management capability/logic.

In what follows, the two cases of counterfeit scenarios mentioned earlier are examined using value chain models. Case 1 covers the threat scenario when the counterfeit value is distributed through the personal contacts with the potential buyers – "street corner counterfeit value distribution." Case 2 examines the threat scenario when a member bank is owned by the criminal organization, and it is used to distribute the counterfeit value.

2.2 Case 1: Examination of Primary Activities of Counterfeiter's Value Chain of the Street Corner Counterfeit Value Distribution Threat Scenario

There are a few ways to obtain economic gains from the counterfeit value. We discuss only a few just to illustrate the counterfeiter's challenges. One way is to purchase goods and services, which imposes physical constraints on the return of counterfeit investment, and logistic problems (e.g., transporting goods.) Alternatively, agents can deposit the counterfeit value into the financial institutions. Both approaches require agents to reveal themselves either face to face or on-line.

Another approach is to sell, at a discount, counterfeit electronic cash to a fraudulent population, in exchange for "real" local currency. The fraudulent population is defined as the one that would engage in such transactions knowingly and willingly. The fraudulent population is not necessarily as loyal as agents of counterfeit organization and the "secret" is bound to be leaked to the law enforcement institutions or electronic cash issuing institution.

Figure 3 shows the counterfeiter's value chain for this scenario. Vertical items on the left of the chain show organizational functions of both primary and support activities. Horizontal items represent a series of objectives that need to be accomplished to produce a profit.

As the counterfeiter's value chain shows, due to the product features (as described in the next section), it requires some formidable organization and resources, up front capital investment, and flawless executions of technical as well as operational tasks against determined foes (various authorities and electronic cash organizations such as Mondex) to make a financial gain. Another prerequisite for a business success is a well financed, functioning, controlled, and coordinated organization with extremely loyal followers. Moreover, it needs people with a variety of technical and operational skills. Some of them have to be world class experts in various fields (e.g. cryptography). Finally, one has to establish a country wide or even world wide network to be able to "cash in" large amounts of counterfeit values in a very short time before the incidence responses are triggered by the electronic cash operators.

The following illustrates some activities that have to be successfully carried out.

Security break (in research & development): This task, difficult by itself, requires an access to or purchase of very specialized equipment. Moreover, a complete secrecy has to be maintained over an extended period of time while various tasks are performed to break security. A success requires not only cryptographic or physical break, but other layers of security measures would have to be compromised as well.

	Capital Investment & Setup	Research & Development	Logistics & Transport	Sales & Operations	
Counterfeit Organization Infrastructure	Country wide or World wide				
Technology Development		Defeat Security		Defeat On-chip And Off-chip RM	
Human Resources (Hire)	Sophisticated Support Staffs	World Class Cryptographers	Dedicated Agents	Large Number Of Conspirators	Profit
Procurement (Obtain)	Specialized Equipment			Large Numbers Of Off the Shelf Equipm	
Primary Activities	Deploy Capital, Product Intelligence, Hardware & Software, Physical Infrastructure, In Secrecy	Break "All" Security Layers In Secrecy	Distribute Counterfeit Values & Associated Equipment To Agents In Complete Secrecy	Pass On-chip & Off-chip Detection and Containment, Avoid False-Positives, Sell Large Volume of Counterfeit Value Fast, In Secrecy	

Figure 3. Counterfeiter's Value Chain Model of the Street Corner Counterfeit Value Distribution Threat Scenario

Creation of counterfeit electronic cash application (in research & development): Assume that the security was broken in the lab environment. The next challenge is to create a "shrink wrap" product of "golden goose" that can generate counterfeit electronic cash with flawless imitation of electronic cash application (e.g., Mondex purse) functionality. If the agents use legitimate electronic cash cards such as Mondex purses for their distribution, on-chip risk management feature will quickly pick up and disable these cards[4]. It has to be robust enough to be operated by technically less sophisticated people. One has to pass quality control that wrong operations or malfunctions will not leak the counterfeit activity information to the authorities and/or electronic cash issuing institutions.

Counterfeit value distribution channels (in logistics & transport): It has to solve the logistics. A counterfeiting organization has to be able to distribute "golden goose" or counterfeit values to its agents in complete "security" and secrecy. It takes time to set up secure and trustworthy channels of distribution. The "product" is a very tempting target for "interceptions" by the agents inside as well as outside the

---

[4] This has been confirmed in the various counterfeit threat scenarios using the Mondex Micro Dynamic Simulator.

organization (such as competing "firm".) And there's always a problem of "informants".

Marketing and sales - false positive problem (in sales & operations): A critical challenge for the counterfeiter/agents is to correctly identify "fraudulent" population whose size is small. If they approach a normal/honest person, he or she might inform the financial institution or authority (statistically speaking, this is called a false positive problem for the counterfeiter.) It is a difficult task to identify a small population, and it's statistically nearly impossible not to have false positives. But the counterfeit organization has to avoid false positives.

Behavioral problem of fraudulent population due to on-chip risk management capability (in sales & operations): Now, even if the false positive problems are solved, there remains a behavioral challenge posed by the fraudulent population. Legitimate electronic cash cards, such as Mondex purse, of the fraudulent population still have active and functioning on-chip risk management on them. It detects unusual flow of values from/to the card, and in some specific cases it disables certain card functionality. As a result, the card owner has to contact the issuing financial institution[5], if she/he wants to bring back this functionality. If the card is linked to the individual's bank account, such a contact is a necessary step to regain access to the bank account, thereby passing the information of potential counterfeit value transactions to the financial institutions. Alternatively, a card owner may choose just to report lost or stolen card, but this very act would trigger some investigation as well. Quantification of impact of this on-chip risk management capability is discussed in section 3. The counterfeiting organization has to solve these fraudulent population's behavioral problems.

Avoidance of off-chip detection (in sales & operations): Then, there is the off-chip (host system based) risk management capability. The counterfeit value bought by the fraudulent population has to be spent to obtain economic gain. Sudden rise in redemption of value can be detected quickly.

Various types of models are used for the detection tasks at various stages and layers of the scheme in the case of Mondex. Mondex risk management philosophy calls not for the adoption of one technology or method, but a balance of different methodologies complementing each other. For example, advanced statistical methods are used in the currency (float) monitoring systems, merchant and consumer monitoring systems, etc. And the Bayesian machine learning method [1,2, and 3] is used for monitoring transactions that are "flagged" by the on-chip risk management. Other complementary detection methods will be used as needed.

---

[5] Suppose a fraudulent person paid "real" $100 for $300 Mondex counterfeit value and cannot spend the acquired counterfeit value due to the on-chip risk management; such person has an incentive to contact the issuing financial institution for the release of value, or request "money back" from the agent.

The counterfeit value distribution activities have to clear the barriers imposed by these detection models.

Consideration of incidence response (in sales & operations => termination): As illustrated by the credit turnover limit example, some of the on-chip risk management capability contains on-chip incident response mechanism in an autonomous mode. On the other hand, one of the most effective ways to respond to the counterfeit contingency is to activate, by a central command, on-chip incidence response to affect a contaminated segment of purses (cards.) It will then function autonomously without outside intervention. It is the fastest way to respond to a potential incident. It can trigger a various incidence responses, including on-chip incidence response [e.g., migration]. This will stop the cash flow to the counterfeiting organization. Therefore the organization has to gain enough profit before the counterfeit activities are shut down.

In theory, any of the above links in the "from security to risk management" chain can be broken. However, as shown above, it is an extremely difficult task to carry out flawlessly in the real world in every step of the way, and against technological, organizational, and human behavioral challenges. Moreover, the tasks have to be accomplished while facing powerful and determined foes, such as government authorities and the electronic cash institutions. Therefore, it is very unlikely that the business case for counterfeiting be attractive enough to justify the overall investments needed against other alternative "business" opportunities.

2.3 Case 2: Examination of Primary Activities of Counterfeiter's Value Chain of the Member Counterfeit Value Distribution Threat Scenario

Now consider the threat scenario that a member (bank) is involved in the distribution of counterfeit activities. Figure 4 shows the counterfeiter's value chain model of the member counterfeit value distribution threat scenario. There are some critical differences from the Case 1. It assumes that the member bank is distributing counterfeit value to the consumers. It provides a portion of consumer withdrawals with counterfeit values (i.e., skimming strategy) to avoid detection by the originator.

The criminal organization may control a bank to cover its criminal activities. If the bank is owned by the criminal organization, it may perform many of the most critical functions from distribution of financial assets to investment of illegally accumulated fund in the legitimate markets.

Business Case (evaluation to enter counterfeit business): Before a criminal organization commits its bank to the counterfeiting an electronic cash, its business case of counterfeiting has to pass not only the return on the investment criteria of the crime organization, but also the contingency of losing the bank due to the "exposure" through the counterfeit detection and incident response. One has to consider not only the lost investment for the counterfeiting but also the loss of the critical element of the criminal organization, the loss caused by the termination of other criminal activities, and, last but not least, the loss of accumulated financial investments and assets if the bank is seized by the authority. Investments in the Mondex member license and the Mondex infrastructure for the bank are lost as well.

In the following, we discuss some of the activities that have to be successfully carried out by the counterfeiter.

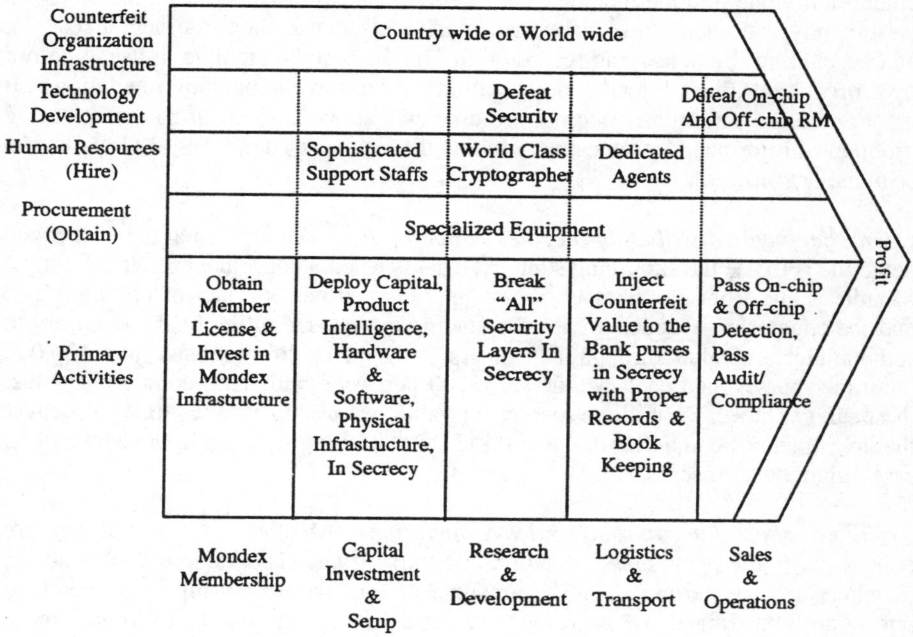

Counterfeit Organization Infrastructure	Country wide or World wide				
Technology Development			Defeat Security		Defeat On-chip And Off-chip RM
Human Resources (Hire)		Sophisticated Support Staffs	World Class Cryptographer	Dedicated Agents	
Procurement (Obtain)		Specialized Equipment			
Primary Activities	Obtain Member License & Invest in Mondex Infrastructure	Deploy Capital, Product Intelligence, Hardware & Software, Physical Infrastructure, In Secrecy	Break "All" Security Layers In Secrecy	Inject Counterfeit Value to the Bank purses in Secrecy with Proper Records & Book Keeping	Pass On-chip & Off-chip Detection, Pass Audit/ Compliance
	Mondex Membership	Capital Investment & Setup	Research & Development	Logistics & Transport	Sales & Operations

Figure 4. Counterfeiter's Value Chain Model
of the Member Counterfeit Value Distribution Threat Scenario

Member License (in Mondex membership): The member has to pass the minimum requirement to qualify for the member license. All critical aspects of the member including internal controls, security, and operations are reviewed carefully by the originator. Although the funds may not directly come from the criminal organization, the bank has to invest in the creation of Mondex infrastructure to provide Mondex services.

Security Break (in research & development): Availability of member purses are limited, their uses are restricted, and carefully monitored on line. Higher value limit purses are stored in the physically secure and restricted area. Note that although the bank is owned by the criminal organization, not all the employees are its agents (different skill sets required to run banks.) Member to member transactions are not permitted. Hence there's no special advantage attributed to counterfeiting member purse which is more difficult to obtain than that of the consumer's. The counterfeiter can create the consumer counterfeit purse and inject the counterfeit value to the member purse directly or indirectly through colluding merchants. The technical difficulty to break the layers of the security is the same as Case 1.

Injection of counterfeit value to the member purse system (in logistics & transport): The scenario assumes that the consumer counterfeit purse is used to inject counterfeit value into the member purse system. The agents have to have access to various physical and data security, and modify associated data transaction records, and accounting (book keeping records.) For the bank to be credible, it has to be run by professionals, have a formal organization, and follow the banking regulations. It has to pass the scrutiny of internal professionals as well. Also, it has to solve the problem of informants. One cannot assume that all bank employees are loyal to the criminal organization.

Counterfeit value distribution (in sales & operations): One way to avoid immediate detection is to use the skimming strategy. That is when a consumer withdraws (buys) Mondex value from the member, the counterfeiter provides a mix of the legitimate and the counterfeit Mondex value. Depending on the size of the bank, an ability to sell counterfeit value through consumers is limited. If the bank has 100,000 consumer purses, and each withdraws $100 per week with 10% counterfeit value, the bank can inject $1 million counterfeit value per week. It takes time to recover the investment of counterfeiting, and if the counterfeiting is found in the bank, all its asset might be confiscated.

Avoidance of on-chip control (in sales & operations): Member purse transactions are controlled by the purse class structure, and purse limit. The value transfers across members are not permitted. The amounts of transfers to consumer or merchant purses are constrained by the respective purse limits. One has to overcome these obstacles.

Avoidance of off-chip detection (in sales & operations): The counterfeiter has to pass the off-chip (host system based) monitoring by the originator that deploys and operates the currency monitoring and the member monitoring systems. Members are the critical focus of monitoring by the originator. Any unusual behaviors are immediately reviewed and inspected. As for detection models, the impact of skimming attacks have been quantified and analyzed using various techniques. Statistical detection models for the skimming threat scenarios have been developed to monitor such attacks. One has to clear these off-chip detection screens.

Passing audit/compliance/inspection (in sales & operations): Every bank is subject to audit, compliance, and inspections by various authorities, and some private organizations including Mondex. It has to pass regular and ad-hoc visits of auditors and other inspectors. The banks that are suspected to be owned by criminal organizations are objects of continuous surveillance by the authorities.

Anticipation of incident response (in sales & operation => termination): Once the counterfeit is detected, on-chip incident response can be invoked to stop the infusion of counterfeit value. Furthermore, even if the counterfeiter may not be captured, but the critical asset, the bank, is left for seizure by the authority. Assets that the counterfeiter has accumulated in the past through various other criminal activities as well as "legitimate" activities would be lost as well. The counterfeiting organization has to generate enough profit before the termination of counterfeit activities, and not to leave a trace to the bank. Note that all the cards issued by the bank have the unique bank identification number that is recorded as a part of transaction log whenever transaction occurs. Hence the value transfer from the bank can be traced.

In summary, considering all the assets the counterfeiter has in the bank put at risk, the relatively moderate counterfeit profit that requires flawlessly execution of all the primary tasks doesn't seem to justify the counterfeiting business case.

3 Quantitative Assessment of Threats Using Micro Dynamic Simulation

As we discussed in the previous section of qualitative assessment, once the additional need for the analysis is identified, the quantitative assessment of the threat scenario is performed using various analytical tools. In this section we discuss the use of the simulation model. To quantify a threat scenario, one needs to observe or model, the following phases: 1) Creation of counterfeit value, 2) Interaction of electronic purses (transactions), 3) Diffusion of both legitimate and counterfeit value throughout the economy, and 4) Incident responses (countermeasures).

At the moment, no actual data on the counterfeit activities exist in the new electronic cash economy. Moreover, it is extremely unlikely that any actual observations regarding counterfeit value will be available in the foreseeable future. Therefore a quantification of a given threat scenario has to be based on the observations generated in a laboratory-like environment. Simulation modeling offers such an environment. It allows, through setting distributions of various parameters, to control and observe the behavior of all phases of a threat scenario. Depending on their properties and underlying techniques, different classifications of simulation models can be used. The simulation models can be classified based on the level of aggregation of modeled phenomena and the role played by the "time" variable. According to the first criterion, the simulation models are assigned into *macro* or *micro* categories. The second criterion differentiates the *dynamic* models from the *static* ones. A more comprehensive discussion of these model classes can be found in [5], where a number of static and dynamic micro simulation models to evaluate tax, social and general economic polices are introduced.

The task to quantify a threat scenario requires, among other information, data on individual purses' transactions as well as on the effectiveness of the on-chip based response. Therefore we use the *micro dynamic simulation model*. In general, it is a computer model that imitates the dynamics of the electronic cash scheme. It has the following important features: 1) Mimics the expected longer term evolution of the electronic cash scheme, 2) Reflects, through respective model parameters, short term behavioral patterns, e.g. seasonal fluctuations, 3) Follows the transaction behavior of individual purses, e.g. a number and frequency of transactions, and 4) Keeps a complete record of all individual transactions.

The above features allow an analyst to perform various experiments. The essence of every experiment is to: 1) Design a threat scenario and inject the related counterfeit value into the system, and 2) Build in and invoke during the simulation the on-chip and off-chip based responses.

The simulated diffusion of the counterfeit value and an effectiveness with which it can be detected and contained provide the critical information that allows us to quantify a threat scenario in question.

3.1   Mondex Micro Dynamic Simulator

Mondex Micro Dynamic Simulator (simulator for short) is a particular application of the micro dynamic simulation concept to the Mondex electronic cash scheme. The model's design is flexible enough to reflect not just today's but also other possible future scheme structures. The simulator was used to assess the effectiveness of the selected responses against the likely threats.

The attached appendix shows examples of input and output screens of the simulator. To increase model's flexibility and the level of detail, as far as the transaction patterns are concerned, each level of scheme participants can be further segmented. Segments within the same level of participants differ from each other by their respective transaction patterns, as defined, for instance, by number and type of daily transactions.

Figure 5 in the Appendix shows a window that defines a member segment given the originator. It allows the user to specify various characteristics of the member segment, ranging from, for example, member type (merchant bank, consumer bank, or both) to birth/death rates for members, merchants and consumers (i.e. population growth and decline.) Member segments can be declared as counterfeit segments by clicking the corresponding "counterfeit" check box. Note that, at the purse level, the simulator keeps tracks of individual purse setting such as purse limit, value balance and on-chip risk management functionality.

Figure 6 in the Appendix shows the impact that counterfeit activities have on the number of locked up purses. This is the direct effect of the on-chip risk management functionality. The locked up purses are the legitimate ones that happen to be contacted by the counterfeit purses in order to receive the created counterfeit value. When a preset condition is met, the on-chip risk management functionality turns on on-chip response autonomously in this case locking up the purses.

An ability to produce and analyze multiple runs of the simulator model under different scenarios allows the user to experience the management of the electronic cash economy before the scheme is actually rolled out.

The risk management capabilities need to be continuously upgraded to match new potential threats in the rapidly evolving electronic commerce. The simulator model plays a critical role in the evaluation of both on-chip and off-chip new risk management tools to anticipate and prepare for the future counterfeit challenges.

In addition to being a tool to evaluate the impact of counterfeit scenarios, the simulator model also generates transactions that can be used to train off-chip detection model(s). The simulator model is to be calibrated for every respective currency originator (i.e. country) to reflect the particular behavior of its purse users and their transaction patterns of their territories.

4   Summary

We discussed the qualitative and the quantitative assessment of threats for smart card based electronic cash.   In the qualitative assessment section we discussed the counterfeiters' enormous technical as well as organizational / behavioral challenges that go far beyond the security break which itself constitutes a formidable barrier to overcome. The counterfeiting organization's value chain and its associated tasks are examined. We discussed two cases of threat scenarios and concluded that it would be very difficult to justify a "business case" for undertaking counterfeiting activities in both cases.

We also discussed the evaluation of the counterfeit threat scenarios using micro dynamic simulation. This modeling technique provides information needed for the quantification of economic risk exposure in conjunction with other analytical tools. It also allows the evaluation of the effectiveness of various on-chip risk management capabilities.   And by generating test data, it allows the assessment of the effectiveness of the host system based counterfeit transaction detection models.

References

1. Ezawa, K.J. and Schuermann, T., "Fraud/Uncollectible Debt Detection Using a Bayesian Network Based Learning System: A Rare Binary Outcome with Mixed Data Structures," *Proeedings of the 11th Conference Uncertainty in Artificial Intelligence*, Morgan Kaufmann, pp. 157-166 (1995).
2. Ezawa, K.J., Singh, M., and Norton, S.W., "Learning Goal Oriented Bayesian Networks for Telecommunications Risk Management", *Proceedings of the 13th International Conference on Machine Learning*, Morgan Kaufmann (1996).
3. Ezawa, K.J., and Norton S., "Constructing Bayesian Networks to Predict Uncollectible Telecommunications Accounts," *IEEE EXPERT*, Vol. 11, No. 5, pp. 45-51 (1996).
4. Maher, D.P., "Fault Induction Attacks, Tamper Resistance, and Hostile Reverse Engineering in Perspective," *Financial Cryptography '97 – First International Conference*, Springer Verlag (1997).
4. Porter, M.E., "Competitive Advantage," Free Press (1985).
5. Harding, A.(editor), "Microsimulation and Public Policy", North-Holland (1996).
6. Napiorkowski, G. and Borghard, W., "Modeling of Customer Response to Marketing of Local Telephone Services" in Dynamic Competitive Analysis in Marketing, Springer Verlag (1996).

Appendix

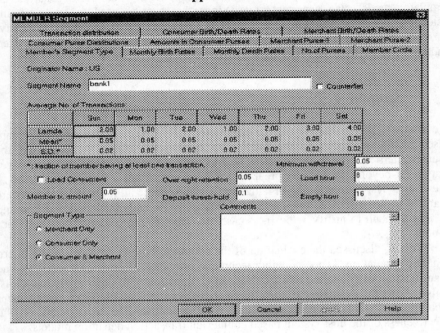

Figure 5. Example Input Screen - Member Segment Specification

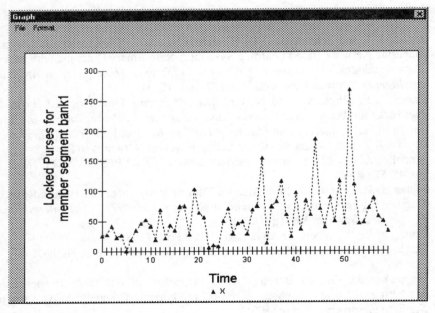

Figure 6. Example Output - Impact of Counterfeit Activity

Using a High-Performance, Programmable Secure Coprocessor

Sean W. Smith, Elaine R. Palmer, Steve Weingart

Secure Systems and Smart Cards
IBM T.J. Watson Research Center
P.O Box 704, Yorktown Heights NY 10598   USA
{sws, erpalmer, c1shw}@us.ibm.com

Abstract. Unsecure computational environments threaten many financial cryptography implementations, and other sensitive computation. High-performance secure coprocessors can address these threats. However, using this technology for practical security solutions requires overcoming numerous technical and business obstacles. These obstacles motivate building a high-performance secure coprocessor that balances security with easy third-party programmability—but these obstacles also provide many design challenges. This paper discusses some of issues we faced when attempting to build such a device.

1   Introduction

Using secure coprocessors to build practical e-commerce applications requires practical secure coprocessors.

Previous work [6, 13, 18, 20, 21] explores the feasibility of building general-purpose, computationally powerful secure coprocessors that carry out computation without observation or interference by a well-funded adversary with direct physical access. Subsequent work [11, 14, 16, 22, 23] demonstrates that such hardware could be the foundation for secure applications in electronic commerce—including nearly every aspect of financial cryptography.

However, bringing any one application vision to reality requires addressing the problem of building and distributing the hardware. Simultaneously enabling the practical realization of a broad family of applications by building general-purpose, customizable hardware introduces the additional trust and security problems of multiple, mutually suspicious authorities, and the inevitability of flaws in complex software.

This paper discusses some of our research on these issues, as part of our efforts to produce such a tool as a mass-produced, commercial product. [10, 15] Sect. 2 discusses the fundamental threat that unsecure and untrusted computing platforms present to financial cryptography implementations, where the stakes may be considerable but where trust and privacy are also significant issues. Section 3 discusses how high-performance secure coprocessors would comprise a near-universal tool for solving these problems. Section 4 discusses the practical barriers that must be overcome for such a tool to be widely used. Section 5 quickly reviews the design decisions we made in building our architecture.

Section 6 discusses the flexibility this architecture brings to development and deployment of security solutions.

2 The Threat of Unsecure/Untrusted Environments

2.1 Security

It is probably indisputable that security is critical for many financial and e-commerce systems. However, an often overlooked aspect of these systems are the machines and data storage environments themselves. No one would argue that it is inadvisable to leave a stack of $100 bills lying on a counter while one walks away to get a deposit form; the time-honored method of storing money in a mattress is certainly less secure than keeping that money in a vault. In the same way, an unsecured computer is not a much better place to leave money than is a counter or a mattress. Data or algorithms can be modified—and control over the assets may be usurped or lost.

Because of this situation, many computational and storage operations must take place in an environment that is secure, in the sense that the parties who need to can trust that the operations satisfy some set of correctness properties, despite potential malice.

These properties may describe storage of critical data. For example:

- Has the private key been exposed?
- Did the quantity of stored funds spuriously change?

The properties also include correctness of the operation itself:

- Was the keypair generated randomly—or or was it predictable by an adversary?
- Were the funds transferred transactionally—or did a communication error result in creation of spurious funds?

Even harder to articulate is the correctness of the invocation of these operations on this data:

- Did the private key generate only the signatures its owner authorized?

2.2 Threats

However, some of the security threats most difficult to thwart stem from potential adversaries with access to the hardware or software that carries out a sensitive computation, and can benefit from modifying it—an exposure which the advent of e-commerce has only amplified.

This risk can have several manifestations, including physically exposed machines and circuitry, software flaws, dishonest employees and customers, and channels for backup and disaster recovery. We visit each in turn.

Exposed Machines. Physically exposed machines are particularly vulnerable to attack, either by mischievous vandals or serious attackers. Anyone with access to a machine can attempt to reboot it, alter its files, load rogue software, or steal the whole machine to hack away at it in private.

Recent business trends exacerbate this threat. For example, the finance industry is increasing its deployment of customer self-service systems via telephone, the Internet, and at physical locations beyond the confines and protection of the conventional service counter. These remote systems allow the business to expand service locations, extend service hours, and reduce costs. The remote systems are more vulnerable to attack than those safely locked within the four walls of the home office.

Exposed circuitry is also vulnerable to attack (e.g., [2, 3]). A physical attacker can quite quickly and unobtrusively clip diagnostic equipment onto a printed circuit board to observe and record cryptographic keys as they leave main memory on the way to an encryption chip. Electrical engineering lab students at the University of Delft in the Netherlands routinely practice opening, reading, and reprogramming smart card chips.

Software Flaws. Software flaws, whether inadvertent or intentional, can also offer an avenue to compromise secure computations and storage.

Consider, for example, a bug in one application of a hypothetical multi-application smart card. Current smart card processors lack the hardware memory protection required to protect the memory space of one application from that of another or the operating system. An errant frequent shopper application on today's smart cards can inadvertently destroy (or increment!) the balance of an electronic purse sharing the same card.

Flaws in operating systems are also a threat. Typically, an operating system has unlimited privileges and access to the entire memory space of the system. But what if a bug in the software causes the operating system to overwrite and thus destroy the rewritable firmware of the machine? The result can be that the system is unable to boot or reload a new, corrected operating system.

Web connectivity, and shipping functionality with Java, introduce even more issues.

Another class of threats from software flaws arises from cryptography. Cryptography is at best a panacea if the implementation itself is somehow compromised. Yet in recent years we have seen both practical demonstrations of real vulnerabilities (e.g., badly chosen random keys in Kerberos [7] and Netscape [9]) as well as theoretical demonstrations of weaknesses in key generation (e.g., [17, 24]) and other aspects of cryptographic mathematics, such as differential fault analysis (e.g., [4, 5]).

Dishonest Employees, Contractors, and Customers. Dishonest employees pose a rather vexing problem. As employees, they must have access to information and systems in order to carry out their jobs, but often that access cannot be finely controlled. For example, a computer system administrator (*sysadmin*) must have unrestricted access to a machine in order to perform software updates, system backups, add new users, etc. Unfortunately, many systems do not have fine-grained access. The sysadmin can copy files to tapes either for legitimate backup purposes or to sell to the competition. Unencrypted financial data can be quite valuable, and is an easy target for employees who succumb to blackmail or temptation. Dishonest contractors or temporary employees pose an even greater threat, since they typically neither go through the vetting nor hold the stake that regular employees do.

Dishonest customers pose an interesting challenge to a merchant. Merchants cannot usually distinguish between an honest customer and a dishonest one, but must nevertheless treat all with courtesy, not suspicion. Furthermore, merchants exert little or no control over their customers and their customers' employees, except to deny a sale or discount (or to litigate). Merchants cannot fire a dishonest customer, and the dishonest customer can return again and again to cheat. New business practices allow customers to have access to product databases, online catalogues, custom pricing algorithms, and other information potentially valuable to one's competitors. How, then, can a merchant prevent a customer's disgruntled, overworked, underpaid purchasing agent from selling the merchant's confidential price list to the merchant's competitors?

Backup and Disaster Recovery. The explicit purpose of backup and disaster recovery service is to replicate mission critical data in sufficiently many places to recover from any single point of failure. But how does one protect numerous, widely-distributed copies of critical data from theft, modification, or misuse, particularly when the backup tapes are stored offsite in facilities managed by third-party vendors?

2.3 Hostile Environments

We reiterate that financially sensitive computations are piles of money, stacked in the platforms, networks, and disks involved, and those with access to this infrastructure have potential access to this money. In many electronic commerce applications, *everyone* with access to the infrastructure—including the *end user* himself—is potentially an adversary. (Who wouldn't like to have a bottomless electronic wallet?) The *entire environment* must be considered hostile.

3 Secure Coprocessors as a Potential Solution

3.1 The Technology

Section 2 outlined threats from adversaries tampering with computation or data storage. As a device that carries out computation despite attempts to tamper with it, a *secure coprocessor* provides a tool that helps systematically address these threats—and potentially enable new applications that are otherwise not feasible.

Figure 1 sketches a generic device. A physically secure boundary protects a CPU and memory. A subset of the memory is specified as *secure*. The physical

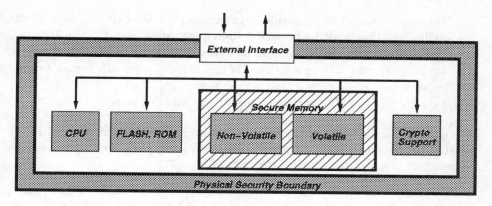

Fig. 1. A generic secure coprocessor. Tamper *zeroizes* the secure memory (or somehow renders it unavailable). As a consequence, with properly designed software, the device can provide privacy and/or integrity for data and/or operations.

security design aims to ensure that attempts to penetrate or tamper with the device will result in the contents of the secure memory being destroyed.

This secure memory enables secure applications. For example, putting a private key in this memory allows the device to act as a trusted witness, since a remote party can trust that a message correctly signed by this key must have been produced by an untampered device. Such messages might include assertions about data the device is storing, or about more complex computations it is carrying out. This foundation can extend to securing the entire on-device application; putting an entire program in secure memory might provide even more advantages. Yee's work [16, 22, 23] explores these issues; [14] provides a taxonomy of potential applications.

The effectiveness of a secure coprocessor as a tool for building secure applications depends on the effectiveness of its memory protections and the power of its computational engine. This previous research considered the implications of a high-end, high-performance device, which provides a general-purpose computing environment that withstands nearly all foreseeable physical and logical attacks. Such a device requires additional properties: it runs only the programs it is supposed to; it runs them unmolested; and one must be able to distinguish between a real program and a clever impersonator, even if the secure coprocessor is thousands of miles away.

Typically, secure coprocessors incorporate high-performance cryptography, but they need not be just fast crypto boxes—since computation besides cryptographic operations can go inside them.

3.2 High-End Secure Coprocessors Counteract Threats

By providing computational horsepower but resisting and responding to physical attacks, a high-end secure coprocessor is ideally suited for security in hostile environments:

- The coprocessor, in the hostile environment, can execute the part of the application that must be protected from adversaries.
- The device is sufficiently powerful for this computation to be fairly complex.
- An attacker who attempts to modify this computation will trigger tamper response.
- An attackers who disassembles a device will learn no secrets.

With proper software design, such a device provides a trusted witness, wherever trust is needed. As a result, an easily programmable, high-performance secure coprocessor is a tool can address the risks of Sect. 2.

Physically Exposed Machines and Circuitry. High-end secure coprocessors are designed to be placed in physically exposed environments. Vandals may attack at will, but will not discern secrets inside the tamper-responding coprocessor. Nor can they load rogue software into the coprocessor. The device will erase its secrets and shut itself down on any attempt to penetrate the tamper-responding enclosure, in order to learn secrets or modify execution.

Software Flaws. High-end secure coprocessors offer both hardware and software isolation of applications from each other, and of the operating system from applications. (Indeed, we found it necessary to protect regions of memory from even the operating system.) Thus, an application running inside a high-end secure coprocessor cannot inflict damage on one of its peers inside the coprocessor. Nor can the operating system damage the highly-critical microcode nor its protected storage inside the coprocessor. The threat of compromised cryptography can be addressed by hardware support for basic operations (such as a hardware source for randomness), and authentication of software configuration. Some approaches to high-end tamper protection can also shield against differential fault analysis.

Dishonest Employees, Contractors and Customers. High-end secure coprocessors can be used to control and audit the access rights of both employees and customers to sensitive data. Furthermore, because of the programmability of the coprocessor, access controls can be quite complex, for example, limited to certain hours of the day, days of the week, etc.

Backup and Disaster Recovery. High-end secure coprocessors enable high speed encryption (backup) of sensitive data before it is sent off to remote sites for backup. High speed decryption facilitates recovery of the data. Furthermore, the keys can be stored in numerous secure coprocessors spread about the world, and accessed only on appropriate conditions. Employees at the remote backup sites see only encrypted data; the plaintext emerges only during bona fide recovery.

3.3   The Family of Secure Coprocessors

Our research interests focus on building and using high-end, programmable secure coprocessors. However, devices meeting the generic pattern of Fig. 1 encompass a wide range of capabilities; various devices in the secure coprocessor family embody various trade-offs between security, computational and cryptographic power, and cost. We review the entire family.

Chip Card. The least powerful member of the secure coprocessor family is the *smart card*[1] (also known as *chip card*). A typical smart card of today includes a tiny 8-bit processor, 512 bytes RAM, 8K bytes ROM, 8K bytes EEPROM, and a hardware accelerator for cryptographic operations. Smart cards must be programmed at the factory, since their software is permanently burned in mask ROM when the chips are manufactured—typically in quantities of at least 10,000 units. Because the memory space is so limited, the software inside the smart card is written in hand-tuned machine code.

Smart cards offer some limited detection of physical attacks. However, the response to such attacks depends on whether the device is powered on or not—for example, the response when inserted into a smart card reader may substantially differ from the response when lying unpowered on an attacker's workbench. Without power, the device is unable to erase sensitive data stored in EEPROM. Even with power, erasure within a very small time window is unlikely or impossible.

Smart cards also offer only limited protection against logical attacks. The processors on current smart cards lack the combination of "supervisor state" with hardware protection of memory regions (including RAM), the cornerstone of preventing one application from accessing and modifying the data of another application on the card. For that reason, most smart card vendors carefully inspect and test all code that must co-exist on the same card (although recent efforts at JavaCard attempt to remedy this). Cryptographic throughput is severely limited by the serial interface into and out of the card, with a typical speed of 9600 bit/second.

Smart cards offer the undeniable advantages of being inexpensive, portable, and physically robust.

Personal Tokens. The personal token, such as a PCMCIA card or "smart button," is usually the next step up in crypto performance and capability. In some cases, these devices are little more than a repackaged chip card—except the larger packaging gives the advantages of greater I/O bandwidth and real estate for more hardware, such as more memory, a battery, or stronger protections. At the other end of the spectrum, a personal token could theoretically have many of the features and capabilities of crypto accelerators and/or high-end secure processors.

---

[1] Unfortunately, the term "smart card" is sometimes used for nearly everything in this family, and other devices besides.

Personal tokens are often tamper-resistant and in some cases have reasonable tamper evident and perhaps tamper-responsive features. (However, tamper evidence is of little value without a well planned audit policy.) The typical token will be able to perform user functions such as authentication, file encryption (albeit with low performance), and storage of secrets off of the host system. Most of the PCMCIA cards available are fixed function devices and are not programmable, though some offer some programming capabilities if the work is done by, or in cooperation with the manufacturer. (Again, recent efforts JavaCard attempt to remedy this for low-end tokens.)

Crypto Accelerators. The next device in the secure coprocessor family is the cryptographic accelerator. Such devices typically include a small microprocessor (e.g. the ARM7), a reasonable amount of memory (e.g. 2 megabytes EEPROM, 512K RAM) and chips to boost cryptographic performance. The primary purpose of these devices (e.g., [1]) is to accelerate cryptographic operations while offering some degree of physical protection of cryptographic keys. These devices are often tamper-resistant, but seldom tamper-responding. (For example, their external cases resist attack because they are difficult to pry open, but they do not erase sensitive data if they are opened.) They are not widely programmable by any customer, but are sometimes programmable under special contract by the manufacturer, given sufficient sales volumes.

High-End Secure Coprocessor. The most sophisticated device in the secure co-processor family is a high-end secure coprocessor, with a powerful microprocessor (e.g. 486), megabytes of RAM and FLASH memory, chips to boost cryptographic performance, a time-of-day clock, and a hardware random number generator, all within a tamper-responding enclosure. Such a device should provide computationally verifiable untamperedness with a nearly open programming environment, but immediately erase sensitive data when under attack.

An example of such a high-end coprocessor is the recent IBM 4758, the product [10] which we explicitly designed to address the issues raised in this paper.

4   Obstacles to Practical Deployment

The feasibility of high-end secure coprocessors (e.g., [21]) and their application potential (e.g., [22, 23]) had been well-established. However, realizing the vision of Sect. 3.1 and Sect. 3.2 required overcoming the significant obstacles that confront an organization wishing to develop and deploy real applications using this technology.

This section reviews these obstacles. Section 5 and Sect. 6 below discuss how we designed our coprocessor to try to eliminate them.

4.1   Hardware

We have repeated allusions to a "high-end secure coprocessor" that provides:

- *highly reliable* tamper-response
- *high-speed* cryptographic support
- a *powerful, general-purpose* computational environment

Until recently, this hardware was not available beyond prototype quantities.

Tamper-Response. Most discussions of secure hardware usually use phrases like "tamper-proof," "tamper-resistant," "tamper-evident" or "tamper-responsive." Any realistic assessment recognizes that "tamper-proof" hardware is unattainable; however, the solutions of Sect. 3.2 all assumed that the secure coprocessor somehow *responded* to tamper by *zeroizing* (or somehow rendering unrecoverable) some stored information.

But how should this happen?

- *Active* tamper-response relies on the device itself to detect tamper attempts and destroy its secrets. Active response can be computational—which requires that during tamper, the processor remain alive long enough to destroy the secrets—or depend instead on independent special-purpose circuitry that more quickly *crowbars* the memory.
- *Passive* techniques rely on physical or chemical hardness (and sometimes on explosives).

Passive protection is difficult to carry out effectively (witness the continued permeation of smart card technology) and difficult to apply to multi-chip modules. But on the other hand, using active protection requires recognizing that the device is only as secure as long as the necessary environment exists for the active protection to function. Minimally, this recognition requires grappling with some difficult issues:

- The continuous existence of this environment requires a continuous source of power.
- What exactly do we know about the device after an interval in which this environment fails to exist?
- Does the device always protect itself, or only between visits by a security officer?
- What should happen to a device that zeroizes its secrets?

Exactly how the zeroizable secrets should be stored raises additional design issues. For example, using Static RAM requires considering the *imprinting* effects of low-temperature and long-term storage.

Trusted I/O Path. Effectively using a trusted device in human-based applications often requires effective authentication of communications between a human and their trusted device. [8] A human-usable I/O path on the secure device itself makes these problems simpler—but although a nice abstraction, such a path can greatly compromise the physical security.

Hosts. Almost tautologically, a secure coprocessor requires a host system. Wide deployment of a secure coprocessor application requires considering the population of host machines:

— What physical interface should be used? How does this choice affect ease of installation, number of potential platforms, and performance of coprocessor? (For example, the PCMCIA, chip-card, and PCI-bus interfaces all give different answers to these questions.)
— What device drivers and other associated host-side software are required? How does this software get to the host? What possibilities exist for attacking the application by attacking the host-side software?

Cost and Durability. For an application to succeed, someone needs to create and distribute a population of secure coprocessors. This task requires balancing the cost of the device with its power and protections, as well as considering longer-term reliability issues. (Indeed, the often-lamented computational restrictions of chip cards are a consequence of the requirement to keep them highly robust to physical wear-and-tear.)

Depending on the tamper-protection methods used, additional environmental factors such as heat and radiation need to be considered.

Exportability. Another challenge facing any practical development and deployment of cryptographically powerful devices is compliance with the U.S. export laws.

4.2 Software

Development. A cornerstone of secure coprocessing applications is putting a substantial portion of application-specific computation into the secure device—not just using it for basic cryptographic operations. Developing and deploying secure coprocessing applications thus requires the ability to develop software for the device. This requirement leads to many challenges, even with current-generation low-end devices:

— Is development possible on a *small scale* with small numbers of devices—or must the application developer first convince a hardware manufacturer of the business case for thousands or millions of units?
— Is development possible *independent* of the hardware manufacturer—or must the application developer work closely and expose plans and code?
— Does a robust *programming environment* exist for the device, or must code be hand-tuned? What about debugging and testing?
— If independent development is possible, what *prevents* malicious or faulty software from *compromising* core device keys? Do these protections consist of verified hardware and software, or depend solely on complex software with a track record of flaws?

Installation. How does the deployer ensure that the potentially untrusted user, in a potentially hostile environment, ends up with an authentic, untampered device that is programmed with the right software?

Installing the software at the factory forces the application developer to have a substantial presence in the factory, and the factory to customize their processes to individual application developers. This approach may complicate small-scale development.

However, installing the software at any later point raises a number of additional issues.

- What about the security of the shipping channel? What if the device is modified between the time it leaves the factory and the time the software is installed?
- How does the device know what software to accept? (Accepting just anything opens the possibility of tamper via false software load.)
- Does a device carry a key whose exposure compromises that device, or other devices?
- Installing the software at the deployer's site forces the deployer to ship the hardware to the end-users.
- Installing the software at the end-user's site requires the need for security officers, or for the device itself to exert fairly robust control, authentication, and confirmation of software loads.
- With general-purpose programmable hardware intended for multiple deployers, installation after the factory needs to ensure that hardware loaded with one deployer's software cannot claim to be executing software from a different deployer.

The software installation process may also have unpleasant interactions with the desired security model. For example:

- If the application developer requires that their software itself be secret, but the hardware only provides a limited amount of tamper-protected storage, then the installation process must include some way of installing the software decryption key in that storage.

Most post-factory installation scenarios require that the devices leave the factory with some type of security/bootstrap code, which raises additional issues.

Software Maintenance. After installation, how does the deployer then proceed to securely carry out the maintenance and upgrades that such complex software inevitably requires?

- How does the device authenticate such requests? Must the deployer use an on-site "security officer," or can they use remote control? If the latter, how much interaction is required? Does the deployer have to undergo a lengthy handshake with each deployed device? Does the deployer need to maintain a database of device-specific records or secrets?

- How can participants in an application know for certain that an upgrade has occurred? (The purpose of the upgrade might be to eliminate a software vulnerability which an adversary has already used to explore the contents of privileged memory.)
- What should happen to stored data when software is upgraded? Not supporting "hot updates" is cleaner, but can greatly complicate the difficulty of performing updates.
- What atomicity does the device provide for software updates? Can failures (or malice) leave the device in a dangerous or inoperable state? What if the software that cryptographically verifies updates is itself being updated?

To avoid grappling with these issues, some deployers may choose simply to not allow updates. However, the decision certainly needs to be balanced against hardware expense and software complexity (hence likelihood of upgrade).

Multi-Party Issues. The foregoing discussion largely focused on a model where basic device hardware had one software component that needed to be installed and updated. In reality, this situation may be more complicated. Multiple software layers may lie beneath the application software:

- The presence of a device operating system (in order to make software development easier) raises the questions of when, where, and how the OS is installed and updated.
- The OS may come from an independent software developer, like the application does.
- The more tasks assigned to the basic bootstrap/configuration, the more likely this foundational software might also require update.

Multiple layers each controlled by a different authority makes the software installation and update problem even more interesting. For example, the ability to perform "hot-updates" potentially gives an OS vendor a backdoor into the application secrets.

The simple answer of "not allowing any OS updates" avoids these risks, but introduces the problem of what to do when a flaw is discovered in security-critical system software—especially if this software is too complex to have been formally verified.

Some scenarios may additionally require multiple sibling software components, at the same layer (although this flexibility must be balanced against the risks of potentially malicious sibling applications, the hardware expense and the sensitivity of the application).

Comparison to PCs. It might be enlightening to compare this situation with software development for ordinary, exposed machines, such as personal computers. For PCs, software developers do not need to build and distribute the computers themselves. Software developers never need meet or verify the identity of the user. Software developers do not need to worry about how or where the user obtained the machine; whether it is a genuine or modified machine, or whether the software or its execution is being somehow modified. Furthermore, developers of the application software usually do not also have to develop and maintain the operating system or the ROM BIOS.

5 Building Technology to Overcome These Obstacles

The list of obstacles to deploying secure coprocessor applications naturally leads to design issues for those hoping to minimize these obstacles by building a *high-end, programmable* secure coprocessor. Although Sect. 4 presented a quick enumeration, we stress that the design choices often interact in subtle ways. For just one example, the business decisions to support remote update of potentially buggy supervisor-level software requires the ability to remotely authenticate that this repair took place, which in turn may require changing the hardware to provide a region of secure memory that is private even from a defective supervisor-level operating system.

Indeed, the issues in Sect. 4 arose from our group's long-term research into secure coprocessing technology, and more recent efforts to produce a commercially available, general-purpose device. Our design choices for this product were driven not just by academic analysis, but also by more practical factors such as expected business case for such devices, and "lessons learned" from previous IBM experience with similar technology. Some of these factors include:

- Software is less stable than hardware—especially if the time delay between manufacture and end-user installation is considerable.
- The complexity of manufacturing and maintenance support appears to increase exponentially with each shippable variation of a commercial product.
- No one wants to trust anyone else more than necessary.
- Expensive hardware must be repairable.

We decided on building a board-level coprocessor assembled, as much as possible, from existing commercial technology. For protection, we chose active tamper response (electrical, not computational). In an attempt to broaden the family of compatible hosts, we use a PCI interface and are developing host-side software for several popular operating systems. Our device supports separate bootstrap, operating system, and application layers, each potentially controllable by different authorities with minimal involvement by IBM. To simplify the production process and comply with export laws, all devices are shipped the same: with only the bootstrap layer. Software installation (and update) can occur at any point thereafter, including at the end-user site, via broadcast-style commands from remote authorities.

The device is shipped already initialized with device-generated secrets protected by the tamper-response circuitry, in order to defend itself. Each untampered device computationally establishes its untamperedness beginning with its creation at the factory, and continuing throughout shipment, software installation and updates—even if some of this software turns out to be defective or malicious.

Our device is not a portable user token (although we see no substantial engineering barriers to moving this to PCMCIA format). Because of our choice of active tamper response, factors such as low temperatures, x-rays, and bungled battery changes may all trigger zeroization—since otherwise, these are avenues for undetectable tamper.

A separate report [15] discusses the technical details of our architecture.

6 Usage Scenarios

From our analysis in Sect. 4, we concluded that enabling widespread development and deployment secure coprocessing applications required a tool that was easily programmable. Adding sufficient computational power and physical security resulted in a device sufficiently expensive that the ability to update software became necessary. The fact that our device is more a fixed extension of the host[2] than a highly portable user token (due to the large form-factor of a PCI-card) makes supporting field installation of software a necessity.

Essentially, we converged on the generic PC model discussed in Sect. 4, attempting to maximize independence between the development/distribution of the hardware, and the development/distribution of the software. As with PCs, end users can obtain their hardware from anywhere, and install the software on their own. But unlike PCs, bona fide software installed into an untampered device can authenticate itself as such—thus providing the necessary cryptographic hooks for the solutions of Sect. 3.2.

Designing for this "worst-case" approach—software from multiple parties gets installed and updated in the hostile field, without security officers—permits a wide range of development, deployment, and usage scenarios:

Application Development.

- **Off-the-shelf Applications** A party wishing to deploy an application may find that suitable software (for example, application-layer code that transforms the device into a crypto accelerator providing whatever crypto API and algorithms are currently fashionable) is already available.
- **Off-the-shelf Operating Systems** A party wishing to deploy a more customized application may choose an OS that is already available, register with that vendor, and build on that programming environment.
- **Debug and Development** Debug and development environments become just another variation of the operating system—the developer can use an off-the-shelf device, with a different OS load.
- **On the Metal** A party wishing complete on-the-metal control of the device can register with the manufacture, and take control of the OS layer in new off-the-shelf devices.

---

[2] In fact, some IBM hosts may be shipped with the device already installed.

- **Incremental FIPS** Secure field upgradability makes a device not a "FIPS 140-1 Module" per se [12], but rather a partially certified "meta-module." If the hardware and bootstrap software have FIPS validation, a developer need only submit their additional code to obtain a fully validated module for their application.

Application Deployment.

- **Remote Broadcast** A deployer can *avoid the hassle of distributing hardware themselves* by just registering as a code vendor and publishing a download command on the Web. The end-users can purchase the hardware from any standard manufacturer channel.
- **Remote Handshake** If the deployer would like more control, he can use targeting and authentication features of the device bootstrap to interactively install software into a particular device, remotely over an open network.
- **Local Security Officer** The deployer can always eliminate the open network, and send an authorized security officer with their own trusted device to perform installation.
- **Direct Shipment** A deployer can also follow the traditional model of obtaining the devices, install the software, and ship them to their users.

Use.

- **Commerce among people who have never met** The ability for devices to authenticate themselves and their software configurations permits users of such secure devices to securely interact with each other remotely, across an open network—even if these users have met neither each other nor the application deployer.

7 Conclusions

With the growth of the Internet, electronic commerce is becoming central to the way business is conducted. However, this great advance for business carries with it tremendous risks. Specifically, the electronic representations of value can often be modified or stolen or otherwise fraudulently manipulated more easily than physical assets—and in many cases this malfeasance is undetectable.

Clearly, cryptography and other computational tools can protect electronic representations of value. But tamper-protection of the hardware itself is necessary for these tools to be effective—the computation that occurs must be the computation that was intended to occur, despite physical and logical attack. But to be useful and acceptable, tamper-protected hardware must fit into the emerging business models. Flexibility and configurability are as necessary as security and integrity for acceptance.

We offer our research as a step toward meeting these new requirements, and our resulting technology as a tool to allow data and computations to be protected in a way sufficiently flexible and configurable to meet the new needs of business.

Acknowledgments

The authors gratefully acknowledge the contributions of entire Watson development team, including Suresh Chari, Joan Dyer, Gideon Eisenstadter, Bob Gezelter, Juan Gonzalez, Jeff Kravitz, Mark Lindemann, Joe McArthur, Dennis Nagel, Ron Perez, Pankaj Rohatgi, David Toll, and Bennet Yee; the IBM Global Security Analysis Lab at Watson; and the IBM development teams in Vimercate, Charlotte, and Poughkeepsie.

We also wish to thank Ran Canetti, Michel Hack, and Mike Matyas for their helpful advice, and Bill Arnold, Liam Comerford, Doug Tygar, Steve White, and Bennet Yee for their inspirational pioneering work, and the referees for their helpful comments.

References

1. D. G. Abraham, G. M. Dolan, G. P. Double, J. V. Stevens. "Transaction Security Systems." *IBM Systems Journal.* 30:206-229. 1991.
2. R. Anderson, M. Kuhn. "Tamper Resistance—A Cautionary Note." *The Second USENIX Workshop on Electronic Commerce.* November 1996.
3. R. Anderson, M. Kuhn. *Low Cost Attacks on Tamper Resistant Devices.* Preprint. 1997.
4. E. Biham, A. Shamir. *Differential Fault Analysis: A New Cryptanalytic Attack on Secret Key Cryptosystems.* Preprint, 1997.
5. D. Boneh, R. A. DeMillo, R. J. Lipton. *On the Importance of Checking Computations.* Preprint, 1996.
6. D. Chaum. "Design Concepts for Tamper Responding Systems." *CRYPTO 83.*
7. B. Dole, S. Lodin, E. H. Spafford. "Misplaced Trust: Kerberos 4 Session Keys." *ISOC Conference on Network Security.* 1997.
8. H. Gobioff, S. W. Smith, J. D. Tygar and B. S. Yee. "Smart Cards in Hostile Environments." *The Second USENIX Workshop on Electronic Commerce.* November 1996.
9. I. Goldberg, D. Wagner. "Randomness and the Netscape Browser." *Dr. Dobb's Journal.* January 1995.
10. *IBM PCI Cryptographic Coprocessor.* Product Brochure G325-1118. August 1997.
11. M. F. Jones and B. Schneier. "Securing the World Wide Web: Smart Tokens and their Implementation." *Fourth International World Wide Web Conference.* December 1995.
12. National Institute of Standards and Technology. *Security Requirements for Cryptographic Modules.* Federal Information Processing Standards Publication 140-1, 1994.
13. E. R. Palmer. *An Introduction to Citadel—A Secure Crypto Coprocessor for Workstations.* Computer Science Research Report RC 18373, IBM T. J. Watson Research Center. September 1992.
14. S. W. Smith. *Secure Coprocessing Applications and Research Issues.* Los Alamos Unclassified Release LA-UR-96-2805, Los Alamos National Laboratory. August 1996.

15. S. W. Smith, S. H. Weingart. *Building a High-Performance, Programmable Secure Coprocessor.* Resarch Report RC21102, IBM T.J. Watson Research Center. February 1998.

16. J. D. Tygar and B. S. Yee. "Dyad: A System for Using Physically Secure Coprocessors." *Proceedings of the Joint Harvard-MIT Workshop on Technological Strategies for the Protection of Intellectual Property in the Network Multimedia Environment.* April 1993. (A preliminary version is available as Computer Science Technical Report CMU-CS- 91-140R, Carnegie Mellon University.)

17. S. Vaudenay. "Hidden Collisions on DSS." *CRYPTO 1996.* LNCS 1109.

18. S. H. Weingart. "Physical Security for the μABYSS System." *IEEE Computer Society Conference on Security and Privacy.* 1987.

19. S. H. Weingart, S. R. White, W. C. Arnold, and G. P. Double. "An Evaluation System for the Physical Security of Computing Systems." *Sixth Annual Computer Security Applications Conference.* 1990.

20. S. R. White, L. D. Comerford. "ABYSS: A Trusted Architecture for Software Protection." *IEEE Computer Society Conference on Security and Privacy.* 1987.

21. S. R. White, S. H. Weingart, W. C. Arnold and E. R. Palmer. *Introduction to the Citadel Architecture: Security in Physically Exposed Environments.* Technical Report, Distributed Systems Security Group. IBM T. J. Watson Research Center. March 1991.

22. B. S. Yee. *Using Secure Coprocessors.* Ph.D. thesis. Computer Science Technical Report CMU-CS-94-149, Carnegie Mellon University. May 1994.

23. B. S. Yee, J. D. Tygar. "Secure Coprocessors in Electronic Commerce Applications." *The First USENIX Workshop on Electronic Commerce.* July 1995.

24. A. Young and M. Yung. "The Dark Side of Black-Box Cryptography— or—should we trust Capstone?" *CRYPTO 1996.* LNCS 1109.

Secure Group Barter:
Multi-party Fair Exchange with
Semi-trusted Neutral Parties

Matt Franklin[1], Gene Tsudik[2*]

[1] AT&T Labs Research, Florham Park, NJ 07932 *franklin@research.att.com*
[2] USC Information Sciences Institute, Marina del Rey, CA 90292 *gts@isi.edu*

Abstract. The recent surge in popularity of e-commerce prompted a lot of The recent surge in popularity of e-commerce prompted a lot of activity in the area of electronic payments. Solutions have been developed for cash, credit card and check-based electronic transactions. Much less attention has been paid to non-monetary commerce such as barter. In this paper we discuss the notion of "secure group barter" or multi-party fair exchange. We develop a classification of types of barter schemes and present new cryptographic protocols for multi-party exchange with fairness. These protocols assume the presence of a "semi-trusted neutral party".

1 Introduction

This paper is concerned with the barter of digital goods among groups of participants in the electronic world. The kind of barter we envision is an instantaneous, one-time, discrete trade arrangement by an *ad hoc* group of participants. A crucial issue for this kind of barter situation is "fairness". This is a kind of atomicity property for the exchange, whereby no participant gives anything away unless she gets everything she wants.

The problem of multi-party fair exchange has received some attention, but it has not been studied as widely as the more fundamental problem of 2-party fair exchange. In a 2-party fair exchange, each party holds a digital document. They want to engage in a protocol to swap the documents fairly, in the sense that neither party should gain an informational advantage by quitting early or otherwise misbehaving. In the next subsection, we consider a simple but useful taxonomy for 2-party fair exchange.

1.1 A Taxonomy of Protocols for Two-Party Fair Exchange

In a 2-party fair exchange, there is nothing to prevent a "malicious party" from behaving honestly throughout the protocol, while contributing a digital document which contains meaningless or valueless junk. To address this, it is typical

---

* Research supported by the Defense Advanced Research Project Agency, Information Technology Office (DARPA-ITO), under contract DABT63-97-C-0031.

to assume that each main party has committed to its document beforehand, e.g., by publishing a cryptographic checksum thereof. Then we assume that each main party is satisfied if it receives a digital document that is consistent with the checksum. In some sense, this commitment-before-exchange approach defers rather than solves the issue of document quality or value. This issue, which also arises in the certification of public keys, is outside the scope of this paper.

Protocols for 2-party fair exchange can be divided into two categories, on the basis of the possible use of an additional, neutral participant. A number of theoretically important protocols, beginning with [6, 14, 16], avoid the use of a neutral party altogether. A number of practically important protocols use a neutral party, with the requirement that the neutral party should not learn any useful information about the documents being exchanged by the two main parties.

Within the category of neutral party protocols, it useful to make the further distinction of "on-line" versus "off-line" participation by the neutral party. Some protocols, such as [2, 1], require the neutral party to participate actively only when there has been misbehavior by one of the two main parties ("off-line"). These off-line protocols are also called "optimistic", because they are most efficient in the (hoped-for) case when the main parties are honest. Other protocols, such as [15, 7, 11], require the neutral party to participate in every exchange ("on-line").

The class of on-line fair exchange protocols can be further subdivided into those offering "certified delivery" versus "expected delivery". A protocol achieves certified delivery [15] if each main party gets either the document it expects or proof that the other main party misbehaved. A protocol achieves expected delivery if each main party gets the document it expects. The protocols in [11] achieve expected delivery under the assumption that the neutral party does not collude with either of the main parties; they call this a "semi-trusted neutral party".

Given a choice of protocols that were otherwise equally efficient, we might prefer expected delivery to certified delivery, and prefer optimistic to on-line, and no neutral party whatsoever most of all. However, the best protocols in the literature for each category are not otherwise equally efficient. In fact, the on-line protocols with certified delivery require the least computation and communication, and the perfect protocols require the most. On-line protocols with expected delivery require a few more public key operations (e.g., modular multiplications) than for certified delivery. Optimistic protocols such as [1] require two to three orders of magnitude more public key operations than for on-line protocols. Perfect protocols perform the exchange one bit at a time, or even a fraction of a bit at a time, with a lot of cryptographic computations required by both parties to prove that they are behaving properly; these protocols are typically not not considered suitable for practical applications.

1.2 Contribution of Our Work

Work in multi-party fair exchange can be categorized as in the 2-party case. Asokan et al. [2] proposed an optimistic multi-party fair exchange protocol fashioned after an optimistic 2-party fair exchange protocol developed earlier in [3]. In the same vein, work is on-going in the context of the EC-sponsored project SEMPER to refine and extend the results in [3]. In addition, Ketchpel and Garcia-Molina [13] developed multi-party fair exchange protocols that are on-line and achieve certified delivery.

This paper is concerned with the case of multi-party fair exchange that is on-line and achieves expected delivery. We envision an environment where large groups of parties are involved in complex transactions and continuous surveillance by an on-line or an in-line neutral party is impossible or impractical. There may not even be a designated *full-time* neutral party to rely on. Finally, parties are mutually suspicious and cannot be assumed to have any prior association. This, coupled with the consideration that different parties can be subject to very different administrative, legal and political controls, makes this kind of an environment unsuitable for optimistic fair exchange.

All this leads us to extend the "semi-trusted neutral party" setting from 2-party fair exchange [11] to multi-party fair exchange. A semi-trusted neutral party can be selected on a case-by-case basis and asked to aid in the execution of a fair multi-party exchange. However, while an semi-trusted neutral party is trusted to ensure the *fairness* of the multi-party exchange, it is not trusted with the actual commodities involved in the exchange. This means that a malicious semi-trusted neutral party must be unable to cheat as long as the other parties remain honest.

The remainder of the paper is organized as follows. In Section 2 we review the previous work on 2-party fair exchange with a semi-trusted neutral party. A classification of multi-party exchanges is given in Section 3. In Section 4, our protocols for multi-party fair exchange are specified and analyzed. Additional security issues are considered in Section 5: concealment of the exchange topology, defense against passive conspiracies, and identification of barter opportunities. Section 6 gives some conclusions and open problems.

2 Two-Party Fair Exchange with a Semi-Trusted Neutral Party

In this section, we review the semi-trusted neutral party setting and the 2-party fair exchange protocol of [11]. We begin with some useful notation and acronyms.

FE	Fair Exchange
TNP	Trusted Neutral Party
STNP	Semi-Trusted Neutral Party
OWF	One-Way Function
P_i	Protocol participant (indexed)
K_i	Secret quantity held by P_i

The 2-party FE protocol with STNP works through 2-out-of-2 verifiable secret sharing [9, 10]. It can be built from any one-way function f with certain algebraic properties, based for example on the hardness of factoring, discrete log, or graph isomorphism. For convenience, we assume the example based on the hardness of factoring: $f(x) = x^2 \bmod N$, where N is the product of two large distinct primes. For notational convenience, we will omit $\bmod N$ whenever it is obvious from context.

Initially, party X holds a secret key K_X and party Y holds a secret key K_Y. Somehow, X and Y agree on (i.e., select) a semi-trusted neutral party Z that will aid them in the exchange. All three parties (X, Y and Z) know K_X^2 and K_Y^2. X chooses random x_1, x_2 such that $x_1 x_2 = K_X$. Y chooses random y_1, y_2 such that $y_1 y_2 = K_Y$. X sends x_1 to Y and Y sends y_1 to X. Then X sends x_2, y_1^2 to Z and Y sends y_2, x_1^2 to Z. This puts Z in a position to *verify* the consistency of the shares: Does $K_X^2 = x_1^2 (x_2)^2$? And does $K_Y^2 = y_1^2 (y_2)^2$? If so, then Z completes the exchange by sending y_2 to X and sending x_2 to Y.

At the end of the protocol, if all three parties are honest, X learns $K_Y = y_1 y_2$ and Y learns $K_X = x_1 x_2$. If X and Z are honest, then Y learns nothing useful about K_X unless X learns K_Y. If Y and Z are honest, then X learns nothing useful about K_Y unless Y learns K_X. If X and Y are honest, then Z learns nothing useful about K_X or K_Y. These are the properties needed for a fair exchange.

The protocol can be optimized so that there are normally only four flows: (1) from X to Y; (2) from Y to Z; (3) from Z to Y; and (4) from Y to X. It is also not necessary for Z to know K_X^2, K_Y^2 at the start. It is also possible to *blind* the protocol so that Z cannot recognize different exchanges of the same document (unlinkability).

In this paper, we will have n main parties in the exchange, together with a single semi-trusted "neutral party". The trust assumptions for this more general case will be discussed in a later section.

3   Classification of Multi-Party Exchanges

Let $\{K_1, \ldots, K_d\}$ be the types of commodities that will be involved in the exchanges, with a well-defined notion of unit for each commodity. We will express trades and trading preferences as d-dimensional vectors of integers. A positive integer $+m$ in the ith position indicates that m units of commodity K_i are received or desired. A negative integer $-m$ in the ith position indicates that m units of K_i are given or offered.

First, we define a single-unit cyclic exchange (see also Figure 1):

Definition: An *n-party single-unit cyclic exchange is a cycle of length n where for every $i \le n$, the corresponding party P_i, trades one unit of commodity K_i by offering it to $P_{(i+1)}$ for one unit of commodity $K_{(i-1)}$ offered by $P_{(i-1)}$. (Note: all indices are mod n.)*

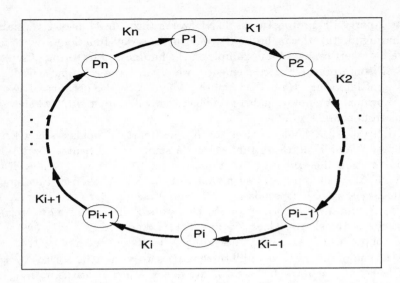

Fig. 1. Single-Unit Cyclic Exchange

The trade performed by party P_i in a single-unit cyclic exchange can be expressed as a d-dimensional vector, all of whose entries are zero except for -1 in the ith location, and +1 in the $i-1$st location. Next, we define a single-unit general exchange:

> **Definition:** *An n-party single-unit general exchange is a permutation σ on $\{1\ldots n\}$, where each party P_i offers a single unit of commodity K_i to $P_{\sigma(i)}$, and receives a single unit of commodity $K_{\sigma^{-1}(i)}$ from $P_{\sigma^{-1}(i)}$.*

The trade performed by party P_i in a single-unit general exchange can be expressed as a d-dimensional vector, all of whose entries are zero except for -1 in the ith position, and +1 in the $\sigma^{-1}(i)$th location. Next, we define a multi-unit cyclic exchange and a multi-unit general exchange. A "basket" of commodities is a d-dimensional vector all of whose entries are nonnegative.

> **Definition:** *An n-party multi-unit cyclic exchange is a cycle of length n where for every $i \le n$, the corresponding party P_i, trades a basket of commodities B_i by offering it to $P_{(i+1)}$ for a basket of commodity $B_{(i-1)}$ offered by $P_{(i-1)}$.*

> **Definition:** *An n-party multi-unit general exchange is a matrix of baskets, where the entry B_{ij} in row i and column j is the basket of goods given by P_i to P_j.*

The trade performed by party P_i in a multi-unit cyclic exchange is the vector $B_{i-1} - B_i$. The trade performed by party P_i in a multi-unit general exchange is the vector $(\sum_j B_{ji}) - (\sum_j B_{ij})$.

Any permutation can be decomposed into disjoint cycles. Given a protocol for (single-unit, multi-unit) cyclic exchange, we can construct a protocol for (single-unit, multi-unit) general exchange by performing each disjoint cyclic exchange independently. For our model, the fairness properties of the cyclic exchange will carry over to the general exchange. In the remainder of this paper, we focus on the problem of fair single-unit cyclic exchange.

4 Fair Single-Unit Cyclic Exchange

In this section, we consider fair protocols for single-unit cyclic exchange. We assume that, initially, each party P_i is in sole possession of a secret quantity K_i. The ideal outcome of a group barter is the simultaneous exchange of secret quantities as depicted in Figure 1, i.e., each P_i trades its K_i to P_{i+1} in return for K_{i-1} from P_{i-1}. The desired properties of a group barter are essentially nothing more than the properties of 2-party FE extended to groups:

1. If all parties are honest, then, for $0 < i \leq n$, P_i obtains K_{i-1}.
2. If all P_i-s are honest, then Z (the STNP) cannot obtain any K_i.
3. Let $\mathcal{P} = P_1, \ldots, P_n$. $\forall \mathcal{S} = \mathcal{P} - P_j$ $(0 < j \leq n)$:
   if all parties in $\mathcal{S}$ and Z are honest, then:
   (a) P_j obtains K_{j-1} iff
       $\forall P_i \in \mathcal{S}$, P_i obtains P_{i-1}.
   (b) P_j cannot obtain any K_i for $i \neq j$ and $i \neq j - 1$.

These properties collectively translate into 1-resilience, i.e., as long at most one of protocol parties is dishonest, it can gain no advantage over the rest. For the moment, we consider this to be sufficient.

Similar to the 2-party case described in [11], we require that all protocol messages be **private** and **authentic**. Also, as in [11], we select an OWF $f :$ $G \rightarrow G$ where G is group in which membership testing, group operation and inverse computation are efficient.

We also require an n-variable function $F_n(X_1, \ldots, X_n)$ with a property that:

$$F_n(X_1, f(X_2), \ldots, f(X_n)) = f(X_1 X_2 \cdots X_n)$$

One example of a suitable $< F_n, f >$ function pair is:

- $F_n = (X_1^2) X_2 \cdots X_n$
  and
- $f = X^2 mod N$
  where N is a product of two large distinct primes.

Each party P_i holds a secret quantity K_i and knows all $f(K_j)$ $(0 < j \leq n)$.

4.1 Protocol for Fair Single-Unit Cyclic Exchange

Our protocol (called SUCEX-1) begins with each P_i generating at random a quantity $R_i \in_R Z_q$ and computing its inverse R_i^{-1}. Then, each P_i sends R_i in secret to P_{i+1}, the intended future recipient of K_i. (See also Figure 4.1.)

Before contacting STNP Z, each P_i also computes the following:

1. $A_i = F_n(K_i, f(K_1), \ldots, f(K_{i-1}), f(K_{i+1}), \ldots, f(K_n))$
2. $C_i = K_i \cdot R_i^{-1}$

Then, each P_i forwards to Z its $< A_i, C_i, f(R_i) >$. In turn, Z does the following:

1. Matches all A_i fields; if everything matches, proceed to next step. Otherwise output ERROR and halt.
2. Computes $C = C_1 \cdots C_n$ and then computes

$$F_{n+1}(C, f(R_1), \ldots, f(R_n)) = f(K_1 R_1^{-1} \cdots K_n R_n^{-1} \cdot R_1 \cdots R_n) = f(K_1 \cdots K_n)$$

and compares to A_i. (The choice of i is unimportant since all A_i's are the same.) The function F_{n+1} is an $(n+1)$-variable version of F_n.

The first step is basically a sanity check; it establishes that all K_i's and all R_i's are consistent and have been properly committed. The second step establishes the coherence of all K_i values, i.e., C_i actually proves P_i's possession of K_i and R_i^{-1}.

In the last protocol round, Z broadcasts to all parties the set $\mathcal{C} = \{C_j \mid 0 < j \leq n\}$. This enables each P_i to compute $K_{i-1} = R_{i-1} \cdot C_i = R_{i-1} \cdot K_{i-1} \cdot R_{i-1}^{-1}$.

4.2 Analysis

Correctness: (sketch) we claim that protocol SUCEX-1 satisfies the requirements stated above:

1. If everyone is honest, then at the end of the protocol each P_i can compute:
   $K_{i-1} = R_{i-1} \cdot C_{i-1} = R_{i-1} \cdot K_i \cdot R_i^{-1}$
2. If all parties in $\mathcal{P}$ are honest (but Z is not) and, as required, all R_i values are pre-distributed securely, Z cannot obtain any K_i.
3. Suppose that exactly one (say, P_j) protocol participant is dishonest:
   (a) P_j has only $f(K_{j-1})$ and R_{j-1} in its possession unless the protocol terminates normally, i.e., it receives C_{j-1} in the last round. Then, P_j obtains K_{j-1}. However, the last round includes the atomic distribution of all C_i values; consequently, K_j is at the same time computed by P_{j+1}. (Since in this case Z is honest.)
   (b) P_j similarly learns nothing about any other K_i where $i \neq j-1$. This is because P_j's *view* of any such K_i is equivalent to that of Z; it only "sees" C_i in round 3 and never learns any R_i which is transmitted in secret to R_{i+1} in round 1.

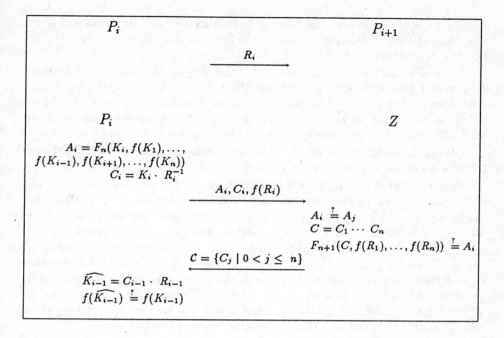

Fig. 2. SUCEX-1: Fair Cyclic Exchange with STNP

4.3 Neutral Party Variations

There are a number of possible variations on the STNP scenario. The role of the STNP could be distributed among two or more neutral parties. Alternatively, the role of the STNP could be played by one or more of the n parties themselves. We have focused on the setting of a single STNP primarily for reasons of efficiency. The communication pattern is particularly simple. The applicability of modular squaring as the underlying cryptographic mechanism simplifies the computational effort by all participants as well.

5 Other Security Issues

In this section, we consider some other security issues associated with multi-party fair exchange: hiding the cycle topology, defending against passive conspiracy, and identifying barter opportunities.

5.1 Hiding the Cycle Topology

In a 2-party exchange, the *topology* of the exchange is obvious: P_1 trades K_1 for K_2 with P_2. This is evident to anyone, including, of course, an STNP. In the multi-party case, however, **the barter topology cannot be inferred from the indentities of the participants.** In fact, for a group of size n, there are $(n-1)!$ distinct barter topologies.

This observation leads us to consider the topology as an additional and unique property of group barter. Furthermore, the topology is something that barter participants may not want revealed to outside parties. We also note that an STNP is essentially an outside party; its task is to ensure the fairness of the exchange and it has no inherent "need-to-know" as far as the topology.

Claim: Although it has not been an explicit design goal, the SUCEX-1 protocol keeps barter topology secret from the STNP.

Proof: (sketch) To support this claim consider that the construction of the barter topology is assumed to have been completed amongst the participants ahead of time. Moreover, the first protocol round (distribution of R_i values) takes place before the STNP (Z) is contacted or perhaps even selected.

In the second round, Z is made aware of the participants' number and identities. The computations of both C and F_{n+1} requires Z to assemble all indexed C_i and $f(R_i)$ values. However, the order of assembly is unimportant due to commutativity of multiplication. Finally, in round 3, Z needs to broadcast a set C to all participants. Once again, the ordering within the set can be arbitrary since each P_i is able to discern its C_{i-1} by testing (for a given C_j):

$$f(C_j \cdot R_{i-1}) \overset{?}{=} f(K_{i-1})$$

Therefore, SUCEX-1 prevents Z from learning the topology.

A related issue is that of group size, i.e., the number of barter participants. While it appears difficult to hide this parameter from an STNP altogether, it is possible to *pad* it. Nothing prevents a *bona fide* participant from enlisting the help of one or more dummy participants whose only function is to make the barter group appear larger than it really is. It is also possible for a participant to take on "multiple personalities", i.e., to play multiple roles (in the SUCEX-1 protocol) only one of which is real.

We have shown that SUCEX-1 hides the barter topology from the STNP, although each main participant P_i knows the complete topology. It is possible to modify SUCEX-1 so that the opposite is true. Only Z learns the barter topology, while P_i is concerned only with the local knowledge that it is giving K_i and K_{i-1}. This is probably not a useful design goal when the STNP is a *stranger* randomly pulled out of the crowd. However, this reverse restriction of the cycle information may be important under other circumstances. The modified protocol, SUCEX-2, is shown in Figure 3.

SUCEX-2 is, in fact, a straightforward extension of the original 2-party STNP protocol. Each P_i goes through the same steps and performs the same computations as in the 2-party case. We also no longer need the cumbersome F_n construct; a much simpler F_2 suffices. (Choice of F_2 is the same as in the 2-party protocol.)

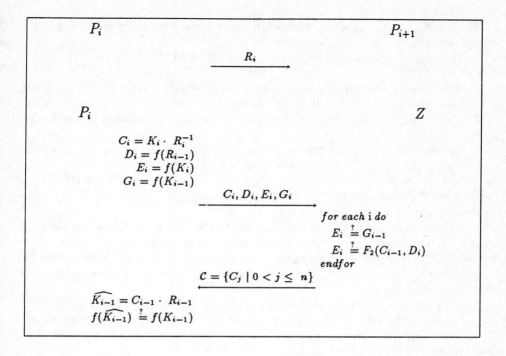

$$R_i$$

P_i $\qquad\qquad\qquad\qquad\qquad\qquad\qquad\qquad\qquad$ Z

$$C_i = K_i \cdot R_i^{-1}$$
$$D_i = f(R_{i-1})$$
$$E_i = f(K_i)$$
$$G_i = f(K_{i-1})$$

$$C_i, D_i, E_i, G_i$$

$$for\ each\ i\ do$$
$$E_i \overset{?}{=} G_{i-1}$$
$$E_i \overset{?}{=} F_2(C_{i-1}, D_i)$$
$$endfor$$

$$\mathcal{C} = \{C_j \mid 0 < j \leq n\}$$

$$\widehat{K_{i-1}} = C_{i-1} \cdot R_{i-1}$$
$$f(\widehat{K_{i-1}}) \overset{?}{=} f(K_{i-1})$$

Fig. 3. SUCEX-2: Fair Cyclic Exchange with STNP

5.2 Defending Against Passive Conspiracies

A *passive conspiracy* (PC) occurs whenever a dishonest party (or a group thereof) *conspires* with an honest party without the latter's consent. PCs were first brought up by Beaver in [4]. The 2-party STNP paper also mentions their relevance to STNP-based fair exchange. The following PC scenarios are given:

1. P_1 could misbehave in a way that causes Z to learn K_1.
2. Z could (without any consent) favor P_1 over P_2 and cause it to learn K_2 without P_2 learning K_1.

Both types are still applicable in a group setting. Furthermore, a new PC type occurring only in groups is:

3. P_i conspiring to reveal K_i to P_{i+1} before SUCEX-1 completion thereby "framing" P_{i+1}.

The first PC type is not of interest to us since, while Z can be tricked into learning some K_i, it will remain utterly oblivious to this fact (unless it is dishonest which puts it out of the realm of passive conspiracies).

In contrast, PC types 2 and 3 are of some concern. Type 3 can be effectively countered by requiring that each participant only accept a message in round 3

if it is signed by Z. This is not an additional requirement since message privacy and authenticity are already assumed in SUCEX-1.

Recall that in round 3 of SUCEX-1, Z is supposed to broadcast: $\widehat{\mathcal{C}} = \{\widehat{C_j} \mid 0 < j \leq n\}$

We consider two sub-types of type 2: one in which Z selectively broadcasts (i.e., directs its message to some participants but not to others) and one in which Z intentionally sends corrupt $\mathcal{C}$, i.e., some C_i values are genuine and some are fake.

In order to prevent an honest participant P_i from becoming and unwilling co-conspirator of Z, the following measures need to be taken:

Before proceeding to search for C_{i-1} in $\widehat{\mathcal{C}}$, P_i computes $C' = \Pi(\mathcal{C})$, i.e., a product of all elements in $\mathcal{C}$. Next, P_i computes $F_{n+1}(C', f(R_1), \ldots, f(R_n))$ and compares it to A_i computed earlier.

In the event that $\mathcal{C}$ does not pass muster, an honest P_i must halt the protocol and not compute K_{i-1}. Otherwise, P_i proceeds to locate C_{i-1} within $\mathcal{C}$ and compute K_{i-1}. Finally, it broadcasts $\mathcal{C}$ to all other participants. This is done for the benefit of other participants who may not have received $\mathcal{C}$ perhaps because of a misbehaving Z.

This procedure ensures that a participant P_i does not learn its barter secret P_{i-1} while some other participant is denied the opportunity to learn its secret. In other words, P_i checks the integrity of the entire set $\mathcal{C}$ – the correctness of all C_i values – before computing K_{i-1}.

5.3 Identifying Barter Opportunities

At the start of a multi-party exchange, the parties to the exchange are fixed, as are the goods that will be exchanged. It is interesting to consider how the parties might arrive at this starting point. After all, there may be many potential barterers, each holding many items for potential exchange. There are a number of ways in which barter opportunities may be identified out of the larger population. In an open outcry system, desired trades might all be public, and possible exchanges could be broadcast to the larger population. Anyone could suggest new exchanges, or insinuate himself into a previously suggested exchange (e.g., "breaking" a link in a cycle to create a larger cycle). Mechanisms for identifying exchanges out in the open, although possibly inefficient, are easy to devise.

If individuals desired privacy, so that trading preferences remained secret whenever possible, then cryptographic techniques could be useful. Recall that potential trades are expressed as d-dimensional vectors over a space of commodities. An exchange is a subset of trades that sum to the all-zero vector. If each trade in the subset has all zeros except for one +1 entry and one -1 entry, then the potential exchange will decompose as a collection of single-unit cyclic exchanges. In principle, finding such subsets can be done using techniques from secure multiparty computation [12, 5, 8]. Since the bulk of the computations are simple sums and comparisons, it is possible that efficient protocols could be found for this problem using existing techniques. This is an interesting area for further investigation.

6 Conclusions

In conclusion, we have presented a classification of barter scenarios. For the case where each participant gives a single item and receives a single item, we have constructed fair exchange protocols in the semi-trusted neutral-party setting. One important open question is how to extend these protocols to the problem of multi-item exchange. Another interesting question concerns the *identification* of barter opportunities. Another interesting open question is to develop efficient protocols for identifying barter opportunities with privacy, as discussed in the preceding section. It would also be valuable to develop algorithms for composing barter cycles (and groups thereof) in the context of both multi-unit and single unit general exchanges.

References

1. N. Asokan, V. Schoup, and M. Waidner. Optimistic fair exchange of digital signatures. Research Report RZ 2892 (# 90840), IBM Research, December 1997.
2. N. Asokan, M. Schunter, and M. Waidner. Optimistic protocols for multi-party fair exchange. Research Report RZ 2892 (# 90840), IBM Research, December 1996.
3. N. Asokan, M. Schunter, and M. Waidner. Optimistic protocols for fair exchange. In *ACM Conference on Computer and Communication Security*, April 1997.
4. D. Beaver. Security, fault tolerance and communication complexity in distributed systems. Ph.D. Thesis, Harvard University, May 1990.
5. M. Ben-Or, S. Goldwasser, and A. Wigderson. Completeness theorems for non-cryptographic fault tolerant distributed computation. In *Proceedings of ACM STOC 1988*, 1988.
6. M. Blum. How to exchange (secret) keys. *ACM Transactions on Computer Systems*, 1:175–193, 1983.
7. J. Camp, M. Harkavy, J. Tygar, and B. Yee. Anonymous atomic transactions. In *2nd USENIX Workshop on Electronic Commerce*, pages 123–134, November 1996.
8. D. Chaum, C. Crépeau, and I. Damgård. Multiparty unconditionally secure protocols. In *Proceedings of ACM STOC 1988*, 1988.
9. B. Chor, S. Goldwasser, S. Micali, and B. Awerbuch. Verifiable secret sharing and achieving simultaneity in the presence of faults. In *IEEE Fondations of Computer Science*, 1985.
10. P. Feldman. A practical scheme for non-interactive verifiable secret sharing. In *IEEE Fondations of Computer Science*, 1987.
11. M. Franklin and M. Reiter. Fair exchange with a semi-trusted third party. In *ACM Conference on Computer and Communication Security*, April 1997.
12. O. Goldreich, S. Micali, and A. Wigderson. How to play any mental game. In *Proceedings of ACM STOC 1987*, 1987.
13. S. Ketchpel and H. Garcia-Molina. Making trust explicit in distributed commerce transactions. In *IEEE ICDCS*, 1996.
14. M. Luby, S. Micali, and C. Rackoff. How to simultaneously exchange a secret bit by flipping a symmetrically-biased coin. In *IEEE Symposium on Foundations of Computer Science*, pages 11–21, November 1984.

15. J. Tygar. Atomicity in electronic commerce. In *ACM Symposium on Principles of Distributed Computing*, pages 8–26, 1996.

16. U. Vazirani and V. Vazirani. Trapdoor pseudo-random number generators, with applications to protocol design. In *IEEE Symposium on Foundations of Computer Science*, pages 23–30, 1983.

A Payment Scheme Using Vouchers

Ernest Foo[*]
ernest@fit.qut.edu.au
and Colin Boyd
boyd@fit.qut.edu.au

Information Security Research Centre
School of Data Communications
Queensland University of Technology
Brisbane, Australia

Abstract. Electronic payment schemes are traditionally based on the physical model of commerce where customers withdraw cash from bank accounts and spend it at merchants' establishments in return for goods and services. This may not be the most ideal model on which to base electronic payment. A new payment scheme using a different paradigm has been developed. Vouchers are prepared by the bank and the merchant. These are distributed to customers who can redeem them for electronic goods with the help of the bank. This new scheme requires fewer online messages to be transmitted than previous payment schemes involving electronic goods such as NetBill and thus also requires less online processing. The voucher scheme also provides some properties desired by payment schemes based on electronic coins.

1 Introduction

It seems that the future of commercial transactions will be electronic payment over the Internet. For several years now, it has been the expectation of industry that the medium of the Internet will be the future of commercial and private trading. Electronic payment over the Internet has great potential in terms of banking because much of the transaction may be automated. Also many users perceive that the use of the Internet will allow more convenient purchasing. Indeed some believe that electronic payment over the Internet will become an integral part of commercial culture, in the same way that this has happened for automatic teller machines and credit cards. Unfortunately, due to the insecure nature of the Internet, the security of

[*] Sponsored by Commonwealth Bank and the Australian Research Council

electronic payment is unsure. In general the current public opinion is that transactions over the Internet are extremely risky and until the much awaited SET protocol [13–15] is widely deployed few banking corporations are willing to guarantee the safe transaction of funds over the Internet.

One of the main problems with electronic payment on the Internet is that the transaction occurs remotely. Unlike normal payment there is no physical proof of the transaction occurring. Cryptographic tools are required in payment protocols to provide this proof in the electronic medium. But electronic payment protocols are also different from other secure protocols in that they have two kinds of threat: external threats and internal threats. External threats have been an issue which has been widely addressed by other secure protocols; the processes for dealing with these threats are widely documented [1, 2]. Internal threats are unique to electronic commerce. These are due to entities which legitimately take part in the protocol but attempt in some way to gain unfairly from the transaction. Designers usually develop a series of proofs and commitments to prevent or detect internal threats.

These issues are directly, and sometimes indirectly, addressed by a multitude of payment protocols [4–7, 9, 10, 16–20, 23] each of which provides many different useful properties. The voucher payment scheme described in this paper addresses external threats in much the same manner as other payment schemes but the treatment of the internal threat is unique.

All payment protocols intended for practical use need to take into account their efficiency with regard to processing, communications and storage requirements. Cryptographic processing, particularly with asymmetric algorithms, is computationally expensive, so it is important to minimise the use of cryptography to where it is really required. The SET protocol has been criticised for its intensive use of asymmetric cryptography. Some protocols, particularly those for *micropayments*, are willing to sacrifice some security in return for large gains in efficiency. The voucher protocol proposed in this paper maintains high security, but is more efficient in terms of online messages transmitted and online computer processing required than other protocols with similar aims.

1.1 Related Work

The design of most electronic payment protocols exists within a common framework. This framework is traditionally based on credit card payment models and consists of three entities. The *customer entity* is the user and the entity which wishes to make a purchase of goods or services. The *merchant entity* is the shopkeeper who uses the payment scheme to offer goods and services to the customer entity. The *bank entity* is responsible for transfer of funds between the other entities.

The establishment and distribution of cryptographic keys and other data flows between the different entities in payment protocols exhibit the following common properties.

- A bit string containing certain information is used to convey value. The information varies depending on the type of payment protocol. This bit string is often called a *coin* or *payment commitment* in the literature, and we call it here the *proof of transaction*. Once transmitted it can be used as proof that an entity agrees or commits to the terms of the transaction.
- The proof of transaction is usually digitally signed to indicate who transmitted it or is encrypted in such a way that it is known as to who sent the message.
- This proof of transaction is created by the bank and the customer. During the payment process it is usually sent from the customer to the merchant. The merchant sends it to the bank to verify its authenticity and thus verify the payment transaction.

The integrity of the proof of the transaction is used to prevent or discourage internal threats. The protection of the proof of transaction during transmission is important to defend against both external and internal threats. That is why the proof of transaction is almost always transmitted along authenticated channels.

The voucher scheme employs a proof of transaction but is unique in the way the payment commitment is distributed. Specifically, in comparison with all the known schemes in the literature, the transmission of the proof of transaction is reversed: instead of being transferred from customer to merchant to bank, it is transmitted from merchant to customer to bank. In the voucher scheme the payment commitment (called a voucher) is created by the merchant with the assistance of the bank. The payment commitment is then distributed to potential customers. The customer has the option to complete the transaction by signing the bit string. The payment commitment is then sent to the bank to verify the validity of the transaction.

The major advantage of the voucher scheme, in comparison to known schemes, is that it allows the merchant to act in a completely passive way. This makes the scheme ideal for use in an Internet environment where merchants already almost universally provide web sites where their customers can download product information. With the voucher scheme merchants can provide goods to be downloaded by customers, but these goods remain encrypted until the customer has committed to payment. As a result the merchant performs no on-line processing. A major benefit of this is that network processing on the merchant side is completely unchanged from the current technology.

It should be made clear that, in comparison with previously proposed schemes, the reduction in merchant processing is accompanied by a consequent shift in processing to the bank. However, overall there is a saving in the online processing required. Moreover, this shift is away from the widely distributed merchants to the central banking facility where it is natural to concentrate processing power, and where processing may be aggregated.

1.2   Outline of Paper

The following section describes the overall idea of the voucher payment scheme and then the detailed protocols are presented. In section 4 a comparison is made with the existing NetBill payment scheme which has many features in common with the voucher scheme.

2   A Voucher Payment Model

In a real world voucher scheme, merchants create vouchers which allow customers to receive discounts for the purchase of goods or even allow the customer to redeem them for the actual goods. This is the basis of the electronic voucher payment scheme. This payment scheme is ideal for processing of electronic goods in a communications network, such as software or electronic news and information. However, it could be modified to work for physical goods as well by substituting an authorisation message or a release signal for the electronic goods package.

The transaction model has a traditional configuration consisting of merchant, bank and customer. We assume that the bank is trusted by both the merchant and customer entities. In reality the bank entity often represents two separate parties: the acquirer and the issuer. The acquirer is the merchant's bank and the issuer is the customer's bank. If the acquirer and the issuer are separate entities we assume that they share a secure private communications link. This scheme consists of three parts. Each of these parts must have been completed to successfully conduct a transaction.

1. The merchant and the bank work together to create a voucher which contains the important transaction commitment. A major saving of the scheme is that this process is only required once for a particular item. Since electronic items are likely to be purchased many times, this is a significant advantage.
2. The merchant allows the free distribution of the voucher to customers. For electronic goods this would typically mean that the voucher is placed on the merchant's web site. The voucher will be distributed together with the actual electronic goods. However, the goods are encrypted so that during this phase the customer cannot access the goods.
3. The customer and the bank co-operate and enable the customer to decrypt the electronic goods and thus allow the customer to access the goods.

The voucher protocol is designed to achieve the following main objectives. These are common objectives which well-known schemes such as iKP [3] and NetBill [8] payment systems attempt to achieve.

1. The customer and merchant are able to agree on the details of the transaction.
2. The customer can only receive the specified goods if she has paid for them.

3. The customer and merchant have proof that a successful transaction has occurred.
4. The customer is able to protect her identity from the merchant.
5. The transaction cannot be adversely affected by external threats. This means that a malicious party (which is not included as part of the payment model) cannot prevent the transaction from succeeding. This can either be by causing the merchant not to be paid or preventing the customer from receiving the goods.
6. The transaction is efficient in terms of processing and in the number of messages required to complete the protocol.

3 The Voucher Protocol

The protocol description will use the notation $i. X \rightarrow Y$ to indicate that the ith message of the protocol is transmitted by entity X to entity Y. The customer entity is represented by C, the merchant entity is represented by M and the bank or notary is represented by B. The basic voucher protocol consists of five steps:

1. $M \rightarrow B$: Request key
2. $B \rightarrow M$: Return key
---
3. $M \rightarrow C$: Distribute voucher
4. $C \rightarrow B$: Redeem voucher
5. $B \rightarrow C$: Release goods

The horizontal line after the first two steps separates the protocol part that need be performed only once, in an offline exchange between bank and merchant. The remaining steps may be run repeatedly with different customers at any time. Thus the merchant engages in no online processing.

Objective 1 is achieved in steps 3 and 4 of the protocol. The merchant determines the price for his goods and sets this in the merchant signed voucher. The customer agrees to this price by cashing in the voucher.

The customer can only decrypt the goods by using the correct key. This key is received by the customer after the bank has determined that the transaction should go ahead and the funds have been transferred from the customer's account. Thus Objective 2 is realised.

The goods decryption key received by the customer is her proof that the bank has successfully conducted the transaction. The merchant's proof of transaction is the bank signed product identification code sent in step 5 of the protocol. Objective 3 has been achieved.

The customer's identity is protected from the merchant because the merchant does not transmit any encrypted messages directly to the customer. Also even if the customer does receive a voucher, she is under no obligation to cash in the voucher and decrypt the goods. Thus Objective 4 is attained. Note that anonymity is not obtained because the bank will be able to identify the customer and the goods that she purchases.

Objective 5 is achieved because no messages within the protocol contain data which is either unsigned or unencrypted.

Objective 6 is discussed in later sections. But steps 1 and 2 of the protocol only need to be conducted on a regular basis and do not need to be conducted for every transaction. This decreases the number of messages required for an average transaction. The voucher payment scheme only requires 1 signature from each entity (the merchant does not even need to do this on line) and a one way hash calculation from the bank and the merchant (who also does not need to do this on line).

3.1 Notation

The following notation is used to denote cryptographic operations. X and Y always represent communicating parties. K always represents a cipher key. When describing the following protocols, the sequence of messages is exchanged among three parties: C, the customer, M, the merchant; and B the bank, acquirer or notary entity.

$E_{XY}(Message)$ *Message*, encrypted with the key XY using symmetric key cryptography. It is assumed that the key is known only by X and Y and that only these entities may know the contents of *Message*.

$Sig_X(Message)$ *Message*, digitally signed by X using a suitable signature algorithm, such as RSA [21]. This implies that X's public key is used to ensure that the message was transmitted by X.

$H(Message)$ A cryptographic function which results in a digest and checksum of $Message$, using an algorithm such as the Secure Hash Algorithm (SHA) one-way hash function.

3.2 Voucher Creation Phase

This phase assumes that the merchant and the bank have exchanged RSA public keys so that they are able to verify the authenticity of digital signatures created by the other entity.

1. $M \rightarrow B : Sig_M(MID, E_{MB}(MerchantAccountDetails))$

2. $B \rightarrow M : Sig_B(E_{MB}(K), Expiry)$

In step 1 the merchant makes a request of the bank for a voucher key. This key will be used to provide the security required by the voucher. The merchant must provide his merchant identification as well as details of his account with the acquiring bank. The acquiring bank stores this information so that any funds which are owed to the merchant by customers may be deposited in that account. It is optional that this message be correctly authenticated with a digital signature. In essence this will allow anyone to sell goods and become a merchant provided that they have a unique merchant identification number. This number may be chosen by the merchant. Merchant account details, like all other account details, must not be allowed to be sent across open networks in the clear.

After it has generated a symmetric key for the merchant the bank encrypts it and sends it to the merchant with an expiry date which indicates when this key is no longer valid. As this key is the only element in the protocol which provides security for the transaction it is essential that it be encrypted so only the merchant and the bank know it. The bank must sign the key and expiry to prevent the merchant from receiving a false key from an external party.

At this point the merchant can create a voucher for each product. The merchant voucher will contain the actual electronic goods which the customer is purchasing. First, the merchant generates the key which will encrypt his goods in the following manner:

$$K_P = H(K, MID, PID, Value)$$

K is the key provided by the bank. This key is only known to the merchant and the bank. MID is the merchant identity which the bank already knows. The product identity (PID) is used to indicate the product which this voucher contains. The merchant can choose to have a different PID for each copy of the product he sells or he can choose to have one product identity for each product or even for a range of products. The PID and MID are used to provide a unique identifier for the voucher which cannot be tampered with. The cost of the product is also included in this key so that customers cannot adjust the value to be paid for the product. It is assumed the the one way hash function is such that the key K cannot be determined, even if multiple valid values for K_P, MID, PID, and $Value$ are known. Now the goods must be encrypted with the key which has been generated by the merchant. The next section will describe the contents of the voucher in more detail.

If the merchant issues one product identity for a number of products or if the merchant has many copies of the same product with the same product identity the customer who has purchased the goods may freely distribute the key K_P to other customers. This would mean that a customer can then obtain certain goods from the merchant and release them using the key she has been given by a friend who has purchased the goods. Unfortunately this protocol cannot prevent this scenario which is in essence the same as software piracy. However, only the legitimate customer has a receipt from the bank which can be used to prove custody of a legal copy. This is the same situation as with purchase of electronic goods on physical media.

This phase of the payment system only has to be conducted once. The merchant can continue to use the key K provided by the bank to prepare vouchers for all of his products indefinitely. In practice it is advisable that the merchant request a new key at regular intervals to maintain the security of the voucher. This is the reason for the inclusion of an expiry date when the key is issued by the bank.

3.3 Voucher Distribution Phase

Vouchers can be freely distributed by the merchant with the associated encrypted goods. The additional data which is included in the voucher is shown below. It is not essential for the security of the payment scheme that the merchant sign the voucher but as this signature need only be constructed once when the voucher is created it does allow the customer to verify that the voucher and goods she has downloaded originate from the correct source.

$$3.\ M \rightarrow C : Sig_M(E_{K_P}(Goods), MID, PID, Description,$$
$$Value, Expiry)$$

The voucher package includes the encrypted goods which the voucher will allow the customer to access. The voucher package also includes the merchant and product identities. These are required to uniquely identify the product which the customer is purchasing. Also included is a human readable description of the product so the customer has some indication of the type of product she is purchasing. The value of the product must also be included so the customer can determine whether the cost of the product is worthwhile. The expiry date is also included for the customer as an indicator of how long the voucher will be valid. The customer may download the voucher and decide not to purchase the goods without any loss. Because the voucher is signed by the merchant, the customer can be sure that the goods and the voucher contents have been received correctly providing, of course, that the merchant is not cheating.

3.4   Redeeming Vouchers

Now that the customer has obtained the encrypted goods and the voucher from the merchant and she has decided to purchase the goods, she must request the key from the bank to release the goods. Again it is assumed that the customer is able to establish a secure connection with the bank.

$$4.\ C \rightarrow B : Sig_C(MID, PID, Value, E_{CB}(Customer\,Account\,Details),$$
$$Counter)$$
$$5.\ B \rightarrow C : E_{CB}(K_P)$$

In step 4 of the protocol the customer sends to the bank the merchant and product identity and the value of the product as well as details of her account and a counter value. The merchant and product identity and the value of the goods are obtained from the voucher the customer has received. The counter is a value which must be maintained by the bank and the customer. The purpose of the counter is to uniquely identify this message and prevent an external entity from replaying the message and thus draining the customer's account of funds. A timestamp could be used instead of a counter provided that problems associated with synchronisation are properly addressed.

It is only when the customer signs this message that the voucher is given value. Up till this stage the customer can abort the transaction. If the customer chooses to accumulate vouchers over a period of time, the customer may concatenate multiple sets of merchant identity, product identity and value bit strings and sign them all once. This will reduce the amount of processing required by the customer.

The bank now makes a decision as to whether the transaction should take place. The bank must consider things like the availability of the customer's funds, and the trustworthiness of both the merchant and the customer and check that the counter value is valid. If the bank decides that the transaction should occur, the bank moves the correct amount of funds from the customer's account to the merchant's account using the details provided by the customer and the merchant during the transaction. At this point the bank may also deduct any transaction, handling or other fees.

As the bank already knows the merchant's key K, the bank uses these additional values to calculate the key K_P. In step 5 of the protocol the bank returns the key K_P to the customer. When the customer obtains the key K_P she is able to decrypt the goods she received with the voucher and complete the transaction.

After the funds transfer has occurred the bank has the option of notifying the merchant that the transaction took place. This notification is only to assist the merchant in updating his inventory and may not be essential for online software goods. When, or if, this notification occurs can be determined by agreement between the bank and merchant. For large value transactions immediate notification may be appropriate; for small values notifications could be batched and sent at the end of each working day. Unfortunately if the merchant chooses not to be notified by the bank he has no indication that a transaction has occurred.

3.5 Disputes

If the merchant or the customer is not satisfied that the transaction has been conducted successfully a dispute has occurred. The voucher payment scheme has a process which is able to deal with most disputes. It is assumed that both the customer and the merchant can trust the bank to be fair in all decisions.

The voucher dispute resolution protocol consists of the following step:

$$1.\ C \rightarrow B : Sig_C(K_P, Sig_M(E_{K_P}(Goods), MID, PID,$$
$$Description, Value, Expiry))$$

The message consists of the key K_P which the customer received from the bank in step 5 of the payment protocol. The remainder of the message is the merchant signed voucher the customer received in step 3 of the payment protocol. Because the voucher is signed by the merchant the customer is unable to alter the contents of the voucher without detection. The re-transmission of the voucher, including the goods, in the dispute protocol will increase the amount of traffic on the network but it is expected that the dispute protocol will not be required very often.

The resolution of the dispute need not necessarily be referred to the bank. Any trusted third party may be used as a judge, provided that party has access to the transaction key K. The following sections describe how the judge may deal with potential complaints.

Incorrect Key In the case of this dispute, the customer claims that the key that she received from the bank does not correctly decrypt the goods which were received in the voucher.

When the judge receives the message from the dispute protocol he calculates the disputed key K_D using the MID, PID and $Value$ fields from the voucher and the key K which is already known to him.

$$K_D = H(K, MID, PID, Value)$$

The judge then compares K_D and the key K_P received from the customer. If they match then the customer has received a legitimate key and the transaction should be rolled back. If the keys do not match, either K_P was altered by the customer or the customer has transmitted an incorrect K_P as part of the dispute protocol. In this case the transaction is not altered. It is assumed that the transmission of each message in the protocol occurs successfully and that the contents of each message is not altered by any network interference.

If the customer is not satisfied with this result it is possible that the incorrect goods have been delivered in the voucher.

Incorrect Goods The customer may not be satisfied that the goods that she received are the correct goods that she has purchased. It could be that the merchant has incorrectly constructed the voucher, or that the merchant has encrypted goods which do not match the goods description included in the voucher.

To check the goods, the judge verifies that the merchant has constructed the voucher correctly by calculating the key K_D and checking for the correct key K_P as described in the previous section. The judge then decrypts the goods using K_D. A human arbitrator determines if the decrypted goods match the description provided in the voucher. If the goods cannot be decrypted, the merchant has incorrectly constructed the voucher by providing an incorrect merchant or product identity or key K. In both of these cases the transaction is rolled back and the money returned to the customer.

Incorrect Payment Amounts This type of dispute includes any disagreement on the amount charged for the goods. This includes both the possibility that the customer has been charged too much or the merchant has been paid too little.

In the voucher payment scheme the value that the merchant assigns to the product cannot be maliciously altered by the customer because the value is part of the key which is required to decrypt the electronic goods. Both the customer and the merchant indicate their agreement to the value to be paid for the goods by transmitting the value field correctly. The merchant indicates his requested goods *Value* within the signed voucher and the customer indicates her agreement to that *Value* by signing it and sending it to the bank in return for the key K_P.

4 Some Implications of Using Vouchers

By using the concept of vouchers, the resulting payment scheme has several interesting properties. These include greater efficiency than existing payment schemes like *iKP* and *NetBill*, as well as the advantage of requiring no online processing by merchants. The following sections provide a more detailed comparison of payment schemes.

4.1 Comparisons with NetBill

The NetBill protocol [8], like the current proposal, was designed especially for payment of information goods over the Internet. Because of this the NetBill protocol may be used as a benchmark for comparison with the voucher payment protocol. The voucher protocol provides many of the objectives which the NetBill designers required. A brief description of the NetBill protocol is given in Figure 1. Like the voucher protocol the NetBill scheme involves three parties: a customer, a merchant and the NetBill server which is the equivalent to voucher scheme's bank entity. NetBill also involves three phases: price negotiation, goods delivery and payment. During a NetBill transaction, the customer and the merchant interact with each other during the price negotiation and goods delivery phases to exchange the transaction request and encrypted goods. In the payment phase the merchant sends the transaction request to the bank. When the bank is satisfied that the transaction is in order he sends a signed receipt back to the merchant who also signs the receipt and passes it onto the customer along with the decryption key for the goods. The bank is able to handle disputes because he also receives the decryption key with the transaction request.

Table 1 compares the efficiency of the NetBill payment scheme against the voucher payment scheme. The main advantage the voucher payment scheme has over the NetBill payment system is that it requires a smaller number of messages to be transmitted for each transaction. The voucher scheme has only three messages which must be transmitted for a transaction to be successfully completed. The first two messages in the voucher payment protocol which involve the creation of vouchers may be conducted offline prior to the transaction. A new voucher does not need to be created for each purchase. The

Price Negotiation Phase
1. $C \rightarrow M : C, E_{CM}(Product, RequestFlags, TID)$
2. $M \rightarrow C : E_{CM}(ProductID, Price, RequestFlags, TID)$

Goods Delivery Phase
3. $C \rightarrow M : C, \{TID\}_{K_{CM}}$
4. $M \rightarrow C : E_K(Goods), E_{CM}(H(E_K(Goods)), EPOID)$

Payment Phase
5. $C \rightarrow M : C, E_{CM}(Sig_C(EPO))$
6. $M \rightarrow B : M, E_{MB}(Sig_M(Sig_C(EPO), Macct, K))$
7. $B \rightarrow M : E_{MB}(Sig_B(Receipt), E_{CB}(EPOID, Cacct, Bal, Flags))$
8. $M \rightarrow C : E_{CM}(Sig_B(Receipt), E_{CB}(EPOID, Cacct, Bal, Flags))$

Component	Description
Product	Bit string representing goods involved in the transaction
RequestFlags	Flags which indicates the customers specification for the transaction. Includes delivery instructions
TID	Transaction ID
ProductID	Human readable description of the goods
Price	Price of the goods
Goods	The electronic goods involved in the transaction
EPO	Bit string representing the Electronic Payment Order. Includes the Customer's ID, Product ID, Price, Merchant's ID, Request Flags, Cacct and EPOID data
EPOID	Unique ID for EPO
Macct	Merchant account number
K	The goods decryption key
Receipt	Response from the bank indicating a successful transaction
Cacct	Customer account number
Bal	Balance of customer's account
Flags	Bit string representing messages from the bank to the customer

Fig. 1. Summary of the NetBill Payment Protocol

NetBill payment scheme requires all eight messages to be transmitted for each successful transaction.

Because the voucher system requires fewer total online messages to be transmitted less online symmetric encryption is required; furthermore, the processing involved is concentrated more at the bank and less at the customer site. In terms of distributed networks centralised processing may not be optimal but it does allow the bank to easily handle dispute situations and allows the owner of the bank server to charge both customers and merchants. The voucher system does move a lot of online processing away from the merchant when

	NetBill	Voucher
Messages for successful payment	8	6
Online Messages	8	3
Offline Messages	0	3
Symmetric Encryptions	11	5
Customer	4	1
Merchant	5	2
Bank	2	2
Hash Calculations	4	2
Customer	3	0
Merchant	1	1
Bank	0	1
Signatures	3	3
Customer	1	1
Merchant	1	1(may be off line)
Bank	1	1

Table 1. A comparison of voucher and NetBill payment protocol processing and message transmission.

compared with the NetBill scheme. The voucher payment system requires the same number of digital signatures as NetBill for purchase of a single item, but one of these is not conducted during run time and may be re-used in subsequent transactions. The merchant need not sign the voucher as the payment protocol is run unlike the Net-Bill protocol. The voucher system also requires a smaller number of one-way hash functions but the processing for these functions is insignificant when compared to constructing digital signatures.

One of the differences between NetBill and the voucher system, which increases the number of messages required, is that the Net-Bill scheme distributes a receipt. When NetBill does this, all messages must pass through the merchant. In the voucher system, the bank transmits the proof of transaction directly to the customer. The merchant does not receive a receipt but may optionally request notification from the bank.

One of the advantages of the NetBill system is that it contains a bidding process which allows the merchant to discount the price of goods for groups of customers or individual customers. The voucher payment scheme does not include this facility. Merchants fix the price of goods when the voucher is created. The merchant would most likely advertise the price of the goods or services separately from the voucher protocol on a web page. If the messages required for downloading the web page are included the total number of messages, both online and offline, for the voucher scheme and NetBill are very similar.

4.2 Comments Regarding Micropayment and Coin Based Payment Protocols

We are unable to fairly compare the voucher payment system with micropayment and coin based payment protocols because these payment systems have different design goals. The main reason for the introduction of electronic coins and the complexity and the large amount of processing associated with them was to enable the complete anonymity of the customer. The anonymity of the customer from the bank was not a design goal of the voucher system. Micropayment protocols such as Payword [22] are specially designed for efficiency. The voucher payment scheme is not as efficient as these schemes but it does include security features which have been dropped from micropayment schemes.

However, it is interesting to note how some design issues which designers of micropayment and coin based payment protocols wrestle with have been addressed or avoided by the voucher payment protocol.

The voucher payment protocol has an advantage over coin based payment protocols. The customer does not commit to the purchase of the goods until the voucher has been signed and received by the bank. No value is given to the voucher until the customer signs the goods. Thus in the situation where the customer's hard drive is accidentally erased, vouchers can be obtained again from the merchant with no loss to the customer. On the other hand if electronic coins are stored on the hard drive their value is lost to the customer. This is especially the case for anonymous cash systems.

The voucher payment scheme also avoids some of the issues, documented in [11], which Payword and other coin based payment schemes must address. One of these issues is divisibility. All of Payword's hash calculations are required to enable the customer to pay out small divisions of her Payword chain. In the voucher system, all goods are paid for without the need to divide the voucher.

Double spending is also not an issue for the voucher system. If a voucher is cashed in more than once to the bank, the correct merchant will always receive the correct value for the goods assuming attackers are unable to substitute their own signature and merchant identity within the voucher.

The property of transferability is also provided by the voucher scheme. Vouchers can be passed from one customer to the next and provided that the customer's acquiring bank has secure communications with the merchant's issuing bank, the voucher can be correctly cashed in. Given the secure communication of funds and keys assumed for transferability, the services of acceptability and scalability will also be provided. It is not unreasonable to assume that this network will be similar to the existing EFTPOS and other electronic funds transfer systems.

References

1. Martin Abadi and Roger Needham. Prudent Engineering Practice for Cryptographic Protocols. *Proceedings of the 1994 IEEE Symposium on Security and Privacy*, pages 122–136, May 1994.
2. Ross Anderson and Roger Needham. Robustness Principles for Public Key Protocols. In *Advances in Cryptology - Proceedings of CRYPTO '95*. Springer-Verlag, 1995.
3. Mihir Bellare, Juan A. Garay, Ralf Hauser, Amir Herzberg, Hugo Krawczyk, Micheal Steiner, Gene Tsudik, and Micheal Waidner. iKP – A Family of Secure Electronic Payment Protocols. In *Proceedings of the First Usenix Workshop on Electronic Commerce*, New York, July 1995.
4. Jean-Paul Boly, Antoon Bosselaers, Ronald Cramer, Rolf Michelsen, Stig Mjolsnes, Frank Muller, Torben Pedersen, Birgit Pfitzmann, Peter de Rooij, Berry Schoenmakers, Matthias Schunter, Luc Vallee, and Michael Waidner. The ESPRIT Project CAFE - High Security Digital Payment Systems. In *Computer Security - ESORICS '94*, pages 217–230. Springer-Verlag, 1994.
5. Stefan Brands. Electronic Cash on the Internet. In *Proceedings of the Internet Society 1995 Symposium on Network and Distributed System Security*, pages 64–84, 1995.
6. David Chaum. Online Cash Checks. In *Advances in Cryptology - Proceedings of EUROCRYPT '89*, pages 288–301, 1989.
7. David Chaum, Amos Fiat, and Moni Naor. Untraceable Electronic Cash. In *Advances in Cryptology - Proceedings of CRYPTO '88*, Lecture Notes in Computer Science, pages 319–327. Springer-Verlag, 1990.
8. Benjamin Cox, J. D. Tygar, and Marvin Sirbu. NetBill Security and Transaction Protocol. In *Proceedings of the First Usenix Workshop on Electronic Commerce*, New York, July 1995.

9. Tony Eng and Tatsuaki Okamoto. Single-Term Divisible Electronic Coins. In *Advances in Cryptology - Proceedings of EUROCRYPT '94*, number 950 in Lecture Notes in Computer Science, pages 306–319. Springer-Verlag, 1995.

10. Niels Ferguson. Single Term Off-Line Coins. In *Advances in Cryptology - Proceedings of EUROCRYPT '93*, pages 318–328. Springer-Verlag, 1994.

11. Ernest Foo, Colin Boyd, William Caelli, and Ed Dawson. A Taxonomy of Electronic Cash Schemes. In *Proceedings of IFIP/SEC '97 13th International Information Security Conference*, pages 337–348. Chapman and Hall, 1997.

12. Matthew Franklin and Moti Yung. Secure and Efficient Off-Line Digital Money. In *Proceedings of ICALP '93*, number 700 in Lecture Notes in Computer Science, pages 265–276. Springer-Verlag, 1993.

13. VISA/MasterCard International. Secure Electronic Transaction (SET) Specification Book 1: Business Description. http://www.visa.com/cgi-bin/vee/sf/standard.html.

14. VISA/MasterCard International. Secure Electronic Transaction (SET) Specification Book 2: Programmer's Guide. http://www.visa.com/cgi-bin/vee/sf/standard.html.

15. VISA/MasterCard International. Secure Electronic Transaction (SET) Specification Book 3: Formal Protocol Definition. http://www.visa.com/cgi-bin/vee/sf/standard.html.

16. Markus Jakobsson and Moti Yung. Revokable and Versatile Electronic Money. In *Third ACM Conference on Computer and Communications Security*, pages 76–87. ACM Press, 1996.

17. Wenbo Mao. A Simple Cash Payment Technique for the Internet. In *Computer Security - ESORICS '96*. Springer-Verlag, 1996.

18. Gennady Medvinsky and B. Clifford Neuman. NetCash: A Design for Practical Electronic Currency on the Internet. In *Proceedings of First ACM Conference on Computer and Communications Security*, pages 102–196. ACM Press, 1993.

19. Tatsuaki Okamoto. An Efficient Divisible Electronic Cash Scheme. In *Advances in Cryptology - Proceedings of CRYPTO '95*, pages 438–451. Springer-Verlag, 1995.

20. Tatsuaki Okamoto and Kazuo Ohta. Universal Electronic Cash. In *Advances in Cryptology - Proceedings of CRYPTO '91*, pages 324–337. Springer-Verlag, 1992.

21. A. Shamir R. Rivest and L. Adleman. A Method for Obtaining Digital Signatures and Public Key Cryptosystems. *Communications of the ACM*, pages 120–126, 1978.

22. Ronald L. Rivest and Adi Shamir. PayWord and MicroMint: Two Simple Micropayment Schemes. http://theory.lcs.mit.edu/ rivest/RivestShamir-mpay.ps, January 1996.

23. Yacov Yacobi. Efficient Electronic Money. In *Advances in Cryptology - Proceedings of ASIACRYPT '94*, pages 153–163. Springer-Verlag, 1995.

A Formal Specification of Requirements for Payment Transactions in the SET Protocol

Catherine Meadows and Paul Syverson

Center for High Assurance Computer Systems
Naval Research Laboratory
Washington DC 20375, USA
{meadows,syverson}@itd.nrl.navy.mil

Abstract. Payment transactions in the SET (Secure Electronic Transaction) protocol are described. Requirements for SET are discussed and formally represented in a version of NPATRL (the NRL Protocol Analyzer Temporal Requirements Language). NPATRL is language for expressing generic requirements, heretofore applied to key distribution or key agreement protocols. Transaction vectors and other new constructs added to NPATRL for reasoning about SET payment transactions are described along with properties of their representation.

1 Introduction

The SET Protocol [5] is a protocol sponsored by major credit card companies and others that is intended to provide a standard for safe, secure credit card transactions over the Internet. ('SET' stands for 'Secure Electronic Transaction'.) As such, it is intended to supply an electronic version of the paper system that exists today. However, there are a number of risks connected with use of the Internet that do not arise in the paper world, or at least are not considered as severe. These arise from the difficulty of identifying participants in transactions and the difficulty of ensuring the private information sent over the Internet remains so. SET is intended to reduce these risks by introducing cryptographic means to protect sensitive information such as credit card numbers and to provide authentication of parties involved in a credit card transaction.

SET is a complex protocol. This has caused a certain amount of concern, since it is well known that even simple cryptographic protocols can have subtle flaws that can go undetected for a long time. This realization that correct protocols are difficult to write has led to an increasing amount of work in the application of formal methods to the analysis of cryptographic protocols, with some notable successes. However, most of this work has concentrated on key distribution protocols, which are intended to distribute keys among parties for secure communication. A key distribution protocol is required to safeguard the secrecy of the key and provide authentication of the key, that is, provide a secure binding between the key and the parties that are intended to use the key to communicate. But protocols such as SET have much more complex requirements than do key distribution protocols. A key distribution protocol provides authentication and secrecy for an atomic object: the key. SET is intended to provide secrecy for the credit card number, which may be considered an atomic object, but the entity authenticated is the credit card transaction itself, which evolves over time. The issue is complicated further by the fact that not all components of the transaction may be known to all parties, even after they have been established. For example, the credit card number, which is an integral part of the transaction, may never be revealed to the merchant.

In this paper, we show how a requirements language developed for the NRL Protocol Analyzer, a formal tool for the analysis of cryptographic protocols, can be used for specifying the security requirements of a complex protocol such as SET. This is part of ongoing work on use of the NRL Protocol Analyzer for the specification and analysis of the SET protocol.

We have found that the flexibility of our simple temporal language has allowed us to specify requirements for the authentication of an evolving transaction without any major modification to the language itself. This is because the language is used to define correctness simply in terms of what events must precede others. The content of the events is left to the specification writer, and in this case we have let them be the components of the transaction.

The remainder of the paper is organized as followed. In Section 2 we describe the SET protocol. In Section 3 we describe the NRL Protocol Analyzer and its associated requirements language. In Section 4 we describe our specification of the SET requirements. In Section 5 we compare our work with others. Section 6 concludes the paper.

2   The SET Protocol

A payment transaction in the SET protocol involves three parties: a customer, a merchant, and an application payment gateway. The customer presents a purchase request to the merchant, which includes credit card information and a proposed purchase amount. The purchase request is identified with a transaction ID. The merchant then passes the request along to the gateway, together with a request that a certain amount (not necessarily equal to the purchase amount) be authorized. The gateway then checks the customer's credit, authorizes a certain amount, and passes this information back to the merchant. The merchant passes this information back to the customer. Either at the same time as the authorization request, or later, the merchant presents a capture request to the gateway for the same transaction, requesting that a certain amount of money be captured. The gateway approves a certain amount which may or may not be equal to the amount requested. The merchant then passes this information back to the customer.

The authentication structure of the SET protocol is complex. Messages between merchant and gateway are always authenticated using digital signatures, as are messages from the merchant to the customer. Digital signatures for authentication for messages from customer to merchant are optional, although they may be made mandatory by a particular application. However, it is in the authentication of forwarded messages that the structure really becomes interesting. The message from customer to merchant includes information that is needed by the gateway but may be hidden from the merchant, such as credit card number (PAN, i.e., Primary Account Number) and expiration date. Also included, when customer digital signatures are used, is a data item called the PANSecret, which is known only by the customer and gateway, but not the merchant. This is not available when customer digital signatures are not used, since it is generated as part of the certificate registration process. This information is protected by the use of a *dual signature*. Two hash functions are computed, one over the the data to be kept hidden from the merchant, and the other over the data to be revealed to it, which includes a hash over the purchase amount and order description that the customer and merchant agreed to offline. The hidden data is encrypted using the gateway's public key. The customer then computes a digital signature (if customer signatures are used) over the two hashes. The signature, the two hashes, and the encrypted and unencrypted information are sent to the merchant. The merchant verifies the signature and forwards the information, including the signature if any, to the gateway. When the gateway receives the message, it verifies the signature, if any, and also verifies the PAN and PANSecret. Whether or not signatures are used, it also verifies the PAN and and the customer's portion of the PANSecret (if any) with the credit card issuer, although this may be done offline.

Authentication of gateway to customer via the merchant is much simpler: there is none. Any information from the gateway that the merchant passes on to the customer is authenticated only by the merchant's signature.

There are also a number of options available. A customer has the option of sending an initialization message prior to its purchase request, which allows it to obtain more up-to-date certificates from the merchant, and allows the merchant to send back a random challenge which it can use to verify the freshness of the customer's subsequent purchase request. When an initialization message is sent, the transaction ID is jointly created by customer and merchant. When no initialization message is sent, the customer may create the transaction ID, or it may be jointly created by the customer and merchant. The gateway also has the option, depending upon the policy followed, of sending the customer's PAN to the merchant (the PANSecret, however, is never sent). There are also protocols for inquiring about the status of an order, cancelling an order, etc.

For the purposes of this paper, we will make some assumptions to simplify our discussion. We will assume that authorization and capture are requested in the same message and granted in the same message. We will ignore the optional protocols for inquiring about the status of an order, cancelling an order, and so on. We will also assume that the customer alone generates the transaction ID when no initialization message exists. This will allow us to assume that the customer knows the entire transaction ID when it sends the purchase request, and so simplify our analysis. However, we will consider the customer options of signing or not signing the purchase request message, and sending or not sending the initialization messages, as well as the gateway option of sending or not sending the PAN to the merchant, since these are directly relevant to the security of the central payment protocol. But we will assume that the gateway will not send a customer's PAN to the merchant if it allows unsigned purchase requests on that PAN. This is to foil the obvious attack in which the gateway sends the PAN to a dishonest merchant, and that merchant uses the PAN to impersonate the customer in an unsigned purchase request.

3   The NRL Protocol Analyzer and Its Requirements Language

3.1   The NRL Protocol Analyzer Model

In the NRL Protocol Analyzer (NPA), protocols are modeled in terms of communicating state machines. Each state machine represents an "honest" participant of the protocol, that is one that obeys the rules of the protocol. The state machines send messages across a network that is controlled by a hostile intruder that can read all traffic, modify traffic, create messages, and normally perform all operations that are available to a legitimate user of the system. The intruder is not itself modeled as a communicating state machine but is identified with the network—likewise all "dishonest" nodes that are assumed to be in cooperation with, and thus identified with, the intruder. In particular, any word that would be available to a dishonest node, such as master keys belonging to that node, or random numbers generated by that node, are assumed to be known by the intruder.

A state in the NRL Protocol Analyzer model consists of three things. The first is the set of local state variable values of the honest nodes. The second is the set of words known by the intruder. These consist of all messages that have been passed by legitimate parties, words created by the intruder's performing operations on messages and words, and words that were initially known by the intruder. The third is the sequence of state transitions that have occurred, where each state transition involves some combination of the sending and receiving of messages (the intruder's operating on a set of words counts as its sending messages to itself) and the assignment of values to local state variables.

NPA works by having the user specify an insecure state. The Analyzer works backwards from that state and attempts to show that every path to it begins in an unreachable state. If it succeeds, then it has proved that the path is unreachable, given the assumptions of the Analyzer model. If on the other hand it finds a path that begins in an initial state, it may have found an attack on the protocol. The Analyzer includes inductive techniques for proving that infinite classes of states are unreachable. These can be used to prove lemmas about unreachability of infinite classes of states that can be used to assist the Analyzer in its search.

The NRL Protocol Analyzer makes very simple assumptions about the strengths of the crypto-algorithms involved. Cryptographic algorithms are modeled as operations which may obey certain algebraic properties, such as the fact that encryption and decryption with the same key cancel each other out. However, more subtle properties of cryptographic algorithms are usually not modeled, and notions relying on probability theory or complexity theory, such as polynomial indistinguishability, are completely beyond it. Thus, the assurance it gives is based on fairly strong assumptions about the cryptographic algorithms used. However, since many protocol failures have been shown to arise even when the cryptographic algorithms used behave perfectly, it remains a valuable tool for reasoning about security at the protocol level.

3.2 NPATRL (The NRL Protocol Analyzer Temporal Requirements Language)

Our language, NPATRL (pronounced N-patrol) contains a denumerable collection of constant singular terms, typically represented by letters from the beginning of the alphabet. We also have a denumerable collection of variable terms, typically represented by letters from the end of the alphabet. We also have, for each $n \geq 1$, n-ary function letters taking terms of either type as arguments and allowing us to build up functional terms in the usual recursive fashion. (We will always indicate whether a term is constant or variable if there is any potential for confusion.) We have a denumerable collection of n-ary action symbols for each arity $n \geq 1$. These will be written as words in typewriter script (e.g., accept). The first argument of an action symbol is reserved for a term representing the agent of the action in question. An atomic formula consists of an n-ary action symbol, e.g., 'act' followed by an n-tuple of terms. We have the usual logical connectives: ¬, ∧, ∨, →, and ↔, and also one temporal operator: ⋄, which stands for "happened previously". Complex formulae are built up from atomic formulae in the usual recursive fashion. (Note that this is only a formal language, not a logic; hence there are no axioms or inference rules.) We also include quantifiers. Earlier version of NPATRL did not use them, but we have found that the introduction of projections which could be defined over a number of possible vectors necessitated their use for the SET requirements specification, and so we now include them in the language.

In general, an action symbol will be of the following form. It will have four arguments, the first representing the agent of the action in question, the second representing the other principals involved in the action, the third representing the words involved in the action, and the fourth representing the local round number of the agent of the action, where a round number local to a principal identifies all actions pertaining to a single session as far as that principal is concerned. Action symbols can describe such events as a principal sending a message, the learning of a word by the intruder, or a principal's making a change to one or more of its local state variables. An action symbol may map to more than one event, and for a given event, there may be more than one action symbol mapping to it. Requirements are stated in terms of conditions on traces of action symbols. For example, we may require that an event indicated by an action symbol can only take place if some event indicated by another action symbol has taken place previously.

For example, suppose that we wish to require that a party A accept a key as good for a session with another party B only if that key was sent by a key server. This would be done as follows:

accept($principal(A, [honest]), principal(B, [X]), [KEY], N?$)
$\rightarrow \Diamond$ send($server(S), (principal(A, [honest]), principal(B, [X])), [KEY], N?$)

Note that the $N?$ is a 'wild-card' symbol. Thus, when $N?$ is used in more than one place, it does not necessarily meant that the two round numbers are the same. Instead, it means that we do not care what the round numbers are.

There are several types of action symbols that we use: these are **receive**, **accept**, **send**, **request**, **learn**, and **compromise**. A **receive** event is one in which a party receives a message. An **accept** event is one in which a party accepts a message as genuine. A **send** event is one in which a party sets in motion a chain of events in which a message will be sent to another party. A **learn** event in one in which the intruder learns a word. A **compromise** event is an event in which a secret such as a session key is compromised and made available to the intruder.

The interpretation of **receive**, **learn**, and **compromise** events are straightforward. However, the interpretation of **accept** and **send** events is deliberately left up to the protocol specifier. This is because what the protocol specifier is trying to determine is whether or not what he or she thinks of as adequate **send** and **accept** events are actually the ones that are necessary to make the protocol function properly. Thus, for example, the **send** event

send($server(S), (principal(A, [honest]), principal(B, [X])), [KEY], N?$)

could describe the server sending a key to A who will then forward it to B, the server sending a key to A and B simultaneously, or even the server sending the key to some fourth party who will then forward it to A and B. The point is that, whatever interpretation is used, in each case the server has set into motion a chain of events by which A and B are supposed to receive the key.

Of course, since the Analyzer reasons about the unreachability of insecure states, it does not use the requirements language directly. Instead, it is necessary to define insecure states in terms of negations of the requirements. The Analyzer can then be used to reason about the unreachability of these insecure states. Details of how this is done are given in [8]. A briefer, earlier description of the language and its application is given in [6], and an analysis of protocols for repeated authentication using NPATRL and NPA is given in [7]. NPATRL is a fairly flexible language. This is reflected by the fact that all of the constructs set out below are application details specified in NPATRL. We have, however, found it necessary to make one addition to NPATRL itself. Previous applications have not required the use of quantifiers, but they appear to be unavoidable in this context. Nonetheless, the requirements that make use of them seem to be normally amenable to NPA analysis, and we will not here discuss any details of adding quantifiers to the language.

4   SET Requirements Specification

Having described the basic ideas behind payment transactions in SET and the language NPATRL, we now present a formal specification of requirements for SET in NPATRL. The chief problem faced in developing formal requirements for SET is the complex nature of the construct that is being verified by the three parties. We thus begin with a presentation and discussion of the constructs that we develop to allow the representation of SET requirements in NPATRL, before proceeding to the requirements themselves.

4.1   Constructs Used

Most work on developing formal requirements for cryptographic protocols has concentrated on key distribution and agreement protocols, in which the construct being agreed upon, the key, is an atomic object that is visible to all parties. The transaction agreed upon in the SET protocol is much more elaborate. It contains a number of components that are added as the protocol progresses. Thus, the transaction agreed upon by merchant and customer in the first part of the protocol will not be the same as the one agreed upon by merchant, customer, and payment gateway at the end. Things are made even more difficult by the fact that some components of a transaction may be hidden from one of the parties. For example, both the customer and payment gateway have access to the customer's credit cared number (PAN), but this may be hidden from the merchant. Thus we need to be able to specify an evolving construct, some parts of which may be hidden from the parties involved.

Our solution is to model a transaction as a vector. We define a set of projection functions that give each party's view of a transaction at each point in the protocol. Note that this use of projection functions defined in terms of both the relevant party and that party's place in the protocol allow us to model both that party's ignorance of terms that have not yet been generated and its ignorance of terms that it is not supposed to know.

We define our projection functions and related notions as follows.

Definition: Let $\mathcal{V}$ be the set of n-vectors over $C \cup \{\bot\}$, where C is some alphabet, and let $\mathcal{W}$ be the set of n-vectors over C. If $V \in \mathcal{V}$, we define the *support* of V to be the set of all i between 1 and n such that $V[i]$ is not $\bot$. We say that V *agrees with* V' (written $V \sim V'$) if they agree on their common support, i.e., if for all $i \in support(V) \cap support(V')$, $V[i] = V'[i]$. A *projection*, proj, is a function mapping $\mathcal{W}$ to $\mathcal{V}$ such that there exists a set X such that $i \in X$ implies that $proj(V)[i] = V[i]$ and $i \notin X$ implies that $proj(V)[i] = \bot$. In such a case we say $X = support(proj)$.

We note that the agrees relation is not necessarily transitive. However, the following lemma does hold. We leave its proof as an exercise to the reader:

Lemma 1: Suppose that $support(proj_1) \subseteq support(proj_2)$, and that $\mathcal{W}$ is as in the above definition. Then, for all V, V', and V'' in $\mathcal{W}$, if $proj_3(V'') \sim proj_2(V')$, and $proj_2(V') \sim proj_1(V)$, then $proj_3(V'') \sim proj_1(V)$.

The following lemma also helps us to simplify our requirements in some cases:

Lemma 2: Suppose that $support(\text{proj}_1) \subseteq support(\text{proj}_2)$, and that $\mathcal{W}$ is as in the above definition. Then, for all V, V', and V'' in $\mathcal{W}$, $\text{proj}_1(V') \sim \text{proj}_2(V)$ if and only if $\text{proj}_1(V) = \text{proj}_1(V')$.

Lemma 2 will allow us to replace $\text{proj}_1(V')$ with $\text{proj}_1(V)$ in any requirement involving $\text{proj}_1(V')$ where $\text{proj}_1(V') \sim \text{proj}_2(V)$ and $support(\text{proj}_1) \subseteq support(\text{proj}_2)$.

We define the transaction vector as follows. Let V be a transaction vector. Its components are defined by:

- $V[1a]$ = Portion of the Transaction ID generated by customer
- $V[1b]$ = Portion of the Transaction ID generated by merchant
- $V[2]$ = customer
- $V[3]$ = hash of order data
- $V[4]$ = customer's PAN
- $V[5]$ = customer's PANSecret
- $V[6]$ = purchase amount
- $V[7]$ = merchant
- $V[8]$ = authorized purchase amount
- $V[9]$ = capture amount
- $V[10]$ = authorized capture amount
- $V[11]$ = *signed* or *unsigned*

Some comments:

1. We will assume that $V[1b]$ is zero if no initialization message is sent, and that $V[5]$ is zero if no PANSecret in used.
2. The hash in $V[3]$ is taken over the purchase amount and the order description that was agreed to by the customer and merchant offline. The order description may or may not be sent to the gateway, but the hash always is sent, and can be used by the gateway to verify that the customer and merchant agreed on the same order description.
3. The value *signed* or *unsigned* does not actually appear in the SET protocol. It refers to whether or not the customer's purchase request was signed with a digital signature or not. Since the type of security that may be guaranteed will be different in each case, it is important that this be accounted for.

The projections for honest principals are constructed as follows. We first give projections describing the knowledge that each principal has. This information will be used in 'accept' actions.

1. $cust\_req(V) = [1a, 1b, 2, 3, 4, 5, 6, 7, \perp, \perp, \perp, 11]$
   (information known by customer when it sends purchase request)
2. $merch\_req(V) = [1a, 1b, 2, 3, \perp, \perp, 6, 7, \perp, 9, \perp, 11]$
   (information known by merchant when it sends request to bank)
3. $apg\_resp(V) = [1a, 1b, 2, 3, 4, 5, 6, 7, 8, 9, 10, 11]$
   (information known by bank when it accepts a merchant's authorization request)

4. $merch\_resp(V) = [1a, 1b, 2, 3, \perp, \perp, 6, 7, 8, 9, 10, 11]$
   (information known by merchant when it accepts a customer's purchase request)
   (in some cases $merch\_resp(V) = [1a, 1b, 2, 3, 4, \perp, 6, 7, 8, 9, 10, 11]$)
5. $cust\_accept(V) = [1a, 1b, 2, 3, 4, 5, 6, 7, 8, \perp, 10, 11]$
   (information known by customer when it accepts a transaction)

We next give projections describing the information that each honest principal sends, to be used in 'send' actions. Note that a single party's send projections are not monotonically increasing, as in the case of the accept actions, since once a data item is sent it may not be sent again. Note also that we do not define a projection for the merchant's response to the initialization request. That is because the merchant's response does not appear in our requirements.

1. $cust\_pinitsend(V) = [1a, \perp, 2, \perp, \perp, \perp, \perp, 7, \perp, \perp, \perp, \perp]$
   (information sent by customer in initialization request to merchant)
2. $cust\_reqsend(V) = [1a, 1b, 2, 3, 4, 5, 6, 7, \perp, \perp, \perp, 11]$
   (information sent by customer in purchase request to merchant)
3. $merch\_reqsend(V) = [1a, 1b, 2, 3, \perp, \perp, 6, 7, \perp, 9, \perp, 11]$
   (information sent by merchant in authorization request to bank)
4. $apg\_respsend(V) = [1a, 1b, 2, \perp, \perp, \perp, \perp, 7, 8, 9, 10, \perp]$
   (information sent by bank to merchant in response to authorization request)
   (in some cases $apg\_respsend(V) = [1a, 1b, 2, \perp, 4, \perp, \perp, 7, 8, 9, 10, \perp]$)
5. $merch\_respsend(V) = [1a, 1b, 2, \perp, \perp, \perp, \perp, 7, 8, \perp, 10, \perp]$
   (information sent by merchant to customer in response to purchase order)

A table summarizing the content of all these projections is given in Figure 1.

We now consider how to map transaction vectors to the NRL Protocol Analyzer model. In the case of honest participants, components of accept transaction vectors can be represented by values of local state variables. Thus, when a customer requests a purchase amount, that will be stored in a local state variable representing $cust\_req(V)[7]$, and so forth. Components of send transaction vectors can be represented by components of messages.

In the case of dishonest participants, projections can no longer represent beliefs, since beliefs of dishonest participants are not represented in the NPA model. However, dishonest participants do send messages, and we can determine what the appropriate values of the send projections should be from messages received by honest participants. For example, let X be the result of encrypting a customer P's PAN, PAN_P, with the gateway's public key. If an honest merchant receives the message X attributed to dishonest customer P, we can conclude that the value of $cust\_reqsend(V)[4] = PAN_P$, whether or not PAN_P is P's actual PAN.

4.2   SET Payment Protocol Requirements

We are now ready to begin with the actual requirements. In each case, we give an informal account, followed by the NPATRL specification.

Replay Requirements We have a general requirement that no projection of a transaction (for the same role) should be accepted twice. We must be careful, though, to exclude from this requirement any fields that the principal generated itself when accepting that transaction. Thus, we phrase our requirement as follows: If an honest principal accepts a projection $\text{proj}_1(V)$, such that $\text{proj}_2(V') \sim \text{proj}_1(V)$ for some other projection proj_2, where proj_1 and proj_2 are from the set of projections defined in section 4.1, then no other principal in the same role previously accepted any $\text{proj}_1(V'')$ such that $\text{proj}_1(V'') \sim \text{proj}_2(V')$.

$$(\textbf{accept}(role(\textbf{P}, [honest]), -, \text{proj}_1(\textbf{V}), \textbf{N}?) \land (\text{proj}_1(\textbf{V}) \sim \text{proj}_2(\textbf{V}')))$$
$$\rightarrow ((\text{proj}_1(V'') \sim \text{proj}_2(V'))$$
$$\rightarrow \neg\diamondsuit\textbf{accept}(role(\textbf{Q}, [honest]), -, \text{proj}_1(\textbf{V}''), \textbf{N}?)))$$

This is a fairly simple requirement. But, as in the rest of SET, nothing is ever quite this simple. This is so in the case of $merch\_req(V)$, if the optional customer initialization message is used. In that case, the merchant sends a random challenge in response. The presence of this challenge, together with the customer's digital signature, protects the merchant against replay of the purchase request message. If these features are not present, the merchant can be protected against replay by the gateway's checking against the forwarded customer request against its database, but the merchant itself apparently does not check for the freshness of its data directly. Our requirement thus becomes: if the merchant accepts $merch\_resp(V)$, and previously the customer sent $cust\_pinitsend(V')$, where $merch\_resp(V) \sim cust\_pinitsend(V')$ and $merch\_resp(V)[11] = signed$, then the merchant did not previously accept $merch\_resp(V'')$, where $merch\_resp(V'') = merchresp(V)$.

$$(\textbf{accept}(merchant(\textbf{Q}, [honest]), customer(\textbf{P}, [\textbf{X}]), merch\_resp(\textbf{V}), \textbf{N}?) \land$$
$$\diamondsuit\textbf{send}(customer(\textbf{P}, [\textbf{X}]), merchant(\textbf{Q}, [honest]), cust\_pinitsend(\textbf{V}'), \textbf{N}?) \land$$
$$merch\_resp(V) \sim cust\_pinitsend(V') \land merch\_resp(V)[11] = signed)$$
$$\rightarrow (merch\_resp(V'') = merch\_resp(V)$$
$$\rightarrow \neg\diamondsuit\textbf{accept}(merchant(\textbf{Q}, [honest]), customer(\textbf{P}, [\textbf{X}]), merch\_resp(\textbf{V}''), \textbf{N}?))$$

Faithful Protocol Execution This requirement states that honest principals will faithfully execute the protocol. Thus, if a send event occurs, then the corresponding accept event occurred previously. In other words, if an honest principal P, playing a given role, engages in the send event $role\_eventsend(V)$, then it should have previously engaged in a corresponding accept event $role\_event(V')$, where $role\_event(V') \sim role\_eventsend(V)$.

$$\textbf{send}(role(\textbf{P}, [honest]), -, role\_eventsend(\textbf{V}), \textbf{N})$$
$$\rightarrow \exists V'((role\_eventsend(V) \sim role\_event(V')) \land$$
$$\diamondsuit\textbf{accept}(role(\textbf{P}, [honest]), -, role\_event(\textbf{V}'), \textbf{N}))$$

Customer Requirements The customer's main requirement is that he be given a guarantee that he will receive the goods in return for his money, or if he has already received the goods, that he be given notification that the merchant agrees that the bank has agreed to pay for the goods, that is, that the customer has obtained the goods legally. In other words, if the customer accepts $cust\_accept(V)$, then there should exist a V' such that $merch\_respsend(V') \sim cust\_accept(V)$ and the merchant sent $merch\_respsend(V')$. However, Lemma 2 and the fact that $merch\_respsend(V') \sim cust\_accept(V)$ allow to simplify this to the requirement that, if the customer accepts $cust\_accept(V)$, then the merchant should have sent $merch\_respsend(V)$. This requirement may be stated as follows:

$\texttt{accept}(customer(\texttt{P}, [honest]), merchant(\texttt{Q}, [\texttt{X}]), cust\_accept(\texttt{V}), \texttt{N?})$
$\rightarrow \diamond \texttt{send}(merchant(\texttt{Q}, [\texttt{X}]), customer(\texttt{P}, [honest]), merch\_respsend(\texttt{V}), \texttt{N?})$

We also have a requirement that the customer and an honest merchant should have the same view of what is going on. The merchant's view of the transaction is not captured by $merch\_respsend(V)$, but rather by $merch\_resp(V')$, for some V'. Thus, we must add the new requirement that, if the customer accepts $cust\_accept(V)$, then there exists a V' such that $merch\_resp(V') \sim cust\_accept(V)$ and the merchant accepted $merch\_resp(V')$. This requirement may be stated as follows.

$\texttt{accept}(customer(\texttt{P}, [honest]), merchant(\texttt{Q}, [honest]), cust\_accept(\texttt{V}), \texttt{N?})$
$\rightarrow \exists V'((cust\_accept(V) \sim merch\_resp(V')) \wedge$
$\diamond \texttt{accept}(merchant(\texttt{Q}, [honest]), customer(\texttt{P}, [honest]), merch\_resp(\texttt{V'}), \texttt{N?})))$

We now move to requirements concerning the gateway. We note that, in the case in which the merchant is dishonest, the customer has no way of knowing that the merchant even communicated with the gateway, so we can make no requirements in that case. However, in the case of an honest merchant, it is reasonable to require that the customer and the gateway share the same view of the transaction, and that the gateway actually communicated with the merchant.

We first consider the requirement that, if the customer accepts $cust\_accept(V)$, then there is a V' such that $apg\_respsend(V') \sim cust\_accept(V)$ and the gateway sent $apg\_respsend(V')$. As it turns out, we do not need to state this requirement explicitly; it results from Lemma 1 and the following:

1. Our previously stated requirement that there exists a V'' such that $merch\_resp(V'') \sim cust\_accept(V)$ and the merchant accepts $merch\_resp(V'')$;
2. A requirement to be given in the Merchant Requirements section saying that, if the merchant accepts $merch\_resp(V'')$, then there is a V' such that $merch\_resp(V'') \sim apg\_respsend(V')$, and the gateway sent $apg\_respsend(V')$, and;
3. The fact that $support(apg\_respsend) \subseteq support(merch\_resp)$.

We do not have such a convenient subset relation for the requirement that the customer and the gateway share the same view of the transaction. Thus, it is necessary to introduce an explicit requirement here: if the customer accepts $cust\_accept(V)$ from an honest merchant, then there is a V' such that $cust\_accept(V) \sim apg\_resp(V')$ and the gateway accepted $apg\_resp(V')$. This may be stated formally as follows.

accept($customer(\mathbf{P}, [honest]), merchant(\mathbf{Q}, [honest]), cust\_accept(\mathbf{V}), \mathbf{N}?$)
$\rightarrow \exists V'((cust\_accept(V) \sim apg\_resp(V') \wedge$
$\diamond$accept($gateway(\mathbf{R}, [honest]), customer(\mathbf{P}, [honest]), apg\_resp(\mathbf{V}'), \mathbf{N}?$))

Finally, there is a less obvious requirement that, if the customer receives notification that he will receive or has paid for goods, then these should be goods he already ordered. In other words, if the customer accepts $cust\_accept(V)$, then the customer should have sent some $cust\_reqsend(V')$, where $cust\_reqsend(V') \sim cust\_accept(V)$. By Lemma 2, this can be simplified to the requirement that, if the customer accepts $cust\_accept(V)$, then the customer sent $cust\_reqsend(V)$. This is stated as follows.

accept($customer(\mathbf{P}, [honest]), merchant(\mathbf{Q}, [\mathbf{X}]), cust\_accept(\mathbf{V}), \mathbf{N}$)
$\rightarrow \diamond$send($customer(\mathbf{P}, [honest]), merchant(\mathbf{Q}, [\mathbf{X}]), cust\_reqsend(\mathbf{V}), \mathbf{N}$)

Merchant Requirements The merchant's main requirement is that, if the merchant agrees to deliver the goods to the customer, then it should have received a guarantee from the gateway that it will receive its money. In other words, if the merchant accepts $merch\_resp(V)$, then the gateway should have sent $apg\_respsend(V')$ for some V' such that $apg\_respsend(V') \sim merch\_resp(V)$. Since $support(apg\_respsend) \subseteq support(merch\_resp)$, Lemma 2 allows us to replace this with the requirement that the gateway send $apg\_respsend(V)$. Likewise, if the merchant passes on a response to a customer, than it should have previously requested that response from the gateway. This will prevent the merchant from agreeing to supply goods that it never offered for sale. In other words, if the merchant accepts $merch\_resp(V)$, then it should have previously sent $merch\_reqsend(V)$. Finally, we require that the merchant and the gateway have the same picture of the transaction. This is captured by requiring that, if the merchant accepts $merch\_resp(V)$, then the gateway should have accepted $apg\_respsend(V')$ for some V' such that $apg\_resp(V') \sim merch\_resp(V)$. These three requirements may be stated as follows.

accept($merchant(\mathbf{Q}, [honest]), customer(\mathbf{P}, [\mathbf{X}]), merch\_resp(\mathbf{V}), \mathbf{N}?$)
$\rightarrow \diamond$send($gateway(\mathbf{R}, [honest]),$
$(customer(P, [X]), merchant(Q, [honest])), apg\_respsend(V), N?$)

accept($merchant(\mathbf{Q}, [honest]), customer(\mathbf{P}, [\mathbf{X}]), merch\_resp(\mathbf{V}), \mathbf{N}$)
$\rightarrow \diamond$send($merchant(\mathbf{Q}, [honest]), gateway(\mathbf{R}, [honest]), merch\_req(\mathbf{V}), \mathbf{N}$)

accept($merchant(\mathbf{Q}, [honest]), customer(\mathbf{P}, [X]), merch\_resp(\mathbf{V}), \mathbf{N}?$)
$\rightarrow \exists V'((apg\_resp(V') \sim merch\_resp(V)) \wedge$
$\diamond$accept($gateway(\mathbf{R}, [honest]),$
$(customer(P, [X]), merchant(Q, [honest])), apg\_resp(V'), N?$))

We now turn to requirements concerning the merchant's interaction with the customer. We first want to show that the merchant accepts a transaction only if the customer has requested it, that is, the merchant accepts $merch\_resp(V)$ only if there exists a V' with $merch\_resp(V) \sim cust\_reqsend(V')$ such that the customer sent $cust\_reqsend(V')$. We leave it as an exercise to the reader to show that this requirement is implied by Lemma 1 and the fact that $support(cust\_reqsend) \subseteq support(apg\_resp)$, together with the requirements expressed in this section and the Gateway Requirements section, and thus does not need to be stated explicitly.

We may also want to require that, when the merchant is aware that digital signatures are used by the customer ($merch\_req(V)[11] = signed$), and the merchant accepts $merch\_req(V)$, then the customer must have sent $cust\_reqsend(V')$, where $merch\_req(V) \sim cust\_reqsend(V')$. This may be stated as follows.

$$(\texttt{accept}(merchant(\texttt{Q}, [honest]), customer(\texttt{P}, [\texttt{X}]), merch\_req(\texttt{V}), \texttt{N})$$
$$\wedge (merch\_req(V)[11] = signed))$$
$$\rightarrow \exists V'((cust\_req(V') \sim merch\_req(V)) \wedge$$
$$\diamond \texttt{send}(customer(\texttt{P}, [honest]), merchant(\texttt{Q}, [honest]), cust\_req(\texttt{V}'), \texttt{N}))$$

There is also an implicit requirement that the merchant be able to prove that the customer initiated the transaction in the event of a later dispute. This is indeed the reason for allowing the gateway to send the PAN to the merchant. However, since the protocol for verifying the merchant's claim is not explicitly defined in SET 1.0, we do not include this as a formal requirement.

Gateway Requirements The gateway's job is to mediate between the customer and the merchant. To do this, it must be able to determine that both the customer and the merchant have actually sent their requests. Thus, the gateway will not accept $apg\_resp(V)$ unless the merchant and the customer have already sent **merch_reqsend(V')** and **cust_reqsend(V'')**, respectively where $merch\_reqsend(V') \sim apg\_resp(V)$ and $cust\_reqsend(V'') \sim apg\_resp(V)$. Again, Lemma 2 and the fact that the supports of both merchant and customer projections are subsets of $support(apg\_resp)$ allows us to replace $merch\_reqsend(V')$ with $merch\_reqsend(V)$ and $cust\_reqsend(V'')$ with $cust\_reqsend(V)$. We do not make any requirement on the order in which the merchant and customer requests are sent. This raises the possibility of a 'psychic merchant' who anticipates a customer's request and sends his request to the gateway before receiving it from a customer. Although this is nonsensical, we don't consider it a security violation, so we don't attempt to guard against it.

The formal version of this requirement is as follows:

$$\texttt{accept}(gateway(\texttt{R}, [honest]),$$
$$(merchant(Q, [honest]), customer(P, [honest])), apg\_resp(V), N?)$$
$$\rightarrow \diamond(\texttt{send}(customer(\texttt{P}, [\texttt{X}]),$$
$$(customer(P, [X]), merchant(Q, [Y])), cust\_req(V), N?) \wedge$$
$$\texttt{send}(merchant(\texttt{Q}, [\texttt{X}]),$$
$$(customer(P, [X]), merchant(Q, [Y])), merch\_req(V), N?))$$

In the case that the customer is honest, we also make the requirement that her view of the transaction agrees with the view of the gateway, that is, that the customer previously accepted $cust\_req(V')$, where $cust\_req(V') \sim apg\_resp(V)$. In this case, however, the fact that $support(cust\_req) \subseteq support(apg\_resp)$, together with the faithfulness requirements and the requirements given just above on the gateway's accepting requests, allows us to use Lemma 1 to derive this requirement from the others. We again leave the proof of this as an exercise to the reader.

Likewise, when the merchant is honest, we make the requirement that if the gateway accepts $apg\_resp(V)$, then the merchant previously accepted $merch\_req(V')$, where $merch\_req(V') \sim apg\_resp(V)$. The proof that this requirement is derivable from the others is also left to the reader.

Requirements for customer, merchant, and gateway are represented diagrammatically in Figure 2.

Secrecy Requirements The SET protocol makes use of the PAN and the PANSecret to provide authentication. Since the PAN is also used for authentication outside of the SET protocol, it is the responsibility of the protocol to protect the PAN. As we have seen, if a misjudgment is made and the PAN is delivered to a dishonest merchant, then it can be compromised. Thus we need to guarantee that, if the intruder learns the PAN (from runs of the protocol), then this was done as a result of the gateway's sending the PAN to a dishonest merchant. Similarly, the protocol should not reveal the PANSecret of an honest customer under any circumstances. These requirements are specified formally as follows.

$\texttt{learn}(intruder, -, pan(customer(\texttt{P}, [honest]), \texttt{N}?)$
$\rightarrow \exists V(V[4] = pan(customer(P, [honest]) \wedge$
$\quad \diamondsuit \texttt{send}(gateway(\texttt{R}, [honest]), merchant(\texttt{Q}, [dishonest]), apg\_respsend(\texttt{V}), \texttt{N}?))$

$\neg(\texttt{learn}(intruder, -, pansecret(customer(\texttt{P}, [honest]), \texttt{N}?))$

The SET protocol is also intended to protect the secrecy of the monetary values passes in the protocol: that is, the purchase amount, the amount authorized by the gateway, and the amount captured by the gateway. The secrecy protection is very weak: ratios of authorization amount to purchase amount and of capture amount to purchase amount are sent in the clear. But we still need to guarantee that these data are not revealed otherwise than by a direct attack on this weak method of encryption. This we can do by modeling the ratio function in the Protocol Analyzer specification, requiring that one element of the ratio is required in order to reveal the other, and then requiring that the intruder could not have learned these data unless the customer were involved in an interaction with a dishonest merchant. This will be done in two parts:

1. If the intruder learns the purchase amount of a transaction involving an honest customer, then that customer must have initiated the transaction with a dishonest merchant.
2. If the intruder learns the authorization or capture amounts of a transaction involving an honest customer, then that customer must have initiated a

transaction $cust\_reqsend(V)$, with a dishonest merchant, Q, and then the gateway must have sent $apg\_respsend(V')$ to Q, where $cust\_reqsend(V) \sim apg\_respsend(V')$.

The formal versions of these requirements are given below. We are not actually concerned with the intruder learning purchase, authorization, or capture dollar amounts; we are concerned with her learning the association of these with a given transaction. However, there are difficulties in the representation and analysis of that association itself. Therefore, as a quick solution, we assume that a purchase/authorization/capture amount chosen by a principal at any time T is unique. While perhaps not reflective of reality, the only practical limitation this has for us is the inability to represent attacks depending on the identity of two such amounts in different transactions. We may seek a more elegant solution in the future. The requirement for the intruder learning the capture amount is virtually identical to the requirement for learning the authorization amount, and so we omit it.

$\text{learn}(intruder, -, purchamt(customer(\text{P}, [honest]), T), \text{N}?)$
$\rightarrow \exists V(\diamondsuit \text{send}(customer(\text{P}, [honest]),$
$\qquad merchant(Q, [dishonest]), cust\_reqsend(V), N?) \wedge$
$\quad V[6] = purchamt(customer(P, [honest]), T))$

$\text{learn}(intruder, -, authamt(customer(\text{P}, [honest]), gateway(\text{R}, [honest]), T), \text{N}?)$
$\rightarrow \exists V(\diamondsuit \text{send}(customer(\text{P}, [honest]),$
$\qquad merchant(Q, [dishonest]), cust\_reqsend(V), N?) \wedge$
$\quad \exists V'(cust\_reqsend(V) \sim apg\_respsend(V') \wedge$
$\quad \diamondsuit \text{send}(gateway(\text{R}, [honest]),$
$\qquad merchant(Q, [dishonest]), apg\_respsend(V'), N?) \wedge$
$\quad V'[8] = authamt(customer(P, [honest]), gateway(R, [honest]), T)))$

5 Comparison with Other Work

As we mentioned at the beginning of this paper, most work on developing requirements for cryptographic protocols has concentrated on secure agreement on atomic object such as keys. However, there has been some work closely related to ours on developing requirements for agreement on more complex transactions. In [2] Bolignano describes the following approach to specifying requirements for complex protocols such as SET. According to Bolignano's definition, a requirement is divided into two parts: a regular language L, and a filtering function ff_x on sequences of messages so that the requirement is satisfied on sequence M if and only if $ff_x(M)$ is in L. Bolignano shows how filtering functions can be used to express requirements on sequences of messages in a protocol in terms of conditions on individual components in the messages. Thus, like us, he can require that different components of different messages in a sequence must agree in order for a protocol to execute correctly. Although we have not attempted to verify this, we believe that Bolignano's approach could be used to specify the requirements we have set out in this paper. Indeed, in [2] he reports that he is applying this technique to the analysis of the SET protocol. We believe that the advantage of our approach lies in the fact that the use of projections and the agreement relation allows us to simplify greatly the expression of the requirements, and thus makes them easier to work with. The complex part of requirements specification for protocols such as SET appears to lie mostly in the definition of the projections. Once this was done, the remaining portion of the requirements turned out to be not that much more complex than requirements for protocols for secure agreement on atomic objects such as keys. It might be interesting to see if a similar approach could be used to simplify the requirements in [2].

Another approach to formal analysis of complex payment protocols is given by Brackin [3]. He describes the analysis of two large protocols for electronic commerce developed by CyberCash. These protocols are similar to SET in their primary respects. Brackin uses an automated theorem prover based on HOL. He specifies the protocol in an extension of GNY [4], itself an extension of BAN [1]. Thus, protocol goals are specified in terms of the beliefs of the principals, e.g., that the gateway believes that the merchant has sent a *merch_req*. The analysis appears to be at a higher level of abstraction than either the present work or that of Bolignano. It thus potentially assumes away some significant features and possibly even vulnerabilities. It is also in some ways not as abstract as the present work. For example, agreement on a transaction is not represented at all; rather, agreement on individual fields within the transaction is analyzed. However, Brackin's analysis is able to highlight, e.g., some of the trust assumptions in the protocols and to provide assurance against some common high level protocol vulnerabilities.

6 Conclusions

We have presented a formal specification of requirements for the payment portion of the SET protocol in the language NPATRL. By introducing transaction vectors, projections thereon, and the vector agreement relation we have been able to present requirements that are completely formal and capture much detail yet are quite readable representations of intuitive goals. Understanding the goals of SET, even informally, has previously been difficult. Since we have been able to represent the SET requirements in NPATRL, they are now amenable to analysis using the NRL Protocol Analyzer to evaluate. This is the focus of future work.

Acknowledgements

David Goldschlag took part in most of the early meetings when this work was taking shape. We thank him for much helpful input given at that time. This work was supported by DARPA.

References

1. M. Burrows, M. Abadi, and R. Needham, *A Logic of Authentication*, SRC Research Report 39, Digital Systems Research Center, February 1989.

2. D. Bolignano, "Towards the Formal Verification of Electronic Commerce Protocols", *Proceedings of the 10th IEEE Computer Security Foundations Workshop*, pp. 133–146, Rockport Massachusetts, IEEE CS Press, June 1997.

3. S. Brackin, "Automatic Formal Analyses of Two Large Commercial Protocols", *DIMACS Workshop on Design and Formal Verification of Security Protocols*, Rutgers New Jersey, September 1997. (Paper available at http://dimacs.rutgers.edu/Workshops/Security/program2/brackin.html)

4. L. Gong, R. Needham, and R. Yahalom, "Reasoning about Belief in Cryptographic Protocols", *Proceedings of the 1990 IEEE Computer Society Symposium on Research in Security and Privacy*, pp. 234–248, IEEE Computer Society Press, Oakland California, May 1990.

5. SET Secure Electronic Transaction Specification, Version 1.0, May 1997. (Downloaded from http://www.visa.com/set/)

6. P. Syverson and C. Meadows, "A Logical Language for Specifying Cryptographic Protocol Requirements", *Proceedings of the 1993 IEEE Computer Society Symposium on Research in Security and Privacy*, pp. 165–177, IEEE Computer Society Press, Oakland California, May 1993.

7. P. Syverson and C. Meadows, "Formal Requirements for Key Distribution Protocols", *Advances in Cryptology — EUROCRYPT '94*, LNCS vol. 950, A. De Santis, ed., pp. 320–331, Springer-Verlag, Perugia Italy, 1994.

8. P. Syverson and C.Meadows, "A Formal Language for Cryptographic Protocol Requirements", *Designs, Codes, and Cryptography*, vol. 7, nos. 1 and 2, pp. 27–59, January 1996.

No. Value	c_init	c_req	c_reqsend	m_req	m_reqsend	apg_resp	apg_respsend	m_resp	m_respsend	c_accept
1a CTransid	✓	✓	✓	✓	✓	✓	✓	✓	✓	✓
1b Mtransid		✓	✓	✓	✓	✓	✓	✓	✓	✓
2. Customer	✓	✓	✓	✓	✓	✓	✓	✓	✓	✓
3. hash of Order Desc.		✓	✓	✓	✓	✓		✓		✓
4. PAN		✓	✓			✓	✓?	✓?		✓
5. PANSecret		✓?	✓?			✓?				✓?
6. Purch. amt		✓	✓	✓	✓	✓		✓		✓
7. Merchant	✓	✓	✓	✓	✓	✓	✓	✓	✓	✓
8. Auth. p. amt.						✓	✓	✓	✓	✓
9. Capt. amt.				✓	✓	✓	✓	✓		
10. Auth. c. amt.						✓	✓	✓	✓	✓
11. Signed or unsigned		✓	✓	✓	✓	✓		✓		✓

Fig. 1

Summary of Requirements

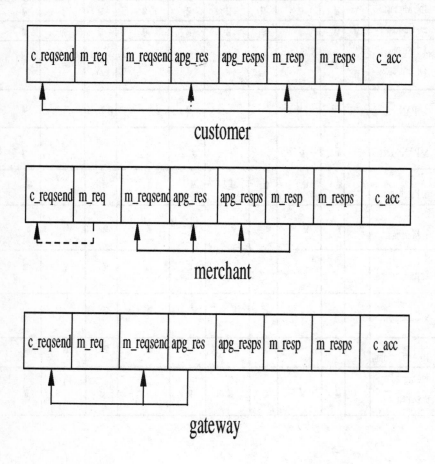

Fig. 2

On Assurance Structures for WWW Commerce

Markus Jakobsson*   Moti Yung**

Abstract. We argue that the true potential of the World Wide Web will not be fully unleashed until the web "becomes civilized," by the implementation of *assurance structures*. These structures will complement means for concerns like privacy and transaction enablers like e-payment mechanisms. We first present our position, then we suggest and survey technical mechanisms to reach these goals, and show how these can be put together to provide a backbone (architectural framework) of civilized web commerce. Being a "position paper" we cannot hope to cover all the issues we touch upon in order to convey the needs and goals, neither do we attempt to provide a system design.

1 Introduction

Just like the pioneers settling in the Americas a number of centuries ago, pushing the frontiers and their civilization into the wild and wooly west (www), individuals and businesses are now settling the World Wide Web (WWW)[1]. The WWW opens up new possibilities by its high accessibility and availability, and permits new social and commercial structures to be built. However, we argue that civilization has yet not arrived to the WWW, and the lawlessness hampers further advances. Commercial transactions on the web have not yet become very common, in spite of the great possibility for entrepreneurship opened up by the net. This is because common "rules of the game" are not yet set up, and no one understands yet the business models and how the new medium enables new ways of human activities which involve willingness to spend money. This is also partly because of the lack of a common and working payment system of high reliability and lack of secrecy and other controls in network operation. We argue that both reasons are influenced by the lack of common rules as well as the lack of trust and its maintenance via acceptable infrastructure that must support organized and civilized society.

We observe that, currently, buying goods or information over the web corresponds, security- and liability- wise, to buying merchandise from a street vendor. Until structures for well-defined security and access control are built, the web inhabitants will still be like the crowd we often see in western movies representing

---

* Information Sciences Research Center, Bell Labs, Murray Hill, NJ 07974. markusj@research.bell-labs.com
** CertCo LLC, New York, NY. moti@cs.columbia.edu
[1] We deliberately do not mention many controversial issues regarding the wild west and our analogy has to be taken with a grain of salt (we admit that we could not resist the "similarity in initials" which has motivated this analogy).

the wild life of the pioneers in the www, i.e., a population where insecurity, lawlessness and arbitrariness rules. (This, of course, excludes the fact that certain known firms and enterprises have established themselves via association with the traditional brand name or via the media, e.g., the first Internet Bookstore is well known, also the manufacturers of Internet technology's web page is highly available and is embedded in various sign-up procedures. In contrast, for massive scale of "new opportunities" and "free enterprise" what we argue above seems to hold).

The WWW is an excellent example of how technology is creating new types of social structures: Suddenly, entrepreneurship and telecommuting are combined, creating a new type of employment opportunities. As another example, spontaneous availability of business to customers is made possible, and self advertising is made easy. More generally, the web changes the nature of communication and creates opportunities for new interactions, some of which can produce new lines of business (which are unpredictable at the moment). However, these will not happen on a large scale until the web becomes civilized. Thus, we need mechanisms that assure certain characteristics of commercial transactions (and related transactions).

We are also aware that the web has a special nature which made it evolve essentially on a voluntary base and that it will continue evolving perhaps dynamically as the population needs change. As a result of such an environment, a general framework with interfaces and service description is what is typically needed (rather than an architecture which dictates specific mechanisms and is cast in concrete). Such frameworks will enable growth and competition within the web environment (and consortiums being created to develop various frameworks). As a negative example, note that recent attempts (by big companies) to dictate commerce via "shopping malls" where merchants gets presented to customers via a special mechanism, seem to have failed. We will therefore avoid getting into detailed designs (this paper should not be mistaken as a specific architecture/ product describing paper). Rather we will concentrate on what our position imply on a generic mechanism and general technical needs level. The suggested framework (ideas) can be in turn included in various paradigms for commercial transactions and the detailed mechanisms themselves can vary. We note that the underlying technology to assure assurance at these more detailed levels is cryptography (the technology assuring integrity and limits in distributed and network environments).

Access control and security: The WWW vs. File Systems In some sense, the problem above can be put in analogy to the simpler problem of "security and access control in file systems". There, different users have different capabilities, and these enable them to access different resources, and in different ways (e.g., read / write/ execute.) While for the file system the access rights are evaluated perhaps statically according to only one strategy in the system, the access rights on the WWW should be evaluated according to dynamic and distributively determined rules. The rules may change according to different strategies, dynamic state, and risk management philosophies (which dynamically change). Thus, the file system can be viewed as a "closed physical system" whereas the WWW can be viewed as an open one.

A user's rule for agreeing to grant access rights to some information can be thought of as a boolean formula of predicates, some of which need to be evaluated in order to satisfy the formula. Typically, these predicates are of the form "someone that I trust, trusts the accessing party," "someone I trust, does not endorse the accessing party," or longer chains of the same formats. Here, the assurances are based on personal trust, legal responsibility, reputation, or monetary responsibility. Whereas in a file system, the evaluation of rights whether to give or deny access, the assessment of predicates in commercial settings may be a quantity calculated based on statistics and other factors, as not all business decisions are based on full knowledge. This is a second difference: we are not performing strict access control but rather we evaluate the trust and risk involved in granting a transaction.

Remark: One problem that is extensively dealt with is the issue of payments. This is an important component of overall commerce, however what we will deal with here is a more general problem of making web commerce trustworthy in more ways than just assuring proper payments.

Organization: The rest of the paper is organized as follows: we start by reviewing positive and negative aspects of the WWW (section 2), then present what we think is needed (section 3), after which we present where, in terms of solutions and problems, we are now (section 4). In section 5, we discuss components for implementing the assurance framework, assemble these into building block, and discuss trust issues. We end, in section 6, by exemplifying transaction scenarios for our proposed generic architecture.

2 Positive vs. Negative Aspects of the WWW

Next we exemplify some basic problems connected with the wide possibilities that the web provides. We believe that by now these issues are well known, but we point at them as a starting point to our position.

The WWW has the capability to supply its users with new services, and makes information collection dramatically easier. The latter is not only true because of the ease of access, but also, with the introduction of payments, by an increased number of service providers. Namely, the web enables small entrepreneurs to find business opportunities without having to go through the bureaucracy and delays of current establishments. Therefore, it will be possible to be a "free-lancer to the masses," instead of going through traditional agencies such as publishers. However, even traditional structures will benefit from the lower costs to access and disseminate information, which can be done across across traditional borders. Thus, new social structures can be built across traditional social and geographical boundaries, benefiting trade and friendship between regions previously isolated from each other, making de-provincialization and de-isolation easier, boosting business and supporting awareness. The "electronic town-hall" idea, a hot topic during the 1993 U.S. presidential campaign, will find itself a natural host in the World Wide Web. Moreover, the WWW, apart from being very useful for the collection of marketing related information, will also become a tool in making sociological and human research in a scientific way. The ingredients for a successful civilization are definitely present in the WWW!

However, all tools (and especially strong ones like the web) can be abused. In order to prevent this brave new world from becoming that of surveillance of users (bothersome big brotherhood), or the lawlessness of a wild and wooly west, we have to take preventive measures against unwanted practices. The lack of trust is inherent in a distributed system without physical contacts and an agency representing the law. The users must be protected from bad service providers, both those who voluntarily provide a bad service, as those who do it unintentionally. Criminality, both in the sense of the sale of bogus services, and of the kind supporting physical world criminality, must be controlled, as must the distribution of misinformation, and of unwanted information such as recipes for bombs and child pornography. At the same time, which can be a very difficult balance act, the user must be protected with respect to his or her privacy, both from businesses and governments. Just like borrowing Marxist books from the library during the McCarthy area had direct implications on the personal level, accessing certain information may be incriminating in the eyes of some governments. Similarly, extracting and abusing personal information is made easy by businesses with daunty practices. For example, insurance companies may base decisions whether to offer or not to offer life insurance to people on information whether this person may have accessed gay chat lines. Similarly, "sucker lists" containing people known to have a low resistance to buying certain services or products can be established and used to further squeeze these users for money.

3 A Position: What Is Basically Needed?

The open-ended nature of the WWW systems makes it necessary to maintain assurance structures that support the dynamic policies, and design processes that employ these structures. Due to its global nature, assurance structures have to be based on "trust infrastructure" that provides "trust relationships" among entities, whereas processes can evaluate "subjectively" the available structure and generate "quantitative access-control entity" that allows for "civilized transaction" to take place. The bottom line is that entities will have the means to assess the "value" and "risk" involved, in a reliable fashion (e.g., a customer is assured that "what you see is what you get!" or an institute is assured that the customer's credentials seem ok given the statistical data about them. The assurance is a combination of evaluating "trust relationships" and perhaps evaluating the evaluation process. Each participant, in turn, may affect the relationship upon participating in a transaction (e.g., via a consumer survey).

It is a central goal of this paper to investigate the need and mechanisms that allow for predicates and access rights to be first accessed correctly; to be evaluated properly on a first level; and to be dynamically maintained on a second level, by providing the necessary structures and processing techniques.

The components that are needed are:

- **Access structure**: First, there is a need for *categorization for simple access*. This is analogous to the business pages of a phone book, but need not be implemented as a static list, but can favorably be achieved by dynamic searches of links. The potential exponential growth of such a search, if clumsily performed, has drawn a lot of attention to the problem of intelligent search methods in the artificial intelligence community. Self-imposed rating of services, combined with lists provided by endorsement agencies can simplify searches. A specific type of self rating that may be of interest is that of self-censorship by categorization. This is analogous to what the movie industry does, and helps movie-goers select what they want to see.
- **Trust Structure**: Then, we argue that in order to make the World Wide Web an organized and civilized society, we need to build structures to protect its inhabitants against unfair and potentially criminal acts. As mentioned above, one of the issues is to *establish trust* between customers and merchants. This can be achieved using endorsements, either in the form of agencies, or in the form of customer feedback. The former has a physical-world counterpart in the Better Business Bureau, which can be contacted and asked whether they endorse a certain business, or if they have customer complaints on it. The second type, which to a certain degree already exists on the Internet, is a media that allows discussions, warnings and recommendations without any established endorser. The need for a structure permitting endorsement becomes clear in the light of how easy it is to set up a store front, generate some sales, and then "leave town" when the going gets tough, only to resurface under a different alias later. Endorsement structures would not only benefit the buyers, but also make it easier for honest businesses to get established, opening up new commercial possibilities. Licensing and attaching liability via insurance providers may add trust as well. (The issue of provision of such trust in the distributed systems context was first dealt with in [3]). The fact that statistical tools and built-in surveys can generate automatically such a function when the web commerce is used extensively is observed here. The mechanism will associate brand-name recognition and will establish reputation. It has to be assured that only "actual" customers who participated in buying and only a sample of those take part in this action, to prevent competitors from taking part in (or significantly influencing) these automatic actions. In short, the mechanisms apply "access control like" decisions whereas the goal is not to deny access to resources, but rather to assist users and institutes in evaluating quality and liability of required transactions. The model will provide quantitative assessment of commercial actions based on assurances which will be maintained dynamically.
- **Provisions for Individual/Institutional Needs:** The establishment of trust in the context of sales is not the only area where the user needs protec-

tion against malicious businesses. It is easy to see that the WWW allows the individual users access to large amounts of information, and also that the information provider can easily control what information is disseminated. Conversely, it is not true that the individuals surfing the net can control what information the providers are allowed to extract about them. Whereas access patterns of users can be put to great use in making marketing surveys and also help the user directly (via profiling and individual promotions), it is also easy to intrude in the privacy of individuals, as the provider easily can find out the (network) identity of the accessing party. This can be abused in the "real world" for political purposes, to deny services to certain groups of people, overzealous direct marketing, and in the extreme, for blackmail and similar. We see nowadays that anonymous access has been recognized as a major component of web technology and it is aimed at solving such problems. Similar to individual needs, there are needs of institutions where the concerns are analogous. Also, users may want to have various trade-offs of anonymity vs. profiling ability. Like anonymity there should be other protective properties that users and businesses may need. Generally, users need guidance and awareness which allow them to act while they also need shielding from side-effects of their actions.

- **Assurance Structure Maintenance**: The trust and relationships that assure the various needs and access rights, limitations and other controls, need mechanisms to maintain the various relationships in a reliable and authenticated fashion. This will require dynamic processes inside the systems and also outside the systems (in the real world) to assure continuity and growth of the web. There are social, organizational and technical issues related to introducing a law, means for trust, selection and censorship on the World Wide Web, to a large degree using mechanisms already existing in other contexts. Drawing knowledge from analogous mechanisms makes the establishment of a civilized society much easier, and just like the founding fathers of the United States used ideas surfacing during the French revolution when writing the constitution, our suggested methods are inspired by structures in the real world. The maintenance involves dynamic changes as well as adaptation of a given basic structure to various cultures and business models at the same point of time. We will suggest ways and methods of maintaining the structures and making sure it is available in a reliable form to users, both to automated agents and to human interfaces.

Again, we wish to remind the reader that this is a position paper, and that there are many opposing positions. Some of these are as follows:

- **Economic Issues:** It may be too costly to implement and maintain the required structure.
- **Legal Issues:** It may be too difficult (and costly) to implement the legal changes and additions needed to support the structure, especially so since the structure geographically encompasses several jurisdictions.
- **Ergonomics:** It may not be possible to design an interface simple enough to be understandable to the average user (e.g., given the intricate decisions

sometimes required for trust evaluation, the average user would not understand how certain settings translate to an acceptable risk). A global system which is culture-independent will be impossible.

- **Anarchistic view:** It may not be desirable to implement the suggested structure.
- **Evolutionary view:** It may not be necessary to make an effort to implement a structure - this will eventually happen by itself[2].

4 Where Are We?

In this section, we discuss the currently used solutions to the problems of the WWW and their shortcomings, and then look at the mechanisms we suggest for civilizing the web.

4.1 Current Solutions

Currently, there is no clear way to judge whether a service provider offers a quality service or not, particularly so for small and unknown providers who do not generate enough sales [3]. However, assume that you are interested in buying a product advertised on the web. *How would you know what the quality of the product is? Can you trust that you will get the merchandise after paying? Can you trust the guarantee?* These are problems also existing in the mail order business, but enlarged by the low costs of a store-front on the web, and the ease with which a new alias can be produced by a criminal shop-keeper. The problem gets even more obvious when the sale of information is considered: Picture a dating company who displays personals and charges for giving out addresses, or a job-search service promising to find you companies where your C.V. has good chances of being successfully reviewed. How can one know that the person or company behind the ad really exists, and is not just a figment of the match making company's imagination?

However, let us assume that you indeed do trust that the merchandise or service you buy from the provider is real. Now, the question is how the payment can be performed. The best existing solutions are based to some degree on sending your credit card information over the network, but leave a lot to wish for. One shortcoming of some solutions of this type is that only registered shops can receive payments, and that it is rather difficult (and expensive) to establish such a status with a credit card company, at least in the perspective of the small entrepreneur. Some solutions overcome this problem by introducing an intermediary, and only this intermediary, run by the provider, needs to be registered as a credit card merchant. Another issue (neglected till recently but

---

[2] Whereas this is not necessarily a counterpoint, it does not stress the importance of careful analysis of the given possibilities before a choice is made.

[3] One exception is providers of connection to the web, where it is easy to compare the service given between different companies, and also has an anchor in the physical world.

more active recently) is anonymity, both regarding payments and accesses, a problem which is not solved by the introduction of the intermediary, who, on the contrary, obtains large amounts of sale-related information. Furthermore, the service provider can, without the knowledge of the user accessing his service, obtain information about the latter, constituting a breach in the privacy of users.

4.2 Promoting and Protecting

There are two types of methods to promote good service providers and punish bad ones: by direct intervention and through the market forces. Although the web, with its distributed nature, is better suited for a distributed, market force driven legal system, the number of potential victims makes some type of direct intervention desirable.

The market forces would most likely express themselves through hierarchical positive and negative endorsements, the trust in which is based on brand name recognition and reputation: A good service provider does not want to associate with a disreputable endorser, and vice versa, and good endorsers can lose their reputation by endorsing bad services. Similarly, well reputed search engines would rather use reliable endorsers, just as the clients will be likely to favor endorsers and search engines with a good record. Endorsements could be performed either by professional organizations (e.g., IEEE,) by commercial bodies (e.g., Consumer Reports), special-interest organizations or congregations (e.g., labor unions,) or government and other organizational entities (e.g., the Chamber of Commerce.)

The endorsements can either be for free to the inquirer (e.g., endorsement agencies charging their clients, selling statistical information, or providing a free service for the common good) or purchased (e.g., insurance companies setting a price for endorsing a service, where the price of the insurance depends on the provider's previous record and therefore approximating the amount of future complaints and lawsuits). The insurance companies makes it possible for providers without a record to establish themselves, by buying support, thereby transferring trust from the physical world. Again, brand name recognition and reputation would be paramount, but now of the insurance companies, or the endorser of these.

Market forces will punish malicious providers by exclusion from lists of recommended providers, or by increasing insurance costs. Direct punishments, i.e., punishments more severe than the exclusion from a list of recommended providers, are difficult to implement in a distributed system without censuring, but could be achieved through voluntarily used filters, where well-known offenders are filtered out, through blacklisting, and by using "traffic polices;" agents listening in to the page requests, and sending out warnings whenever a service provider with a bad track record is contacted. These filters and "early warning systems" can be either officially run, or run by endorsement agencies as above.

The establishment of maps of the web landscape is closely related to the promotion of good providers, and can be obtained using the same vehicles, namely endorsers, directories, and search engines, which will establish pointers to providers that are likely to please the client.

4.3 Data Mining for Marketing and Research

Just as the WWW provides users with a valuable and easy accessible source of information, the users can in turn provide service providers and others with valuable statistical information. By observing user behavior and purchase patterns, a lot of very precise marketing information can be automatically collected, and marketing approaches tested on a large population for a small cost. Similarly, researchers can will be able to collect important information of a similar kind from access and purchase patterns, and performing experiments whose results are easily quantified through the precise collection of data and the large sample size, making the web population the ultimate ant-farm of social studies. (However, and as earlier pointed out, the goals of the marketers can sometimes be in conflict with the goals of supporters of privacy, making it important to regulate what type of information can be obtained without a previous agreement.)

4.4 Enforcing Policies

Currently, one may use the off-line mechanisms to complain and to assure trust. However, such traditional enforcement mechanisms may become a bottleneck. (In fact we see that such services also made themselves available on the web).

We are aware that it will take a lot of user education to assure that users and institutions use automatic tools to assure commercial transactions (and other transactions). We therefore assume that the sooner we think about them, the easier it will be for new and unpredictable commerce to find its way to the web (e.g., the intergalactic paradigm put by Rivest [4] hints about such unpredictabilities).

We next start describing the framework we try to put forth here.

5 Assurance Framework: Components

Here, we concentrate on technical solutions to implement the mechanisms of civilization. After introducing all the building blocks, we look at how these can be assembled to produce the desired structures.

5.1 Building Blocks

In order to achieve the goals, we suggest the following building blocks:

- *Endorsing Agencies and Rating Agencies*
  In order for consumers to know what businesses to trust and which ones to avoid, different types of endorsing agencies can be employed. Here, it is possible to picture an active agency who goes out and samples the services,

in order to produce what compares to the Michelin guide rating of good restaurants. This agency can then either produce a time-stamped certification (using digital signatures and related standard cryptographic methods) that the business could display, or could make itself available on-line for advice. Alternatively, a parallel to the Better Business Bureau or the Chamber of Commerce could be established, keeping statistics of user complaints and endorsing (either off-line or on-line, as above) businesses with a good track record. The collection of consumer opinions could be automated by asking for user feedback after each major transaction, or could solely rely on negative feedback in the form of complaints. Furthermore, a forum for user opinions can be useful guidance. This can either be organized and centralized (as a digital version of *Consumer Reports*) or distributed and open for discussions (as many newsgroups currently are.) In those cases where feedback is given by users it has to be made certain that the feedback is valid, e.g., does not originate from the organization judged or a competitor, or at least not to a significant share.

— *Insurance Companies*

Another way trust can be established is by the endorsement of a third party in the sense that if the service provider fails to provide the promised service (by accident or intention) then the third party, the *insurance company*, will pay the customer for its damages. The cost of buying insurance will depend on the history of the service provider, the expected risks and the extent of the insurance, just as for "real world" insurance companies. Furthermore, insurance companies may be structured hierarchically to establish trust and ascertain availability of funds for payments. This issue is treated in detail in [3].

— *Directories*

In order to allow the users to find the services they are interested in, directories of services will be useful. These can as part of their function perform a selection of services that have been well received by previous users, and therefore take part in the quality control practiced by the endorsement and rating agencies. Individual directory services may interface each other, exchanging information and enabling searches. An example of a service of this type, already existing on the web, is dating services.

— *Brokerages*

Brokerages are institutions devoted to find information, services and merchandise for their customers, and are related to the directories in functionality, although they may not themselves have any information, only the capability of finding it. Examples of such services that already exist on the net are general search engines and job-finding agencies (some of which are more closely related to directory services.)

— *Banks*

In order for commerce to be made possible, there must exist means for exchanging tokens denoting value electronically. Several different approaches to solve this problem have been suggested, and financial institutions are showing the issue much attention. There are many systems suggested, extending the use of cash or credit cards. Extension of cash allow a high or perfect degree of anonymity, but at the same time, many schemes of this type introduce possibilities for crimes like money laundering and blackmail using the perfect anonymity. Recently, the cryptographic community has given attention to payment forms implementing an anonymity that can be revoked in special cases of suspected criminal behavior, thereby removing this problem.

– *Drive-through Booths*

In order to achieve anonymity, we must provide means to access a service under an alias, since it is possible for a service provider to read the IP address of an individual accessing the service, and also to query the gateway of the accessing party in order to obtain more information about the user. We call this service the *drive-through booth*, as it would funnel all its traffic through, establishing an alias for outgoing traffic, and de-anonymize returning traffic in order to send it to the accessing party. This way, using one or more drive-through boots on the way to a service provider, it will be possible to implement anonymity. An example of such a service is [2]. We note that, in the context of digital cash, it does not make sense to implement a higher degree of anonymity in the payment scheme than is obtained by the use of (possibly multiple) drive-through booths. High throughput is an issue of major importance to the drive-through booths, as they would otherwise constitute unnecessary bottlenecks. Therefore, it makes sense to combine the drive-through booths with a directory service, an on-line service provider, etc., i.e., where the traffic goes through anyway. To obtain further privacy, encryption can be employed.

– *Toll Booths*

A toll-booth is a service that allows charging for traffic. In order to make sure that over-charging by a service provider does not take place, the toll both will constitute the trusted interface between the user and the merchant, making sure that the proper amount is charged and clearly displaying this to the customer. The honesty of the toll booths, in its turn, can be inspected and kept track of by endorsement agencies. The toll booths may have the added functionality of recording transactions in order to enable legal actions to be taken, should the service paid for not be what was promised. We note that this does not need to compromise anonymity, as the transactions can be recorded w.r.t. the secret alias used. With the help of the drive-through booth, the user would still, however, be able to show that a certain payment took place.

– *Arbitrage Agencies*

An arbitrage agency implements the legal function of a judge, receiving complaints, ruling in specific cases, and making policy decisions. The decisions of such a judge can be implemented in a distributed system like the WWW by voluntary agreement to its decisions by service providers such as network providers, directories, endorsement agencies and similar. Since a working society is in the common interest of the majority of the players, the rulings of **arbitrage agencies will be meaningful.**

– *Certification Agency*

Users will have a need to identify themselves, sign contracts, etc. In order to achieve this, each user will select a secret key and calculate the corresponding public key. Knowledge of a secret key corresponding to a certain public key allows the user to prove his identity as that of the owner of the public key, sign documents with the name connected to the public key, etc. The certification agency certifies the public keys connected to the name of participants, using digital signatures.

One recent idea of relevance is Blaze, Feigenbaum and Lacy's [1] work which identified the issue of "trust management" and suggested mechanisms to achieve it in the context of network services via certification authorities of extended roles. Another related idea is the distributed security infrastructure suggestion by Rivest and Lampson [5] which suggests grouping. Indeed, assurance structured are processes which should be supported by trust management and aggregation mechanisms which become part of the processes as will be described in this work.

– *Traffic Polices*

The traffic police could implement a warning system, where users accessing the pages of known offenders could be warned, and pointers to complaints and lawsuits be given. This can be implemented in conjunction with e.g., drive-through booths, or by agents residing in the physical switchboards of the net, listening in to the page requests.

– *Tax Collectors*

When commerce becomes common on the WWW, it will become of importance for the local authorities to be able to derive the amount of income from transactions on the network, so that they can tax the related companies and individuals correspondingly. In order to achieve this, one possibility is to obtain revenue information from the toll-booths. Although sales can take place without the toll-booths taking part in it, in order to evade taxes, it may not be wanted by the customer since the toll-booth gives security to him by overseeing and possibly also recording the transaction. We note that the existence of tax collectors further motivates the use of toll booths. Another way of taxing (with a flat rate) would be to let all coins in an e-cash setting lose value between withdrawal and deposit.

– *Customs*

The customs make sure that the transfer of information and funds is performed according to the rules. This may include the banning of certain services into the country, taxation of others, and the control of money flow in order to prevent tax evasion.

– *Marketing Agencies*

The marketing agencies, who with advantage can cooperate with the directory agencies, brokerage agencies and endorsing agencies, perform market surveys and do research on consumer behavior. The amount of information given to them can be controlled by means of the drive-through booths, making sure that no personal information is used without the agreement of the provider of the marketing information (i.e., the user). As noted before, the value of web-based surveys can give be very high, given the high precision of the experiments, aided by the objective measurability, and the high throughput of the media used.

— *Standardization Body and Form Providers*
The standardization body decides on the proper format for queries of different types. There may (although there is no direct benefit) be several co-existing standards, in which case we can envision a type of party that "translates" queries between different formats. The proper formats may be provided by "form providers". Note here that the proper format may be an executable description of the expected merchandise, and that these descriptions then can be both provided and certified by such an entity.

5.2 Assembling the Building Blocks

We show one example of how the above building blocks can be put together to form service units, which together obtain the means for trust, payments, privacy and structure that we require.

1. *Connection unit*
   The Internet access provider can at the same time as providing a connection implement the functions of directories, brokerages, banks, drive-through booths, toll booths, certification agencies, marketing agencies and form providers. Furthermore, they can to some degree be endorsing agencies, and insurance companies to its users.

2. *Commercial unit*
   We combine directories, brokerages, drive-through booths and marketing agencies to form a commercial unit. Such a unit provides information about services, implements anonymity, and uses access patterns of users for marketing surveys.

3. *Charging unit*
   We can combine banks, drive-through booths and toll booths, tax collectors and customs to a unit supervising payments, implementing anonymity, and verifying that no "illegal material" is imported.

4. *Endorsement unit*
   The endorsement unit contains endorsement and licensing agencies, possibly combined with directories and brokerages. If the endorsement unit provides traffic through it (and not only is a consulary service) then it will also implement a drive-through booth.

5. *Privacy Unit*
   The privacy unit solely implements a drive-through booth, enabling users concerned with privacy to access information anonymously. The privacy unit would not have any conflict of interests, would be run by privacy advocates, and would therefore give a more trustworthy anonymity than the other units

implementing drive-through booths. We note that a multiplicity of privacy units may be employed to strengthen the degree of privacy.

6. *Legal unit*
   We combine arbitrage agencies and certification agencies to form a legal unit. This unit may also implement a directory of legal services, and similar.

5.3 Trust between Components

The establishing of trust is central to the issue of obtaining secure WWW commerce. There are three types of trust involved: (1) the trust each entity has to put in his or her own machine, (2) the static trust between entities, and (3) dynamically established trust. Let us consider these one by one:

1. **"Self" trust**
   Each participant needs to trust the operating system on his or her machine to give access appropriately. For example, a charging unit will be allowed to open a window with a certain appearance (indicating its authenticity) and interact with the wallet of the participant. The same access rights must of course not be given to a merchant. The operating system should use the so called sandbox concept, in which different processes are given a "sandbox" of their own, in which they may access any information, but from which they are not allowed to leave.

2. **Static trust**
   The user needs to trust the different parties differently; with money (his bank, and to some extent the charging unit, and indirectly, the endorsement unit), with privacy (that not all drive-through boot units on the path collaborate against him), and with "good advice" (that all units giving referrals or recommendations are properly updated and maintained.) The money related trust and the trust of "good advice" are related in the sense that entities giving bad advice may be economically liable for this.

3. **Dynamic trust**
   During any transaction, the user will have to establish a chain of trust, based on a hierarchy of positive endorsements or a lack of negative endorsements (two paths with different risks associated with themselves.) This process is partially automatic (by automatic verification of credentials and endorsements, some of which may require communication with other entities) and partially manual (driven by user decisions based on the user's own business decisions and preferences.)

6 Assurance Framework: Generic Architecture

Once the building blocks are identified, relationships and interactions between them can be designed and then "transaction scenarios" can be built. We will exemplify some of those.

We want to envision the establishment of trust in a setting using generic access mechanisms with standardized protocols for interacting with each other.

For example, we want not to restrict the type of payment scheme used, the type of browser, or the root of the trust in the establishment of trust. We give three examples of flows of information, closely related to chains of trust, in figures 1 to 3. In these figures, we sketch how three common types of transactions can be viewed. These are *searching for a product* (figure 1), *performing a barter* (figure 2), and *filing a complaint* (figure 3.) In these figures, filled lines indicate communication; dotted lines indicate endorsement; and flash-lines the potential revocation of endorsements.

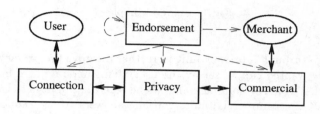

Fig. 1. Searching for a product.

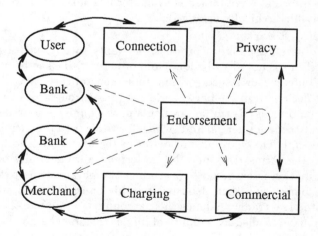

Fig. 2. Performing a barter.

1. Searching for a product *(Figure 1.)*

When searching for a product, the user connects through the connection unit, where he obtains forms for the query, and pointers to appropriate commercial units, after which he goes through a drive-through booth for privacy. Second,

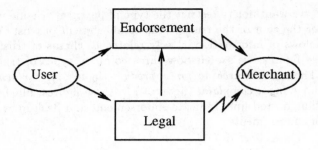

Fig. 3. Filing a complaint.

he may go through a privacy unit to further improve the privacy (the degree of privacy wanted can be set by the user). This anonnymizes his request for information from the commercial units he received pointers to by his connection unit. The commercial units compile answers to the requests, possibly using other commercial services, and possibly in cooperation with different merchants. These answers are returned to the user through the privacy unit and his connection unit. The process may be interactive, and the above may be repeated several times. All the different units above may be positively endorsed (or negatively, in which case that will be taken into consideration when the information obtained is evaluated) by a set of endorsement units, potentially hierarchically arranged.

2. **Performing a barter** *(Figure 2.)*

When the user has found a product, he wants to establish a price for the product (if this is not already done) and procure it. Backed by a bank, he has some digital currency issued (or, in a more general case, something that the merchant desires from the barter). He connects through his connection unit, which again funnels the traffic through a privacy unit, if desired. The request is then sent to a commercial unit, which forwards it to the merchant through a charging unit. The charging unit performs the barter after both parties have agreed to the terms (this may be performed automatically or manually). The information is exchanged by sending the obtained merchandise to the acquiring party, who then deposits it in his bank (where applicable.) The banks of the two traders balance their accounts to complete the transaction, after they have verified availability of funds (this may be done in a way that is supervised by the charging unit in order to establish availability of funds for both traders before the barter is performed.) As before, all units may be endorsed.

3. **Filing a complaint** *(Figure 3.)*

If a user (or more general, any participant) is unhappy with the service he or she received from another participant, he can file a complaint. This may be done with the appropriate endorsement agencies, and with the appropriate legal units. These consider the complaint, and the history of complaints on the potentially misbehaving party, and takes appropriate action. This may involve the issuing of negative endorsements, or the refusal to perform positive endorsements onwards. This is a process of strongly hierarchical nature, where one entity may suggest another to change its future behavior (e.g., in terms of referrals) in order for the first entity to continue to trust the second.

References

1. M. Blaze, J. Feigenbaum and J. Lacey, "Decentralized Trust Management," IEEE Security and Privacy, 1996
2. E. Gabber, P. Gibbons, Y. Matias, A. Mayer, "How to make personalized web browsing simple, secure, and anonymous," Financial Cryptography '97, pp. 17 - 31.
3. C. Lai, G. Medvinsky, B.C. Neuman, "Endorsements, Licensing, and Insurance for Distributed System Services," 2nd ACM Conference on Computer and Communications Security, pp. 170-175
4. R. Rivest, "Perspectives on Finacial Cryptography," Financial Cryptography '97, pp. 145 - 149.
5. R. Rivest and B. Lampson, "SDSI– A simple distributed security infrastructure."
6. J. M. Tenenbaum, C. Medich, A. M. Schiffman, and W. T. Wong, "CommerceNet: Spontaneous Electronic Commerce on the Internet," Compcon '95, pp. 38-43

Certificate Revocation: Mechanics and Meaning

Barbara Fox* and Brian LaMacchia

Microsoft Corporation
One Microsoft Way
Redmond, WA 98052 USA
{bfox,bal}@microsoft.com

Abstract. Revocation of public key certificates is controversial in every aspect: methodology, mechanics, and even meaning. This isn't so surprising, though, when considered in the context of current public key infrastructure (PKI) implementations. PKIs are still immature; consumers, including application developers and end-users, are just beginning to understand the implications of large-scale, heterogeneous PKIs, let alone PKI subtleties such as revocation. In this paper, which is the product of a panel discussion at Financial Cryptography '98, we illustrate some of the semantic meanings possible with current certificate revocation technology and their impact on the process of determining trust relationships among public keys in the PKI. Further, we postulate that real-world financial applications provide analogous and appropriate models for certificate revocation.

1 Introduction

At this stage of PKI deployment we've figured out how to issue certificates and evaluate them in a reasonably interoperable manner but not how to revoke them. In fact, when it comes to revocation, we can't even agree on who should do it, how it should work or even what it means.

In the most literal sense, to *revoke* a digital certificate is to *UNDO* a persistent signed statement. Revocation doesn't sound controversial or, at first glance, even very hard. At the root of the problem though is the maturity of the technology itself. While the concept of digital certificates has been around since the late seventies, only now do we see any plans by commercial certificate authorities and enterprise PKIs to issue them on a large scale. And as technologists, we've done a terrible job of explaining certificates and digital signatures.

Viable trust models already exist that do not include explicit "identity" certificates, most notably PGP ("Pretty Good Privacy" [2]). In key-centric PGP, key holders are responsible for notifying their correspondents of a key compromise — a form of self-revocation. After all, key compromise is what they *should* care about; for it allows the crook to impersonate them in a transaction. We do not tend to think of the *subject* of a certificate being able to unilaterally revoke that certificate, but that's exactly what is necessary if the subject knows its private key has been compromised. Key holders could "bulk" revoke all their certificates acquired with the same key through some kind of registry. This is a natural analog of credit card registries with the convenient side effect that multiple certificates issued against the same key establish an alias: Bfox@microsoft.com can easily become barb@skijump.com when two certificates are bound to the same key pair.

To make this phenomenon clear to consumers of public key systems including application developers and end-users, we first need to position certificates as merely *evidence for a decision* that the certificate acceptor needs to make. The certificate (or a chain of them) is intended to provide enough information for an acceptor to determine whether he will accept the bound signature for a transaction, period. Confusion arises however because actual certificate evaluation is usually buried deep

---

* The opinions expressed in this paper are those of the authors and are not necessarily those of Microsoft Corporation.

under the covers in some application or system. Most Internet-savvy users understand the concept of trusted *root certificates*, which are usually either "baked into" or installable in their browsers, and that a digital signature/certificate chain ending in one of these root certificates constitutes validation. Revocation, however, is a different matter — because it doesn't work yet. In other words, there's still time to make revocation make sense.

So far, though, we've manage to confuse certificates, which are solely intended to establish transitive trust through public keys, with lots of real-world analogies like driver's licenses and credit cards. In retrospect, this was probably a bad idea because many of these examples lose sight of the function and value of the signature key. The long-term cost of these false similes is that before revocation can make any sense we have to start over in explaining certificates themselves.

2 Meaning

What really matters in a public key certificate? For practitioners looking at this problem for the first time, the answer is obvious: *the issuer and subject public keys*. But those familiar with X.509-based public key infrastructures could counter that *the distinguished names of the issuer and subject* alone provide enough information to verify a certificate chain.

The process of certificate path validation from an end-entity certificate of interest to a trusted root is the algorithmic foundation of establishing trust in public key systems. In turn, checking to determine whether a certificate has been revoked is just a function of the underlying algorithm.

The proposed IETF public key infrastructure standard, PKIX Part 1 [4], specifies the algorithm for determining whether a particular certificate chain is valid but does not describe how to discover certificate chains in the first place. Moreover, the semantics of PKIX certificate revocation are also underspecified, which puts crucial issues of meaning in the hands of individual implementations. In every case, the actual process of certificate revocation is deemed the responsibility of the signer even if it is at the request of the subscriber. In theory, the certificate authority has the most to lose with continued circulation of a bad certificate.

Let $C = c_0, c_1, ..., c_n$ be a chain of certificates where c_n is the end-entity certificate of interest, c_0 is a self-signed trusted root certificate, and c_k is signed by the subject of c_{k-1} for all $k = 1, ..., n$. By definition, if any certificate c_i in C is revoked then C is not a valid chain. Assume that no c_i in C is revoked, and let $C' = c_0', c_1', ..., c_{k-1}', c_k, ..., c_n$ be a second chain of certificates from c_n to a trusted root (c_0'), with c_{k-1}' distinct from c_{k-1}. Certificates c_{k-1} and c_{k-1}' have the same subject public key (the issuer of the statement in c_k).

Now, because revocation in the PKIX model applies to a particular certificate, it is possible to revoke c_{k-1}' without revoking c_{k-1}. Then chain C' is an invalid chain while C is still valid. Is this consistent? It depends on the semantics of the revocation. The certificate c_{k-1}' is a statement by an issuer $I_{c_{k-1}'}$ that binds together *subject name* $SN_{c_{k-1}'}$ and a *subject public key* $SPK_{c_{k-1}'}$. That is:

$$I_{c_{k-1}'} : SN_{c_{k-1}'} \longleftrightarrow SPK_{c_{k-1}'}$$

where this statement is read, "Issuer $I_{c_{k-1}'}$ states that there is a binding (or relationship) between the public key $SPK_{c_{k-1}'}$ and the identity information $SN_{c_{k-1}'}$."

So, revoking c_{k-1}' (e.g. adding c_{k-1}' to a "certificate revocation list" (CRL) signed by $I_{c_{k-1}'}$) could mean "UNDO" any of the following:

(a) UNDO $SPK_{c_{k-1}'}$, the subject public key (that is, no longer trust the subject public key for anything because it has been compromised),

(b) UNDO $SN_{c_{k-1}'} \longleftrightarrow SPK_{c_{k-1}'}$, the relationship between the subject public key and the subject name/identity information, because that binding is no longer valid, or

(c) UNDO $I_{c'_{k-1}}$:<binding>, the relationship between the certificate issuer and the binding between subject public key and identity information, because the issuer is no longer willing to vouch for the binding, although it may still be true.

Each of these cases means something different, and chain processing in the presence of revocation information acts differently in each case.

Consider the first case (a) above, where revocation of c'_{k-1} denotes compromise of the subject public key. In this case, the fact that c'_{k-1} is revoked should cause *all* certificate paths that involve the subject public key $SPK_{c'_{k-1}}$ to no longer be valid. So, not only is C' now invalid, but C itself is now invalid as:

$$SPK_{c_{k-1}} == SPK_{c'_{k-1}} == I_{c_k}$$

Ideally, if any certificate for a given subject public key is revoked for reasons of key compromise, all such certificates would immediately be revoked, but obviously we cannot guarantee this behavior. Thus, it may be argued that relying parties have a duty to check revocation status on all certificates naming a particular subject public key even if they themselves are not relying on those certificates for chain-building.

Case (b), direct revocation of the subject name-subject public key binding by the issuer, is a fuzzier situation. If the subject names in the two certificates c_{k-1} and c'_{k-1} are distinct (i.e. $SN_{c_{k-1}} \neq SN_{c'_{k-1}}$) then revocation of c'_{k-1} should have no impact on acceptance of c_{k-1} itself. That is, chain C' is invalid because of the revocation but C is still a perfectly valid chain. Notice, however, that if the subject names in the two certificates *are* equal then relying parties could reasonably choose to reject C (or at least suspect it) if the name information $SN_{c_{k-1}} == SN_{c'_{k-1}}$ is important to their particular application.

Finally, in case (c) we have revocation of certificate c'_{k-1} because the issuer of that certificate no longer has a relationship with the subject public key. Revocation here speaks not to the validity of the name-key binding but rather to a lack of contractual obligation. Revocation of c'_{k-1} should not in any way impact chain C as there is no authorization statement from the issuer of c'_{k-1} concerning the validity of the subject public key $SPK_{c'_{k-1}}$ itself (which would make it case (a)) or the name-key binding (case (b)).

The fact that the act of revoking a particular certificate needed to be qualified with intended semantics was recognized by the authors of the X.509 standard. In X.509 Version 2 Certificate Revocation Lists (CRLs), it is possible to include a *reason code* extension on each and every entry in the CRL. Reason codes are semantics modifiers and can specify situations such as:

- Key compromise
- CA compromise
- Affiliation change (including subject name changes)
- Superseded
- Cessation of operation (the certificate is no longer needed for its original purpose)

Thus, one could conceivably decide whether a particular revocation fell into cases (a)–(c) above based on reason code, assuming one was present in the CRL and that each possible reason code could be assigned to a particular case. (This is not currently true in the PKIX specification as some reason codes have semantics orthogonal to the separation described above. For example, reason code 6, "certificateHold," means that the certificate in question has been "suspended" pending the outcome of some process. Clearly the suspended certificate could fall into any of cases (a)–(c).)

Even if reason codes were always present (which is not required by PKIX) and defined to fall into exactly one semantic category for meaning, they only solve the problem if this information is always available to the chain-building algorithm. This is clearly not the case, as any revocation that falls into case (a) (including reason code 1, "keyCompromise") may impact certificate chains that do not include the particular revoked certificate. Thus, until we come up with a better mechanism for moving revocation information around, and binding that revocation information to the proper statement being undone by the revocation, use of revocation information can add significant ambiguity to the chain-building process.

3 Mechanics

So, how does the revocation notification get propagated? Certificates come attached to all kinds of mobile objects ranging from signed forms to ActiveX controls, so considerable thinking has been put into how to avoid having revocation notices chase certificates. These include simple techniques like issuing certificates with short validity periods (certificates just expire on their own), directory-based revocation certificates (in effect an "anti-certificate") and online status checking. While each of these approaches may reduce the problem to some extent, they all rely on two independent but closely related factors:

- Good network connectivity, to either perform online status checks or frequently refresh certificates; and
- The certificate acceptor application (or person) has to care enough to check.

Technically, the "revocation mechanics problem" boils down to *on-line vs. off-line* operation and *open vs. closed* systems. In the traditional closed, on-line system, for example within an enterprise, a trusted directory is the obvious repository for key status information. But how realistic is this model in the long term? Gartner [3] estimates that by 2001, 60 million users will be relying on intermittent, low bandwidth, unreliable network connections and notebooks continue to be the fastest growing segment of the PC market? Furthermore, in the age of the Internet where are the examples of truly closed systems?

Possibly the only large-scale specimen of a closed system is the bank credit card authorization network within the United States, and in its Internet implementation (SET), there is currently no support for revocation. It has been argued that SET does not need a revocation mechanism because a SET certificate is just a proxy for a credit card that exists in the physical world. Only the account number requires verification — and legacy systems work fine for this task. Thus, if the rest of public key systems are trending towards *all open* and *often off-line* in their degenerate state, we have to make some form of revocation work within those constraints.

The most common proposed method for distributing revocation information requires an issuing certificate authority to publish a signed list of revoked certificates (a CRL). These lists may be actively distributed to users or simply made available to interested applications via cached file references, URLs, or directory queries. In any case, it is up to the individual application to determine whether it will enable CRL checking by default and how it will handle revoked certificates. In practice, applications that must rely on HTTP do not generally check CRLs by default for performance reasons, and even when such applications do perform revocation checks they only warn users of revoked certificates. These are two separable problems.

Applications' not checking for revocation should not be wholly credited to some fear of degraded performance. Robust revocation information just isn't available yet and, more importantly, the legal landscape isn't littered with case law allocating liabilities for misinformation. After all, revocation of a certificate only means that *either* one of the two parties chose to terminate the binding of the public key to some identity or authorization.

A possibly larger issue is timeliness. There is no magic in how revocation data gets to a client in an enterprise setting: it's either a signed wad of certificates or their hashes pushed at some designated time, or, if he happens to be online, the client can fetch it. In either case, there is some amount of latency. Revocation is after all a *process*, not an event, and as such implies some responsibility (if not outright liability) for correctness. Due diligence requires the expenditure of time and effort somewhere in the system.

Perhaps the whole certificate revocation concept itself is too blunt an instrument to be really useful without some re-engineering. While PKI architects are worrying about hundreds of millions of certificates floating around, systems designers are trying to figure out how to "recall" individual Java applets without impacting code size or runtime overhead. Revoking a software publisher's certificate clearly doesn't solve the problem.

Dealing with revoked certificates presents another set of problems for applications. When a revoked certificate is encountered, can an application simply prompt the user for a decision, or must it invoke some policy to determine what to do? There isn't a definitive answer yet; the only widespread applications that actually use certificates are secure channels and mail. In fact, the only people talking about public key infrastructures these days are technologists and lawyers; the business types haven't shown up yet to the party.

When those business types *do* arrive, though, the applications in which they will most likely be interested deal with something everybody cares about: money. Signed transactions with assigned monetary value and properties of non-repudiation are the obvious next step to legitimacy for public key systems and the certificates that support them. Revocation will begin to *mean* something.

The credit card system provides both bad and good examples of how things could work. *Bad* because the issuer of the "certificate" (aka the credit card) is always a party to any transaction using it, and because the certificate remains the property of its issuer (which means he can govern its use through subscriber agreements). For example, the card cannot legally be used for identification (cashing a check) and no other identification (a driver's license) may be required by a merchant to accept it.

Credit cards provide a *good* example because the card itself is only a small component of a complete (and highly mature) risk management system. When a merchant goes online to authorize a credit card he not only associates a value and a signature with a transaction, but he simultaneously *sells his own risk* to his bank for a fixed discount rate. His bank, in turn, sells that risk to the card's issuer or assumes it himself (which, by the way, is the default outside the US where communication costs are high). As soon as the merchant makes the decision to authorize the transaction, he's *committed* to sell it. The same holds true for his bank. In each case, though, the decision to sell the risk (i.e. go online) is the decision of the risk holder.

The critical point here is that the *transaction* is being traded (i.e. bought and sold) between cardholder and merchant, between a merchant and his bank, and ultimately between banks. Each participant in the value chain discounts, or more precisely, *factors* it. The only difference between the certificate acceptance model and the old credit card acceptance model is that the risk metrics of the latter are built on years of experience with billions of transactions.

So, how does risk management relate to public key certificate revocation? It's possible that the controversy surrounding such basics as whether certificates state the right relationships for keys, who should be trusted to issue and revoke them, and how far that authority extends will go on as long as there are no risk models in place to test the assumptions. If the credit card system is any indicator of how public key infrastructures will actually roll out, then revocation will start with a simplistic blacklist like the "card recovery bulletin" and evolve based on something as fundamental as who's willing to pay for revocation information. The value of the transaction, or rather the effect of fraud, will determine whether it is verified off-line or on-line and what kinds of checks are performed.

In terms of the *revocation data*, credit card companies price this kind of information based on the risk characteristics of the individual transaction. For example, a bad merchant could be blacklisted for free because that information benefits the entire infrastructure, but individual cardholder status costs something. Again, it's all about risk. For certificate revocation lists, this would imply that revocation lists and online status checking of individual certificates would be available at different prices – but in no case free!

The core question then resolves down to, "To an acceptor, does a certificate have any independent value, or does it rely on *his* trust in its issuer?" Who is trusting whom? When the issuer *is a party to the transaction*, a certificate can certainly provide authentication along with some form of authorization. What's more interesting, though, is what happens when the issuer *is not a party* to the transaction. Will the acceptor of a certificate pay any attention to what an issuer intended as its use when issued, and does the acceptor even care that the stated binding is still valid?

It is still too early in the process of gluing public key infrastructures together to predict how relying third parties will view their relationships, real or implied, with certificate issuers. As we saw with credit cards in the seventies, it all resolves to a "certificate acceptance" problem. And this is the tough infrastructure play.

In a world where certificate issuers acquire some reputation (through a brand even?) then it might follow that the possession/revocation of a particular certificate carries more weight than the possession/revocation of another. Likewise, having ten certificates against a single signature key could pass for some form of digital credit rating. Sound familiar? If we're actually facing the digital variant of a known risk model, then elaborate infrastructures will almost certainly grow up to support certificate revocation and every intermediate state on the way to it.

The most obvious of these is aggregation of certificate-linked information into some "universal" revocation service paid for by the at-risk stakeholders. The Visa and Mastercard associations are existence-proofs of this concept at work for banks, but it's not clear that banks are going to be the only risk stakeholders in PKIs. Key-holders of all kinds, along with certificate acceptors, may well pay for some trusted, instant, and always available revocation registry — but only if the risk profile of the transactions justifies its cost.

This kind of service would undoubtedly have to offer more than notice of revocation. The real value in the credit card authorization network is that it provides fraud detection as well. If it's worth the trouble for a crook to compromise a signature key, then he's bound to use it in transactions. How can these be detected and what accompanying consumer protection must be in place?

4 Summary

Credit cards took almost twenty years to gain ubiquitous acceptance. While on the surface it appears to be a simple model, it isn't. But it just works. If the analogy holds and certificate revocation tracks with credit card authorization, the technology isn't really the gating factor. It's the infrastructure required to support it. Until *what the certificate stands for can be reliably verified and undone* — and the decision to status check it on-line or accept it off-line can be done seamlessly based on risk characteristics – then issuing it in the first place probably isn't worth doing.

5 Acknowledgements

The authors wish to acknowledge the Public Key Infrastructure Group at Microsoft, members of the Public Key Infrastructure (PKIX) Working Group within the IETF, and panel members (Joan Feigenbaum, Paul Kocher, Michael Myers, and Ron Rivest) at Financial Cryptography '98 for their valuable contributions to this paper.

References

1. Warwick Ford and Michael Baum, Secure Electronic Commerce, Prentice Hall, 1997.
2. OpenPGP Working Group, Internet Engineering Task Force. "OP Formats - OpenPGP Message Format," Jon Callas, Lutz Donnerhacke, Hal Finney, and Rodney Thayer, eds., work in progress. (Draft as of March, 1998, available from http://www.ietf.org/internet-drafts/draft-ietf-openpgp-formats-01.txt.)

3. J. O'Reilley. Information Security Strategies (ISS), Research Note, Key Issue Analysis, The Gartner Group, 21 July 1997.
4. PKIX Working Group, Internet Engineering Task Force. "Internet Public Key Infrastructure: X.509 Certificate and CRL Profile," R. Housley, W. Ford, W. Polk, D. Solo, eds., work in progress. (Draft as of March, 1998, available from http://www.ietf.org/internet-drafts/draft-ietf-pkix-ipki-part1-07.txt.)

Revocatoin: Options and Challenges

Michael Myers

VeriSign, Inc.
mmyers@verisign.com **

Abstract. Public keys can be trusted if they are digitally signed by a trusted third party. This trust is most commonly conveyed by use of a digital certificate. However, having once established trust in a public key, means must exist to terminate that trust should circumstances dictate. The most common means to do so is through revocation of the corresponding digital certificate. This paper identifies and discusses options that may be considered by those undertaking to address the revocation of digital certificates.

1 Introduction

Who do you trust? And why? And will you be protected if something goes wrong? These are tough questions facing the builders of PKI today as we move beyond the initial broad releases of products and services and into more value-added realms. As we do so, one fact is glaringly obvious: while the current crop of commercial products and services today have done a fair job of turning on the PKI machine, there is yet no means in place to shut it off; there is no revocation.

This paper adopts the somewhat constrained view that a successful infrastructure must provide well-understood and broadly deployed capabilities. A freeware toolkit that parses an X.509 CRL does not form an infrastructure. Rather, infrastructure is formed when capabilities are uniformly deployed in large scale such that services or derivative products can be developed with an assumption of the existence of these capabilities.

In view of this claim, we are today faced with applications that implement but a portion of standards-compliant logic necessary for a globally scaleable public key infrastructure. Correspondingly, PKI service providers, self-certifying enterprises and various industry consortia are foreclosed from a complete solution. The time is rapidly approaching when revocation capabilities will become essential if the marketplace often predicated on PKI is to emerge.

2 Characteristics

This paper examines several means by which digital certificates may be revoked. To do so it's important to establish the metrics with which these various approaches can be analyzed. We claim there are at least four such characteristics:

** The opinions expressed in this paper are those of the author and not necessarily those of VeriSign Inc.

1. Population size and symmetry;
2. Timeliness of revocation information;
3. Connectivity and bandwidth utilization; and
4. Responsiveness to security-critical needs.

2.1   Population Size and Asymmetry

The absolute size of a population of potentially revocable certificates can strongly influence the approach taken. Absolute size can range across orders of magnitude. At one end of this spectrum we have closed communities with, say, fifty members, to in the worst case the entire Internet. Quite obviously a solution that meets the needs of the former in all likelihood may fail to adequately address the latter. Conversely a solution intended to address Internet-scale populations may in many cases require more resources and complexity than is necessary for more modestly sized enterprises.

One must also take into account the effects of population asymmetry. Efficiencies can be gained when the set of potentially revocable certificates is considerably smaller than the set of relying parties. While other architectures may emerge over time, there exist today two well-known instances of this situation: client-server type services and signed objects. In both cases the number of relying parties would exceed by orders of magnitude the number of certificates issued.

2.2   Timeliness of Revocation Information

How soon after a certificate is revoked does a relying party wish to know of the revocation? Within a week? A day? Immediately? The degree of timeliness relates to the interval between when a Certification Authority made a record of the revocation and when it made that information available to its relying parties. At first it would seem that CAs should strive to make this information available as soon as possible. All other things being equal, this is certainly a legitimate requirement. However the mechanism used to convey this information may consume an appreciable level of bandwidth. While it might be prudent to publish CRLs on an hourly basis, in all likelihood CRL(n+1) will contain no more information than CRL(n).

2.3   Connectivity and Bandwidth Utilization

Does the approach require the relying party to be online, or can the relying party ascertain a certificate's reliability using cached data? Clearly there exists scenarios where a relying party will be attempting to validate a certificate in off-line modes of operation. Online mechanisms further create a mission-critical component in the overall security design. However, online mechanisms can be applicable to a wide variety of electronic exchanges that already assume connectivity. This dimension to the problem can inform the designers of online mechanisms of the need to facilitate off-line caching of prior results.

2.4 Security Considerations

In the overwhelming majority of cases a certificate will expire without ever having been revoked. It is however those few circumstances when a certificate needs to be revoked that causes one to carefully consider the above mentioned characteristics. Without a doubt the most troubling scenario involves the compromise of a private key. Without an effective compromise recovery capability, a security solution based on PKI is at risk of general system compromise.

3 Certificate Revocation Options

3.1 Certificate Revocation Lists

The Certificate Revocation List has been a fixture of PKI standards for several years. The mechanism is well understood and is well supported across the relevant standards. The concept does however suffer from some widely recognized shortcomings.

First and perhaps most significantly, CRLs can grow arbitrarily large. One may delete expired certificates from a CRL, but the CRL remains a linear function of the population of certificates it covers. One means of reducing the size of a CRL is through partitioning. There exist proposals that partition CRLs according to some partitioning rule and include in the certificate the location of the partial CRL where that particular certificate would be listed should it be revoked. While this approach shows promise of managing CRL size, it remains to be seen if this capability will be implemented in anything other than a few proprietary systems.

Closely related to the sizing criticism, frequent distribution of CRLs may unnecessarily consume bandwidth. Assuming that a CRL listing 1000 certificates may run to about 50kb in size, periodic updates listing one additional certificate will transmit roughly 50 bytes of new information in addition to 50kb-50 bytes of redundant information.

CRLs do not provide a positive response; they do not speak to a certificate's existence. Another way to look at this aspect of CRLs is to ask: Does the absence of a certificate on a CRL imply the certificate exists? While in most cases a certificate processing system would have on hand the certificate in question, it is foreseeable that certificate processing systems can be developed and deployed that rely exclusively on a certificate identifier.

All that said, CRLs have their place in the global scheme of PKI. They form a least-common-denominator baseline. Even in the instances where alternative methods are used to enforce revocation locally (as will be discussed momentarily), CRLs may serve a role as a common interchange format across autonomous PKIs.

To place CRLs against the metrics defined earlier, they are most useful where:

1. Populations on the order of 10,000 certificates. An order of magnitude larger requires infrastructure capabilities that are both beyond the state of the art and further may not be operable in practice.

2. The number of relying parties is considerably larger than the number of certificates issued. Client-server architectures are one such system design pattern, as is the practice of signed code.
3. Timeliness is not the top priority. For the purposes of comparison, this would amount to a daily update vs. hourly or realtime updates.
4. High bandwidth environments that can easily handle the redundancy inherent in CRL distribution. CRLs are also useful in instances where the certificate processing system is not connected to the CRL distribution network, bearing in mind that the weight of this advantage is inversely proportional to the periodicity of CRL update.
5. CRLs provide basic mechanisms to deal with key compromise. Reason codes can be embedded into CRLs that can be used to partition key compromise CRLs from all other reasons.

In summary, CRLs are best used within an enterprise that is handling more or less typical PKI-secured traffic. To the extent that these characteristics defines a non-trivial subset (or market), CRLs can and must be considered a viable solution to the revocation problem.

3.2 Online Certificate Status Checking

It has been long known that timely reporting of unreliable public keys is crucial to the safety and security of a secure message handling infrastructure. In the absence of commercially available options, mission-specific solutions were developed that met this need in a DoD context. To move the matter forward into the commercial sector, the IETF's PKIX working has established that some means of online status checking can and should be anticipated over the evolution of PKI on the Internet. A recent proposal has been put forward to drive this solution to reality.

Status checking is particularly relevant to environments with severe time constraints. Federal reserve loans among major banks are a prime example. In that environment, interest is charged by the minute. To the extent that trades and transfers in this environment are secured using public key technology (and consequently public key certificates), there exists a compelling need for very timely status on the reliability of a certificate prior to accepting its use to validate a transfer. Does this type of solution bear risk of lost connectivity? Absolutely—to the same extent that those electronic transfers are themselves at risk of connectivity loss. Dimensions of timeliness, service availability and reliability would all serve to characterize the value of the service.

Online status is well suited to environments where:

1. Populations on the order of 10,000 certificates. An order of magnitude larger requires infrastructure capabilities that are both beyond the state of the art and further may not be operable in practice.
2. As with CRLs, efficiencies can be achieve in instances where the number of relying parties is considerably larger than the number of issued certificates.

3. Timeliness is of the highest priority, notwithstanding the ability to produce status responses that have a validity interval similar to that used in CRLs. This capability would allow for offline operations.
4. Online-oriented security protocols. In most client-server and server-server design patterns, connectivity is already an assumption. Online status can also be relevant to firewalls that are set up to assess the reliability of signed objects entering a secure enclave. In-band inclusion of status responses in security protocols can improve bandwidth utilization.
5. To the extent that online status is a direct reflection of CRLs, this mechanism can effectively address key compromise. A "push" model of online status responses can also be used to broadcast key compromise data in the instance where a wide-scale alert of such information is relevant to the overall security of the system.

3.3 Trusted Directory

Within an enterprise, one can effectively "revoke" a certificate on the basis of its absence in a trusted directory. Such can be the case when an employee leaves a company. Her account is deleted from the system, including its content of digital certificates. To the extent that applications are designed to check for certificates in the directory prior to relying on them, this enables an expedient solution to the immediate crisis of revocation capability. It does however invoke severe penalties. Simply put, the directory and all its components now become trusted elements and thus are prime targets for attack. This option thus transforms the proven reliability of a digital signature on a CRL to trusted software development, secure systems engineering, trusted operational procedures and trusted operating personnel. An independent, cryptographically trustworthy assertion— either as a CRL or a signed status response message—significantly reduces the costs, risks and complexity of this option.

The trusted directory approach is largely limited to a closed, well-connected enclave. It requires continuous connectivity to the directory for every certificate acceptance decision. In most cases a corporation's internal directory is not made available to external parties for reasons of privacy and security. While replication of internal directory content to external servers may reflect the existence of certificates, there nonetheless exists concern that the certificates themselves may contain proprietary information. Thus external parties will very likely have no means to determine if a certificate is revoked.

Despite these limitations it is nonetheless foreseeable that the trusted directory approach will be taken by some environments due to the expediency of its default behavior. With this eventuality in mind, the trusted directory approach:

1. Is as scaleable in population as the underlying directory technology reaches across inter-departmental and branch-office boundaries.
2. Can be responsive to timeliness concerns in that the absence of a certificate in its assumed directory entry would inhibit further reliance regardless of cause.

3. Requires constant connectivity to the directory if timeliness benefits are to be achieved. This approach however fundamentally fails to address the needs of the off-line user.

4. Can enforce compromise if connectivity can be assumed. The absence of a certificate in its assumed directory entry would inhibit reliance regardless of cause.

3.4 Short Lived Certificates

The presumption underlying this option is that in the absence of any other act, a certificate with a short validity interval will naturally bound the effects of revocation causes. Proposed intervals are typically on the order of weeks where current practice is on the order of years. There are some fundamental questions that need answering however:

Are new key pairs generated for each new certificate, or is the same key pair simply recertified? Public key validity renewal is today absent from commercial products as well, although sorely needed. Short certificates amplify the urgency of this requirement. In its absence one is led to conclude that new key pairs are generated for each new "ticket". This is a good deal of keying material to be generating, placing a greater reliance on key generation performance than has to date been asserted with well-defined models of PKI key management requirements.

Do the validity intervals overlap from certificate to certificate for the same subscriber? If not, then an enterprise PKI being sustained by this model must carefully consider the effects of delayed propagation of one's "next" certificate in the event of network failure. It's worth noting that short validity intervals reverse the freshness requirement, the need to distribute information to maintain freshness and the criticality of doing so reliably. This option does nothing to eliminate these essential requirements. If however validity intervals do overlap, will applications be savvy enough to disambiguate from among several equally valid subscriber certificates? Perhaps, but only at the expense of additional user interface and operational complexity.

This option also completely ignores the essential need to recovery from compromised private keys. It is not enough to simply require the owner of a compromised key to stop using it in favor of a fresh key pair. Outlying relying parties must be provided notice that the signatures they are processing—which validate with the still valid public key of the prior certificate—are no longer reliable.

As it relates to the proposed metrics, this option:

1. Responds effectively to population effects. Regardless of the size or symmetry of the population, the essential requirement to inhibit reliance on the certificate can be achieved to a first-order degree of compliance.

2. As it relates to timeliness metric, it fails to provide an asynchronous mechanism to notify relying parties of revocation events.

3. Suffers seriously from a need for frequent refreshes from centralized recertification services. In short, this option reduces public-key infrastructure to secret-key management.

4. Provides no means to deal with key compromise.

4 Conclusions

Independent of the technology and solution options there exists a less tractable problem of trust policy. Clearly the impact of state, national and international legislation bears respect in defining the extent of the revocation solution space. While the law historically describes actual usages of trade rather than create them, certificate issuance and acceptance policy has established a respected level of maturity. This body of knowledge would maintain that a CA not only has the right but may be held accountable for providing notice of revocation to its relying parties. Technologists considering options for revocation need to take into account their role as a enabler of such policies and practices.

On Certificate Revocation and Validation

Paul C. Kocher

Chief Scientist, ValiCert
3160 Bayshore Rd., Palo Alto, CA 94303, USA.
e-mail: pck@cryptography.com.

Abstract. Cryptosystems need to check whether the certificates and digital signatures they are given are valid before accepting them. In addition to providing cryptographically secure validity information, certificate revocation systems must satisfy a variety of challenging technical requirements. The traditional revocation techniques of Certificate Revocation Lists (CRLs) and on-line checking are described, as well as a newer technique, Certificate Revocation Trees (CRTs), based on Merkle hash trees. CRTs provide an efficient and highly-scalable way to distribute revocation information. CRT-based systems include Tree Issuers who compile revocation information, Confirmation Issuers who distribute elements from CRTs, and users who accept certificates. CRTs are gaining increased use worldwide for several reasons. They can be used with existing protocols and certificates, and enable the secure, reliable, scalable, and inexpensive validation of certificates (as well as digital signatures and other data).

1 Brief Introduction

Industry is embracing public key cryptography and certificates as a practical and secure way express privileges, relationships, and trust in a digital form. Without revocation support, however, many of the advantages of public key cryptography are lost.

For example, consider code signing. Before running a digitally signed program, the operating system might verify that the code has a signature from someone with a developer certificate. Without revocation checking, however, any signature made with any certified application developer's private key will be accepted. As a result, the compromise of any one developer's private key compromises the entire system unless users are able to reject signatures made with the compromised key. Without revocation, the security model is little better than having only one signing key and giving copies to all application developers.

Certification Authorities (CAs) and others who issue certificates and digital signatures are granting privileges, usually to a person, computer, or some data. In any large system, some digital signatures will be misused or need to be revoked. Secure revocation checking is essential because, unlike passports and other forms of physical identification, a compromised private key can be copied easily.

2 Technical Requirements

Implementing a good revocation system is difficult. The revocation status of any certificate (or signature, etc.) can change at any time, so certificate acceptors have to obtain fresh information quickly enough that attacks can be stopped. While specific requirements vary somewhat, a typical revocation system must provide the following:

Security Users must receive cryptographic assurance as to whether or not certificates are valid. An attacker should not be able to make a user accept a revoked certificate or reject a valid certificate as revoked. If required, the time and reason of revocation should also be provided securely.

Reliability The service must be available at all times, even if individual network components fail or are attacked. Reliability is essential for security so that a denial of service attack cannot be used to cause applications or users to accept bad certificates.

Scalability In a large system, such as secure e-mail on the Internet, revocation information must be provided from thousands of CAs to millions of users conducting billions of transactions, all at low cost.

Performance The entire system must be fast and efficient, without requiring excessive computational complexity or network overhead for any participant.

Memory Validation often has to be performed in constrained environments. Smartcards, for example, often can have less than a kilobyte of available RAM.

Bandwidth Communication bandwidth should be small and should scale well. By minimizing the amount of data that has to be exchanged, users experience shorter validation delays, less burden is placed on the network infrastructure, and the cost of providing the service is reduced.

Auditability While the requirements for the actual revocation decision itself vary widely between implementations, the cryptographic operations should be auditable.

Practicality The system must be easy to integrate into existing protocols and applications.

Manageability It must be possible to operate the system in a secure manner. Whenever possible, critical keys should be stored off-line where they are least vulnerable to attack.

Simplicity The cryptographic design must be unambiguous and easy to review and evaluate.

3 Certificate Revocation Lists

The traditional revocation technique is for CAs to issue Certificate Revocation Lists[1] (CRLs), which are digitally signed lists of the serial numbers of the certificates revoked by a CA. To test the validity of the certificates in a chain, a user obtains current CRLs from each CA in the chain and checks for the certificates' serial numbers. To be secure, CRLs must be issued regularly and frequently so that users can reject stale CRLs. Otherwise attackers could exploit compromised keys by preventing victims from receiving fresh CRLs. (The CRL expiration period determines the time required to halt the use of revoked certificates.) Users must thus download a new CRL with each transaction, unless a fresh CRL is cached.

Certificate revocation is not widely used today because CRLs fail to meet many of the needs listed above:

Reliability The CRL distribution mechanism is not standardized, and depends on the CA and the application. While big commercial CAs can issue CRLs on a predictable schedule and operate reliable servers, smaller CAs (such as companies issuing certificates to their employees or participants in systems with non-hierarchical trust models) often cannot.

Scalability A CRL's size is proportional to the number of revoked certificates, which in turn is some fraction of the total number of issued certificates. A large system can easily have many thousands of revoked certificates. CRLs of many megabytes are possible, particularly if revocation occurs often. Techniques such as CRL segmentation can help somewhat, but do not solve the problem.

Performance Validation performance is likely to be slow, since users have to make separate network connections to obtain the CRLs from each CA in a chain, download the CRLs, and verify each.

Memory Because CRLs do not have a maximum size, they often cannot be processed by smartcards or in other constained environments.

Bandwidth CRLs can require very large amounts of bandwidth. For example, the CRLs needed to validate an S/MIME message will often far exceed the size of the message. Bandwidth requirements for CRL distribution alone can potentially exceed a network's entire capacity.

Practicality Today, certificates seldom specify if CRLs are available or where they can be downloaded. As a result, it is often impossible for applications to find CRLs.

4 On-line Verification

Revocation systems can be on-line or off-line. In off-line systems (such as CRLs and CRTs), validity information is precomputed then distributed. In on-line schemes, validity proofs are constructed for each request, such as by a digitally signing a certificate identifier, the certificate status, and a user-specified challenge value (to prevent replay attacks).

On-line schemes are much more expensive to operate than CRT- based systems because the signer is involved in every secure transaction where validation is required – potentially requiring computing resources and tremendous bandwidth. Also, key management is difficult because the validation keys must be stored securely yet be connected to an untrusted network. However, true on-line schemes have the advantages that status information is always up-to-date and they are simpler to design and implement.

5 Background: ValiCert

My involvement with the revocation problem started with trying to design a secure electronic financial transaction system. The encryption algorithms, certificate issuance processes, etc. were available, but the system could not be built because existing certificate validation technologies were unworkable. My work on the problem led to the development of the (currently patent-pending) Certificate Revocation Tree (CRT) technology [2].

ValiCert, Inc. was founded to implement solutions to the revocation problem using CRTs and other technologies. Today ValiCert has developed a great deal of experience addressing real-world revocation requirements and is the only company in the world specializing in certificate validation and revocation.

6 Introduction to Certificate Revocation Trees

Certificate Revocation Trees (CRTs) are designed to solve the problems associated with CRLs and other revocation approaches.

The basic technology is best outlined with an example. Imagine a simple case where CA "Q" has revoked its certificates with serial numbers 5, 12, 13, 15, 20, 50, and 99. To build a CRT, the information from the CRLs is divided into a series of ranges that describe certificate statuses. For example, the range (5,12) for CA Q denotes "certificate 5 is bad, but any certificates larger than 5 and less than 12 are good." There exactly one range that describes each possible certificate serial number. For example, the range for certificate 12 would be (12,13), which means "certificate 12 is bad, but any certificates larger than 12 and less than 13 are good."

The ranges are packaged (with the reason for revocation, date of revocation, etc.) as data structures $L_0...L_{N-1}$, which are then used as leaf nodes to build a Merkle hash tree[3]. The tree's root and accompanying information such as when the tree expires are digitally signed (for example by ValiCert). Figure 1 illustrates the structure of a hash tree for the example above. In the hash tree, each node $N_{i,j}$ is formed by concatenating the values connecting from its left. For example, $N_{2,1}$ equals the hash of $N_{1,2}$ and $N_{1,3}$.

The tree and digitally signed root are distributed to Confirmation Issuers, servers that provide validation data to users. A user wishing to validate a certificate chain sends a data structure identifying the issuer and serial number of each certificate to any Confirmation Issuer. The Confirmation Issuer responds with the Merkle tree leaf for each certificate, the hashes that bind the leaves to the root, and the signed root. No cryptographic operations are required in this

176

process, as the tree's intermediate nodes can be precomputed. Thus, a single Confirmation Issuer can easily process millions of transactions per day.

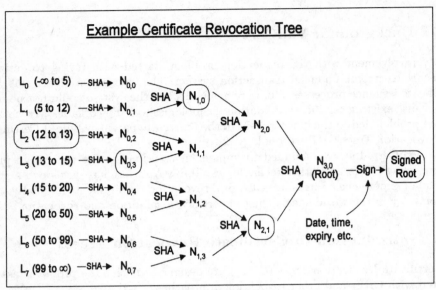

Figure 1: Sample Certificate Revocation Tree

The user confirms that the leaves describe the certificates in question, that the hashes correctly bind the CRT leaves to the root, and that the root is properly signed and not expired. Additional information, such as the date and reason for revocation, are also provided in the leaf nodes. As necessary, the user may also validate the root key (e.g., by verifying that it has been signed by the CA as authorized to provide validity status).

In Figure 1, the elements of the confirmation for certificate 12 are circled. The range L_2 is valid because it includes the correct serial number (i.e., indicates that 12 is revoked). Using the hash algorithm (e.g., SHA[4]), the user can derive $N_{0,2}$ from L_2. With the circled value $N_{0,3}$, the user can find $N_{1,1}$ by hashing the concatenation of $N_{0,2}$ and $N_{0,3}$. Next, $N_{2,0}$ can be found from $N_{1,0}$ and $N_{1,1}$. Finally, $N_{3,0}$ can be found from $N_{2,0}$ and $N_{2,1}$. If the derived value of $N_{3,0}$ matches the value in the signed root, the user is assured that L_2 is valid (assuming that the hash function and digital signature are secure).

Confirmations do not need to come from a trusted source because they are self-verifying; defective or expired confirmations will be rejected. Locations for Confirmation Issuers can thus be chosen for their network connectivity.

Users can even provide their own confirmations with their certificates. For example, senders of e-mail messages can include their own confirmations so that recipients need not fetch them separately. For receive-only wireless devices, piggybacked confirmations are essential.

The CRT architecture meets the technical requirements for most applications. The cryptographic security is provably as good as the underlying hash and signature functions. The only digital signing process (for the tree root) is performed off-line, so signing keys do not need to be managed on computers connected to the network. CRTs issuance is also auditable, since the process of repackaging revocation information into a CRT is predictable and verifiable using the CRT issuer's public key. Performance is excellent, since confirmation issuance requires almost no computational effort and only one signature verification is required to validate a certificate chain. For reliability, multiple Confirmation Issuers can be deployed, so any single failure will not cause an outage.

Communication bandwidth is small and extremely scalable, since the size of a confirmation only increases as the logarithm (base 2) of the number of leaves in the tree. (For example, in a tree with one trillion leaves, there will be 40 connecting hashes, requiring 800 bytes of hashes using 20-byte SHA hashes. With a 1028-bit (128-byte) RSA signature, the confirmation is still less than one kilobyte.) Because confirmations are small and the Confirmation Issuers can be placed close to the users (rather than at the CAs), network latency is minimized. For example, ValiCert's public Confirmation Issuers are placed on major Internet backbones. When an acceptable confirmation is piggybacked with a certificate, no extra network round trips are required.

While CRT systems are well suited to large infrastructures, they can be used in smaller environments as well. In a corporate network, for example, an internal confirmation issuer can provide confirmations for both internal certificates (for which revocation information is not globally distributed) as well as external certificates. In such cases, separate CRTs are typically used.

7 The Future

The need for fast, efficient revocation is not yet clearly understood by many customers, but will become crucial as public key systems are increasingly used to protect valuable assets and attackers learn to profit from compromised keys. Revocation checking will inevitably become a standard, required step whenever a certificate or digital signature is accepted.

References

1. "Information Technology - Open Systems Interconnection - The Directory: Authentication Framework," ITU-T Recommendation X.509 (1197 E), June 1997.
2. P. Kocher and A. Malpani, "Certificate Revocation Trees," ValiCert Inc. Technical Specification, http://www.valicert.com.
3. R. Merkle, "Secrecy, Authentication, and Public Key Systems," Ph.D. Dissertation, Department of Electrical Engineering, Stanford University, 1979.
4. National Institute of Standards and Technology, "Secure Hash Standard," Federal Information Processing Standards Publication 180-1, April 1995.

Can We Eliminate Certificate Revocation Lists?

Ronald L. Rivest

rivest@theory.lcs.mit.edu

http://theory.lcs.mit.edu/ rivest

MIT Laboratory for Computer Science, Cambridge, Mass. 02139

Abstract. We briefly consider certificate revocation lists (CRLs), and ask whether they could, and should, be eliminated, in favor of other mechanisms. In most cases, the answer seems to be "yes." We suggest some possible replacement mechanisms.

1 Introduction

The notion of a "digital certificate" was introduced by Kohnfelder in his 1978 MIT bachelor's thesis[2]. The idea, now common, was that a certificate is a digitally signed statement binding the key-holder's name to a public key. The signer (or issuer) is often called a certificate authority (CA). Since then, the notion of a certificate has been expanded to include:

- Labeling a public key with a label or attribute, such as a nickname, group name, SDSI name, account number, photo, etc.
- Authorizing a key (or all keys with a given label or name) to do something.

The SPKI/SDSI effort[1, 6] explores some of these varieties of certificates. In any case, a certificate typically specifies the issuer, the subject, an issue date, and an expiration date.

Certificates are an essential component of any infrastructure to support digital signatures. Suppose a "signer" Alice sends a signed message M to an "acceptor" (or "verifier") Bob. Alice signed the message with her private key, and Bob can verify her signature with her public key. The message M might be a piece of email, a request for a copy of a document that Bob has, or a contract.

Presumably, Bob is making some decision about the message, such as whether to ignore it altogether, or to reply to the request it contains. Otherwise why should Alice bother to sign it? And Bob's decision presumably depends on *which* key signed it, and the properties that have been associated with that key. If Bob makes a favorable decision, he *accepts* the message (and sends Alice a reply, or the document, or whatever).

In addition to the message M and her signature on M, Alice may send along other evidence or credentials that will help induce Bob to accept the message. Such evidence typically takes the form of a set of certificates. For example, Alice may include a certificate binding the name "Alice Smith" to her public key. Or, she may include a certificate authorizing her public key to request a copy of a confidential corporate memo.

The standard problem we now address, is that certificates have the potential of going "stale." Alice may change her last name, or be fired from the company. The name-binding certificate or the authorization certificate may no longer be appropriate, and the issuer may thus wish to "revoke" a previously-issued certificate.

Periodically-issued "certificate revocation lists" are one common approach to revoking certificates; each such list specifies what unexpired certificates have been revoked, and when the next CRL will be issued. (See, for example, Menezes et al.[3], section 13.6.3.) The CRL is signed by the issuer. For example, a company might issue a weekly CRL for its employee's certificates. The acceptor has to download the most recent CRL from each relevant CA in order to check the validity of the signer's certificates.

2 The acceptor should set recency requirements

Bob, the acceptor, will care that the certificates that Alice supplies as evidence in support of her message are not stale (e.g. revoked). He wants her evidence to be *recent*; he wants to see recently-issued certificates. Alice may supply day-old, week-old, or year-old certificates. Bob must decide whether they are acceptable evidence or not. He will need to set *"recency requirements"* for the decision he is going to make about whether or not to accept and act upon Alice's message.

We now come to one of the major points of this paper:

Proposition 1: *Recency requirements must be set by the acceptor, not by the certificate issuer (CA).*

The reason is that *the acceptor* is the one who is running the risk if his decision is wrong, not the CA. If "Bob" is an electronic badge-checker at a door to a sensitive room, he may want at most day-old evidence of employment at the company. Weekly-issued CRL's can't meet his requirements.

We thus have as a corollary:

Corollary 1: *Periodically-issued CRL's are wrong, because they are inconsistent with Proposition 1.*

One can also criticize CRL's since they make "negative statements." In line with the principles of good writing, one would prefer only to make "positive statements." One of the goals of this paper is to explore the extent to which a certificate infrastructure can be built entirely around positive statements.

3 The signer should supply all relevant evidence

This section proposes a design principle for certificate infrastructures. The justification for this principle is economy, rather than security. Nonetheless, we give it here as it helps round out our vision for certificate infrastructures.

Proposition 2. *The signer can (and should) supply* all *the evidence the acceptor needs, including recency information.*

Instead of having the *acceptor* query the CA for CRL's or the like, we ask that the *signer* obtain any such necessary evidence, and present it with his signature. We argue that

- The signer can query the CA just as well as the acceptor can.
- The recency information obtained may be useful again later to the signer.
- This structure puts any burden on the signer (the client), rather than on a possibly overworked acceptor (the server).
- In many case, this allows the acceptor (server) to be implemented in a *stateless* manner. For example, Bob can reply to Alice, "Sorry, please make sure that all of your evidence is at most one week old," and then forget about Alice until she comes back again, rather than having to rummage all over the Internet to see if Alice's certificates are still OK. A stateless server design is less vulnerable to denial-of-service attacks.

The only exception to having the signer provide all necessary evidence might be when the acceptor wants an "absolute recency check," for which he can do an on-line check himself.

4   New certificates are the best evidence

If Alice needs to get more recent evidence to convince Bob, then she might just as well get the relevant certificates re-issued.

Proposition 3. *The simplest form of "recency evidence" is just a (more-) recently-issued certificate.*

While this may seem to require an on-line CA, we note that a two-level scheme such as the elegant one suggested by Micali[4] can be used to allow an on-line agent to re-validate certificates previously issued by an off-line CA. Naor and Nissim[5] and Kocher[this proceedings] have related proposals.

This structure seems to give the right sort of behavior. If Bob is willing to take a month-old employment certificate, even if it might now be inaccurate, fine. If he demands a certificate that is at most a day old, then a recently-fired Alice won't be able to provide one.

5   Certificate guarantees

Of course, an issuer may know something about when or how often he might change his mind about the statement he is making in a certificate. A "standard" certificate says something like,

> [Standard certificate guarantee] "*This certificate is good until the expiration date. Unless, of course, you hear that it has been revoked.*"

Not a very useful statement. The acceptor is *always* required to check to see if a certificate has been revoked. SPKI/SDSI is at the other end of the spectrum:

[SPKI/SDSI certificate guarantee] *"This certificate is good until the expiration date. Period."*

This is much better for the acceptor; he *never* has to check whether a certificate has been revoked. In many cases, this can be made to work well enough by having certificates with reasonably short validity periods, or by restricting such certificates to applications where the issuer has the authority to make his statement valid for the stated validity period. However, in other cases an issuer might be tempted to have validity periods that are too long, and cause an acceptor to suffer some undue risk.

In addition, the issuer may not be willing to re-issue certificates arbitrarily; there may be some limits to what he is willing to do. We imagine that a more general guarantee might take this into account, as well as any other information about when the validity of the statement might change. We suggest the following sort of guarantee.

[Proposed general certificate guarantee] *"This certificate is definitely good from (date-time-1) until (date-time-2). The issuer also expects this certificate to be good until (date-time-3), but a careful acceptor might wish to demand a more recent certificate. This certificate should never be considered as valid after (date-time-3)."*

The certificate goes through three phases: (1) guaranteed, (2) probable, and (3) expired, in contrast to the standard certificate, which goes through (1) probable (2) expired, or the SPKI/SDSI certificate, which goes through (1) guaranteed, (2) expired. An acceptor may reasonably accept a certificate in its "probable" phase if there is little at risk. If necessary, the acceptor may insist that the signer go back to the issuer and get a certificate that is still in its guaranteed phase.

We conjecture that such a structure can yield great benefits in helping both signers and acceptors clearly define their intentions and security policies. By giving certificates a nonempty guaranteed phase, the issuer is informing potential acceptors about the length of time that the certificate is necessarily valid, and simultaneously protecting himself from needless queries for more recent certificates within this period. This is definitely an improvement over CRL's, whose certificates have no guaranteed period. Furthermore, the probable phase allows low-value or low-risk transactions to proceed without needless checking.

6   Key compromise is different

One of the standard reasons why a certificate might be revoked is that there is evidence that the key-holder has lost control of, or lost, his private key. We suggest that this issue should be separated out and handled differently. Ordinary certificates should not be revoked merely because the key is compromised. Rather, the signer should present separate evidence to the acceptor that the key has *not* been compromised. Since, in this framework, the no-compromise evidence is separate, the ordinary certificates can continue to be "valid" even though the key has been compromised. In this way, ordinary CA's do not have to deal with this issue at all.

How does this work?

First of all, we propose that the "standard" way of declaring a key to be compromised is to publish a note, *signed by that key* declaring it to be compromised, or dead. We call this note a "suicide note." PGP uses this mechanism. So the key-holder can notify anyone that his key has been compromised by signing and distributing such a note. The key-holder might save such a note in a safe place, in case his private key is lost. Note that if a key gets published on the Internet, anyone can sign such a suicide note.

There is a very interesting question, which is seldom addressed in the conventional certificate literature, regarding the question as to *who should be allowed to declare a key as compromised or lost, and on what basis?* Clearly the original owner of the key should be able to; but who else?

For example, suppose Bob makes up a public-key pair, and then registers to use this pair with an on-line service that charges an annual fee. In return for his fee, Bob obtains an authorization certificate that enables him to use the service. Bob then distributes the private key to all of his friends so that they may obtain the service for free. Should the service, which now has evidence that Bob has distributed his key, be able to declare the key as compromised? Perhaps. It is reasonable to suppose that some services might want to receive an escrowed copy of a suicide note in return for the authorization certificate they are issuing, so that the signer would be discouraged from sharing his key. We'll see a slightly better approach in a second.

Now, back to the basic scenario. Alice presents a signed message M to Bob, together with a collection of certificates. Bob is happy with the certificates, but wants to know if Alice's key has been compromised. How can Alice convince Bob that her key has *not* been declared compromised?

We propose the use of a new kind of agent, called a "key compromise agent" (KCA), or a "suicide bureau"(SB). There may be many such agents; they form an association that certifies its members, and they share a high-speed reliable network. When Alice creates her public key pair, she registers the public key with one such SB. The suicide bureaus listen attentively to their network and elsewhere for any suicide notes signed by keys belonging to users registered with them. Anyone who receives a suicide note can forward it to any SB, who will broadcast it on the SB network.

Alice's SB can then give Alice a "certificate of health" of the form:

[Certificate of health] *"The public key (....) was registered with this bureau on (date). Since then, no evidence has been received that the key has been lost or compromised."*

Alice can then present this certificate of health to Bob with her other certificates. Bob can demand a more recent health certificate, if he wishes.

With this, we see that we have now eliminated CRL's entirely, and can have a signer present evidence of the desired sort entirely in the form of certificates.

The signer and acceptor can negotiate the recency required on these certificates, and the signer can go off and obtain more recent ones as necessary.

As a final wrinkle, we note that the signer might not need to give a suicide note to a service provider. A weaker form of delegation might be better. The signer could sign an authorization certificate authorizing the service provider to transmit a "bill of bad health" to the SB's. The SB might then no longer issue a certificate of health to the signer. This is not much different than giving a suicide note in escrow to the service provider, but it does help the SB's clearly identify the source of their information. (A suicide note sent by anonymous email would be acted upon, but it is preferable to have the sources of such information identified when possible. The authorization certificate allows that.)

7 Conclusions

We see that one can do without CRL's. Indeed, it is possible to organize a certificate infrastructure so that a signer can present just a collection of certificates to the acceptor as evidence in support of the signature and the signed message. The acceptor and signer might negotiate about the recency of some of the certificates, in which case it is the signer's responsibility to get more recent replacements. We suggest that such a framework would be an improvement over the use of CRL's.

Acknowledgments

I'd like to thank Stuart Stubblebine for useful comments and suggestions. The reader might profitably refer to some of his very relevant related work [7].

References

1. Carl M. Ellison. SPKI certificate documentation. (See http://www.clark.net/pub/cme/html/spki.html), 1998.
2. Loren M. Kohnfelder. Towards a practical public-key cryptosystem. B.S. Thesis, supervised by L. Adleman, May 1978.
3. Alfred J. Menezes, Paul C. van Oorschot, and Scott A. Vanstone. *Handbook of Applied Cryptography*. CRC Press, 1997.
4. Silvio Micali. Efficient certificate revocation. Technical Report TM-542b, MIT Laboratory for Computer Science, March 22, 1996.
5. Moni Naor and Kobbi Nissim. Certificate revocation and certificate update. In *Proceedings 7th USENIX Security Symposium (San Antonio, Texas)*, Jan 1998.
6. Ronald L. Rivest and Butler Lampson. SDSI–a simple distributed security infrastructure. (see SDSI web page at http://theory.lcs.mit.edu/ cis/sdsi.html).
7. Stuart Stubblebine. Recent-secure authentication: Enforcing revocation in distributed systems. In *Proceedings 1995 IEEE Symposium on Research in Security and Privacy*, pages 224–234, May 1995. (Oakland).

Group Blind Digital Signatures: A Scalable Solution to Electronic Cash

Anna Lysyanskaya[1] and Zulfikar Ramzan[1]

Laboratory for Computer Science,
Massachusetts Institute of Technology,
Cambridge MA 02139,
{anna, zulfikar}@theory.lcs.mit.edu

Abstract. In this paper we construct a practical group blind signature scheme. Our scheme combines the already existing notions of blind signatures and group signatures. It is an extension of Camenisch and Stadler's Group Signature Scheme [5] that adds the blindness property. We show how to use our group blind signatures to construct an electronic cash system in which multiple banks can securely distribute anonymous and untraceable e-cash. Moreover, the identity of the e-cash issuing bank is concealed, which is conceptually novel. The space, time, and communication complexities of the relevant parameters and operations are independent of the group size.

1 Introduction

1.1 Distributed Electronic Banking

Consider a scheme in which there is a large group of banks, monitored by the country's Central Bank (e.g. the US Treasury), where each bank can dispense electronic cash. We want such a scheme to have the following properties:

1. No bank should be able to trace any e-cash it issues. Therefore, just as with paper money, people can spend their e-cash anonymously.
2. A vendor only needs to invoke a single universal verification procedure, based on the group public key, to ensure the validity of any e-cash he receives. This procedure works regardless of which bank issued the e-cash. This makes the vendor's task much easier since he only needs to know the single group public key.
3. There is a single public key for the entire group of banks. The size of this public key is independent of the number of banks. Moreover, the public key should not be modified if more banks join the group. Thus, the scheme is still practical even if there are a large number of participating banks.
4. Given a valid piece of e-cash only the Central Bank can tell which bank in the group issued it. No vendor can even determine the bank from which the customer got her e-cash even though the vendor can easily check that the e-cash is valid. This restriction gives an extra layer of anonymity since we conceal both the spender's identity and the bank she uses.

5. Neither the Central Bank nor any bank can issue cash on behalf of another bank; i.e. no bank or any other entity, including the Central Bank can "frame" another bank.

In this paper we implement such a scheme using Group Blind Digital Signatures. Many previous electronic cash schemes focus on a model in which a single bank distributes all the e-cash. In real life, one would like for more than one bank to be able to dispense electronic money. Our scheme is unique since it considers scalability as a criterion in the design of electronic cash systems. Moreover, our scheme is conceptually novel since we conceal the bank's identity in addition to the spender's.

1.2 Blind Digital Signatures

Blind Digital Signatures were introduced by Chaum [7] to allow for spender anonymity in Electronic Cash systems. Such signatures require that a signer be able to sign a document without knowing its contents. Moreover, should the signer ever see the document/signature pair, he should have no recollection of it (even though he can verify that the signature is indeed his). In the electronic cash scenario, a document corresponds to an electronic coin, and the signer represents a bank. The spender retains anonymity in any transaction that involves electronic coins since they are blindly signed.

Blind Signatures have been looked at extensively in the literature [6, 16, 14]. Like some of the previous schemes, the security of our scheme is proven under the random oracle model [16, 1, 11]. Complexity based proofs of security are, however, considered much stronger. Unfortunately, the only known Blind Signature Scheme with such a proof is far too impractical [14].

1.3 Group Digital Signatures

In a group digital signature scheme, members of a given group are allowed to sign on behalf of the entire group. In addition, the signatures can be verified using a single *group public key*. Also, once a document is signed, no one, except a designated group manager, can determine which member of the group signed it. Companies can use group signatures to validate price lists, press releases or digital contracts; customers would only need to know a single company public key to verify signatures. Companies can then conceal their internal structure, but can still determine which employee signed a given document. Group Digital Signatures were first introduced and implemented by Chaum and van Heyst [9]. Recently, Camenisch and Stadler [5] presented the first group signature scheme for which the size of the group public key remains independent of the group size, as do the time, space, and, communication complexities of the necessary operations; in previous schemes [9, 3, 10] the size of the public key grew with the size of the group which is impractical for large groups. We extend [5] by showing how to add the blindness property to their scheme. This may have applications besides the electronic cash and voting schemes described below.

1.4 Using Group Blind Signatures for Electronic Cash

If we combine the properties of Blind Signatures and Group Signatures, we get what we call *Group Blind Digital Signatures*. We now show how to use group blind digital signatures to achieve a scheme in which multiple banks can securely distribute anonymous and untraceable electronic cash. First we give the main ideas, and then we address some of the relevant problems. The basic techniques are due to Chaum [7].

All the banks form a group and their manager will be the country's Central Bank (e.g. U.S. Treasury or the Federal Reserve). If Alice wants to withdraw e-cash from her bank, she first creates an electronic coin C. Her bank applies a *group blind signature* to C and it withdraws the appropriate amount from Alice's account. Alice now gives C and the bank's signature on C to a vendor. The vendor uses the *group public key* to verify the bank's signature on the coin. If the coin is valid, the vendor gives Alice her merchandise, and gives the coin to his bank. The vendor's bank double checks the coin's validity, adds it to a global list of coins that have already been spent (to prevent Alice from double spending), and credits the vendor's account. Now, since Alice's bank is signing blindly, it is possible for Alice to trick her bank by having it sign something other than what it was supposed to sign. We can prevent this by requiring that the bank have different secret signing keys to authorize different dollar amounts. For example, one key could correspond to a \$5 withdrawal, another to a \$10 withdrawal, and so on [15]. There are several other ways to prevent this kind of fraud [21], but we omit them here.

1.5 Advantages of Our Scheme

Previous work on electronic cash systems focused on models in which a *single* bank distributes all the e-cash. We, on the other hand, show how to implement an efficient *multiple* bank model. Our scheme is useful for several reasons. First, the vendor only has to know a single group public key to check the validity of any e-cash he receives. Second, the spender's identity is completely anonymous to both the vendor and his bank since the signature is blind. Third, neither the vendor nor the vendor's bank can determine the user's bank (thus providing an extra layer of anonymity). Fourth, the bank which receives the e-cash just needs to check it with the group public key. Finally, if there are any conflicts regarding which bank issued some piece of e-cash, the group manager (e.g. the U.S. Treasury) can intervene and establish the identity of that bank.

1.6 Disadvantages of Our Scheme

Our scheme is an *online* scheme. That is, the vendor must engage in a protocol with the bank each time he receives an e-coin from Alice. Otherwise Alice could potentially use the same electronic coin for several different transactions because her identity is concealed. This extra interaction between the vendor and bank each time a transaction is made is a disadvantage. It is especially costly for small transactions. We can convert our scheme into an offline scheme if we make a minor modification to our underlying model. We outline this modification later in the paper. Another important drawback of our scheme is that Alice must engage in an expensive several round interactive protocol with her bank each time she wants a new e-coin. Also, our scheme requires $O(l)$ exponentiations per signature, where l is the security parameter. Unfortunately, this parameter must be set to at least 64 for the scheme to be secure. Finally, our scheme does not address issues such as *divisibility* and *transferability*. We leave these issues as open problems.

1.7 Making Our Scheme Offline

We can make our scheme offline under a slight compromise in spender anonymity. In this case we allow for a *passive trustee* who can revoke the anonymity of the spender. To start with, in addition to the banks forming a group, all the spenders in our system form a group – and a trusted third party (passive trustee) can act as the group manager of the spender group. The spender engages in the withdrawal protocol as specified earlier. In addition, after she receives a piece of e-cash, she applies the spender group signature to it. Now, no one, except the group mangager (trusted third party) can determine the identity of the spender, so her identity is still somewhat anonymous. The vendor verifies the validity of e-cash he receives just like he did before, except he must also check that the spender's group signature is authentic. Now, because the identity of the spender is encoded into the cash via a group signature, the vendor doesn't have to worry about dealing with the bank whenever he receives an electronic coin. He can wait until the end of the day and cash all his coins in one shot. If there are any conflicts, then the trusted third party can intervene and determine the identity of the spender. These trusted third parties are commonly refered to as passive trustees because they only have to be present when the user opens her bank account, and when there is a dispute [4].

2 The Group Blind Signature Model

Our group blind signature model extends Camenisch and Stadler's [5] group signature model by adding blindness. Our scheme consists of several signers (members of the group), their group manager, and several users. We combine two concepts: blind signatures [6, 16, 14] and group signatures [5, 9, 3, 10]. Our model allows the members of a group to sign messages on behalf of the group such that the following properties hold for the resulting signature:

1. **Blindness of Signatures:** The signer is unable to view the messages he signs. Moreover, the signer should have no recollection of having signed a particular document even though he can verify that he did indeed sign it. This is new with our scheme.
2. **Unforgeability:** Only group members can issue valid signatures.

3. **Undeniable Signer Identity:** The group manager can always establish the identity of the member who issued a valid signature.
4. **Signer Anonymity:** It is easy to check that a message/signature pair was signed by a group member, but only the group manager can determine which member issued the signature.
5. **Unlinkability:** Two message-signature pairs where the signature was obtained from the same signer cannot be linked.
6. **Security Against Framing Attacks:** Neither the group manager, nor the group members can sign on behalf of other group members.

A group blind signature scheme allows the following five procedures:

Setup: a probabilistic algorithm that generates the group's public key $\mathcal{Y}$ and a secret administration key $\mathcal{S}$ for the group manager.
Join: an interactive protocol between the group manager and the new group member Alice that produces Alice's secret key x, her membership certificate v, and her public key z.
Sign: an interactive protocol between group member Alice and an external user, which, on input message m from the user and Alice's secret key x produces a signature s on m that satisfies the properties above.
Verify: an algorithm which on input $(m, s, \mathcal{Y})$, determines if s is a valid signature for the message m with respect to the group public key $\mathcal{Y}$.
Open: an algorithm which, on input $(s, \mathcal{S})$ returns the identity of the group member who issued the signature s together with a proof of this fact.

Our scheme is the first to extend group signatures to allow for blind signing. As in [5], the following parameters are of interest; all but the last one are constant in the size of the group, but linear in the security parameters:

– the size of the group public key $\mathcal{Y}$.
– the length of signatures.
– the efficiency of the protocols **Setup, Join, Sign, Verify**.
– the efficiency of the protocol **Open**.

Just as in [5] the protocol **Open** can be made to execute in constant time with a compromise in security of the scheme; the basic scheme's **Open** takes time linear in the size of the group.

3 Techniques

In this section, we present some well-studied techniques for proving knowledge of discrete logarithms and related problems. We show how they can be extended to serve as blind signatures of knowledge, which are the building blocks of our group blind signature scheme.

3.1 Preliminaries, Assumptions, Notation

Basic Notation We use "," to denote the concatenation of two (binary) strings, or of binary representations of integers and group elements. We use $c[i]$ to denote the i-th leftmost bit of the string c. For a set A, "$a \in_R A$" means that a is chosen uniformly at random from A. For an integer n, $\mathbb{Z}_n$ denotes the ring of integers modulo n, and $\mathbb{Z}_n^*$ denotes the multiplicative group modulo n.

The Discrete Logarithm Problem and Some Variations Let G be a cyclic group of order n generated by some $g \in G$ (hence $G = \langle g \rangle$). Let $a \in \mathbb{Z}_n^*$. The discrete logarithm of $y \in G$ to the base g is the *smallest* positive integer x such that $g^x = y$. The double discrete logarithm of $y \in G$ to the bases g and a is the smallest positive integer x satisfying:

$$g^{(a^x)} = y \, , \tag{1}$$

if such an x exists. G, g, n, and a can be chosen such that the double discrete logarithm problem is infeasible to solve. An e-th root of the discrete logarithm of $y \in G$ to the base g is an integer x satisfying

$$g^{(x^e)} = y \, , \tag{2}$$

if such an x exists. If the factorization of n is unknown, computing e-th roots in $\mathbb{Z}_n^*$ is assumed to be infeasible [17].

Use of a Hash Function We also assume the existence of an ideal hash function $\mathcal{H} \colon \{0,1\}^* \mapsto \{0,1\}^k$ satisfying the following properties ($\mathcal{H}_l$ denotes the first l bits of $\mathcal{H}$):

1. For a specified parameter l, $\mathcal{H}_l(x)$ contains an equal number of 0's and 1's.
2. $\mathcal{H}_l$ is collision-resistant.
3. $\mathcal{H}$ hides all partial information about its input.

If we have a hash function that satisfies the second and third properties, we can convert it into one which satisfies the first property as well: suppose $\mathcal{H}$ satisfies properties two and three. Consider $\mathcal{H}'(x) = \mathcal{H}(x) \circ \overline{\mathcal{H}(x)}$ where $\overline{\mathcal{H}(x)}$ is the bitwise complement of $\mathcal{H}(x)$ and $\circ$ denotes the concatenation operator. Then $\mathcal{H}'(x)$ has an equal number of 0's and 1's.

We use these assumptions to prove security in the random oracle model [16, 1, 11].

3.2 Blind Signatures of Knowledge

A signature of knowledge is a construct that uniquely corresponds to a given message m that cannot be obtained without the help of a party that knows a secret such as the discrete logarithm of a given $y \in G$ to the base g ($\langle g \rangle =$

G). A proof of knowledge is a way for one person to convince another person that he knows some fact without actually revealing that fact. In a signature of knowledge, the signer ties his knowledge of a secret to the message being signed. A signature of knowledge is used both for the purpose of signing a message and proving knowledge of a secret. Signatures of knowledge were used by Camenisch and Stadler [5]. Their construction is based on the Schnorr signature scheme [19] to prove knowledge. All the signatures of knowledge proposed by [5] can be proved secure in the random oracle model and their interactive versions are zero-knowledge.

To construct blind signatures of knowledge, we modify some of the signatures of knowledge constructs proposed by [5]. The proofs of security that work for [5] also work for our signatures of knowledge.

The first signature of knowledge we consider, both in the regular and blind settings, is the signature of knowledge of the discrete logarithm of a given $y \in G$ to a given base g ($\langle g \rangle = G$).

Definition 1. *An $(l+1)$-tuple $(c, s_1, ..., s_l) \in \{0,1\}^k \times \mathbb{Z}_n^l$ satisfying*

$$c = \mathcal{H}_l(m,y,g,g^{s_1}y^{c[1]},g^{s_2}y^{c[2]},\ldots,g^{s_l}y^{c[l]}) \tag{3}$$

is a signature of knowledge of the discrete logarithm of $y \in G$ to the base g on a message m, with respect to security parameter l, denoted

$$SKLOG_l[\alpha \mid y = g^{\alpha}](m) \tag{4}$$

In general we use Greek letters to represent values whose knowledge will be proven by the signer, and Roman letters to denote values that are known to both the signer and the user.

If the signer does not know the discrete logarithm of y to the base G it is infeasible for him to construct the $l+1$ tuple $(c, s_1, \ldots, s_l)$ satisfying the above equation. We can think of the above definition as an interactive protocol in which the $c[i]$'s represent challenges; the hash function $\mathcal{H}$ serves to remove the interaction. If the prover knows x such that $x = log_g(y)$, he computes $r_1, r_2, ..., r_l \in_R \mathbb{Z}_n$, plugs $m,y,g,g^{r_1},g^{r_2},\ldots,g^{r_l}$ to hash function $\mathcal{H}$ to obtain random challenge c, and obtains $s_1, s_2, \ldots, s_l$ by setting

$$s_i = \begin{cases} r_i & \text{if } c[i] = 0 \\ r_i - x \pmod{n} & \text{otherwise} \end{cases} \tag{5}$$

The signature of knowledge constructed above is not blind. There is, however, a way to construct a blind signature that would satisfy Defintion 3.1. Consider the following interactive protocol between a signer and a user:

User Round 0: User wants message m signed and sends a sign request to the signer.
Signer Round 1:
    1. Obtain $\{r_i \in_R \mathbb{Z}_n\}$, $1 \le i \le l$.
    2. Set $P_i := g^{r_i}$, $1 \le i \le l$.
    3. Send $\{P_i\}$ to the user, thus commiting to the $\{P_i\text{'s}\}$.

User Round 2:

1. Obtain a random permutation $\sigma : \{1, \ldots, l\} \mapsto \{1, \ldots, l\}$ and set $Q_i := P_{\sigma(i)}$, $1 \le i \le l$. (σ will be used to blind the result of $\mathcal{H}$.)
2. Obtain random $a_1, \ldots, a_l$, and set $R_i := Q_i g^{a_i}$ $1 \le i \le l$. ($\{a_i\}$ are used to blind the inputs to $\mathcal{H}$.)
3. Calculate $c := \mathcal{H}_l(m, y, g, R_1, \ldots, R_l)$.
4. Calculate c' such that $c'[i] = c[\sigma^{-1}(i)]$.
5. Send c' to the signer.

Signer Round 3:

1. Using secret x (recall $x = \log_g y$) compute for

$$1 \le i \le l, t_i = \begin{cases} r_i & \text{if } c'[i] = 0 \\ r_i - x \,(\text{mod } n) & \text{otherwise} \end{cases} \tag{6}$$

2. Send $\{t_i\}$ to the user.

User Round 4:

1. Verify that $P_i = g^{t_i} y^{c'[i]}$.
2. Compute $s_i := t_{\sigma(i)} + a_i \,(\text{mod } n)$.
3. Output $(c, s_1, \ldots, s_l)$.

Lemma 1. *The protocol described above produces a blind signature, that is, $(c, s_1, \ldots, s_l)$ is a signature on m that cannot be linked to the signer's view of the protocol.*

Informal proof:

1. $(c, s_1, \ldots, s_l)$ is a signature on m, because $c = \mathcal{H}_l(m, y, g, R_1, \ldots, R_i, \ldots, R_l)$, where $R_i = Q_i g^{a_i} = P_{\sigma(i)} g^{a_i} = g^{t_{\sigma(i)}} y^{c'[\sigma(i)]} g^{a_i} = g^{s_i - a_i} g^{a_i} y^{c'[\sigma(i)]} = g^{s_i} y^{c'[\sigma(i)]} = g^{s_i} y^{c[i]}$.
2. $(c, s_1, \ldots, s_l)$ cannot be linked to the signer's view of the protocol, because σ blinds c and $\{a_i\}$ blind $\{s_i\}$.

Also note that since in the proposed protocol the signer does not provide more information than in the regular proof of knowledge, our protocol is zero-knowledge.

We now define signatures of knowledge based on variations of the discrete logarithm problem and extend the protocol above to construct blind versions of these signatures.

One important variation is the representation problem, studied in [2,5]. It is a direct generalization of the signature of knowledge discussed above, except we have $y_1, \ldots, y_w$ instead of just one y, and $g_1, \ldots, g_v$, instead of just one g. We omit a more formal treatment of signatures of knowledge based on the representation problem due to space limitations.

We also employ signatures of knowledge of the double discrete logarithm and of the roots of discrete logarithms introduced in [5] and show how to make them blind signatures.

Definition 2. *A signature of knowledge of a double discrete logarithm of y to the bases g and a, on message m, with security parameter $l \le k$ denoted*

$SKLOGLOG_l[\alpha \mid y = g^{(a^\alpha)}](m)$, *is an* $(l+1)$-*tuple* $(c, s_1, ..., s_l) \in \{0,1\}^l \times \mathbf{Z}^l$ *satisfying the equation*

$$c = \mathcal{H}_l(m,y,g,a,P_1,\ldots,P_l), \ \text{where} \ P_i = \begin{cases} g^{(a^{s_i})} \ \text{if} \ c[i] = 0 \\ y^{(a^{s_i})} \ \text{otherwise} \end{cases} \tag{7}$$

It can be shown, in the random oracle model, that a $SKLOGLOG_l[\alpha \mid y = g^{(a^\alpha)}](m)$ can be computed only if a double discrete logarithm $x \in \mathbf{Z}_n$ of the group element $y \in G$ to the bases $g \in G$ and $a \in \mathbf{Z}_n^*$ is known (where $G = \langle g \rangle$ and $|G| = n$). One does not necessarily know the order of $a \in \mathbf{Z}_n^*$, but it is easy to find λ such that $|\mathbf{Z}_n^*| \leq 2^\lambda - 1$). Knowing x, λ, and a $\mu > 0$ compute the signature as follows (we use μ to make sure that the distribution of r_i is indistinguishable from the distribution of $r_i - x$, for a secret $x \leq 2^\lambda - 1$):

1. For $1 \leq i \leq l$, generate random $2^\lambda \leq r_i \leq 2^{\lambda+\mu} - 1$.
2. Set $P_i = g^{(a^{r_i})}$ and compute $c = \mathcal{H}_l(m,y,g,a,P_1,\ldots,P_l)$.
3. Set $s_i = \begin{cases} r_i & \text{if} \ c[i] = 0 \\ r_i - x & \text{otherwise} \end{cases}$

To obtain a blind $SKLOGLOG_l[\alpha \mid y = g^{(a^\alpha)}](m)$, we propose the following protocol, quite similar to the one we use for $SKLOG$:

User Round 0: User wants message m signed and sends a sign request to the signer.
Signer Round 1:
    1. For $1 \leq i \leq l$, generate random $2^\lambda \leq r_i \leq 2^{\lambda+\mu} - 1$.
    2. Set $P_i := g^{(a^{r_i})}$.
    3. Send $\{P_i\}$ to the user, commiting to them.
User Round 2:
    1. Obtain a random permutation $\sigma : \{1,\ldots,l\} \mapsto \{1,\ldots,l\}$ and set $Q_i := P_{\sigma(i)}$.
    2. For $1 \leq i \leq l$, generate random $2^{\lambda+\mu} \leq b_i \leq 2^{\lambda+2\mu} - 1$, and set $R_i := Q_i^{(a^{b_i})}$.
    3. Calculate $c := \mathcal{H}_l(m,y,g,R_1,\ldots,R_l)$.
    4. Calculate c' such that $c'[i] = c[\sigma^{-1}(i)]$.
    5. Send c' to the signer.
Signer Round 3:
    1. Compute, for $1 \leq i \leq l$, $t_i = \begin{cases} r_i & \text{if} \ c'[i] = 0 \\ r_i - x(\text{mod} \ n) & \text{otherwise} \end{cases}$
    2. Send $\{t_i\}$ to the user.
User Round 4:
    1. Verify that $P_i = \begin{cases} g^{(a^{t_i})} \ \text{if} \ c'[i] = 0 \\ y^{(a^{t_i})} \ \text{otherwise} \end{cases}$
    2. Compute $s_i := t_{\sigma(i)} + a_i$, $1 \leq i \leq l$.
    3. Output $(c, s_1, ..., s_l)$.

Lemma 2. *The protocol described above produces a blind* $SKLOGLOG_l(\alpha \mid y = g^{(a^\alpha)})$.

Informal proof:

1. $(c, s_1, ..., s_l)$ is a signature on m, because $c = \mathcal{H}_l(m,y,g,a,R_1, ..., R_l)$ where

$$R_i = Q_i^{(a^{a_i})} = P_{\sigma(i)}^{(a^{a_i})} = \begin{cases} g^{(a^{t_{\sigma(i)}})(a^{a_i})} = g^{(a^{s_i})} & \text{if } c'[\sigma(i)] = c[i] = 0 \\ y^{(a^{t_{\sigma(i)}})(a^{a_i})} = y^{(a^{s_i})} & \text{if } c'[\sigma(i)] = c[i] = 1 \end{cases}$$

   which satisfies the definition of $SKLOGLOG_l$.

2. $(c, s_1, ..., s_l)$ cannot be linked to the signer's view of the protocol, because σ blinds c and $a_1, ..., a_l$ blind $s_1, ..., s_l$.

Definition 3. *A signature of knowledge of an e-th root of the discrete logarithm of y to the base g, on message m, denoted $SKROOTLOG_l[\alpha \mid y = g^{(\alpha^e)}](m)$, is an $(l+1)$-tuple $(c, s_1, ..., s_l) \in \{0,1\}^k \times \mathbb{Z}_n^{*\,l}$ satisfying the following equation:*

$$c = \mathcal{H}_l(m,y,g,e,P_1, ..., P_l), \quad where P_i = \begin{cases} g^{(s_i^e)} & if\ c[i] = 0 \\ y^{(s_i^e)} & otherwise \end{cases}$$

It can be shown that such signature can only be computed if the e-th root of the discrete logarithm x of y to the base g is known; where $x \in \mathbb{Z}_n^*$, $y \in G$, $|G| = n$, $\langle g \rangle = G$, $e \in \mathbb{Z}_n$. When x is known, construct $SKROOTLOG_l[\alpha \mid y = g^{(\alpha^e)}](m)$ as follows:

1. For $1 \leq i \leq l$, generate random $r_i \in \mathbb{Z}_n^*$.
2. Set $P_i = g^{(r_i^e)}$ and compute $c = \mathcal{H}_l(m,y,g,e,P_1, ..., P_l)$.
3. Set $s_i = \begin{cases} r_i & \text{if } c[i] = 0 \\ r_i/x \pmod{n} & \text{otherwise} \end{cases}$

The $SKROOTLOG_l$ can also be constructed blindly, by applying a similar protocol to the one outlined for $SKLOG_l$ and $SKLOGLOG_l$. We omit this here due to lack of space.

4 Our Group Blind Signature Scheme

Camenisch and Stadler [5] have two schemes for group signatures: their *basic* scheme and their *efficient* scheme. Their *efficient* scheme is less secure and therefore in this extended abstract we concentrate on extending their *basic* scheme to allow for blind signatures. However, our techniques apply to both.

4.1 Setup

To set up the group signature scheme, as in [5], the group manager chooses a security parameter l and computes the following values:

1. An RSA Public Key (n,e), where the length of n is at least $2l$ bits.
2. A cyclic group $G = \langle g \rangle$ of order n for which computing discrete logarithms is hard. In particular, we can choose G to be a cyclic subgroup of $\mathbb{Z}_p^*$ where p is a prime and $n|(p-1)$.
3. An element $a \in \mathbb{Z}_p^*$ where a has large multiplicative order modulo all the prime factors of n.
4. An upper bound λ on the length of the secret keys and a constant $\mu > 1$.

The group's public key is $\mathcal{Y} = (n, e, G, g, a, \lambda, \mu)$.

4.2 Join

As in [5], if Alice wants to join the group she picks a *secret key* $x \in_R \{0, 1, \ldots, 2^\lambda - 1\}$ and calculates $y = a^x \ (mod \ n)$ and the *membership key* $z = g^y$. Alice commits to y and sends (y,z) to the group manager and proves to him that she knows x (without actually revealing x) using techniques similar to the signature of knowledge of discrete logarithm. If the group manager is convinced that Alice knows x he gives her a *membership certificate* $v \equiv (y + 1)^{1/e} \ (mod \ n)$. It is an additional security assumption due to [5] that computing v without factoring n is hard.

4.3 Sign and Verify

Unlike [5], our signature construction protocol is blind. When responding to a sign request, the signer does the following:

1. Obtain $q \in_R \mathbf{Z}_n^*$ and set

$$
\begin{aligned}
\tilde{g} &:= g^q \\
\tilde{z} &:= \tilde{g}^y
\end{aligned}
\tag{8}
$$

2. Obtain random $2^\lambda \leq u_i \leq 2^{\lambda+\mu} - 1$, for $1 \leq i \leq l$ and set

$$
P_i^{SKLOGLOG} := \tilde{g}^{(a^{u_i})}, 1 \leq i \leq l
\tag{9}
$$

3. Obtain random $v_i \in \mathbf{Z}_n^*$, for $1 \leq i \leq l$ and set

$$
P_i^{SKROOTLOG} := \tilde{g}^{(v_i^e)}, 1 \leq i \leq l
\tag{10}
$$

4. Send $(\tilde{g}, \ \tilde{z}, \{P_i^{SKLOGLOG}\}, \{P_i^{SKROOTLOG}\})$ to the user.

In turn, the user does the following:

1. Obtains $b \in_R \{1 \ldots 2^\lambda - 1\}$, and $f \in_R \mathbf{Z}_n^*$, and sets $w := (af)^{eb} \ (mod \ n)$.
2. Set

$$
\begin{aligned}
\hat{g} &:= \tilde{g}^w \\
\hat{z} &:= \tilde{z}^w \\
\hat{P}_i^{SKLOGLOG} &:= (P_i^{SKLOGLOG})^w \\
\hat{P}_i^{SKROOTLOG} &:= (P_i^{SKROOTLOG})^w
\end{aligned}
\tag{11}
$$

3. Execute rounds 2, 3, 4 of the blind $SKLOGLOG$ and blind $SKROOTLOG$ protocols, taking $\{\hat{P}_i^{SKLOGLOG}\}$ and $\{\hat{P}_i^{SKROOTLOG}\}$ as commitment values and adjusting the responses $\{t_i^{SKLOGLOG}\}$ and $\{t_i^{SKROOTLOG}\}$ by adding eb for $SKLOGLOG$ and multiplying by $(af)^b$ for $SKROOTLOG$ to obtain

$$
\begin{aligned}
V_1 &= SKLOGLOG_l[\alpha \mid \hat{z} = \hat{g}^{a^\alpha}](m) \\
V_2 &= SKROOTLOG_l[\beta \mid \hat{z}\hat{g} = \hat{g}^{\beta^e}](m)
\end{aligned}
\tag{12}
$$

The resulting signature on the message m consists of $(\hat{g}, \hat{z}, V_1, V_2)$ and can be verified by checking correctness of V_1 and V_2.

Informal proof of the unforgeability of the signature: It is impossible to construct the signature without the help of a group member, because V_1 proves that the signer must know a membership key, and V_2 proves that the signer also knows the membership certificate that corresponds to that key. That is, V_1 shows that $\hat{z} = \hat{g}^{a^\alpha}$, and therefore:

$$\hat{z}\hat{g} = \hat{g}^{(a^\alpha + 1)} \tag{13}$$

for an integer α that the signer knows. On the other hand, V_2 proves that

$$(a^\alpha + 1) = \beta^e \tag{14}$$

for some β that the signer knows. That can only happen if the signer is a group member, α is his secret key, and β is his membership certificate.

Informal proof of the blindness of the signature: The signer's input into the protocol has been blinded by blinding $\tilde{g}$ and $\tilde{z}$ into random $\hat{g}$ and $\hat{z}$, and constructing two blind signatures of knowledge. Therefore, the resulting signature $(\hat{g}, \hat{z}, V_1, V_2)$ cannot be linked to the signer's view of the protocol.

4.4 Open

Given a signature $(\hat{g}, \hat{z}, V_1, V_2)$ for a message m, the group manager can determine the signer by testing if $\hat{g}^{y_P} = \hat{z}$ for every group member P (where $y_P = \log_g z_P$ and z_P is P's membership key). The group manager can establish the identity of the signer without giving away y_P using the signer's membership key z_P, the signer's commitment to z_P, and a non-interactive proof that $\log_g z = \log_{\hat{g}} \hat{z}$. Since it is considered difficult to test if $\log_{\hat{g}} \hat{z} = \log_{\hat{g}'} \hat{z}'$ members' signatures are anonymous and unlinkable. Thus the running time of this scheme is linear in the size of the group.

4.5 Efficiency of the Proposed Scheme

The proposed scheme is as efficient as the basic group signature scheme proposed by Camenisch and Stadler. That is, for a fixed security parameter l, all of the described operations, except **Open**, take constant time, and the time **Open** takes is linear in the size of the group. All signatures take constant space, and communication complexity per signature is constant. Computational, space, and communication complexities are linear in the security parameter l.

4.6 Security of the Proposed Scheme

Our scheme is exactly as secure as Camenisch and Stadler's Basic Group Signature Scheme [5]. The security of the scheme is based on the assumptions that the discrete logarithm, double discrete logarithm, and the roots of discrete logarithm problems are hard. In addition, it is based on the security of the Schnorr and the RSA signature schemes and on the additional assumption due to [5] that computing membership certificates is hard.

4.7 Improvements on the Efficiency

Camenisch and Stadler [5] also proposed a group signature scheme in which the computational complexity of the **Open** algorithm is constant in the size of the group. This scheme can also be extended to a group blind signature scheme. We chose to omit the details, because the more efficient group signature scheme is also less secure and is known to be broken for certain values of its parameters.

5 Conclusion

We have proposed a group blind digital signature scheme that is secure and efficient, and therefore practical. Our result is an extension of the group signature scheme recently prosposed by Camenisch and Stadler in [5]. We showed how our construction could be used to set up an electronic cash system in which more than one bank can dispense anonymous e-cash.

Acknowledgements

The first author would like to acknowledge the support of DARPA grant DABT63-96-C-0018, the NSF Graduate Research Fellowship and a Lucent Technologies GRPW Program. The second author would like to acknowledge the support of DARPA grant DABT63-96-C-0018. In addition, we thank Ron Rivest for helping us shape our random ideas into a coherent paper. We would never be able to manage without his encouragement. Also, we give many thanks to Eric Lehman, Tal Malkin, Daniele Micciancio, and Amit Sahai for helpful and greatly appreciated discussions. Finally, we thank the anonymous referees for their helpful comments and suggestions.

References

1. Mihir Bellare and Phillip Rogaway. Random oracles are practical: A paradigm for designing efficient protocols. In *First ACM Conference on Computer and Communications Security*, pages 62–73, Fairfax, 1993. ACM.
2. Stefan Brands. An efficient off-line electronic cash system based on the representation problem. Technical Report CS-R9323, CWI, April 1993.
3. Jan Camenisch. Efficient and generalized group signatures. In *Proc. EUROCRYPT 97*, pages 465–479. Springer-Verlag, 1997. Lecture Notes in Computer Science No. 1233.
4. Jan Camenisch, Ueli Maurer, and Markus Stadler. Digital payment systems with passive anonymity-revoking trustees. *Journal of Computer Security*, 5(1), 1997.
5. Jan Camenisch and Markus Stadler. Efficient group signatures for large groups. In *Proc. CRYPTO 97*, pages 410–424. Springer-Verlag, 1997. Lecture Notes in Computer Science No. 1294.
6. D. Chaum, A. Fiat, and M. Naor. Untraceable electronic cash. In S. Goldwasser, editor, *Proc. CRYPTO 88*, pages 319–327. Springer-Verlag, 1988. Lecture Notes in Computer Science No. 403.

7. David Chaum. Blind signatures for untraceable payments. In R. L. Rivest, A. Sherman, and D. Chaum, editors, *Proc. CRYPTO 82*, pages 199–203, New York, 1983. Plenum Press.

8. David Chaum. Blind signature system. In D. Chaum, editor, *Proc. CRYPTO 83*, pages 153–153, New York, 1984. Plenum Press.

9. David Chaum and Eugène van Heyst. Group signatures. In *Proc. EUROCRYPT 91*, pages 257–265. Springer-Verlag, 1991. Lecture Notes in Computer Science No. 547.

10. L. Chen and T. P. Pedersen. New group signature schemes (extended abstract). In *Proc. EUROCRYPT 94*, pages 171–181. Springer-Verlag, 1994. Lecture Notes in Computer Science No. 547.

11. Amos Fiat and Adi Shamir. How to prove yourself: Practical solutions to identification and signature problems. In A.M. Odlyzko, editor, *Proc. CRYPTO 86*, pages 186–194. Springer-Verlag, 1987. Lecture Notes in Computer Science No. 263.

12. S. Goldwasser, S. Micali, and C. Rackoff. The knowledge complexity of interactive proof-systems. *SIAM. J. Computing*, 18(1):186–208, February 1989.

13. Shafi Goldwasser, Silvio Micali, and Ronald L. Rivest. A digital signature scheme secure against adaptive chosen-message attacks. *SIAM J. Computing*, 17(2):281–308, April 1988.

14. A. Juels, M. Luby, and R. Ostrovsky. Security of blind digital signatures. In *Proc. CRYPTO 97*, Lecture Notes in Computer Science, pages 150–164. Springer-Verlag, 1997. Lecture Notes in Computer Science No. 1294.

15. Laurie Law, Susan Sabett, and Jerry Solinas. How to make a mint: the cryptography of anonymous electronic cash. National Security Agency, Office of Information Security Research and Technology, Cryptology Division, June 1996.

16. David Pointcheval and Jacques Stern. Provably secure blind signature schemes. In M.Y. Rhee and K. Kim, editors, *Advances in Cryptology–ASIACRYPT '96*, pages 252–265. Springer-Verlag, 1996. Lecture Notes in Computer Science No. 1163.

17. Ronald L. Rivest, Adi Shamir, and Leonard M. Adleman. A method for obtaining digital signatures and public-key cryptosystems. *Communications of the ACM*, 21(2):120–126, 1978.

18. B. Schneier. *Applied Cryptography: Protocols, Algorithms, and Source Code in C*. John Wiley & Sons, New York, 1993.

19. C. P. Schnorr. Efficient identification and signatures for smart cards. In G. Brassard, editor, *Proc. CRYPTO 89*, pages 239–252. Springer-Verlag, 1990. Lecture Notes in Computer Science No. 435.

20. Daniel R. Simon. Anonymous communication and anonymous cash. In Neal Koblitz, editor, *Proc. CRYPTO 96*, pages 61–73. Springer-Verlag, 1996. Lecture Notes in Computer Science No. 1109.

21. Peter Wayner. *Digital Cash: Commerce on the Net*. Academic Press, 1996.

Curbing Junk E-Mail via Secure Classification

E. Gabber   M. Jakobsson   Y. Matias*   A. Mayer

Bell Laboratories
600 Mountain Avenue
Murray Hill, NJ 07974
{eran, markusj, matias, alain}@research.bell-labs.com

Abstract. We introduce a new method and system to curb junk e-mail by employing *extended e-mail addresses*. It enables a party to use her (core) e-mail address with different extensions and consequently classify incoming e-mail messages according to the extension they were sent to. Our contributions are threefold: First, we identify the components of a system that realizes the concept of extended e-mail addresses and investigate the functionality of these components in a manner which is backwards compatible to current e-mail tools. Secondly, we specify an adversarial model, and give the necessary properties of extended e-mail addresses and of the procedure to obtain them in the presence of the adversary. Finally, we design cryptographic functions that enable realizing extended e-mail addresses which satisfy these properties.

1 Introduction

As more and more people rely on e-mail for daily communication, both for their work and personal use, it becomes increasingly important to sort and classify incoming e-mail. Classification allows users to treat different classes of messages in different ways, e.g., store in different mail folders or delete without inspection. The need for such classification is becoming painstakingly apparent, as e-mail is not only becoming more *used*, but also more *abused*. The most widespread example of abuse is mass mailing of unsolicited e-mail messages based on address lists collected from various sources. The act of sending this "junk e-mail" is called "spamming", and it is now threatening to thwart legitimate e-mail. Since spamming is virtually free, whereas its current methods of prevention are time consuming and expensive, it is becoming alarmingly clear that an inexpensive type of protection must be made available, or both the Internet and individual e-mail accounts will turn into a giant digital traffic jam. However, as backwards compatibility is necessary for a resource as distributed as the Internet, the number of possible solutions are clearly limited.

In this paper, we focus on the problem of how to prevent spamming, which can be viewed as a binary classification problem: a message is either classified

---

* Also with the Department of Computer Science, Tel-Aviv University, Tel-Aviv 69978 Israel; Email: matias@math.tau.ac.il.

as a legitimate e-mail or as spam. We introduce an appropriate adversarial setting, and provide efficient and inexpensive solutions for secure classification of spamming. Our solution easily extend to more general classifications.

1.1 The Problem of Spamming

Spamming is facilitated by the following facts:

— It is fairly easy and inexpensive to obtain a list of valid e-mail addresses and to use it without the corresponding user's consent. Many people give their e-mail address to Web sites where they open accounts. Newsgroups and home pages are other good sources for collection of a large number of valid e-mail addresses.

— The recipient cannot easily distinguish between a personal e-mail message and an unsolicited spam massage. There is no characteristic envelope or sender's address that facilitates easy recognition of spam. The recipient must open the message and read it before deleting it. Spam messages clog the recipient's mailbox and necessitate time-consuming examination prior to removal.

— The cost of generating a relatively large number of spam messages is very low. Sending one million copies of a message is almost as easy sending one thousand copies.

1.2 Current Anti-Spamming Tools

All current tools use one or a combination of the following three methods for detecting and removing spam:

— *Source Address Filtering*: Collect a blacklist of known spammer e-mail addresses. Recognize these *source addresses* and remove their messages automatically. However, most spammers disguise their true address by various means and frequently "mutate" among various bogus return addresses.

— *Keyword Filtering*: Collect a blacklist of keywords often found in the subject-line or body of junk e-mail messages. Recognize these keywords and remove those messages automatically. This has been a somewhat effective method, since spam messages up to now are often characterized by a limited vocabulary. However, automatic removal of messages based on keywords is heuristic at best. It may eliminate some valid messages. Furthermore, spammers have started to adapt to such filtering by changing the vocabulary of their messages, especially after blacklists of keywords become public knowledge.

— *Address Change:* This is a tedious, last-resort action, appropriate when the user's e-mail address is constantly overloaded with spam messages. The corresponding user has to notify all potential senders, from whom she expects to receive e-mail.

1.3 Our Results

We introduce a method to combat junk e-mail via a new kind of e-mail address, termed an *extended e-mail address*. It enables a user to use her core (current) e-mail address with different extensions and consequently classify incoming e-mail messages according to the extension they were sent to. In particular, a user can classify e-mail sent to a particular extension as *spam*. We show how a party (the initiator) can obtain a valid extension from another party (the receiver) via a *handshake* protocol, whereas junk mailers are deterred from doing the same by introducing a "cost" for each handshake.

Our contributions are threefold. We identify necessary components and their functionality for a system to realize the concept of extended e-mail addresses. We specify an adversarial model and necessary properties of extended e-mail addresses in the presence of such an adversary. We then discuss how to realize the handshake by introducing a "cost" for the initiator of the request. Finally, we show a possible realization of the cryptographic functions generating extended e-mail addresses and the handshake. The system may be implemented on top of existing e-mail tools and services. It does not require public key infrastructure. Moreover, the system may be implemented by "agents" that run on behalf of initiators and receivers, so that the operation of the system (beyond the actual sending and receiving of (non-junk) mail) can be made transparent to users.

Organization: Section 2 presents a high-level overview of our approach. In Section 3, we describe the handshake protocol and introduce the main components of our system. Section 4 describes alternate simplified handshake protocols. Section 5 gives the requirements for the address extensions and a generating function, and Section 6 covers the cost function for handshakes. Finally, Section 7 concludes by showing that our system effectively deals with the facts that currently facilitate spamming (as mentioned in Section 1.1).

2 Overview of Our Solution

Currently, most e-mail users have a *very small number* of e-mail addresses. For example, one at the office and one for private use with an ISP at home. In contrast, the principle behind extended e-mail addresses is that each user has *many* e-mail addresses. Possibly, as many as different groups or entities the user is interacting with. Furthermore, a recipient of such an address cannot guess an extended address belonging to the same sender and destined for a different group.

Let Alice be our exemplary e-mail user. Alice wants to communicate with Bob via e-mail, and wants to register at a web-site www.crook.com, which requires her to give a valid e-mail address. Finally, Alice wants to post to a newsgroup. Bob receives e-mail from Alice with an extended return address Alice+xV78Yjklp9@company.com, whereas the folks at www.crook.com will receive the return address Alice+hdfsjg85nK@company.com. Alice's address will appear plainly as Alice@company.com in her newsgroup posting. We call

`Alice@company.com` a *core address* and `xV78Yjklp9` an *extension*. Subsequently, `www.crook.com` sells the obtained address to a spammer. As soon as Alice gets her first junk-mail message from that spammer, she can *classify* the address she gave to `www.crook.com` as "spam". This action is called *address revocation*, and it does not affect Alice's communication with Bob or with any other e-mail user or Web site. Furthermore, `www.crook.com` only knows a revoked e-mail address and cannot guess any other valid extended e-mail address of Alice. Likewise, an arbitrary newsgroup reader will not know a valid extension of Alice's. We note that Alice does not accept messages to her core address; senders (initiators) are requested to obtain a valid extension first by performing a handshake.

Another possible scenario is that Bob inadvertently leaks Alice's address to a database, which gets into the hands of spammers. Alice has the option of *binding* the address `Alice+xV78Yjklp9@company.com` to Bob, by classifying all messages sent to the extension `xV78Yjklp9` as spam, unless the (recognized) sender is Bob.

In order for extended addresses to be of practical use, Bob (the initiator) must have a way to obtain a valid extended address of Alice's (the receiver). For this *handshake* to be effective, it must involve a procedure acceptable for Bob, but unacceptable to a spammer. One possibility for Alice is to ask Bob for a valid return address where she can send the extension. Many spammers do not reveal their real e-mail address. A more sophisticated way is to force Bob to incur *a computational cost* by performing a CPU intensive computation on his machine. Bob might be perfectly willing to "pay" a small amount, but a spammer intending to send a message to a million users, might not. Once the receiver verified that the initiator has actually incurred the cost, she provides a new *extended e-mail address* to the initiator. The initiator can use this address for further communication with the receiver, as long as the receiver does not revoke this address. Thus, the cost of obtaining the extended address is amortized among multiple messages.

Related Work Extended e-mail addresses are similar in appearance to the e-mail addresses generated by the Andrew Message System (AMS) [BT91], which uses addresses of the form `user+text@domain`. AMS classifies incoming messages by executing user-supplied programs. Extensions serve a purpose similar to the target revocable email addresses generated by the LPWA proxy [LPWA97]. The system generates such alias e-mail addresses on the user's behalf within the context of Web browsing. The filtering is done via separate tools, such as the filtering functions of popular client mail programs (see `http://lpwa.com:8000/filter.html`). Extended e-mail addresses are also related to electronic mail channel identifiers (see [Hall98]). Channels, like extended addresses, can be used to block unwanted mail. The channel identifiers contain an indication of the policy for handling incoming mail on this channel. However, individuals who adopt a channelized email system might find themselves receiving significant amounts of spam on public channels but be unwilling to revoke those channels because they are also used for unanticipated, but desired, correspondence. The idea of using computational cycles as "cost", an option how for implementing the handshake in our system, was considered by Dwork and Naor [DN92] and Franklin and Malkhi [FM97] in different settings.

A recent paper by Cranor and LaMacchia [CL98] examines the spam problem and discusses several of the above approaches in more detail.

3   System Operation and Major Components

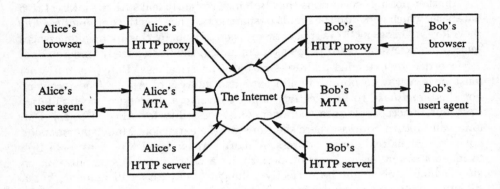

Fig. 1. Basic Communication Structure

In this section we describe the operation of the proposed scheme in some detail. We assume that both senders and receivers use an unmodified *user-agent* for composing and viewing mail messages (e.g., Eudora Pro, Netscape Messenger, etc) and that the actual delivery of the mail is accomplished by a *mail transfer agent* (MTA). The mail agent is typically located on the user's machine, while the MTA might be located on a firewall, Internet access point, etc. A user interacts with a *browser* to visit the Web. That traffic is routed via an *HTTP proxy*, which is typically located at the same place as the MTA; see Figure 1. In addition, the user employs an HTTP server, also often located at the same place as the MTA. The HTTP server allows the user to control the activities of the system and allows external initiators to request an extended address manually. We proceed by presenting in turn the *Extension Generator Module*, the *Destination Lookup Module*, the *Message Receiver Module*, the *Handshake Module*, and the *State Information Database*. We describe the functionality of each logical "module" and point out where a module might physically reside.

The system could be employed either in a fully automatic mode, in which all parties run the entire set of modules, or in a semi-automatic mode, in which some parties use an unmodified MTA without any of the afore-mentioned modules. In the fully automatic mode, the initiator's modules can obtain a valid extended address from the receiver without any interaction with the user. In the semi-automatic mode, the initiator must obtain the extended address from the receiver manually.

The following description should be read in conjunction with Figure 2, which depicts the message flow for obtaining an extended address in the fully automatic mode.

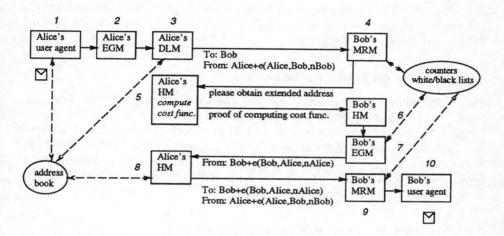

Fig. 2. Message Flow in the Fully Automatic Mode

3.1 Extension Generator Module (EGM)

The EGM computes the appropriate extended address a whenever the e-mail user A (Alice) registers at a Web-site, or sends an e-mail message to another party (Bob), or to a group of parties (Bob and Cathy) or subscribe to a mailing list. The EGM is illustrated in steps 2 and 7 of Figure 2.

When Alice sends a message to Bob, her "From"-address will be calculated as alice+$e(Alice, Bob, n_{Bob})$@company.com, where e is a function generating the appropriate extension. e takes as input Alice's and Bob's core addresses (e.g, alice@company.com and bob@university.edu) and a counter (state information) n_{Bob}, whose use is related to the revocation and immediate reissuing of a valid extension, and which will be elaborated on later. The specification of e is given in Section 5. The EGM updates Alice's state information database, as explained in Section 3.7. Bob can forward a message from Alice to a third party, Charlie. Charlie may communicate directly with Alice using her extended address in the forwarded message.

When Alice sends a message to both Bob and Cathy, the mail transfer agent duplicates the message body, and hence both Bob and Cathy will receive the same From-address. EGM will generate a single extension $e(Alice, Bob, n_{Bob})$, where Bob is the first recipient in the group. Both Bob and Cathy may use the same reply address (extension) in order to communicate with Alice.

Similarly, the EGM needs to compute extended addresses when Alice registers at a Web-site, which asks her to give an e-mail address. The EGM provides a valid extended address alice+$e(Alice, domain(site), n_{domain(site)})$@company.com.

When Alice posts to a Usenet newsgroup, it is a prudent choice that only her core address will be visible in her posting. When a reader of a newsgroup wants to send Alice e-mail directly, he will have to get a valid extension via a handshake (as described in Section 3.4). Hence, the EGM will simply forward Alice's core address to the MTA.

3.2 Destination Lookup Module (DLM)

The destination lookup module replaces the destination's core address (e.g. bob@university.edu) by its latest known valid extended address using the information stored in the *address book*. The DLM is needed only when Alice's user agent cannot access the address book directly to perform this lookup. The DLM does nothing if the destination address is an extended address or if the address book does not contain a valid extended address for this core address. The DLM is depicted in step 3 of Figure 2.

3.3 Message Receiver Module (MRM)

The MRM is responsible for classifying all incoming mail messages into two categories: *valid*, which is passed to the receiver's user agent, and *all others*, which are returned to the sender, who is asked to apply for a valid extended e-mail address. In the description of the MRM we will use the following definitions:

Definition 1. An extension e' is *genuine* for a user A, if $e' = e(A, B, n_B)$ for some party B and a current counter n_B; and *ingenuine* otherwise.

Definition 2. The subset of genuine extensions, which a user no longer wants to accept is denoted *invalid*, all other genuine extensions are *valid*.

For all parties B, the MRM must deliver each message, addressed with a valid $e(Alice, B, n_B)$ to Alice. The action of Alice removing an extension ϵ from the list of valid extensions is equivalent to classifying e-mail addressed with ϵ as junk e-mail. In this way Alice essentially *revokes* an extension she gave out to a party at some earlier point in time. The MRM must support this operation. Alice can further specify what the (different) actions of the MRM should be, when it receives a message addressed with either a invalid (but genuine) extension, a fake (ingenuine) extension, or no extension at all (i.e., Alice's core address). For example, a possible action might be an automatic reply, advising the sender to obtain a valid extension from Alice (via the handshake described in Section 3.4).

The MRM also allows Alice to *bind* an extension ϵ to a group G of other parties. The effect of binding is that only for parties in G the extension ϵ is valid, for all other parties, the extension ϵ is invalid.

When managing an intranet, it is beneficial to eliminate junk e-mail right at the gateway (MTA). Hence, part of this module should reside close to the MTA. Hence, an appropriate location for the MRM is inside the *gatekeeper*, which is a new component that handles all communication between the user agent and the MTA, as depicted in Figure 3. The gatekeeper maintains a database for each user to make a the decision which incoming mail the intended user classifies as junk. The required state information is also discussed in Section 3.7.

One way to control the operation of the MRM is to use an internal HTTP server, which allows the user to specify the desired actions (i.e. filter-like definitions) via a some web interface. The most important action is, of course, the revocation of a certain extended address.

In order to minimize the amount of data storage in the state information database, we introduce the notion of verifiable addresses:

Definition 3. A recipient-address a of a message intended for user A is *verifiable*, if there is an efficient check that a is genuine. This excludes the trivial check of simply going through the list of parties B, for whom A had generated an e-mail address at any point in the past.

The use of verifiable addresses thus allows that the system only has to store those extensions which are genuine, but no longer valid ("blacklist"), a potentially significant reduction in size. We note that a possible way to implement verifiability is to append the output of a keyed MAC to each extension. The input to the MAC is the extension, keyed with the user's secret. The key is shared with the user's MRM for easy discarding of fake (ingenuine) extensions.

3.4 Handshake Module (HM)

The handshake module is employed by the initiator (sender) and the receiver to implement the protocol for obtaining an extended address, as depicted in steps 5 and 8 of Figure 2.

If Alice would like to start exchanging e-mail with Bob, she might not know a valid extension for Bob. The handshake procedure allows Alice to obtain a valid extension for Bob, which she then can store in the address book of her user agent. We assume that Alice knows either Bob's core address or the URL of Bob's home-page (which is consistent with today's e-mail usage). Bob can publish these items on his business card, resume, and other immutable media. Alice initiates the handshake by sending e-mail to Bob's core address. The handshake method must involve a procedure acceptable to Alice, but not to spammers. We observe that spammers often do not give out returnable sender addresses and typically send to a large number (millions) of recipients. This leads to the following desirable properties for a handshake method:

- The handshake requires Alice to give a valid return address.
- The handshake requires Alice to "pay a cost". For example, Alice might be required to spend a certain amount of computing power in order to complete the handshake. We examine suitable cost functions in Section 6.

If Alice's message is satisfactory to Bob, she obtains a reply with a valid extension for Bob. We note that Bob's part in the handshake can be automated, so that Bob's HM handles all messages addressed to Bob's core address: The HM verifies that Alice has paid her cost and then generates a valid extension (which requires that the EGM is also accessible by the HM). In any other case, the HM either ignores a message sent to a core address or executes a user-specified action. HM might reside on the gatekeeper as well.

3.5 HTTP Proxy

Alice must employ a HTTP proxy to compute her extended address whenever she is registering at Web sites that require a valid e-mail address. The HTTP proxy employs the EGM, that was described in Section 3.1. This configuration is similar to the configuration of the Lucent Personalized Web Assistant (LPWA) [GGMM97], that is used to enhance privacy by creating consistent aliases for the user.

3.6 HTTP Server

Alice should also employ an HTTP server that has access to her state information database. This HTTP server is used for controlling the operation of the system and to allow manual requests of extended addresses. Alice could query the internal state information database as well as specify the desired actions of the system by a Web interface, which is maintained by the HTTP server.

3.7 State Information Database

If Alice revokes the extension $e(Alice, Bob, n_{Bob})$, used for communicating with both Bob and Cathy, she might later want to re-establish communication with Bob (alone). EGM uses the counter n_{Bob}, and increments it at the time when Alice re-establishes an extension. The new extension will be $e(Alice, B, n_{Bob+1})$. Initially, the generated extension is $e(Alice, Bob, 0)$. Hence, the EGM needs to maintain a counter for each party Alice is communication with. The HM needs access to these counters as well. This is depicted in Figure 3. The EGM and the HM on the gatekeeper access the counters in the state information database. The mail agent keeps an address book for storing valid addresses of other parties, like most agents do already today (Figure 3). So Alice only needs to tell the mail agent to which party she wants to send a message, and the system supplies the corresponding recipient address and her own extended sender address transparently.

The MRM must keep track of Alice's genuine and valid extensions. Possible solutions range from keeping a simple database of valid addresses ("whitelist") to use *verifiably* genuine addresses, and storing (the potentially much smaller list of) revoked addresses ("blacklist"). In all cases, user updates in the set of valid addresses have to be reflected in the state information database (Figure 3).

Accountability: When Alice qualifies an incoming message addressed to a currently valid address a as junk e-mail, then she might want to find out for whom a was originally computed. This party is directly or indirectly accountable for the junk e-mail message. This information is easily stored with the corresponding counter.

3.8   The Gatekeeper

The EGM, DLM and HM are best located between the user agent and the MTA, inside a new component called the *gatekeeper*, as depicted in Figure 3. The gatekeeper implements the functionality of our system without requiring any change to user agents or to the MTA. In this way, users need not change their user agents (mail readers), and the operation of the system is mostly transparent to the users.

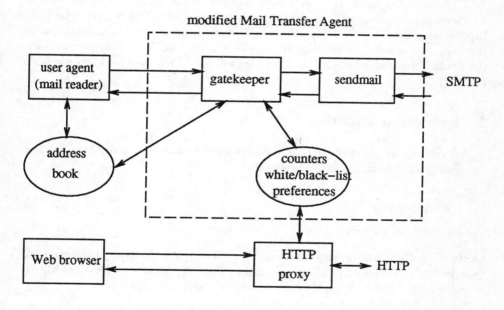

Fig. 3. Enhanced Communication Structure

Other systems, such as the channels system of [Hall98], use a similar component, the Personal Channel Agent (PCA), which also sits between the MTA and the user agents (mail clients).

Deployment

The proposed system may co-exist with other mail tools, and it does not require all parties to use it. The receiver may be protected by the system, while the senders use unmodified mailing tools. The senders have to keep the receiver's extended e-mail address in their address book, which is often maintained by their mailing tool.

The best place for placing the gatekeeper software is at the firewall, so that unsolicited mail can be returned to the sender immediately without the need to store or transfer it.

4 Alternative Protocols

The handshake protocol described in Section 3 involves 5 messages and a considerable internal state, as depicted in Figure 2. In this section we propose a variant that reduces the number of messages by computing the cost function prior to sending the first message to the recipient.

The variant protocol combines steps 3 and 5 in Figure 2 and eliminates step 4. Alice's first message to Bob contains the proof of computing the cost function. In this way, Bob does not have to ask Alice to compute the cost function. In this way, we reduce the number of messages from 5 to 3. If Bob ever revokes the extended address he gave to Alice, he will ask Alice to recompute the cost function.

5 Extension Function

In this section, we give precise requirements for the function e generating a user's extensions and show a possible realization.

5.1 Requirements

We consider the following adversarial model:

Definition 4. The adversary can obtain e-mail addresses from any chosen e-mail "parties" (e.g., Web-site database, Usenet newsgroup, private address book). All addresses stored at such a party are considered *compromised*.

Requirements on Generation of Sender Addresses:

1. *Authenticity:* An adversary cannot do better than guessing an extension of an uncompromised address with negligible probability. Having compromised some addresses of a user does not help an adversary in guessing the user's extension of an uncompromised address with non-negligible probability.
2. *Consistency:* The computed extension for a given party/state-counter is consistent.
3. *Efficiency:* The computation of the extension is efficient.

4. *Acceptability:* The range of generated extensions must be appropriate for e-mail addresses. Furthermore, the length of $e(A, B, n_B)$ is determined to give meaning to "negligible" in the above requirements.

5.2 Realization

The requirements *authenticity, consistency,* and *efficiency* would all be satisfied by the use of a perfect pseudo-random function generator. However, in the absence of such a function, we need to consider reasonably inexpensive approximations to it with respect to these requirements and to ensure *acceptability* at the same time.

We note that this was investigated by Bleichenbacher *et al* [BGGMM97] in the context of secure and pseudonymous client-server relationships. The so-called *Janus* function suggested in [BGGMM97] embodies the requirements we put on our module for generation of sender address extensions. We further note that the Lucent Personalized Web Assistant ([GGMM97] and [LPWA97]) computes a different e-mail address on a user's behalf for each Web-site, which requires registration. More generally, each system which derives different e-mail addresses from a core address under the above properties forms the basis for an effective tool against spam.

6 Handshake Function

The handshake can be implemented by simply having the initiator calling up her intended receiver on the phone, asking for an extension, or by sending an e-mail request of a special format. However, we will consider the somewhat more intricate solution of using a *cost function*, since this allows a considerable amount of automation. Intuitively, we want this function to be such that it has some well known and well regulated generation cost, is fast to verify, and can be easily implemented. Thus, a "friendly" user would not be too inconvenienced by its use (since it only has to be invoked once for each pair of communicating parties), but it would substantially hinder a spammer desiring to send to a large number of parties. In this section, we give precise requirements for the function controlling the cost of a handshake and show a possible realization.

Software implementing (1) a function for generating valid handshakes via the cost function and (2) a verifier of valid handshakes would be made publicly available.

We let c be a parameter describing the cost of performing the handshake; this may be a global parameter, but may also be individually set (and published) to customize the level of resistance to spam. Next, there is a target function T that decides whether its input is the result of a valid handshake or not. This function could simply compare a preset portion of its input to some predetermined pattern (of length corresponding to c). The initiator of a handshake repeatedly attempts to construct a potential handshake using a random approach, and verifies her attempt using the target function. She repeats her attempts until a valid handshake is found (the cost being measured in the expected number of trials.) She then sends her request for an extension to the core address of her desired recipient and encloses the handshake, which we note, is specific to this pair of parties. The handshake module at the recipient will sort out the request and evaluate the target function on it. If the result indicates that it is valid (and the initiator is not on some blacklist), then a valid extension will be generated and returned to the address of the initiator of the handshake. Given the correct extension, the initiator of the request is now able to send an e-mail that will reach the recipient.

6.1 Design Goals

The cost function is used to ensure that the party initiating the handshake has performed a certain expected amount of computation. Thus, this function controls the number of valid handshakes a party can initiate per time period. More formally, the cost function should have the following properties:

1. *Known Generation Cost:* Let c be a security parameter controlling the expected cost for generating a valid cost function. This cost measures the number of operations required and can be set either universally or individually. If the computation can be distributed, the cumulative expected cost per cost function evaluation must be at least c.
2. *Low Verification Cost:* We require that it should be inexpensive to verify that a given handshake is valid, where we leave "inexpensive" to mean considerably less expensive than c, but do not specify the exact maximum cost.
3. *Amortization Freeness:* Assume that E is an adversary who wants to generate k valid and different cost function evaluations: each such cost function transcript may be valid for any two protocol participants (who may not even exist at the time of the computation, but may be named and created afterwards) and for any time in the future. We require that the expected cost for E's computation is at least $\epsilon k c$, for ϵ very close to 1.
4. *Function Familiarity:* For practical purposes, it is an advantage if the cost function is based on a well known family of one-way primitives, for which computational costs are understood.
5. *Software Based:* In order to make the playground level, and not permit an adversary any significant advantage, we choose a cost function where hardware implementations are not giving any drastic advantage over software implementations.
6. *Transferability:* It may be required that a third party can verify that a given cost function evaluation is valid. In this situation, the third party wants the guarantee that the expected generation cost is c, even if all other handshake participants do not collaborate.

6.2 Realization

We will now briefly consider a possible implementation of the cost function, satisfying the most important requirements listed in the previous section. Recall that c is the cost parameter and T the target function. Herein, we will assume that A is the identity of the initiator of the handshake and B is the receiver. Furthermore, we will let d denote the day of the handshake; this is used to force an initiator to perform a new handshake computation if an old extension gets revoked – other degrees of granularity may be employed. The initiator will construct potentially valid handshakes using a probabilistic approach, and verify, using the target function, whether the result is satisfactory or not. A handshake specifies the identity of the sender, the identity of the recipient, and the date, and contains a randomly chosen string. The handshake is valid if a one-way function of it, evaluated by the target function, makes the latter output 1. The initiator of a request therefore tries different random strings until such a result is achieved. Consider now the following cost function:

Given a one-way hash function $h : \{0,1\}^* \to \{0,1\}^n$, a cost parameter $c < 2^n$ and a value $v \in \{0,1\}^*$, the cost function is evaluated by picking a random value $x \in \{0,1\}^*$, and evaluating $T(x,v,c)$. If $T(x,v,c) = 1$ then x is a satisfying choice for v. In other words, x is a valid cost function value. If $T(x,v,c) = 0$ we pick another random value x and repeat the above process. Here, we can choose MD5 for h, let $v = A\|B\|d$, let x be a random string of 128 bits, and let T output 1 when $h(x\|h(v)) < 2^n/c$, otherwise 0. We note that the probability of picking a value x that causes T to accept is $1/c$, and so, the expected number of necessary hash function evaluations required to arrive at a satisfactory value x is $c + 1$. Note that one cannot reduce the effort of computing the cost function by pre-computing $h(x)$ for many values of x, since MD5 works on 512 bit blocks, and its input $(x\|h(v))$ is 256 bit long.

Evaluating the cost function for $c = 2^{20}$ would take about 2 seconds on a 266 MHz Pentium II processor[2]. On the other hand, verifying that a given value x satisfies the target function for a certain sender, receiver and date only takes two hash function evaluations.

Support: We are not able to prove that the suggested function has the desired properties. In particular, we do not know how to prove that the function has a known generation cost and is amortization free, since the area of lower bounds for cryptographic functions still to a large extent is a grey and unknown area. It will therefore have to suffice to explain why the cost function was chosen as it was.

First, the reason why we hash down v first, as opposed to plainly appending it to x, and hash these together, is that this makes the generation cost for the cost function (largely) independent on the length of v, which would not be the case if it were plainly to be appended.

Second, note that it is not possible to reduce the effort of computing the cost function by pre-computing $h(x)$ for many values of x, and then for many values $h(v)$ find a pair that results in a valid output. This is so since MD5 works on

---

[2] Wei Dai reports in http://www.eskimo.com/~weidai/ that a 266 MHz Pentium II processor can compute MD5 hash at the speed of 32MB per second. This is equivalent to 0.5M blocks of 512 bits per second.

512 bit blocks, and its input, $x|h(v)$, is 256 bits long.

We believe that our requirement for known generation cost is satisfied: If we treat the hash function as a random oracle, then we can show that it is not possible to find a valid x in less c trials on average. Without the random oracle assumption, the generation cost depends on possible (today unknown) methods of evaluating hash functions such as MD5 on certain inputs. Similarly, the amortization-freeness can be shown in an idealized setting where we treat the hash function as a random oracle, and appears to hold without this assumption, given the current knowledge about hash functions. It is clear that the suggested function satisfies the rather fuzzy requirement of a low verification cost, since it only requires one function evaluation (of the extended function, including the three individual hash function applications). Also, the fuzzy requirement of function familiarity is satisfied given a choice of MD5, which is a function for hardware support does not gain a significant advantage over software implementations (as opposed to, for example, DES.) Finally, we see that the suggested function satisfies receipt availability, viz. that a third party is able to verify that a given valid cost function evaluation indeed is valid.

7 Discussion and Conclusion

We have proposed a design of a new system to effectively help in curbing junk e-mail. We have made typical sources for spammers to obtain valid e-mail addresses (Web site databases, Usenet newsgroups, ISP lists of (core) addresses of subscribers) much less attractive. Upon receiving a first junk e-mail message, a user will declare the corresponding extension invalid. Hence, a list of extended addresses is useless, if another spammer had access to it before. A core address cannot be used directly for a spamming. We have furthermore introduced a non-negligible cost to obtain a new and valid e-mail addresses, so even if junk e-mailers can use a high speed machine with good price/performance ratio, they must reduce the rate of sending junk messages, which will require them to target their messages carefully and avoid mass mailing. Furthermore, a spammer must provide a working e-mail address in the course of this handshake, which serves as another deterrent and prevents spoofing, currently prevalent among spammers.

We have shown that our system is mostly transparent to an e-mail user and easily integrated with today's e-mail tools. Implementations and practical use will guide in showing the appropriate cost for a handshake, the appropriate degree of automation of the functionalities and other possible trade-offs.

Acknowledgments

The authors would like to thank the anonymous referees for their helpful comments, and Daniel Bleichenbacher for very helpful discussions.

References

[BGGMM97] D. Bleichenbacher, E. Gabber, P. Gibbons, Y. Matias, A. Mayer, *On Secure and Pseudonymous Client-Relationships with Multiple Servers*, submitted, also available at URL http://www.bell-labs.com/projects/lpwa/papers.html.

[BT91] N.S. Borenstein and C.A. Thyberg, *Power, Ease of Use and Cooperative Work in a Practical Multimedia Message System*, International Journal of Man-Machine Studies, Volume 34, Number 2, February 1991, pp. 229–259.

[CL98] L.F. Cranor and B.A. LaMacchia, *Spam!*, to appear in Communications of the ACM. Also available at URL http://www.research.att.com/~lorrie/pubs/spam/.

[DN92] C. Dwork and M. Naor, *Pricing via Processing or Combating Junk Mail*, Crypto'92, pp. 139–147.

[FM97] M. Franklin and D. Malkhi, *Auditable Metering with Lightweight Security*, Proc. of Financial Cryptography'97, Springer-Verlag, LNCS 1318, pp. 151–160.

[GGMM97] E. Gabber, P. Gibbons, Y. Matias, A. Mayer, *How to Make Personalized Web Browsing Simple, Secure, and Anonymous*, Proc. of Financial Cryptography'97, Springer-Verlag, LNCS 1318, pp. 17–31. Also available at URL http://www.bell-labs.com/projects/lpwa/papers.html.

[Hall98] R.J. Hall, *Channels: Avoiding Unwanted Electronic Mail*, to appear in Communications of the ACM. Also available at URL ftp://ftp.research.att.com/dist/hall/papers/agents/channels-long.ps.

[LPWA97] LPWA: The Lucent Personalized Web Assistant, A Bell Labs Technology Demonstration. Available at URL http://lpwa.com.

Publicly Verifiable Lotteries: Applications of Delaying Functions

David M. Goldschlag* Stuart G. Stubblebine**

Abstract. This paper uses *delaying functions*, functions that require significant calculation time, in the development of a one-pass lottery scheme in which winners are chosen fairly using only internal information. Since all this information may be published (even before the lottery closes), anyone can do the calculation and therefore verify that the winner was chosen correctly. Since the calculation uses a delaying function, ticket purchasers cannot take advantage of this information. Fraud on the part of the lottery agent is detectable and no single ticket purchaser needs to be trusted. Coalitions of purchasers attempting to control the winning ticket calculation are either unsuccessful or are detected. The scheme can be made resistant to coalitions of arbitrary size. Since we assume that coalitions of larger size are harder to assemble, the probability that the lottery is fair can be made arbitrarily high. The paper defines delaying functions and contrasts them with pricing functions [8] and time-lock puzzles [15].

1 Introduction

In a typical lottery, one or more winners are chosen using some process that is trusted to give each purchased ticket an equal chance of winning: choosing balls from an urn, for example. The process may be executed or monitored by an outside auditor. Unfortunately, because the process is random, it is not repeatable, and ticket purchasers must trust both the process and the auditing organization.

In this paper, we propose a scheme for fairly selecting lottery winners using information internal to the lottery (e.g., numbers on tickets). The winning number calculation is therefore repeatable. We make the calculation verifiable by obliging the lottery agent to publish all internal information. We put the lottery agent on a level playing field with his customers by obliging him to publish the internal information as he accumulates it. We prevent anyone from taking advantage of this internal information by using *delaying functions* as part of the winning number calculation. These functions require significant computational resources, which are unlikely to be available before the lottery closes.

The winning number calculation produces a random (i.e., fair) result if at least one of the tickets used in the calculation is random (i.e., not under the

---

* Divx, 570 Herndon Parkway, Herndon, VA 20170, USA, +1 703-708-4028 (voice), +1 703-708-4088 (fax), david.goldschlag@divx.com

** AT&T Labs–Research, Rm B235, 180 Park Avenue, Florham Park, NJ 07932, USA. http://www.research.att.com/~stubblebine

control of a colluder). Therefore, the lottery could be controlled if all tickets are purchased by colluders. Since we assume that larger coalitions are harder to assemble, the lottery scheme is designed to detect coalitions of a pre-specified size and to be resistant to attack by smaller coalitions. (If a coalition is detected, the lottery may be extended.) By choosing the hardness of the delaying function and the detectable coalition size appropriately, the probability of a fair lottery can be made arbitrarily high. The lottery is one-pass, except (if tickets are anonymous) the winner may need to return to claim her winnings.

This paper uses three concepts in its lottery design:

1. Delaying functions prevent computationally bounded adversaries from cheating.
2. Trust is distributed by giving everyone equal access to sensitive information. Where one party has a role that makes him more trusted than another (i.e., the lottery agent), that party incriminates himself when cheating. Furthermore, it is easy for individual purchasers to provide the evidence.
3. We detect, instead of prevent, denial of service attacks.

Prior research [10] indicates that it is information theoretically impossible to construct a Boolean function that cannot be controlled by sufficiently large sized subsets of its inputs. In the absence of other assumptions, this work would preclude our result. However, that work does not place computational constraints on the coalition controlling the inputs.

Other work has used calculation time as a barrier [8, 9, 15, 12]. But none of the solutions have all the properties that we require here: Unlike time-lock puzzles [15, 12], the solution should not be known in advance to anyone, not even the puzzlemaker. And, although easy verification of the solution may be convenient, it is not a requirement here. Unlike pricing functions [8, 9], the cost of a security breach is high.

This paper is organized as follows. In section 2, we present definitions. Section 3 describes our solution including lottery registration, ticket purchase, critical purchase phase, and winning entry calculation. In section 5, we present related work. Section 6 presents some concluding remarks.

2 Definitions

Lottery terms and properties. We now present some terminology for describing lotteries. Our cast of characters include the *lottery agent* who runs the lottery, and a *client agent* who represents the *customer*. The client agent and lottery agent interact to generate a *lottery ticket*. Upon completion of this interaction a lottery ticket is said to be purchased. A lottery ticket is a record containing at least a *seed* and a *winning number parameter* of fixed size. Those two parameters may be the same, or be implicit (e.g., the winning number parameter may be a function of the ticket). For the purposes of this paper, we assume that a ticket's winning number parameter is the same as its seed.

The run of a lottery ends at a scheduled *closing time*, t. A distinguished interval called the *critical purchase phase* is represented as a pre-defined period, p. During the critical purchase phase, the required number of distinct client agents purchasing tickets is at least n. The number of lottery tickets sold is represented as L. The sum of what customers pay for tickets is called the *lottery revenue*. The fraction of the lottery revenue that is distributed to winners (according to pre-defined rules of the lottery) is called the *winnings pool*. The time to compute the winning ticket(s) is called the *calculation time*.

We now define properties of lotteries. First, the probability that a lottery is fair is represented using the notation P_f. The fairness of the lottery depends upon three factors: that the calculation used to compute the winning ticket gives all purchased tickets an equal chance of being selected; that the winning number calculation is highly unlikely to be computable before the lottery closes; and that at least one ticket purchased during the critical purchase phase is sold to a non-coalition member. Second, if anyone can calculate the winning ticket based on the parameters of purchased tickets, and the integrity of the winnings pool can be verified, we say the lottery is *publicly verifiable*. Third, if the calculation of the winning number depends only upon purchased tickets and not upon some extra information (such as a "trusted" third party selecting a random number), then we say the lottery is *closed*.

Delaying functions. We borrow complexity terminology from [8]. However, our definitions are not identical. We choose a calculation function that is *moderately hard* to compute, as opposed to *easy* or cryptographically *hard*. Depending on the lottery requirements, this may mean that the calculation time takes several hours, using the fastest known implementation. The critical purchase phase p is set at some fraction of that time, to place an additional measure of safety that the calculation could not be completed while the lottery is running.

A function f is a *delaying function* if:

1. f is moderately hard to compute. Given a minimum operation time p and an interval following p i.e. $[p, q]$, the probability that the function is computable on average is less than or equal to ϵ before the interval and the probability increases monotonically from $[\epsilon, 1]$ over that interval where ϵ can be made arbitrarily small.

   The function f is computationally secure. However, the attack complexity (the dominant of the data, storage, and processing complexities) that we must resist is much lower than that expected in a cryptographic function (i.e., hours of significant effort instead of years).

2. f preserves the information of its inputs. That is, given $Y = f(X)$, where Y and X are random variables representing the range and domain of the function f, $H(X) \simeq H(Y)$ (where $H(X)$ is the entropy of X).

The second requirement may be made clear by example. In our lottery scenario, the delaying function maps random numbers to random numbers and these are mapped to the winning ticket. We must ensure that the lottery is fair.

We caution the reader that delaying functions suffer from *practical* problems common to other cryptographic mechanisms: it is difficult to be sure that the problem can't be shortcutted (with a trap door or another mechanism) or parallelized. It is also difficult to count the number of sequential operations required to solve the problem–for example, people have discovered increasingly efficient ways to implement DES over the years. Finally, estimates of the cost of executing those operations are unlikely to be precise. For our purposes, however, we only require a conservative lower bound on the actual delay.

Syntax. We use "floor brackets" to indicate message authentication and curly braces to indicate message confidentiality. Thus, '$\lfloor X \rfloor_K$' might refer to data X signed with key K or a keyed one-way hash of X using K. '$\{X\}_K$' refers to X encrypted with key K. For our purposes, both of these are used to refer to mechanisms that also provide integrity within the indicated scope.

3 Approach

3.1 Problem and Overview

We place the following three requirements on our lottery design:

R1. The probability that the lottery is fair, P_f, can be made arbitrarily high:
1.1 The winning number calculation gives each purchased ticket an equal chance of being selected.
1.2 The calculation is unlikely to be computable in less than p time.
1.3 The calculation is resiliant to failures: It is random if even one argument is random, and the chance of one random argument is high.
R2. The lottery is publicly verifiable.
R3. The lottery is closed.

We are concerned with the type of lottery where if the entire pool is not distributed to winners, the balance rolls over into subsequent lotteries.

A solution must be secure against an adversary that can purchase tickets, selectively block communications, and control the order of purchased tickets. The lottery agent can be an adversary too. We make a simplifying assumption that the probability of a successful attack on cryptographic mechanisms is negligible.

Our approach divides the lottery into four phases. These phases are *registration, purchase, critical purchase,* and *winner calculation.* The purchase phase contains the entire critical purchase phase. The critical purchase phase defines the distinguished interval p. Prior to the purchase phase, the lottery agent commits to when the critical purchase phase begins.

We now present what happens in each of the lottery phases.

3.2 Registration

In order to detect whether a coalition of a particular size controls the lottery we must be able to count the number of different client agents participating in the lottery. How can we ensure that tickets are from distinct sources? The goal of registration is to enable this identification. This requires mapping between an individual and his client agent. The client agents may use certificates or hardware devices. The integrity of the mapping is maintained in two steps:

- It must be difficult for an individual to obtain more than a small number of certificates or hardware devices.
- Only the owner can prove that he is authorized to use the certificate or box.

We could use certificates issued by certificate authorities that can be trusted to issue only a single certificate to an individual. The individual could prove that he is authorized to use the certificate by signing some challenge with his private key. Anonymous purchases can be done in two ways: Certificate authorities could issue a blinded certificate along with an unblinded certificate. The lottery service may wish to issue its own certificates when presented with third party certificates to simplify ticket purchase. We refer to a client C's private key as K_C and to his certificate as $Cert_C$. This certificate includes the client's public key K_C^{-1}. Similarly, the lottery agent's private key is K_L^{-1}.

3.3 Purchase

During lottery transactions, tickets are only sold to registered client agents. Those are the only clients who know the private signature keys corresponding to the certified public keys. Ticket purchases by the same client agent can be correlated since the certificate is presented during each ticket purchase transaction. Ticket correlation is necessary, since we need to identify n distinct client agents. (This is discussed in further detail in sections 3.4).

Ticket purchase consists of the steps:

Message 1 $C \to L$: $\lfloor Seed \rfloor_{K_C}, Cert_C, Payment^3$

Message 2 $L \to C$: $\lfloor \lfloor Seed \rfloor_{K_C}, seq_L, time_L, Cert_C \rfloor_{K_L}$

In Message 1 the client agent requests a ticket by providing a signed seed, and possibly payment. In Message 2 the lottery agent returns a ticket, in which the lottery agent signs the already signed seed along with other fields: sequence number, timestamp, and purchaser's certificate. The client agent then verifies the ticket. The ticket's construction enables the proper purchaser to claim his winnings since the winner is the only one who can sign a challenge that can

---

[3] The payment must be structured so it cannot be applied with another seed. This level of detail is highly dependent on the payment mechanism and is not included in this description.

be verified with the same key as the winning ticket (e.g., K_C^{-1}). The lottery agent publishes the ticket. Publication enables observers to count distinct ticket purchasers and to calculate the winning ticket. Publication also allows individual ticket purchasers to ensure that their tickets are included in the calculation.

In Message 1, the space of the seed parameter must be at least as large as the number of tickets that can be sold. The client agent randomly generates the seed according to a uniform distribution over this range. Standardized implementations of the client agent can help insure that the client agent correctly generates the seed using available techniques for random number generation [1]. Clients not obeying the protocol specification may be defined to belong to the coalition attempting to control the lottery. (If the set is thus expanded, the number of distinct client agents required may need to increase to achieve the same probability of fairness.)

Message 2 represents the lottery ticket. Lottery tickets contain sequence number and timestamp fields. The goal is for the lottery agent to include information in tickets to incriminate himself if he cheats, while making the collection of this evidence easy for individual purchasers.

Sequence numbers allow the collection of small amounts of inconsistent information (i.e., two tickets with the same sequence number.) One could imagine that the lottery agent publishes both in the database, but not at the same time (in order to make the ticket appear yet make the winnings pool smaller). If sequence numbers are reused, audit queries from client agents searching for a single sequence number can eventually find two tickets with the same sequence number. In the analogous attack on tickets not containing sequence numbers, the lottery agent publishes only a subset of the database at any time. The evidence required to prove the absence of a ticket is to take a snapshot of the entire database without the ticket. (The lottery design may also require that sequence numbers be consecutive.)

Alternatively, tickets may contain signatures of previous tickets. This approach has similar virtues and limitations of the other approaches with the added feature that the lottery agent would not need to create a signature over the entire database after each ticket purchase. However, checking the integrity of the database would require numerous signature verifications. Of course, combinations of these approaches may prove suitable in practice.

The lottery agent includes the current time in message two of the signed ticket. This time is meant to be fairly accurate, and serves to identify which tickets are used in the winning calculation. The client agent can check this time locally, and if the lottery agent's clock is very fast (i.e., the lottery agent is trying to start the critical purchase phase early), then the client agent can immediately send the ticket to law enforcement, who will stamp it promptly. (For this purpose, it is reasonable to assume some form of communication channel, e.g., telephone, is available between a client agent and law enforcement.) Thus, the lottery agent has incriminated himself. The opposite attack, where the lottery agent slows the clock prior to the critical purchase phase, does not help the attacker, since shortening the critical purchase phase makes it even more unlikely that the attacker can solve the delaying function in time.

At any time after the ticket purchase, the client may check to see that his purchased tickets are published properly. If they are not, the client can complain to lawful authorities and provide proof (the ticket or certificate or response to a query). Anyone can verify the number of distinct ticket purchasers.

3.4 Critical Purchase

Before the lottery starts the lottery agent commits to the time of the beginning of the critical purchase phase. The critical purchase phase is entirely within the purchase phase. Consequently, all steps of the purchase phase apply to the critical purchase phase. The critical purchase phase is an interval of size p. The critical purchase phase and the purchase phase end at the close of the lottery, t. We make the following assumptions:

A1. At least n distinct certificates appear in the set of purchased tickets during the critical purchase phase.

A2. The probability that n or more distinct client agents collude can be made arbitrarily small by increasing n.

The choice of n in assumption A2 depends in part on the likelihood that individuals have multiple certificates, and the likelihood of a client agent being a colluder. As discussed later, the values of n and p are chosen to make the probability of a fair lottery, (i.e., P_f) acceptably high.

3.5 Winning Entry Calculation

The winning entry calculation must select among all purchased tickets with equal probability. It operates under the minimal assumption that only a single seed parameter among all tickets sold during the critical purchase phase was chosen randomly. The timestamp within the ticket indicates which tickets fall within the critical period.

The winning entry calculation may be structured into the following steps:

1. Hash computation. Compute $h(s_1, s_2, ...)$ where $s_1, s_2, ...$ represents the concatenation of all seed parameters of tickets purchased during the critical purchase phase p. We require that $h()$ be preimage resistant and non-correlating [13, 19].

2. Delay calculation. Input the result of step 1 to a delaying function (as defined in section 2).

If the range of step 2 does not map directly to a winning ticket (e.g., sequence number) then the following step may be needed:

3. Winner computation. Map the result of step 2 to one or more purchased tickets.

The hashing of step 1 may be necessary if the delaying function does not take input of arbitrary size and the delaying function does not have the non-correlating properties of "distributing" localized randomness to all output bits.

The delay calculation is achieved through a moderately hard calculation that must also preserve the randomness in the input. We may choose the parameters of a delaying function for the calculation to take several hours, using the best known implementation. By choosing p to be some conservative fraction of that time, we can make it very likely that the calculation cannot be completed before the lottery ends. A consequence of our winning entry construction is:

A3. The probability that the winning calculation can be made within p time can be made arbitrarily small.

Where L is the number of lottery tickets sold, an implementation of these three steps may be:

1. Concatenate in some pre-defined order the seed parameters purchased in the critical purchase phase of the lottery. Hash the resulting string.
2. Use bits from the resulting hash as the key for a cipher with a very long period. Run the cipher in output feedback mode (OFB) to generate some pre-defined number of bits. Save the last $\lceil \log L \rceil$ bits.
3. Choose winning entries by computing the Hamming distance between the result of step 2 and the winning number parameter (expressed in binary) in the tickets. (The Hamming distance $d(x, y)$ from x to y is the number of positions in which the two strings differ [16].)

The use of a cipher in OFB mode may be a good delaying function. The cipher should have a large period, large linear complexity, and good statistical properties. Such a construction should be hard to short-circuit, because it is hard to predict how the choice of initialization vector indexes into the keystream. Also, the implementation of many ciphers have been carefully studied for minimizing the number of operations required. By conservatively estimating the cost of the dominating operations (bit permutations) one can predict how much delay a certain keystream length requires.

Notice that this implementation could choose several winners. The lottery policy may allocate the winnings using a tiered approach among the closest Hamming distances.

3.6 Denial of Service

Our lottery is subject to a denial of service attack. If fewer than n distinct sources are detected in the p interval, the winning calculation is considered invalid. A reasonable lottery policy may be to extend the lottery.

Measures to prevent, rather than detect, denial of service attacks are beyond the scope of this paper. But it is easy to imagine engineering approaches that complicate denial of service attacks, if the lottery agent does not participate in the coalition. For example, if sufficient independent network connections connect the lottery agent to his possible customers, blocking communication entirely becomes more difficult. Of course, the lottery agent could be one of the colluders. Unmonitored, he can then deny service. This too may be detectable by monitoring the arrival of tickets during period p.

4 Evaluation

Our lottery operates in the following way: Assume a set of games that is too large to pre-compute. Each game produces a random result, and playing any game takes longer than some period of time, p.

The seeds in tickets purchased during the final p interval in the lottery together define the selected game. The game is played, and the result defines the winning ticket(s).

To fix the lottery, colluders must choose their seeds to select a game with favorable results. Since, any play of any game will extend beyond the close of the lottery, colluders must control all the final tickets sold (and precompute that set). But we assume one random ticket among the set of final tickets sold (contradiction).

In this analogy, the game is the delaying function. It is interesting to note that we could shift the delaying function to the function that amalgamates the seeds–that is, selecting the game could be the expensive operation, instead of playing the game. The resulting lottery would be fair too.

5 Related Work

We use a function of moderate complexity as the delaying function when computing the winner. To increase security, we minimize the requirements placed on that function (i.e., only complexity and randomness). In contrast, for the different problem of controlling access to a resource, Dwork and Naor present a technique requiring a user to compute a moderately hard, but not intractable (cryptographically hard) function which they call a pricing function [8]. They present solutions based on extracting square roots modulo a prime, the Fiat-Shamir signature scheme, and the Ong-Schnorr-Shamir (cracked) signature scheme. These solutions depend on the difficulty of extracting square roots mod p (no known method requires fewer than about $\log p$ multiplications), factoring large numbers, and an algorithm by Pollard for breaking the signature scheme based on quadratic equations modulo a composite, respectively. In a similar fashion, Franklin and Malkhi [9] use repeated hashing as evidence that a certain amount of time has elapsed.

These papers' motivating applications, preventing and/or detecting junk e-mail, and metering web clicks for advertising revenue, have two important properties that are not present in lotteries. The first is that, unlike lotteries, the cost of a security breach is low: some junk mail may get through or an advertiser may be changed for a bogus click. In contrast, the probability that a lottery may be fixed must be insignificant. The second difference is that both the junk mail and Web click metering solutions require asymmetric functions: the calculation must be moderately hard, but verification must be cheap. This is because the moderately hard calculation is used to slow down attackers, but the recipient's filtering process must be fast. If the calculation is not done correctly, the recipient ignores the mail. If the verification was as hard as the calculation, this approach would be ineffective: for example, the denial of service attack that junk mail presents would be transformed into one that consumes cycles.

Can we use pricing functions as our delaying functions? If the pricing function must be built using a shortcut, and one entity knows the shortcut, then one entity can break the scheme. The security of the lottery would then rely both upon the hardness of the non-shortcutted solution, and the confidentiality of the shortcut. Because we want to decentralize trust in the lottery, and do not want to rely upon the confidentiality of the shortcut, such pricing functions would not be suitable.

Pricing functions must allow for easy verifications of solutions that are hard to calculate. We could use this functionality in the lottery solution, but it may complicate the lottery design. For example, if a single ticket's seed parameter was the only input to the winning calculation and the ticket was the winner if its winning number parameter was the result, then each ticket purchaser would face a quandary: He could verify whether his proposed seed and winning numbers parameters would be winners before purchasing a ticket! Since nearly all combinations would loose, purchasers would never purchase tickets.

We have two options: We can either simplify the selection of delaying functions by requiring that they only satisfy the moderately hard to compute property, or we can complicate their selection, but perhaps simplify the lottery design, by requiring them also to be hard to verify. As our lottery design is resistant to the dilemma proposed above, we do not place the hard to verify requirement on our delaying functions.

The class of delaying functions may include the functions of [8, 9]. Since delaying functions do not have the easy to verify or shortcut requirement, they can be easier to construct, simply by choosing functions that have a high operation count and cannot be parallelized.

Rivest et. al. [15] propose time-lock puzzles where a puzzlemaker can create a puzzle that requires a well defined amount of computation time to solve. The proposal is related to [12] but is not parallelizable. Unlike delaying functions, the solution is known to the puzzlemaker, but is then discarded. So the puzzlemaker must be trusted not to cheat. The related work is summarized in Table 1. (A blank space in the table means that the property on the left is not a requirement for the function at the top of the column.)

Beth and Desmedt [3] present a time based solution to the chess grandmaster problem. Their solution involves delay, not expensive computation. They solve the problem of how to prevent a man in the middle from playing two grandmasters against one another, and claiming a significant win. They reduce the problem to one of authentication, and show that if the game setup protocol re-

	Delaying Functions	Time-lock Puzzles	Pricing Functions
Preserve Entropy	*Requirement*		
Easy to Verify		*Requirement*	*Requirement*
Solution Known a-Priori	*Negative Requirement*	*Requirement*	*Requirement* (with shortcut)

Table 1. Required properties of the related functions.

quires each party to commit to an exact delay that will precede their moves, one of the legitimate players will discover the man in the middle. They assume that communication takes some time, and do not require parties to otherwise identify themselves. (This is in contrast to PGP-Phone [20], which requires parties to read the negotiated key–the right sounding voice reading shared keying material is hard to forge in real-time.)

Finally, we briefly touch on other work. Cai et. al use moderately hard functions in the design of uncheatable benchmarks [6]. Benchmarks use problems that take significant computation time. However, if the input data is known a-priori, machine architectures can be optimized for those inputs. A solution is to select inputs randomly for each test. However, this makes independent verification of the result difficult (perhaps the machine computed the wrong result quickly!). Cai et. al. propose functions that have shortcuts that make them easy to verify, and functions that are easier to verify than to compute. Rivest [14] defines several types of electronic lotteries. There has been much work on distributed coin flipping [2, 4, 5, 11]. The protocols are expensive for each participant and are multi-pass. Also, Kahn, Kalai, and Linial [10] prove that it is information theoretically impossible to design functions that cannot be controlled by some strict subset of their inputs. Finally, we note if registration certificates are blinded for anonymity, care must be taken that the communications channel not identify the customer [18].

6 Conclusion

This paper presented a publicly verifiable lottery scheme that can be made fair with arbitrarily high probability. The scheme relies on two assumptions: the existence of delaying functions that are unlikely to be controllable by colluders with limited computational resources and that preserve the entropy in their inputs; and, the likelihood that large coalitions are more difficult to assemble than smaller ones. A candidate delaying function may use a cryptographic cipher with a very long period to generate a sufficient amount of keystream.

Delaying functions are related to pricing functions, time-lock puzzles, and other work that uses calculation time as a barrier [8, 9, 15, 12]. However, none of the previously proposed functions possess all the required properties of delaying functions: the function must preserve the entropy on its inputs, and the solution must not be known in advance to anyone, not even the party controlling the game.

Publicly verifiable lotteries decentralize the auditing of trusted function by enabling many individuals to validate the selected winner(s). To detect lottery fraud, individual customers can independently verify that their tickets were counted, anyone can compute the size of the winnings pool, and anyone with sufficient computational resources can calculate the winning entry. The use of time as a barrier may enable other interesting applications as well.

7 Acknowledgments

This works draws on initial discussions with Paul Syverson about closed lotteries. We are very grateful to him for his contributions. We also thank Matthew Franklin, David Maher, Rafail Ostrovsky, Moti Yung, and the anonymous referees for their suggestions

References

1. W. Aiello, S. Venkatesan, and R. Venkatesan. Design of practical and provably good random number generators. Proceedings of the Sixth Annual ACM-SIAM Symposium on Discrete Algorithms, ACM, New York, NY, Jan. 1995.
2. M. Bellare, J. Garay, and T. Rabin. Distributed Pseudo-Random Bit Generators - A New Way to Speed-Up Shared Coin Tossing, PODC'96, ACM, 1996.
3. T. Beth and Y. Desmedt. Identification tokens-or: solving the chess grandmaster problem. Advances in Cryptology - CRYPTO '90 Proceedings, pp. 169-176.
4. M. Blum. Coin flipping by telephone-a protocol for solving impossible problems. Spring COMPCON 82, IEEE, 1982, pp. 133-137.
5. A. Broder. A provably secure polynomial approximation scheme for the distributed lottery problem. Proceedings of the 4th Annual ACM Symposium on Principles of Distributed Computing, 1985, pp. 136-148.
6. J. Y. Cai, A. Nerurkar, M. Y. Wu. The Design of Uncheatable Benchmarks Using Complexity Theory, technical report 97-10, Department of Computer Science, SUNY Buffalo, 1997.
7. D. Chaum, "Security without Identification: Transaction Systems to Make Big Brother Obsolete", CACM (28,10), October 1985, pp. 1030–1044.
8. C. Dwork, and M. Naor. Pricing via processing or combating junk mail. Weizmann Technical Report CS95-20, 1995 (Also preliminary version in CRYPTO '92, pp. 139-147).
9. M. K. Franklin and D. Malkhi. Auditable Metering with Lightweight Security, Financial Cryptography 1997, LNCS Vol. 1318, Springer-Verlag, 1997.
10. J. Kahn, G. Kalai, and N. Linial. The influence of variables on Boolean functions. 29th Annual Symposium on Foundations of Computer Science, IEEE Washington, DC, USA, 1988, pp. 68-80.
11. E. Kushilevitz, Y. Mansour, and M. Rabin, On Lotteries with Unique Winners, SIAM Journal on Discrete Mathematics, vol. 8, No. 1, pp. 93-98, February, 1995.

12. R. Merkle. Secure Communications Over Insecure Channels. Communications of the ACM, vol. 21, no. 4, April, 1978, pp. 284-299.
13. A. Menezes, P. van Oorschot, and S. Vanstone. *Handbook of Applied Cryptography*, CRC Press, 1997.
14. R. Rivest. Electronic Lottery Tickets as Micropayments, Financial Cryptography 1997.
15. R. Rivest, A. Shamir, and D. Wagner. Time-lock puzzles and timed-release Crypto. Unpublished manuscript, February, 1996. See http://theory.lcs.mit.edu/˜rivest/RivestShamirWagner-timelock.ps.
16. S. Roman. Coding and Information Theory. Graduate texts in Mathematics number 134, Springer-Verlag, 1992.
17. P. Syverson, S. Stubblebine, and D. Goldschlag. Unlinkable Serial Transactions, Financial Cryptography 1997, LNCS Vol. 1318, Springer-Verlag, 1997.
18. P. Syverson, D. Goldschlag, and M. Reed. Anonymous Connections and Onion Routing, *Proceedings of the Symposium on Security and Privacy*, Oakland, CA, May 1997.
19. A. Webster and S. Tavares. One the design of S-boxes, Advances in Cryptology - Crypto 85 (LNCS 218), pp. 523-534, 1986.
20. P. R. Zimmerman. PGPfone Owner's Manual, Version 1.0 beta 7, July 8, 1996, p. 33.

Robustness and Security of Digital Watermarks

Lesley R. Matheson, Stephen G. Mitchell*, Talal G. Shamoon, Robert E.
Tarjan**, and Francis Zane***

STAR Lab
InterTrust Technologies Corporation
460 Oakmead Parkway
Sunnyvale, CA 94086.
{lrm,talal,mitchell,ret,fzane}@intertrust.com

Abstract. Digital watermarking is a nascent but promising technology
that offers protection of unencrypted digital content. This paper is a
brief technical survey of the multimedia watermarking landscape. The
three main technical challenges faced by watermarking algorithms are
fidelity, robustness and security. Current watermarking methods offer
possibly acceptable fidelity and robustness against certain types of processing, such as data compression and noise addition, but are not sufficiently robust against geometric transforms such as scaling and cropping
of images. Theoretical approaches have been developed that could lead
to secure watermarking methods, but substantial gaps remain between
theory and practice.

1   Introduction

The merging of computation and communication, as embodied for example in
the Internet, offers substantial new opportunities for processing and distribution
of valuable digital creations such as audio tracks, still images, and movies. At the
same time, the new technology offers cheap and easy copying and distribution of
pirated material. A standard and well-understood technical approach to reducing
piracy is to use cryptography: valuable material is distributed in encrypted form,
and only authorized users have the decryption keys. A complementary approach
that offers protection of unencrypted material is *digital watermarking*.

This paper is a brief technical survey of the landscape of digital watermarking. Our goal is to understand the general principles that could lead to successful
watermarking methods. Whereas cryptography is a relatively well-studied and
stable field, serious study of digital watermarking began only recently, and much
is not yet known. We begin in Section 2 by describing what we mean by watermarking, what content types might be marked, and what functionality watermarking might provide. In Section 3, we discuss what criteria should be used to

---

*   and School of Electrical Engineering, Cornell University, Ithaca, NY 14853.
** and Department of Computer Science, Princeton University, Princeton, NJ 08544.
*** and Dept. of Computer Science, University of California at San Diego, La Jolla, CA
      92093.

evaluate watermarking methods, and why successful watermarking might even be possible. In Section 4, we discuss the components of a generic watermarking system. In Section 5, we study the issue of robustness of watermarks to standard data processing, and in Section 6 we discuss various issues concerning watermark security. In Section 7, we study theoretical results about the resistance of watermarks to attacks. In Section 8 we offer a few concluding remarks. For a variety of interesting papers on watermarking and related topics, see [1, 33, 14].

2   What Is Watermarking?

By *watermarking* we mean the embedding of encoded information into digital data so that the information is imperceptible, easily read by authorized parties only, and difficult to remove by unauthorized parties without destroying the (value of the) original data. We contrast this with several related, but distinct notions:

Steganography (hidden writing): Steganography is the imperceptible embedding of encoded information in data in a way that may or may not be robust, but with the assumption that a potential adversary is unaware of the existence of the hidden communication channel. Watermarking allows the possibility of an adversary knowing about the channel; ideally, we want methods resistant to malicious attack.

Visible watermarking: Here the mark is designed to be easily read by all parties, but this visibility may (or may not) spoil the original data. Examples of visible image watermarks include the glyph technology of Xerox [12] and a method of IBM [22].

Fragile watermarking: Here we embed information imperceptibly, but so that significant changes to the data destroy the watermark. A fragile watermark can serve as an embedded signature guaranteeing the authenticity of the data. Ideally, a fragile watermark might even reveal, through how it has been distorted, what processing the original data has undergone. Developing fragile watermarking methods is a promising research direction, but it is beyond our scope here.

In watermarking, it is important to distinguish between two broad content types. The first, *perceptual content*, includes audio tracks (speech and wideband), still images, and video clips. The second, *representational* or *abstract content*, includes natural language texts and programs written in general- or special-purpose programming languages. From the standpoint of watermarking, the main distinction between these two content types is the amount and kind of distortion each can tolerate. For perceptual content, it seems easier to make the distinction between "small" distortions of the data, as such those caused by a successful watermarking method, and "large," or value-destroying, distortions. Put differently, in the case of perceptual content, we are dealing with a continuous space of possibilities that has some relatively simple (though high-dimensional) geometry. What the geometry might be for various kinds of representational content is largely unexplored terrain. Here we shall limit our attention to perceptual content, selecting our examples primarily from the realm of still images. Even for perceptual content, identifying the underlying geometry is a challenging problem.

The meaning of the watermark is another important issue. To understand the possible functions of watermarks, let us posit a simplified scenario in which a creator develops a piece of valuable content and sends it through a distribution channel, at the end of which it is released to various customers. The content can be marked in two places: by the creator, before it enters the distribution channel; and, by the distributor, as it leaves the channel. Marks introduced by the creator before distribution can depend only on the material itself, and not upon the recipient. Such watermarks can encode creator identity, copyright information, and content characteristics. These marks can be used to help defend copyright, to identify the creator for advertising and billing purposes, and to identify the content for use in metering and to facilitate database search.

Marking the material as it is released to a consumer affords the possibility of putting consumer identification or transaction information into the content, so that illegitimately-distributed content can be traced back to its point of release. The added flexibility allowed by transaction-based marking (sometimes called fingerprinting, although this word has also been used for other concepts) comes with some costs. First, the marking process must be efficient enough to not unduly impede the transaction. Preprocessing the content to make marking faster, or even pre-marking the content in many different ways and binding a specific mark to a specific consumer at transaction time, are ways to save time in transactions. Second, transactional marking raises the possibility of collusion attacks, in which pirates obtain several differently marked copies of the same material and combine all the copies to remove all the different marks. Most of the theoretical work on watermarking has been devoted to the problem of resisting collusive attacks. We look at this in Section 7.

For more complicated (and more realistic) distribution chains, there are more opportunities to introduce and to use watermarks. Assuming that the watermarking method supports multiple marking, the entire development and distribution history of a piece of content could be encoded in a sequence of successively embedded marks.

Some have suggested that watermarks should be human-readable [6]. We believe strongly that watermarks should be machine-readable, not (necessarily) human-readable. Machine-readable marks allow the possibility of active marking, in which marks are read and appropriate actions are taken in the course of content processing and distribution. A very simple example is copy control: a video player/copier outfitted with a watermark reader could seek a mark indicating "copyrighted material: no copying allowed," and disable the copying function when sensing such a mark. Another reason to use machine-readable marks is that they allow for much more efficient encoding of information into what is inherently a low-capacity communication channel.

3   Quality Criteria for Watermarking Methods

Critical criteria for watermarking methods include the following:

1. **Fidelity:** The changes entailed by marking should not affect the value of the content, and ideally the mark should be imperceptible. Specifically, experts in the medium should not be able to discriminate between the watermarked data and the original.

2. **Robustness:** Watermarks should survive standard data processing, such as would occur in a creation and distribution process. For still images, for example, such processing includes data compression, noisy transmission, digital-to-analog and analog-to-digital conversion (such as printing and scanning), color correction, sharpening and blurring, addition of captions, and geometric modifications such as cropping, scaling and rotation.

3. **Security:** Watermarks should survive deliberate attempts to remove them. Ideally, a watermark should remain readable up to the point where the content becomes modified enough to be of low value. A potential attacker can try standard processing techniques such as those mentioned above, but can also try less natural transformations specifically designed to erase watermarks. Attack becomes easier if the attacker has access to a watermark reader and can measure success. Attack also becomes easier if the attacker has access to differently marked versions of the same material.

Among these criteria, fidelity is usually paramount. The goal in building a successful marking method is to find a way to embed a mark with as much strength as possible (to provide robustness) while still preserving fidelity, by keeping the changes made by the mark under the perceptual threshold. We shall discuss this issue more fully in Section 5.

To obtain watermark security requires another key idea, that of *randomness*. The reason we might expect to be able to watermark perceptual data with some degree of security boils down to the following idea. Perceptual data has a very high number of places to put a mark (consider the number of pixels in a high-quality digital image.) The perceptual threshold allows small changes in a significant but relatively small number of such places. To spoil the mark successfully, an attacker who does not know the location of the mark must alter a large fraction of the places, thereby exceeding the perceptual threshold and destroying the original content. To guarantee that an attacker does not know the marked places, we can choose them randomly (or pseudo-randomly). This argument can be quantified, and (theoretically) gives security even in the presence of collusion. (See Section 7.)

Additional important criteria for watermarking methods include:

4. **Data capacity:** How many bits of information can the mark contain as a function of the size of the original content? How many marks can be added simultaneously?

5. **Accuracy of detection:** How accurately can the mark be read? What is the chance of a false positive (unmarked content appearing to have a mark) a false negative (marked data appearing to be unmarked), or a false reading (a mark misread as another mark)?

6. **Efficiency:** What are the computing time, storage requirements, and software or hardware size of the mark writing and reading processes? Are they real-time, so that they can be incorporated into playback or display mechanisms in an on-line setting? How do they interact with data compression and decompression?

7. **Data secrecy and storage requirements:** What information needs to be retained, or kept secret, about the marks, their meaning, and the marked material? Depending upon the watermarking method, such information can include encryption and decryption keys for computing and interpreting marks, a database mapping marks to their meanings, and a database containing (components of) original content that has been marked. A significant distinction here is between "original-based" watermarking methods, in which the original data is required to read the marks, and "no-original" methods, in which marks can be read without having the original. No-original algorithms are much more flexible and useful but harder to make robust. Many of the early algorithms in the literature are original-based methods, which have restricted practical functionality.

4 The Components of a Watermarking System

There are three components to a watermarking system: a watermark writing algorithm, a watermark reading algorithm, and a database (or databases) to store needed information about marks written and data that has been marked. We shall discuss watermark writing and reading from a generic point of view. When specifics or examples are needed to make concepts concrete, we shall select them from the domain of still images, although the same principles apply to watermarking audio tracks, video clips or similar kinds of data. Since database technology is relatively well-understood, we shall not comment on this component of a watermarking system, except to mention information that might have to be stored in such a database.

The first step in watermark writing is to choose a representation of the original data. An important property of media data is that it is high-dimensional: think of the number of pixels in a high-quality image. The representation may be the original representation (pixels for images); or it may be a transformed representation, such as Fourier components, discrete cosine components, or wavelet components; or some higher-level representation, such as an object or feature representation. If a transformed representation is used, it may be applied to the entire data (the whole image), or on a block-by-block basis. For images, watermarks have been applied to pixels [2], Fourier components [24], whole-image and block-based discrete cosine components [8, 23, 39], wavelet components [23], and Fourier-Mellin components [25, 13]. One use of a transformed representation is to make the components of the data more independent; pixels in an image, for example, are highly correlated locally, which is not true of discrete cosine components.

Once a representation has been determined, a subset of the components must be chosen to be marked. This choice is generally made with the goal of preserving fidelity while enhancing robustness and security as much as possible. One idea in the literature is to mark the largest-magnitude discrete cosine components [8], the justification being that these components are perceptually significant and likely to be preserved by common data processing techniques, such as data compression. Though this may be a good approach for an original-based watermarking scheme, it may not be so useful for a no-original scheme, for reasons discussed below. For typical data, the largest magnitude components are mostly the low-frequency ones, and marking low frequencies may serve just as well. A possibly better idea for a no-original scheme is to mark mid-frequency components [13, 37, 19] with the hope that these components are perceptually significant but relatively low-energy. Herigal, et al. [13] for example, mark in the Fourier domain. They avoid "the largest (high energy) components (at about the lowest 10% of the frequencies)" and use "components at the medium frequencies (about next 30%)." They also suggest the possibility of "marking the largest components (inside the allowed frequency range)."

Another guide to choosing components is to seek some that are invariant to certain kinds of processing. For example, one may choose to represent a color image using a luminosity-chrominance basis, and mark only the luminosity components, thereby rendering the watermark robust to a color-to-grayscale transformation. A similar idea discussed more fully in the next section is to mark certain Fourier-Mellin components of an image [25, 13], thereby obtaining some robustness to the geometric transformations of scaling, cropping and rotation. To enhance security, one may choose to mark only a random subset of the set of components selected for robustness.

Having chosen components (places) to mark, one must choose the mark values and combine them with the chosen components to obtain modified components, which replace the original components and are used to construct a modified copy of the original data. The mark values may be an encoded and possibly encrypted representation of the information to be conveyed by the mark, or they may be chosen randomly and merely associated with the intended information (via a database entry). It is worth noting that encryption by itself will serve the purpose of making the watermark values appear random. A common choice of mark values is $\{0, 1\}$ or $\{-1, +1\}$, although we shall see later that security needs dictate other choices. To deal with the issue of perceptibility, we may choose to multiply each watermark value by a strength parameter, which may be globally chosen or may depend on the particular component being marked and on the particular data being marked: sophisticated marking algorithms use perceptual masking models to choose strength parameters [39, 40, 31], seeking maximum-strength marks that lie within the perceptual threshold.

As a way of combining mark values with original component values, we distinguish between *addition,* in which each strengthened mark value is added to the corresponding original component value, and *replacement,* in which each strengthened mark value replaces the corresponding original component value. Other ways of combining values can generally be reduced to addition by an appropriate transformation. For example, a multiplicative marking scheme can be reduced to an additive marking scheme by applying a logarithmic transformation.

We can represent a generic additive watermark-writing method symbolically as follows. Assume that n components of the data are to be marked, and that the original component values are $d_1, d_2 \ldots, d_n$. Let $w_1, w_2 \ldots, w_n$ be the selected watermark values, and let $s_1, s_2 \ldots, s_n$ be the desired watermark strengths. Then the watermark writing process consists of replacing each $d_i, 1 \leq i \leq n$, by $d_i' = d_i + s_i w_i$. The corresponding replacement watermark-writing method would instead replace each d_i by $d'_i = s_i w_i$. If there is a finite range to each component (as for example with pixels), we must truncate each d_i' to keep it in range.

The second major component of a watermarking system is the watermark reader, which of course must match the writer. To read a mark, we first transform the data into the representation used for mark writing. Then we extract the components $d_1^*, d_2^*, \ldots, d_n^*$ that correspond to the ones that were marked. In a replacement-based scheme, these values should be approximately the strengthened mark values $s_1 w_1, s_2 w_2 \ldots, s_n w_n$. We can merely divide each d_i^* by the corresponding strength s_i and attempt to interpret the resulting vector d_1^*/s_1, $d_2^*/s_2, \ldots, d_n^*/s_n$ as a mark. One way to make the reading process robust is to use an error-correcting code in choosing marks and interpreting them. Another way is to apply signal detection theory [32] (see also [37, 20, 19]) and do a correlation-based hypothesis test. Namely, we compute a correlation (a dot product normalized in some way) between the hypothetical watermark $d_1^*/s_1, d_2^*/s_2, \ldots, d_n^*/s_n$ and an actual watermark $w_1, w_2, \ldots, w_n$, and conclude that the latter is present in the data if the correlation exceeds some threshold.

Virtually the same methods can be used to read additive watermarks. The connection is tightest for original-based additive marking. If we have access to the appropriate components, $d_1, d_2, \ldots, d_n$ of the original data, we can compute a hypothetical watermark by first subtracting these components and then dividing by the strengths: $w_i^* = (d_i^* - d_i)/s_i$. We can then apply error correction or a correlation test to the sequence $w_1^*, w_2^*, \ldots, w_n^*$ to attempt to match it against an actual mark. The CKLS original-based watermarking method [8] uses such a correlation test to read the mark.

Reading a no-original additive watermark is more problematic. Fortunately, the correlation-based method still works if we merely correlate the reduced-strength components $d_1^*/s_1, d_2^*/s_2, \ldots d_n^*/s_n$ with an actual watermark w_1, w_2, $\ldots, w_n$ and apply a threshold test [37, 20, 19]. A corresponding no-original version of the CKLS method is described in [30]. Such an approach works because the reduced-strength components d_i^*/s_i are approximately the watermark values w_i

plus the reduced-strength original components d_i/s_i, and the correlation between the w_i and the d_i/s_i is approximately zero, but with high variance.

A major hurdle in no-original watermarking is to reduce the noise in the detection process caused by the presence of the original data when doing watermark reading [37, 19]. One way to accomplish this is to mark low-energy but still significant components, such as middle-frequency components as mentioned above. Subtracting out the original, when this is possible, can be viewed as just a very powerful noise-reduction technique applied to standard correlation-based signal detection.

5 Robustness

As discussed briefly in Section 3, to be robust, a watermark must survive two types of standard processing techniques: *alignment-preserving transformations*, which include data compression, quantization, data conversion (digital-to-analog and analog-to-digital conversion), and others; and *alignment-altering transformations*, such as (in the case of images), cropping, scaling and rotation (Data conversion with severe distortion or imprecise resampling may actually be alignment-altering rather than alignment-preserving.) The current state-of-the-art is that there are a variety of similar watermarking algorithms for various media types that survive alignment-preserving tranformations reasonably well. Many of these algorithms use frequency-based representations and rely on some kind of perceptual model to embed a maximum-strength imperceptible mark (e.g. [40]).

Lacy, et al. [18] argue that *compressed* data, not the original *baseband* (raw or uncompressed) data, is what should be protected. They propose an audio watermarking algorithm that is tightly integrated with a perceptual audio data compressor. Such an algorithm allows reading a watermark from the compressed data, a capability that may be a requirement in on-line transaction-based systems. Whether such watermarks survive decompression remains to be tested empirically.

Surviving alignment-altering transformations is problematic. For example, devising still-image watermarking methods that are robust to scaling, cropping and rotation is a challenging problem, especially for combinations of these transformations as would occur, for example, in creating a photomontage. Several approaches exist:

1. In an original-based method, one can align a transformed watermarked image against the original, using standard registration or pattern-matching methods.
2. In a no-original based method, one can add a universal *registration* mark and align a transformed marked image against the registration mark.
3. In a no-original method, one can attempt to do a self-alignment of a transformed image, based on some set of distinguishable features.
4. As mentioned in Section 3, one can put the watermark into a set of components that are invariant to certain transformations. For still images the

magnitudes of Fourier-Mellin components are invariant under translation, rotation, and scaling (in an abstract, continuous setting) [5, 36].

Ó Ruanaidh and Pun [25] have explored Method 4, that of marking the magnitudes of the Fourier-Mellin components, as a way to make watermarks robust against translation, rotation and scaling. This idea has been refined by Herigal, et al. [13]. They first take the logarithm of the luminance levels (to match the human visual system) and then do a Fourier transform. They mark the magnitudes of medium-frequency components. Additionally, they add a registration template based on a Fourier-Mellin transform of the magnitudes of the Fourier components. This template is intended to be robust against rotation and scaling. Their approach combines Methods 2 and 4. It is worth noting that taking the logarithm as the first step has the effect of increasing the watermark signal-to-noise ratio and hence of making detection easier.

6 Security

Security of watermarks is receiving increasing attention, especially from the academic community. A variety of attacks on various kinds of watermarking schemes have been proposed and studied [26, 20, 38, 15, 21, 10]. There are a variety of issues concerning watermark security that are properly in the domain of cryptography and cryptographic protocols, and these should be considered separately from the issue of whether marks can be erased. For example, by using standard cryptographic methods, one can guarrantee (up to the security of the cryptographic scheme) that watermarks cannot be read or forged by unauthorized parties, although preventing false claims of ownership may require an appropriate information registry. Craver, et al. [10] observed that additive original-based schemes such as the CKLS algorithm [8] can be subjected to a forgery attack in which a forger creates his or her own watermark and subtracts it from a previously marked original, creating a fake "original" that the forger claims to own. Again, cryptographic techniques are the appropriate way to guard against attacks like this.

Turning to attacks designed to make watermarks unreadable, it is well-known that a simple least-significant-bit scheme can be defeated by randomizing the least-significant bits that contain the watermark, or by setting all these bits to zero. Schemes based on perceptual modeling that attempt to insert maximum-power watermarks are much harder to attack, but small amounts of scaling and cropping will erase many kinds of watermarks. For example, Kilian, et al. [17] observed that the CKLS mark can be rendered unreadable by cropping a few rows and columns of pixels and scaling the image to the original size. Such an attack can be countered by aligning (or registering) to the original image; or, if the original is not available, by aligning to a previously inserted registration mark, or by using a watermark that is robust to such transformations, as discussed in Section 5.

Making watermark writers and readers publicly available creates security risks, even if the algorithms are black boxes. For example, a watermark scheme that uses a universal, additive registration mark can be made unreadable by taking the negative of the marked data and remarking it, thereby subtracting out the registration mark (Bill Horne, oral communication, 1997). A scheme that uses a public reader may be susceptible to a sensitivity-analysis attack such as described by Cox and Linnartz [9] and analyzed by Linnartz and Van Dijk [20]. Fridrich, et al. [11] have proposed a watermarking method that uses key-dependent basis functions and may allow the construction of a secure public reader.

A particularly potent kind of attack is a *collusion attack*, in which an attacker obtains several differently marked copies of the same data, or several different pieces of data marked in the same way. Kilian, et al. [17] have observed that correlative-reader watermarks that use a componentwise $\{-1, 1\}$ or $\{0, 1\}$ distribution (common in the literature) or even a component-wise uniform distribution are at risk of attack with as few as five or six differently-marked copies. Resistance to collusive attack is the main focus of the theoretical work we discuss in the next section.

7 Models of Security

A body of work exists devoted to answering the question of whether truly secure watermarks can exist, and what the characteristics of such marks might be. Most of this work deals with resistance to collusive attacks. Such work is necessarily theoretical and relies on modeling assumptions. A key issue is the extent to which the emerging theories can be applied to practice.

An early and intriguing paper is that of Wagner [43], who proposed the use of randomly selected additive watermarks and did a preliminary study of the resistance of such marks to collusive attacks. Blakely, et al. [3] looked at a combinatorial model for collusion resistance, and proposed a scheme that offers k-way collusion resistance within the model but requires a number of watermark bits exponential in the number of colluders. Chor, et al. [7] worked on a related problem involving tracing pirates in a broadcast distribution system using a multiple-key protocol. Boneh and Shaw [4] combined the Chor, et al. work with a simple collusion-resistant scheme to yield a watermarking method that provides defense against k-way collusion and conveys b bits of information in a watermark of size $O(k^4 b)$ bits. Follow-on work to that of Chor, et al. and Boneh and Shaw appears in [28, 29, 27].

The Boneh-Shaw model is a discrete combinatorial framework that captures the notion of collusion resistance, but ignores other issues of watermark security and robustness. They posit a watermark consisting of n positions, each position selected from an alphabet of size s. An attacker in posession of k differently watermarked copies is allowed to spoil any position in which two of the obtained copies differ. The goal of the watermarker is to identify at least one of the watermarks using only the information contained in the positions in which all k watermarks are the same.

Boneh and Shaw do not address the question of how to provide individual robust marking positions (which cannot be attacked unless detected by difference analysis) nor do they consider the possibility that marked positions, even if detected, might be difficult to spoil (for perceptual or other reasons) This makes their method more suited for representational-content watermarking (see Section 2) than for perceptual-content watermarking.

A model of the latter kind of watermarking has been investigated by Kilian, et al. [17], building on ideas of J. Kilian and F.T. Leighton (oral communications, 1996) and a draft set of notes of Leighton (1996). The model assumes that the original data is an n-dimensional vector, with each component independently distributed according to $N(0, 1)$, the Gaussian distribution with mean zero and variance 1. The model further assumes a perceptual threshold based on Euclidean distance. For an additive watermark that is also an n-dimensional vector with independent components distributed according to $\epsilon N(0, 1)$ (for a suitable choice of ϵ depending on the perceptual threshold) and a correlative original-based watermark reader, Kilian, et al. proved that the watermarks can carry $O(n/k^2)$ bits of information while resisting k-way collusive attacks with high probability. Equivalently, $O(k^2 b)$ watermark components are needed to carry b bits of information while being secure against k-way collusive attack. Further work by Ergun, Kilian and Kumar (unpublished notes, 1997), refined and tightened by Mitchell, Tarjan and Zane (unpublished notes, 1997) has shown that, within the Kilian-Leighton statistical model, no watermarking method can offer better resistance to collusive attacks. Specifically, collusive attack based on averaging and addition of Gaussian noise will erase any watermark with high probability, given $\Omega(n/k^2)$ differently marked copies, if n is the dimension of the watermarks.

Related but independent work has been done by Karakos and Papamarcou [16]. They consider the ability of maximum-strength watermarks with original-based correlative reading to withstand the attack of averaging plus addition of Gaussian noise, within a Euclidean perceptual threshold model. They consider only a single-copy attack and a two-copy attack. They show that such watermarks can convey up to 0.5 bits of information per dimension while being secure against a one-copy attack, and up to 0.146 bits per dimension while being secure against a two-copy attack.

One reason why no-original watermarking works, at least theoretically, is that in high dimensions randomly selected watermarks are, with high probability, almost orthogonal to the data and to each other [20, 37]. Tirkel et al. [42, 34, 35] discuss the issue of orthogonality at length, and propose the construction of watermarks that are exactly orthogonal to each other, but this may be an unnecessary step in practice. (They use pseudo-random bit sequences as watermarks rather than Gaussian noise.) Swanson, et al. [41] suggest a scheme that chooses a random watermark direction and encodes a mark in the hidden direction, with a strength determined by a perceptual model.

Some extensions of the Kilian, et al. results are possible. First, it is straightforward to extend the result to the no-original setting; only the constant factors change. Second, the watermark need not be Gaussian, but can be maximum-strength (or fixed strength) with randomly chosen direction within the Euclidean threshold model, because, for high dimensions, Gaussian and random-direction fixed-strength watermarks behave approximately the same. Thus the Swanson et al. marking algorithm falls within this theory.

Much remains to be done to extend this theoretical work and to determine if it has any practical relevance. The Kilian, et al. Euclidean perceptual model breaks down in reality because small geometric distortions can produce large changes in Euclidean distance. Also, a correlative reader must compute a correlation for each possible watermark, leading to a computation that is exponential in the number of bits of information conveyed. One way to improve the efficiency of the reader is to use a small set of signalling patterns, either combined in all the components or distributed over subsets of components. A third direction to study is the relationship between the combinatorial and statistical models, and to determine whether they can usefully be combined. Finally, the Boneh-Shaw bound on watermark size is $O(k^4 b)$ to protect against k colluders and convey b bits. Reducing this bound, or proving it tight, is an open problem.

8 Remarks

Digital watermarking, though young, is a rapidly expanding field. It combines elements of cryptography, signal processing, information theory, coding theory, probability and statistics, game theory and other disciplines. Whether all the activity in this area will lead to robust, practical watermarking schemes remains to be seen, but certainly the field is full of exciting possibilities.

References

1. R. Anderson, Ed., *Information Hiding, First International Workshop Proceedings*, *Lecture Notes in Computer Science* 1174, Springer-Verlag, Berlin, 1996.
2. W. Bender, D. Gruhl, N. Marimoto, and A. La, "Techniques for data hiding," *IBM Systems Journal* 35 (1996).
3. G.R. Blakely, C. Meadors, and G.B. Purdy, "Fingerprinting long unforgiving messages," *Crypto '85, Lecture Notes in Computer Science* 218, Springer-Verlag, Berlin (1985), pp.180-189.
4. D. Boneh and J. Shaw, "Collusion-secure fingerprinting for digital data," *Crypto '95, Lecture Notes in Computer Science* 963, Springer-Verlag, Berlin, 1995, pp. 452–465.
5. R.D. Brandt and F. Lin, "Representations that uniquely characterize images modulo translation, rotation, and scaling," *Pattern Recognition Letters* 17 (1996), pp. 1001-1015.
6. G. W. Braudaway, "Protecting publicly-available images with an invisible image watermark," *Proc. IEEE Int. Conf. on Image Procesing, ICIP-97* (1997), Vol. I, pp. 524-51.
7. B. Chor, A. Fiat, and M. Naor, "Tracing traitors," *Crypto '94, Lecture Notes in Computer Science* 963, Springer-Verlag, Berlin, 1995, pp. 452-465.

8. I. Cox, J. Kilian, T. Leighton, and T. Shamoon, "Secure spread spectrum watermarking for multimedia," *IEEE Trans. on Image Processing* 6 (1997), 1673-1687.

9. I. Cox and J.-P. Linnartz, "Public watermarks and resistance to tampering," *Proc. IEEE Conf. on Image Processing* (1997), CD-ROM.

10. S. Craver, N. Memon, B.L. Yeo, and M. Yeung, "Can invisible watermarks resolve rightful ownerships?", *IBM Research Report* RC 20509 (1996).

11. J. Fridrich, A.C. Baldoza, and R.J. Simard, "Robust digital watermarking based on key-dependent basis functions," *Preliminary Proc. Second International Information Hiding Workshop* (1998).

12. D.L. Hecht, " Embedded data glyph technology for hardcopy digital documents," *SPIE* 2171 (1995).

13. A. Herrigal, J.J Ó Ruanaidh, W. Peterson, S. Pereira, and T. Pun, "Secure copyright protection techniques for digital images," *Preliminary Proceedings of the Second International Information Hiding Workshop* (1998).

14. *Proceedings of the IEEE International Conference on Image Processing, ICIP-47,* Vols. I-III, IEEE Computer Society, Los Alamitos, CA, 1997.

15. N.F. Johnson and S. Sajodia, "Steganalysis of images created using current steganography software," *Preliminary Proc. Second International Information Hiding Workshop* (1998).

16. D. Karakos and A. Papamarcou, "Some results on the information capacity of authentication channels," Dept. of Electrical Engineering, University of Maryland, College Park, MD, manuscript, 1997.

17. J. Kilian, F.T. Leighton, L. Matheson, T. Shamoon, R. Tarjan, and F. Zane, "Resistance of digital fingerprints to collusional attacks," unpublished manuscript (1997).

18. J. Lacy, S.R. Quackenbush, A. Reibman, and J.H. Snyder, "Intellectual property protection systems and digital watermarking," *Preliminary Proceedings of the Second International Information Hiding Workshop* (1998).

19. J. P. Linnartz, T. Kalker, and G. Depovere, "Modelling the false alarm and missed detection rate for electronic watermarks," *Preliminary Proceedings of the Second International Information Hiding Workshop* (1998)

20. J. P. Linnartz and M. Van Dijk, "Analysis of the sensitivity attack against electronic watermarks in images," *Preliminary Proceedings of the Second International Information Hiding Workshop* (1998).

21. M. Maes, "Twin peaks: the histogram attack on fixed depth image watermarks," *Preliminary Proc. Second International Information Hiding Workshop* (1998).

22. K.A.Magerlein, G.W. Braudaway, and F.C. Mintzer, "Protecting publically-available images with a visible image watermark," *Proc. SPIE Conf. on Optical Security and Counterfeit Deterrence Techniques*, SPIE 2659 (1996), pp. 126-132.

23. J.J.K Ó Ruanaidh, W. J. Dowling, and F. M. Boland, "Watermarking digital images for copyright protection," *IEE Proc. on Vision, Image and Signal Processing* 143 (1996), pp. 250-256.

24. J.J.K. Ó Ruanaidh, W.J. Dowling, and F.M. Boland, "Phase watermarking of digital images," *Proc. IEEE International Conference on Image Processing ICIP-96* (1996), pp. 239-242.

25. J. Ó Ruanaidh and T. Pun, "Rotation, translation and scale invariant digital image watermarking," *Proceedings 1997 IEEE International Conference on Image Processing* (1997), Vol. I, pp. 536-539.

26. F. Peticolas, R. Anderson, and M. Kuhn, "Attacks on copyright marking systems," *Preliminary Proc. Second International Information Hiding Workshop* (1998).

27. B. Pfitzmann and M. Shaunter, "Anonymous fingerprinting, (extended abstract)," *EUROCRYPT '96, Lecture Notes in Computer Science* 1070, Springer-Verlag, Berlin (1996), pp. 84-95.

28. B. Pfitzmann and M. Waidner, "Asymmetric fingerprinting for larger collusions," *4th ACM Conf. on Computer and Communications Security* (1997), pp. 151-160.

29. B. Pfitzmann and M. Waidner, "Anonymous fingerprinting," IBM Research Report RZ 2221 (1996).

30. A. Piva, M. Barni, F. Bartolini, and V. Cappellini, "DCT-based watermark recovering without resorting to the uncorrupted original image," *Proceedings 1997 IEEE International Conference on Image Processing* (1997) Vol. I, pp. 520-523.

31. C. Podilchuck and W. Zeng, "Digital image watermarking using visual models," *IS&T/SPIE Electronic Imaging* 3016 (1997).

32. V. Poor, *An Introduction to Signal Detection and Estimation*, 2nd Edition, Springer-Verlag, New York, 1994.

33. *Preliminary Proceedings of the Second International Information Hiding Workshop*, 1998.

34. R. van Schyndel, A. Tirkel, and C. Osborne, "A digital watermark," *Proceedings 1994 IEEE International Conference on Image Processing*, (1994), pp. 86-90.

35. R. van Schyndel, A. Tirkel, and C. Osborne, "Towards a robust digital watermark," *Proceedings DICTA-95* (1993), pp. 378-385.

36. Y. Sheng and H.H. Arsenault, "Experiments on pattern recognition using invariant Fourier-Mellon descriptors," *J. Optical Society of America A* 3 (1986), pp. 771-776.

37. J.R. Smith and B.O. Comisky, "Modulation and information hiding in images," *Information Hiding, First International Workshop Procedings*, R. Anderson, ed., *Lecture Notes in Computer Science* 1174, Springer-Verlag, Berlin (1996), pp. 207-226.

38. S. Sowers and A. Youssef, "Testing digital watermark resistance to destruction," *Preliminary Proc. Second International Information Hiding Workshop* (1998).

39. M.D.Swanson, B. Zhu, and A.A. Tewfik, "Transparent robust image watermarking," *Proc IEEE Int. Conf. On Image Processing, ICIP-96* Vol. 3, (1996) pp. 211-214.

40. M.D. Swanson, B. Zhu, and A.H. Tewfik, "Robust image watermaking using perceptual models," unpublished manuscipt (1997).

41. M. Swanson, B. Zhu, and A. Tewfik, "Data Hiding for Video in Video," *Proceedings 1997 IEEE International Conference on Image Processing*, (1997), Vol II, pp. 676-679.

42. A. Tirkel, G. Rankin, R. van Schyndel, W. Ho, N. Mee, and C Osborne, "Electronic watermark," *Proceedings DICTA-93* (1993), pp. 666-673.

43. N. Wagner, "Fingerprinting," *Proc. 1983 IEEE Symp. on Security and Privacy* (1983), pp. 18-22.

44. W. Zeng and B. Liu, "On resolving rightful ownerships of digital images by invisible watermarks," *Proc. IEEE Int. Conf. on Image Processing, ICIP-97* (1997), Vol. I, pp. 552-555.

Beyond Identity: Warranty-Based Digital Signature Transactions

Yair Frankel*, David W. Kravitz **, Charles T. Montgomery*, Moti Yung*

Abstract. We distinguish between two types of digital-signature based transactions: *identity-based* and *warranty-granting*. In the relatively static (and traditional) offline "identity-based" transaction, a Certification Authority (CA) vouches for validity and veracity of data in a user's certificate. Whereas, in the more dynamic "warranty-granting" case, which we identify in this paper, a third-party entity vouches for a user on a per-transaction basis while considering the user's history and characteristics. Here, we provide a modeling for a warranty-granting transactions system and demonstrate its importance in the banking/financial/commercial setting. Warranty-granting systems can be implemented in one of several configurations based on the type of transaction and which party pays for the service (of acquiring the warranty). We discuss the primary configurations and then give a detailed specification for one of the discussed configurations.

1 Introduction

The development of public-key and modern cryptography has given us the notion of "digital signature". The role of digital signature is to replace real-life signatures and allow a user in an "electronic world" to have a mechanism for signing documents. The digital signature identifies the signer and unequivocally associates the signer with the document signed. It provides non-repudiation of the sender and enables transitive passing of authenticated messages.

Let us note first that in order to achieve scalability of digital signature, a mere personal digital signature scheme is not enough. In a crude form every user must have the "signature verification key" of every other user. Therefore, the notion and architecture of "Certification Authority" (CA) has been suggested. In fact, a CA is an entity that vouches for the correctness of very specific messages, each of which establishes the association of "user identity" with the user's "signature verification key". Thus, a CA architecture is in fact a bootstrapping of the notion of digital signature. The individual users now do not have to have the verification key of each user, instead they can be presented with a signature and a "certificate" where the CA signs the standard message associating a user with a verification key. To this end there are various schemes (e.g., [X509]).

In a basic CA-based architecture a certificate is either "pushed" to the user by the signer, or the certificate is "pulled" from the CA by the user. The "or" is not exclusive due to the possibility of revocation of certificates. For high scalability,

* CertCo LLC., montgomeryc,moti@certco.com; moti,yfrankel@cs.columbia.edu
** Divx, David.Kravitz@divx.com, Research performed while at CertCo LLC

we will typically have a hierarchy of CA's (CA infrastructure). A user will go up the tree-structure to a CA that it trusts. (The structure does not have to be a hierarchy and may have more semantics; namely various CA's may deal with certain tasks, key types and transactions.)

What we claim is that: a basic CA architecture is there in order to assure that a signature scheme is associated with an identity and its associated static properties. Thus, it will give very good services to transactions where the authenticity of digital signatures is the basic worry. We call such transactions "identity-based".

What has been observed is that once we enter into a commercial setting where financial service support for a transaction is needed, there is much more relevant information in a transaction than what a certificate provides (for example [Froomkin96] describes essential roles for a trusted third party in electronic commerce). We do believe that a certificate is the common information which makes digital signature schemes useful and legally viable [ABA], however we claim there is more which is needed to achieve financial transactions.

Our basic claim is that: once identity is assured, we need to further validate current contextual information which we abstract as a warranty; this validation is the core of smoothly operating business in the electronic world. The granting and validity of warranties should be based on the nature of the transaction, and the characteristics and current states of the parties involved in the transaction. The warranty-granting process can typically be viewed as an augmentation of user certification transactions in a digital signature based context. It melds implicit verification checks on the identity and transaction-specific digital signature authenticity with respect to the subject of the warranty, with access control mechanisms designed to address privacy and warranty-issuance criteria.

We can therefore observe that warranty-granting infrastructure has to support the maintenance of user information and status which is beyond what is provided in a certificate (e.g., it can be built upon anonymity-providing infrastructure). We would also like to mention that a warranty based system might not necessarily be an augmentation of a CA infrastructure. It is rather an infrastructural component with the following properties:

- It is based on pre-established relationships between clients (i.e., users, commercial entities, etc.) and elements of the warranty-granting infrastructure (i.e., banks and financial institutions).
- An established relationship may not exist between clients performing financial transactions.
- The financial transaction may involve more than the clients themselves; e.g., banks may help in controlling risk of transactions.
- Financial institutions may be required to carry users' private and time-sensitive information which may not be appropriate for a public certificate, such as credit rating or financial backing.
- Financial institutions may share information about their clients (shared monetary values and type of fields shared depend on certain circumstances).

– The relevant information per transaction may be dependent upon characteristics of the users performing the transaction, the relationships between them, and the nature of the transaction itself.

The transaction will be associated with a warranty-granting process that precedes the execution of the actual transaction, and is intended to assure that certain terms, conditions, and prerequisites do hold and will make the transaction possible. We assume that connectivity between the clients, and between one of the clients and the system back-end, is available on-line (a varied granularity in which a warranty is given for a transactions which consists of numerous sub-transactions is also possible). The validity of the warranty depends upon the correct representation of information by the clients. Note that the nature of warranty is more refined than that of "authorization certificate" and "transactional certificate" [Froomkin96], as it ties the financial infrastructure with the clients, their state, and the nature of the transaction itself.

2   Requirements

We now list the requirements pertaining to the warranty-granting system, which includes an infrastructure and where users access local representatives of this infrastructure. These requirements follow from the above discussion of properties and connectivity.

1. Each transaction will require access to the supporting infrastructure before a warranty is issued for this transaction. (This is a direct result of the need to obtain current status concerning the subject of the warranty.)
2. The system must provide for high availability and large transaction volume as in any public-key infrastructure that is usable in an electronic commerce environment. Of course, the supporting infrastructure must serve many simultaneous requests including simultaneous requests in which a given client is a requester and others where the given client is the subject of the warranty. This results from the ability of a given client to request service on a new transaction while waiting for a response from a previous transaction, as well as the fact that several clients could request warranties with a single subject of warranty at the same time.
3. The system should support flexible processing in such a way that delays and congestion, which are normally associated with warranty-based systems, can be minimized or avoided. These delays would occur, for instance, when the local representative does (can) not keep all information locally and/or must perform extensive verification with other sources. Accommodation for both completely automated transactions and delayed transactions is an important feature of the system.
4. The payment of fees for services provided by the supporting infrastructure must be consolidated within the supporting infrastructure. This is required both as a throughput issue and in order to ensure payment for services.

5. Amongst the users in a transaction, only the warranty requester needs to contact the supporting infrastructure.
6. A client needs to trust only his local representative.
7. The issuance of a warranty requires that the subject of the warranty provide authorization. This is a result of a desire to allow a client to limit and control the delivery of information concerning him as well as limit the scope of warranties issued with him as the subject.
8. The system must support limiting the amount of information provided to the supporting infrastructure to only the information necessary to support a warranty. It is viewed as neither necessary nor desirable to provide the details of the transaction to the system infrastructure unless a claim against the warranty results. (Notice that claims processing is likely to require exposure of the transaction to the supporting infrastructure.)

3 Warranty-Granting General System Description

The completion of operations within a warranty-based system always involves at least the supporting infrastructure and two or more clients. While the supporting infrastructure is viewed as a unit, it in fact consists of the banking system and contains geographically separated units.

Each client is assumed to have a relationship with their local representative of the infrastructure (business or individual client relationship with bank). The client's local representative has connectivity with other local representatives, banks, CA's, insurance companies, underwriters, etc.

It is also assumed that clients, where appropriate, will periodically receive statements concerning outstanding warranties and related information. This will not be provided on a per-transaction basis, and thus will not be shown in the message flows. The local representative may need to also provide for an electronic payment system as well as documentation, timestamping and other services.

A client can take on any of several roles. The client may be the party in need of a warranty in order to allow a transaction to go forward and thus is the warrantee. Another client will be the "subject" of the warranty, that is the assurance or warranty is provided with respect to the "subject". (While it is possible to provide assurance about a party who is not a client such cases are of less interest with respect to this paper.) An additional role that a client may take on is the requester of the warranty. Notice that the "requester" may be either the warrantee or subject of the warranty.

Notice that the relationship between the supporting infrastructure and the clients has two basic cases. In Case 1 (See Figure 1) the interaction is simplified in the sense that the local representative would be able to both determine the ability of Client 2 to meet the requirements of the transaction as well as arrange for payment of any fees associated with providing the warranty. In case 2 (See Figure 2 which contains additional flows) the situation is more complex since Client 1 is paying for the warranty but the ability of Client 2 to support the transaction is the primary issue.

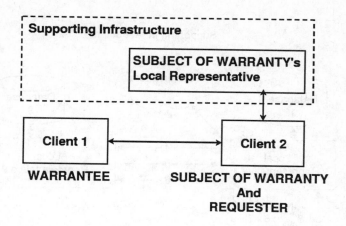

Fig. 1. Case 1: Warranty Subject is the requester for warranty. Client 2 communicates with its own local representative in the supporting infrastructure.

4   Detailed Description

Below we will take a closer look at Case 2 represented by Figure 2. We note that Client 1 has a trust representative in the supporting infrastructure which we call Local Representative 1. Similarly, Client 2 is supported by Local Representative 2. Database 1 is assumed to contain all relevant information on Client 1 and database 2 contains relevant information on Client 2.

It is assumed that any necessary exchange of information required between the WARRANTEE and the WARRANTY SUBJECT to reach agreement on a specific transaction has been completed. Security features required to support this preliminary exchange are not shown.

Message 1: This message contains the final version of the transaction along with information which forms the basis for warranty request. (Notice that there may have been information exchanged between the WARRANTEE and the WAR-RANTY SUBJECT prior to message 1 related to specific aspects of the transaction.) It is expected that the information in message 1 (as well as any preceding messages) would be encrypted and possibly signed. However, such protection is not vital to the proposal in this paper and therefore does not receive additional discussion.

Message 2:

Field 2.1. Identification of the WARRANTY SUBJECT: Unique identifier of WARRANTY SUBJECT which also identifies Local Representative 2.

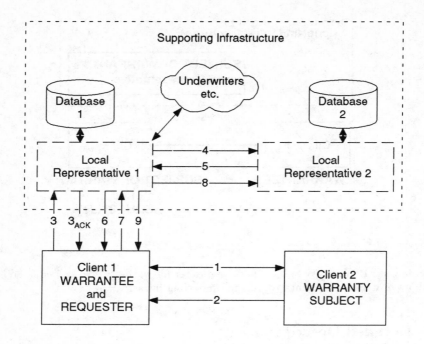

Fig. 2. Case2: WARRANTEE is the requester for warranty. WARRANTEE communicates with its own local representative in the supporting infrastructure.

Field 2.2. Identification of WARRANTEE: Based on information previously received from the WARRANTEE and should support unique identification of the WARRANTEE within the supporting infrastructure.

Field 2.3. Desired class for WARRANTEE: Allows WARRANTY SUBJECT to prescribe minimum standards that the WARRANTEE must meet in order to be issued a warranty on this transaction or to be provided other non-public information about the WARRANTY SUBJECT.

Field 2.4. Transaction count - WARRANTY SUBJECT: A parameter that is meaningful to the WARRANTY SUBJECT and his bank (local representative 2). The WARRANTY SUBJECT will generate the count by increment one from the previous count.

Field 2.5. Warranty parameter categories: Identifies information held by local representative 2 which is believed to be relevant to this transaction. This information is based on such things as the credit rating of the WARRANTY SUBJECT, standing in industry and related information based on the history of the WARRANTY SUBJECT.

Field 2.6. Coverage limit: The warranty coverage limit supported by the WARRANTY SUBJECT for this transaction.

Field 2.7. Effective time period of warranty coverage

Field 2.8. Transaction element categories (discussed below)

Field 2.9. Signature by WARRANTY SUBJECT: The WARRANTY SUB-JECT signs the concatenation of fields (2) through (8) and a hash of the transaction. Notice that the hash of the transaction is not included as an element of message 2.

Let us discuss the Transaction element categories now. In some cases the ability to issue a meaningful warranty must take into consideration the contents of the transaction. Since one of the system requirements (see requirement 8) was to limit the information provided to the infrastructure, the "Transaction element categories" field provides a means of providing limited information related to this specific transaction which would be relevant to supporting the warranty. As examples, the identification of the transaction as covering agricultural goods may be relevant to the time period of the warranty (as it would be to a Letter of Credit issued by the Export Import Bank), or the warranty may be sensitive to the possible military use of the goods. Notice that the difference between "Warranty parameter categories" and "Transaction element categories" is that the first field is a direction from the WARRANTY SUBJECT to Local Representative 2 that identifies information on the WARRANTY SUBJECT which may be released for the purposes of supporting this transaction. While this information may support the transaction, it is based not on the transaction, but on the history and status of the WARRANTY SUBJECT, including the record of the WARRANTY SUBJECT's prior executed transactions. Note that it is outside the flow of the presently described system to track the status of transactions beyond the issuance of the warranty. The "Transaction element categories" are related directly to the nature and content of the transaction.

Message 3: This message may be structured so as to address encryption / authentication aspects of this message and/or subsequent messages between Local Representative 1 and the WARRANTEE. Notice that the Local Representative 1 can uniquely identify the WARRANTEE by the information contained in field 3.5.

The signed message from the WARRANTEE contains:

Field 3.1. Identification - WARRANTY SUBJECT

Field 3.2. Transaction count WARRANTEE: A parameter that is meaningful to the WARRANTEE and his bank (local representative 1). The WARRAN-TEE will generate the count by incrementing one from the previous count.

Field 3.3. Coverage limit requested: This is warranty coverage desired by the WARRANTEE.

Field 3.4. Hash of transaction: A hash of his copy of the final transaction agreement. This hash should be identical to the hash formed by the WARRANTY SUBJECT as a part of computing the signature for message 2.

Field 3.5. Signed portion (i.e., fields 2.2 - 2.9) from WARRANTY SUBJECT

Field 3.6. WARRANTEE Transaction element descriptions. (See below)

In cases in which the agreement or the warranty is based on underlying details contained in the transaction, those elements of the transaction which are important to the WARRANTEE and the usefulness of the warranty he will receive will be listed in the 'WARRANTEE Transaction element descriptions'. It is assumed that the form of this information was based on information obtained from the WARRANTY SUBJECT during negotiation of the transaction, and is related to the 'transaction element categories' identified by the WARRANTY SUBJECT in message 2. These WARRANTEE Transaction element descriptions may be transmitted within message 1. It is in the WARRANTEE's interest to ensure that these descriptions depict an accurate summary of all of the salient characteristics of the transaction. An "illicit" transaction may result in rejection of a warranty claim.

Message 3$_{ACK}$: Message 3 acknowledgment is provided to the WARRANTEE as an indication that message 3 was received and that it contained the required information from the client to support processing. It also would provide a path for immediately indicating that a warranty would not be issued if Local Representative 1 could determine this without additional information. An example of such a situation would be Client 2's identification appearing on a list held by Local Representative 1, which identified clients that were barred from being WARRANTY SUBJECT's.

In the case of complex transactions the time span between the WARRANTEE receiving message 3$_{ACK}$ and message 6 may be unpredictable. This is due to the possible need for Local Representative 1 to obtain additional support for the warranty (such as underwriter support) as well as the possibility that Local Representative 2 may require time in order to obtain additional information. In many cases this additional support may require review by humans and would not be fully automated. To the extent possible, message 3$_{ACK}$ should provide an estimate of the required processing time as well as providing the necessary communication and security basis for future messages. In particular messages from Local Representative 1 to the WARRANTEE would require encryption in order to provide adequate protection of information about the WARRANTY SUBJECT. Of course it is expected that any such information provided to the WARRANTEE would be held as sensitive information. (The WARRANTEE would have agreed to this as part of a contract with his local representative. This could be augmented by signed information within message 3.) This structure for the messages allows fast response where possible while still accommodating delayed responses where required.

Message 4:[1] This message includes the components from message 2 as created by the WARRANTY SUBJECT plus the hash of the transaction created contained in message 3 as created by the WARRANTEE. Notice that since the hash of the transaction as created by the WARRANTEE should be identical to the hash of the transaction as created by the WARRANTY SUBJECT, the signature on this information as created by the WARRANTY SUBJECT should be

---

[1] This message is internal to the supporting infrastructure and as such its security is assumed to be provided by infrastructure components which are not described in this paper.

correct. Message 4 contains:

Field 4.1. Signed message 2 from WARRANTY SUBJECT
Field 4.2. Identification - WARRANTY SUBJECT
Field 4.3. Transaction count WARRANTEE
Field 4.4. Information related to the WARRANTEE

Let us now discuss some of the processing performed at Local Representative 2. The signature on message 2 is verified. In order to detect the presence of a repeated message the database maintains a list of the N most recently processed transaction count values for each client. A message is not considered to be a valid new request unless the 'Transaction count - WARRANTY SUBJECT' is not contained in the database and is greater in value than the lowest transaction count retained in the database.

The "Desired class for WARRANTEE" from message 2 is compared with information provided in Field 4. This will be used by local representative 2 to make a support/non-support decision.

The data available for the WARRANTY SUBJECT will be reviewed for compatibility with maximum reasonable warranty coverage limits as well as the total coverage limits outstanding. This will require that all pending requests for warranties and the related status of these requests (as reported in previous messages of type 8) have been accounted for. As a result a support/not-support decision can be reached.

Notice that the actual processing of the transaction is outside the exchanges covered by this document. As a result the decision process may include consideration of warranties which were issued but did not actually result in completion of the associated transactions. It is expected that the local representatives will use knowledge concerning their clients which is verifiable outside of the exchanges of this system. This is necessary since the system does not in general follow the details of the transaction through its completion.

If the issuing of a warranty is supported, the Transaction element categories will be used to form the 'Database Transaction element descriptions'.

Message 5: [1]

Field 5.1. Identification of WARRANTEE
Field 5.2. Transaction count WARRANTEE
Field 5.3. Support/not-support decision
Field 5.4. Warranty parameters as listed in the warranty parameters categories
Field 5.5. Coverage limit authorized (Not Applicable if not supported)
Field 5.6. Database Transaction element descriptions. (Not Applicable if not supported)
Field 5.7. Reason for a not-support decision (Not Applicable if supported)

Let us now briefly discuss the processing at Local Representative 1. Assuming that message 5 indicated that the transaction is to be supported a comparison will be made between the WARRANTEE Transaction element descriptions (message 3) and Database Transaction element descriptions (message 5).

A discrepancy will prevent providing a warranty. Information available to Local Representative 1 may also be used to adjust relevant parameters (such as time period) in the warranty.

Message 6: The status of the warranty is provided in this message. Assuming that issuance of the warranty has been approved, it can also provide cost information associated with the warranty as well as any information required to initiate receiving of the warranty as well as any restrictions on the purchase of the warranty (for example time limit for purchase). In addition, message 6 will provide a report based on the warranty parameters as provided by the WARRANTY SUBJECT's Local Representative (as extracted from message 5) and may also provide relevant information related to the Database Transaction element descriptions (as extracted from message 5) and contrasted against the WARRANTEE Transaction element descriptions.

In accordance with requirement 7, the transfer of information relevant to the WARRANTY SUBJECT is limited as defined by the Warranty parameter categories and Transaction element categories contained in message 2.

It is important to note that message 6 is not the warranty but is an offer to sell the warranty. It is constructed such that misinterpretation is unlikely.

Message 7: Agreement by the WARRANTEE to accept (and pay for) the warranty is provided by this message.

Message 8: [1]

Field 8.1. Identification - WARRANTY SUBJECT
Field 8.2. Transaction count
Field 8.3. A statement of issued/non-issued status of the requested warranty.
Field 8.4. Final coverage value

Message 9: Message 9 is a signed indication of the warranty. It contains:

Field 9.1. Identification - WARRANTY SUBJECT
Field 9.2. Identification - WARRANTEE
Field 9.3. Transaction count (used with Identification - WARRANTY SUBJECT as pointer in database 2)
Field 9.4. Transaction count WARRANTEE (used with Identification - WARRANTEE as pointer in database 1)
Field 9.5. Hash of transaction
Field 9.6. Final coverage value.
Field 9.7. Time period of coverage

Message 9 may also contain information relating to specific aspects of coverage, such as the warranty parameters, if these values are guaranteed to be "accurate" at the time they were compiled, where the determination of accuracy is in accordance with the initial contract between Local Representative 1 and Client 1, the WARRANTEE.

5   Fees to the Supporting Infrastructure

It is envisioned that a fee will be charged to the REQUESTER (the WAR-RANTEE in the case under consideration) only if a warranty was approved and issued. While this practice does not provide fees for requests which are either denied by the system or not acceptable to the WARRANTEE it does prevent inappropriate fees from being charged to the REQUESTER as a result of requests involving security shortcomings in security structures outside of this system (e.g. an imposter posing as the WARRANTY SUBJECT).

The collection of the fee is enabled by the ability of Local Representative 1 to consolidate payments for services provided (with appropriate payment-authorization provided by the client which directly contacts the warranty-granting infrastructure back-end). No charge is made to the other client involved in the transaction.

While not envisioned as the primary method for providing fees for the supporting infrastructure, a more general fee structure could support a fee for three levels of service. The first level would be a small fee assuming the process ended with the message 3 acknowledgment. The second level would be if the process ended at message 6 without the issuance of a warranty. The third level would include the issuance of the requested warranty.

We remark that the system under discussion does not address any confidentiality requirements between the clients (which is an orthogonal issue in our context. It can, however, be provided as an additional layer).

6   An Exemplifying Scenario

As a conclusion we provide an example warranty issue process. Of course, this is one of many possible examples but was chosen to represent some of the capabilities of the described system.

In this example the WARRANTY SUBJECT is known by the supporting infrastructure to be a provider of software and cryptography. It will also be assumed that the WARRANTY SUBJECT is a company in the US and therefore subject to export controls for the delivery of cryptography outside the US. In this example it will be assumed that the WARRANTEE is a non-US company.

The transaction developed between the WARRANTY SUBJECT and WARRANTEE will be for the delivery of software which contains cryptographic capability. In addition it will be assumed that the WARRANTY SUBJECT is attempting to cheat and has not obtained the necessary US export authorization.

In this case the WARRANTY SUBJECT would include in the "transaction element categories" of message 2 only the category for software and not include the fact that the software also contains cryptography. In message 3 the WARRANTEE should ensure that the "WARRANTEE Transaction element descriptions" include all descriptors which he feels are important to the transaction. It is assumed here that he included both cryptography and software as descriptors.

Message 4 will contain the transaction element categories of message 2 and will return in message 5 matching database transaction element descriptions. Upon receiving message 5 local representative 1 will check for a discrepancy between the "database transaction element descriptions" of message 5 and the "WARRANTEE Transaction element descriptions" of message 3. In this example the discrepancy would prevent a warranty from being issued.

Notice that the WARRANTEE has the burden of insuring that the "WARRANTEE Transaction element descriptions" of message 3 was sufficiently complete to provide protection. If the WARRANTEE had included only software in the "WARRANTEE Transaction element descriptions" the warranty would have been issued. If the transaction had later failed to complete (perhaps as a result of the export controls) the WARRANTEE might have tried to make a claim against the warranty. In processing the claim the supporting infrastructure would have obtained the complete transaction and discovered that it was in violation of law and therefore not subject to warranty protection.

On the other hand if the WARRANTY SUBJECT had included the cryptographic "Transaction element category" in message 2, this along with "information related to the WARRANTEE" of message 4 would allow local representative 2 to detect a questionable transaction, in this case because of the non-US status of the WARRANTEE.

It should be noted that the issue here is not one of export control, but rather the legitimacy or legality of the transaction in the context of warranty coverage as defined in contracts between local representative 1 and client 1 and between local representative 2 and client 2. The extent of the actual coverage provisions may vary. For example, coverage may deal strictly with guaranteeing the accuracy of the delivered warranty parameter information, or may guarantee certain aspects of actual transaction fulfillment to be carried out by the WARRANTY SUBJECT. Even if certain transaction aspects are guaranteed, the WARRANTEE may want to use warranty parameter information to make a judgment on whether to expend the resources necessary to further pursue the transaction. In fact, the entire warranty process, as defined in the message flows, may be iterated during the transaction negotiation between the two clients. The incorporation of transaction element and warranty parameter categories enables automation and facilitates handling of access control and privacy requirements.

Other exemplifying scenarios may deal with the sale and delivery of morphine to licensed pharmacies, or with the shipment of hazardous waste materials to sites which must be licensed as demonstrable proof that they are equipped to deal with containment.

References

[Froomkin96] A. M. Froomkin, "The essential role of trusted third parties in electronic commerce", 75 Oregon L. Rev. 49, 1996. (See also http://www.law.miami.edu/ froomkin/articles/trustedno.htm)

[X509]   CCITT, Recommendation X.509, "The directory-authentication framework," Consultation Committee, International Telephone and Telegraph, International Telecommunications Union, Geneva, 1989.

[ABA]   American Bar Association, "Draft Digital Signature Guidelines", Information Security Committee of the Section on Science and Technology, 1996 (Available online: http://www.state.ut.us/ccjj/digsig/dsut-gl.htm)

Compliance Checking in the PolicyMaker Trust Management System

Matt Blaze   Joan Feigenbaum   Martin Strauss

AT&T Labs – Research
180 Park Avenue
Florham Park, NJ 07932 USA
{mab,jf,mstrauss}@research.att.com

Abstract. Emerging electronic commerce services that use public-key cryptography on a mass-market scale require sophisticated mechanisms for managing trust. For example, any service that receives a signed request for action is forced to answer the central question "Is the key used to sign this request authorized to take this action?" In some services, this question reduces to "Does this key belong to this person?" In others, the authorization question is more complicated, and resolving it requires techniques for formulating security policies and security credentials, determining whether particular sets of credentials satisfy the relevant policies, and deferring trust to third parties. Blaze, Feigenbaum, and Lacy [1] identified this *trust management problem* as a distinct and important component of network services and described a general tool for addressing it, the *PolicyMaker trust management system*.

At the heart of a trust management system is an algorithm for *compliance checking*. The inputs to the compliance checker are a *request*, a *policy*, and a set of *credentials*. The compliance checker returns yes or no, depending on whether the credentials constitute a *proof* that the request complies with the policy. Thus a central challenge in trust management is to find an appropriate notion of "proof" and an efficient algorithm for checking proofs of compliance.

In this paper, we present the notion of proof that is used in the current version of the PolicyMaker trust management system. We show that this notion of proof leads to a compliance-checking problem that is undecidable in its most general form and is NP-hard even if restricted in several natural ways. We identify a special case of the problem that is solvable in polynomial time and is widely applicable. The algorithm that we give for this special case has been implemented and is used in the current version of the PolicyMaker system.

1   Introduction

Blaze, Feigenbaum, and Lacy [1] identified the *trust management problem* as a distinct and important component of security in network services. Aspects of the trust management problem include formulation of policies and credentials, deferral of trust to third parties, and a mechanism for "proving" that a request, supported by one or more credentials, complies with a policy. In [1], the authors describe a comprehensive approach to trust management that is independent of the needs of any particular product or service, and a *trust management system*, called *PolicyMaker*, that embodies the approach. They emphasize the following general principles.

- **Common language**: Policies, credentials, and trust relationships are expressed as programs (or parts of programs) in a "safe" programming language. A common language for policies, credentials, and relationships makes it possible for applications to handle security in a comprehensive, consistent, and largely transparent manner.
- **Flexibility**: PolicyMaker is expressively rich enough to support the complex trust relationships that can occur in the very large-scale network applications currently being developed. At the same time, simple and standard policies, credentials, and relationships can be expressed succinctly and comprehensibly.
- **Locality of contol**: Each party in the network can decide in each transaction whether to accept the credentials presented by a second party or, alternatively, which third party it should ask for additional credentials. Local control of trust relationships eliminates the need for the assumption of a globally known, monolithic hierarchy of "certifying authorities." Such hierarchies do not scale beyond single "communities of interest" in which trust can be defined unconditionally from the top down.
- **General compliance-checking mechanism**: The mechanism for checking that a set of credentials proves that a requested action complies with local policy does not depend on the semantics of the application-specific request, credentials, or policy. This allows many different applications with widely varying policy requirements to share a credential base and a trust management infrastructure.

The algorithmic core of trust management is the *compliance-checking problem*. The inputs to the compliance checker are a request, a policy, and a set of credentials. The compliance checker returns yes or no, depending on whether the credentials constitute a *proof* that the request complies with the policy. Thus a central challenge in building a trust management system is to find an appropriate notion of "proof" and an efficient algorithm for checking proofs of compliance. In this paper, we present the notion of proof that is used in the PolicyMaker compliance checker. We show that, in general, the PolicyMaker version of compliance checking is undecidable and that it is NP-hard even if restricted in a number of natural ways. However, we isolate a polynomial-time solvable case that is general enough to be useful in a wide variety of applications and is implemented and available in the current version of the PolicyMaker system.

1.1 Examples

We now give three examples of application-specific requests and local policies with which they may need to comply. Note that these are realistic examples of the types of transactions that users want to perform; individually, none of them is very complicated. Collectively, they demonstrate that an expressive, flexible notion of "proof of compliance" is needed. More examples can be found in [1–3, 9, 10].

Example 1: Signed Email. Consider an email system in which messages arrive with headers that include, among other things, the sender's name, the sender's public key, and a digital signature. When a recipient's email reader processes an incoming message, it uses the public key to verify that the message and the signature go together, *i.e.*, that an adversary has not spliced a signature from another message onto this message. The recipient should also be concerned about whether the name and the public key go together; for example, might an adversary have taken a legitimate message-signature pair that he produced with this own signing key and then attached to it his public key and someone else's name? The recipient needs a policy that determines which name-key pairs he considers trustworthy. Because signed messages will regularly arrive from senders whom he has never met, he cannot simply maintain a private database of name-key pairs. Here is a plausible policy.

(1) He maintains private copies of the name-key pairs (N_1, PK_1) and (N_2, PK_2). (A reasonable interpretation of this part of the policy is that he knows the people named N_1 and N_2 personally and can get reliable copies of their public keys directly from them.)

(2) He accepts "chains of trust" of length one or two. An arc in a chain of trust is a *certificate* of the form $(PK_i, (N_j, PK_j), S)$ and is interpreted to mean that (i) the owner N_i of PK_i vouches for the binding between name N_j and public key PK_j, and (ii) N_i attests that N_j is trusted to provide certificates of this form. The party N_i signs (N_j, PK_j) with his private key and the resulting signature is S.

(3) He insists that there be two disjoint chains of trust from the keys that he maintains privately to the name-key pair that arrives with a signed message.

Example 2: Banking. Consider a loan request submitted to an electronic banking system. Such a request might contain, among other things, the name of the requester and the amount requested. A plausible policy for approval of such loans might take the following form.

(1) Two approvals are needed for loans of less than $5,000. Three approvals are needed for loans of between $5,000 and $10,000. Loans of more than $10,000 are not handled by this automated loan-processing system.

(2) The head of the loan division must authorize approvers' public keys. The division head's public key is currently PK_3. This key will expire at 23:59:59 on December 31, 1998.

Example 3: Web Browsing. A typical request for action in a web-browsing system is "View URL http://www.coolstuff.org/pictures.gif." In setting a viewing policy, a user must decide what types of metadata or "labels" he wants documents to have before he views them, and he must decide whom he trusts to label documents. If he is concerned about Internet pornography, the user may insist that documents he views be rated according to the Recreational Software

Advisory Council (RSAC) rating system and that they be rated ($S \leq 2, L \leq 2, V = 0, N \leq 2$) on the Sex, Language, Violence, and Nudity scales, respectively. He may trust self-labeling by the Disney Corporation and any labels by a labeler that is approved by Good Housekeeping.

1.2 Related Work

While the concept of a "trust management system" *per se* originated in [1], there is previous work on "protection systems" that is loosely related. We briefly recall two examples of such work here; more recent work that is similarly related to ours can be found in, *e.g.*, [12].

The main thrust of the work we present in this paper is twofold: We define a general "proof-of-compliance problem" that is intractable, and we isolate a special case of the problem that is both tractable and useful. Protection systems, as described by Denning [4], address a similar (but not identical) problem to the one we address, and a similar type of result is sometimes obtained.

Harrison, Ruzzo, and Ullman [7] analyze a general protection system based on the *access matrix* model. In matrix A, indexed by subjects and objects, cell A_{so} records the rights of subject s over object o; a set of transition rules describes the rights needed as preconditions to modify A and the specific ways in which A can be modified, by creating subjects and objects or by entering or deleting rights at a single cell.

Harrison, Ruzzo, and Ullman showed that given

- an initial state A_0
- a set Δ of transition rules
- a right r

it is undecidable whether some sequence $\delta_{i_0} \cdots \delta_{i_t} \in \Delta$ transforms A_0 such that δ_{i_t} enters r into a cell not previously containing r, *i.e.*, whether it is possible for some subject, not having right r over some object, ever to gain that right. On the other hand, Harrison, Ruzzo, and Ullman identify several possible restrictions on Δ and give decision algorithms for input subject to one of these restrictions. One restriction they consider yields a PSPACE-complete problem.

Independently, Jones, Lipton, and Snyder [8] define and analyze *take-grant* directed-graph systems. Subjects and objects are nodes; an arc a from node n_1 to n_2 is labeled by the set of rights n_1 has over n_2. If subject n_1 has the *take* right over n_2, and n_2 has some right r over n_3, then a legal transition is for n_1 to "take" right r over n_3. Similarly, if subject n_1 has the *grant* right over n_2, and n_1 has some right r over n_3 then a legal transition is for n_1 to "grant" right r over n_3 to n_2. Besides these transitions, subjects can create new nodes and remove their own rights over their immediate successors. Although rights are constrained to flow only via take-grant paths, take-grant systems do model nontrivial applications [4].

Jones, Lipton, and Snyder asked whether a right r over a node x possessed by node n_1 but not possessed by n_2 could ever be acquired by n_2. They showed that this question can be decided in time linear in the original graph by depth-first search. Thus Denning [4] concludes that, although safety in protection systems is usually undecidable, the results in, *e.g.*, [7, 8] demonstrate that safety can be decided feasibly in systems with sets of transition rules from a restricted though nontrivial set. The related results on compliance checking that we present in Section 5 provide additional support for Denning's conclusion.

Having reviewed the basics of "protection systems," we can now explain why they address a similar but not identical problem to the one addressed by the PolicyMaker compliance-checking algorithm. In the protection-system world, there is a relatively small set of potentially dangerous actions that could ever be performed, and this set is agreed upon in advance by all parties involved. A data structure, *e.g.*, an access matrix, records which parties are allowed to take which actions. This data structure is *precomputed offline*, and, as requests for action arrive, their legitimacy is decided via a lookup operation in this data structure. "Transition rules" that change the data structure are applied infrequently, and they are implemented *by a different mechanism and in a separate system module* from the ones that handle individual requests for action.

In the "trust management system" world, the set of potentially dangerous actions is large, dynamic, and not known in advance. A system such as PolicyMaker provides a general notion of "proof of compliance" for use by diverse applications that require trust policies. The users of these applications and the semantics of their actions and policies are not even known to the PolicyMaker compliance-checking algorithm; hence it is not possible for all parties to agree in advance on a domain of discourse for all potentially dangerous actions. The compliance-checking question "is request r authorized by policy P and credential set C?" is analogous to the question "can subject s eventually obtain right r by transition rules Δ" in the protection-system world. Part of the novelty of the PolicyMaker system [1] and of its analysis as given here is the realization that *a single instance of request processing*, especially one that involves deferral of trust, can require a moderately complex computation and not just a lookup in a precomputed data structure. The work in this paper, for the first time to our knowledge, formalizes and analyzes the complexity of a general-purpose, working system for processing requests of this nature.

In summary, a general-purpose "trust management system" such as PolicyMaker is, very roughly speaking, a meta-system in the protection-system framework.

1.3 Outline of Paper

In the next section, we explain why an application-independent notion of compliance checking can be useful and can enhance security. Terminology and notation are given in Section 3, followed by a formal statement of the compliance-checking problem in Section 4. Negative and positive results are give in Sections 5.1 and 5.2, respectively. A brief discussion of our formulation of the problem and how it might be extended appears in Section 6.

2 Need for a General Compliance Checker

We now explain why we believe that a general, highly expressive, application-independent compliance checker is a good thing. Readers already familiar with these arguments as put forth in [1, 2, 9, 10] should skip to the next section.

Clearly, any product or service that requires some form of proof that requested transactions comply with policies could implement a special-purpose compliance checker from scratch. So what advantage does a developer gain by using a general-purpose compliance checker?

One important advantage is soundness and reliability of both the design and the implementation of the compliance checker. As will become clear in the following sections, formalizing the notion of "credentials' proving that a request complies with a policy" involves a lot of subtlety and detail. It is very easy to get wrong, and an application developer who sets out to implement something special-purpose and "simple" in order to avoid what he thinks is the overly "complicated" syntax and semantics of a general-purpose compliance checker is likely to find either that he has underestimated the complexity of his application's needs for expressiveness and proof or that his special-purpose compliance checker is not turning out to be as "simple" as he expected it to be. A general-purpose notion of "proof of compliance" can be explained, formalized, proven correct, and implemented in a standard package (such as PolicyMaker), thus freeing developers of individual applications from the need to reinvent the wheel. Applications that use a standard compliance checker can be assured that the answer returned for any given input (*i.e.*, a request, a policy, and a set of credentials) depends only on the input, and not on any implicit policy decisions (or bugs) in the design or implementation of the compliance checker. As policies and credentials become more diverse and complex, the issue of assuring correctness will become especially important, and modularity of function with a clean separation between the role of the application and the role of the compliance checker will make further development more manageable.

Two important sources of complexity that are often underestimated are delegation and cryptography. Products and services that need a notion of "credential" almost always have some notion of "delegation" of the authority to issue credentials. The simplest case, *i.e.*, unconditional delegation, is easily handled by a special-purpose mechanism. However, if the product or service grows in popularity and starts to be used in ways that were not foreseen when it was originally deployed, delegation can quickly become more complex, and a special-purpose language that restricts the types of conditional delegation that can be expressed becomes an impediment to widespread and imaginative use. The general framework that we develop for compliance checking avoids this by allowing delegation to be described by ordinary programs. Similarly, digital signatures and other cryptographic functions may not seem crucial when an application is first designed; for instance, web browsers may be designed to accommodate "safe surfing" policies configurable by Internet-aware parents but may not initially involve cryptographic functions. If the application is subsequently integrated into the wider world of electronic commerce, however (as web browsers have been), the need to accommodate increased use of cryptography will be pressing, and cryptographic credentials (such as public-key certificates) will need to be incorporated into the application's notion of proof of compliance. If the application is already using a general-purpose notion of proof of compliance, this can be done without having to rethink and recode the compliance-checker.

Finally, note that a general-purpose compliance checker facilitates interoperability. Requests, policies, and credentials, if originally written in the native language of a specific product or service, must be translated into a standard format understood by the compliance checker. Because a wide variety of applications will each have translators with the same target language, policies and credentials originally written for one application can be used by another. The fact that the compliance checker can serve as a locus of interoperability may prove particularly useful in e-commerce applications and, more generally, in all settings in which cryptographic credentials are needed.

3 Notation and Terminology

The general problem we are concerned with is *Proof of Compliance* (POC). The question is whether a *request* r complies with a *policy*. The policy is simply a function f_0 encoded in some well understood programming system or language and labeled by the keyword POLICY. In addition to the request and the policy, a POC instance contains a set of *credentials*, also general functions, each labeled by its source. Policies and credentials are collectively referred to as *assertions*.

Credentials are issued by *sources*. Formally, a credential is a pair (f_i, s_i) of function f_i and *source-ID* s_i, which is just a string over some appropriate alphabet. Important examples of source-IDs include public keys of credential issuers, URLs, names of people, and names of companies. With the exception of the keyword POLICY, the interpretation of source-IDs is part of the application-specific semantics of an assertion, and it is not the job of the compliance checker. From the compliance checker's point of view, the source-IDs are just strings, and the assertions encode a set of (possibly indirect and possibly conditional) trust relationships among the issuing sources. Associating each assertion with the correct source-ID is the responsibility of the calling application, and it takes place *before* the POC instance is handed to the compliance checker; the rationale for this architectural decision is given in the original paper on the PolicyMaker trust management system [1].

The request r is a string encoding an *action* for which the calling application seeks a proof of compliance. In the course of deciding whether the credentials $(f_1, s_1), \ldots, (f_{n-1}, s_{n-1})$ constitute a proof that r complies with the policy (f_0, POLICY), the compliance checker's domain of discourse may need to include other action strings. For example, if POLICY requires that r be approved by credential issuers s_1 and s_2, the credentials (f_1, s_1) and (f_2, s_2) may want a way to say that they approve r *conditionally*, where the condition is that the other credential also approve it. A convenient way to formalize this is to use strings R, R_1, and R_2 over some finite alphabet Σ. The string R corresponds to the requested action r. The strings R_1 and R_2 encode "conditional" versions of R that might be approved by s_1 and s_2 as intermediate results of the compliance-checking procedure.

More generally, for each request r and each assertion (f_i, s_i), there is a set $\{R_{ij}\}$ of *action strings* that might arise in a compliance check. By convention, there is a distinguished string R that corresponds to the input request r. The range of assertion (f_i, s_i) is made up of *acceptance records* of the form (i, s_i, R_{ij}), the meaning of which is that, based on the information at its disposal, assertion number i, issued by source s_i, approves action R_{ij}. A set of acceptance records is referred to as an *acceptance set*. It is by maintaining acceptance sets and making them available to assertions that the compliance checker manages "inter-assertion communication," giving assertions the chance to make decisions based on conditional decisions by other assertions. The compliance checker will start with *initial acceptance set* $\{(\Lambda, \Lambda, R)\}$, in which the one acceptance record means that the action string for which approval is sought is R and that no assertions have yet signed off on it (or anything else). The checker will run the assertions $(f_0, \text{POLICY}), (f_1, s_1), \ldots, (f_{n-1}, s_{n-1})$ that it has received as input, not necessarily in that order and not necessarily once each, and see which acceptance records are produced. Ultimately, the compliance checker approves the request r if the acceptance record $(0, \text{POLICY}, R)$, which means "policy approves the initial action string," is produced.

Thus, abstractly, an assertion is a mapping from acceptance sets to acceptance sets. Assertion (f_i, s_i) looks at an acceptance set A encoding the actions that have been approved so far and the numbers and sources of the assertions that approved them. Based on this information about what the sources it trusts have approved, (f_i, s_i) outputs another acceptance set A'.

We close this section by providing two concrete examples that show why we chose to allow assertions to approve multiple action strings for each possible request. That is, for a given input request r, why do assertions need to do anything except say "I approve r" or refuse to say it?

First, we flesh out the "conditional approval" example given earlier. Consider the following "co-signing required" assertion (f_0, POLICY): "All expenditures of \$500 or more require approval by A and B." Suppose that A's policy is to approve such expenditures if and only if B approves them and that B's is to approve them if and only if A approves them. Our acceptance record structure makes such approvals straightforward. The credential (f_1, A), can produce acceptance records of the form $(1, A, R)$ and $(1, A, R_B)$, where R corresponds to the input request r; the meaning of the second is "I will approve R if and only if B approves it." Similarly, the credential (f_2, B), can produce records of the form $(2, B, R)$ and $(2, B, R_A)$. On input $\{(\Lambda, \Lambda, R)\}$, the sequence of acceptance records $(1, A, R_B)$, $(2, B, R_A)$, $(1, A, R)$, $(2, B, R)$, $(0, \text{POLICY}, R)$ would be produced if the assertions were run in the order (f_1, A), (f_2, B), (f_1, A), (f_2, B), (f_0, POLICY), and the request r would be approved. If assertions could only produce binary approve/disapprove decisions, no transactions would ever be approved, unless the trust management system had some way of understanding the semantics of the assertions and knowing that it had to ask A's and B's credentials explicitly for a conditional approval. This would violate our goal of having a general-purpose, trust management system that processes requests and assertions whose semantics are only understood by the calling applications and that vary widely from application to application.

Second, consider the issue of "delegation depth." A very natural construction to use in assertion (f_0, POLICY) is "I delegate authority to A. Furthermore, I allow A to choose the parties to whom he will re-delegate the authority I've delegated to him. For any party B involved in the approval of a request, there must be a delegation chain of length at most two from me to B." Various "domain experts" $B_1, \ldots, B_t$ could issue credentials $(f_1, B_1), \ldots, (f_t, B_t)$ that *directly* approve actions in their areas of expertise by producing acceptance records of the form (i, B_i, R_0^i). An assertion (g_j, s_j) that sees such a record and explicitly trusts B_i could produce an acceptance record of the form (j, s_j, R_1^i), the meaning of which is that "B_i approved R^i directly, I trust B_i directly, and so I also approve R^i." More generally, if an assertion (g_l, s_l) trusts s_k directly and sees an acceptance record of the form (k, s_k, R_d^i), it can produce the acceptance record (l, s_l, R_{d+1}^i). The assertion (f_0, POLICY) given above would approve an action R^i if and only if it were run on an acceptance set that contained a record of the form (k, A, R_1^i), for some k. Note that (f_0, POLICY) need not know *which* credential (f_i, B_i) directly approved R^i by producing (i, B_i, R_0^i). All it needs to know is that it trusts A and that A trusts *some* B_i whose credential produced such a record.

4 Problem Statement

The most general version of the compliance-checking problem is:

Proof of Compliance (POC):
Input : A request r and a set $\{(f_0, \text{POLICY}), (f_1, s_1), \ldots, (f_{n-1}, s_{n-1})\}$ of assertions.
Question : Is there a finite sequence $i_1, i_2, \ldots, i_t$ of indices such that each i_j is in $\{0, 1, \ldots, n-1\}$, but the i_j's are not necessarily distinct and not necessarily exhaustive of $\{0, 1, \ldots, n-1\}$ and such that

$$(0, \text{POLICY}, R) \in (f_{i_t}, s_{i_t}) \circ \cdots \circ (f_{i_1}, s_{i_1})(\{(\Lambda, \Lambda, R)\}),$$

where R is the action string that corresponds to the request r?

This most general version of the problem is clearly undecidable. A compliance checker cannot even decide whether an arbitrary assertion (f_i, s_i) halts when given an arbitrary acceptance set as input, much less whether some sequence containing (f_i, s_i) produces the desired output. In what follows, we consider various special cases of POC and ultimately obtain one that is both useful and computationally tractable.

When we say that "$\{(f_0, \text{POLICY}), (f_1, s_1), \ldots, (f_{n-1}, s_{n-1})\}$ contains a proof that r complies with POLICY," we mean that $(r, \{(f_0, \text{POLICY}), (f_1, s_1),$

..., $(f_{n-1}, s_{n-1})\})$ is a yes-instance of this unconstrained, most general form of POC. If F is a (possibly proper) subset of $\{(f_0, \text{POLICY}), (f_1, s_1), \ldots, (f_{n-1}, s_{n-1})\}$ that contains all of the assertions that actually appear in the sequence $(f_{i_t}, s_{i_t}) \circ \cdots \circ (f_{i_1}, s_{i_1})$, then we say that "$F$ contains a proof that r complies with POLICY."

In order to obtain a useful restricted version of POC, we consider adding various pieces of information to the problem instances. Specifically, we consider augmenting the instance $(r, \{(f_0, \text{POLICY}), (f_1, s_1), \ldots, (f_{n-1}, s_{n-1})\})$ in one or more of the following ways:

Global runtime bound: An instance may contain an integer d such that a sequence of assertions $(f_{i_1}, s_{i_1}), \ldots, (f_{i_t}, s_{i_t})$ is only considered a valid proof that r complies with POLICY if the total amount of time that the compliance checker needs to compute $(f_{i_t}, s_{i_t}) \circ \cdots \circ (f_{i_1}, s_{i_1})(\{(\Lambda, \Lambda, R)\})$ is $O(N^d)$. Here N is the length of the original problem instance, *i.e.*, the number of bits needed to encode r, (f_0, POLICY), $\ldots$, (f_{n-1}, s_{n-1}), and d in some standard fashion.

Local runtime bound: An instance may contain an integer c such that $(f_{i_1}, s_{i_1}), \ldots, (f_{i_t}, s_{i_t})$ is only considered a valid proof that r complies with POLICY if each (f_{i_j}, s_{i_j}) runs in time $O(N^c)$. Here N is the length of the actual acceptance set that is input to (f_{i_j}, s_{i_j}) when it is run by the compliance checker. Note that the length of the input fed to an individual assertion (f_{i_j}, s_{i_j}) in the course of checking a proof may be considerably bigger than the length of the original problem instance $(r, \{(f_0, \text{POLICY}), (f_1, s_1), \ldots, (f_{n-1}, s_{n-1})\}, c)$, because the running of assertions $(f_{i_1}, s_{i_1}), \ldots, (f_{i_{j-1}}, s_{i_{j-1}})$ may have caused the creation of many new acceptance records.

Bounded number of assertions in a proof: An instance may contain an integer l such that $(f_{i_1}, s_{i_1}), \ldots, (f_{i_t}, s_{i_t})$ is only considered a valid proof if $t \leq l$.

Bounded output set: An instance may contain integers m and s such that an assertion (f_i, s_i) can only be part of a valid proof that r complies with POLICY if there is a set $O_i = \{R_{i1}, \ldots, R_{im}\}$ of m action strings, such that $(f_i, s_i)(A) \subseteq O_i$ for any input set A, and the maximum size of an acceptance record (i, s_i, R_{ij}) is s. Intuitively, for any user-supplied request r, the meaningful "domain of discourse" for assertion (f_i, s_i) is of size at most m — there are at most m actions that it would make sense for (f_i, s_i) to sign off on, no matter what the other assertions in the instance say about r.

Monotonicity: Important variants of POC are obtained by restricting attention to instances in which the assertions have the following property: (f_i, s_i) is *monotonic* if, for all acceptance sets A and B, $A \subseteq B \Rightarrow (f_i, s_i)(A) \subseteq (f_i, s_i)(B)$. Thus, if (f_i, s_i) approves action R_{ij} when given a certain set of "evidence" that R_{ij} is ok, it will also approve R_{ij} when given a superset of that evidence — it does not have a notion of "negative evidence."

Any of the parameters l, m, and s that are present in a particular instance should be written in unary so that they play an analogous role to n (the number of assertions) in our calculation of the total size of the instance. The parameters d and c are exponents in a runtime bound and hence can be written in binary.

Any subset of the parameters d, c, l, m, and s may be present in a POC instance, and each subset defines a POC variant, some of which are more natural and interesting than others. Including a global runtime bound d obviously makes the POC problem decidable, as does including parameters c and l.

5 Results

In stating and proving results about the complexity of POC, we use the notion of a *promise problem* [5]. In a standard decision problem, a language L is defined by a predicate R in that $x \in L \Leftrightarrow R(x)$. In a promise problem, there are two predicates, the *promise* Q and the *property* R. A machine M *solves* the promise problem (Q, R) if, for all inputs x for which the promise holds, the machine M halts and accepts x if and only if the property holds. Formally, $\forall x[Q(x) \Rightarrow [M$ halts on x and $M(x)$ accepts $\Leftrightarrow R(x)]]$. Note that M's behavior is unconstrained on inputs that do not satisfy the promise, and each set of choices for the behavior of M on these inputs determines a different solution. Thus predicates Q and R define a family of languages, namely all L such that $L = L(M)$ for some M that solves (Q, R).

The class NPP consists of all promise problems with at least one solution in NP. A promise problem is NP-hard if it has at least one solution and all of its solutions are NP-hard. To prove that a promise problem (Q, R) is NP-hard, it suffices to start with an NP-hard language L and construct a reduction whose target instances all satisfy the promise Q and satisfy the property R if and only if they are images of strings in L.

5.1 NP-Hardness

The following are natural POC variants that we can show to be computationally intractable.

Locally Bounded Proof of Compliance (LBPOC):
<u>Input</u> : A request r, a set $\{(f_0, \text{POLICY}), (f_1, s_1), \ldots, (f_{n-1}, s_{n-1})\}$ of assertions, and integers c, l, m, and s.
<u>Promise</u> : Each (f_i, s_i) runs in time $O(N^c)$. On any input set that contains (Λ, Λ, R), where R is the action string corresponding to request r, for each (f_i, s_i) there is a set O_i of at most m action strings such that (f_i, s_i) only produces output from O_i, and s is the maximum size of an acceptance record (i, s_i, R_{ij}), where $R_{ij} \in O_i$.
<u>Question</u> : Is there a sequence $i_1, \ldots, i_t$ of indices such that

1. Each i_j is in $\{0, 1, \ldots, n-1\}$, but the i_j need not be distinct or collectively exhaustive of $\{0, 1, \ldots, n-1\}$,
2. $t \leq l$, and
3. $(0, \text{POLICY}, R) \in (f_{i_t}, s_{i_t}) \circ \cdots \circ (f_{i_1}, s_{i_1})(\{(\Lambda, \Lambda, R)\})$?

Globally Bounded Proof of Compliance (GBPOC):

<u>Input</u> : A request r, a set $\{(f_0, \text{POLICY}), (f_1, s_1), \ldots, (f_{n-1}, s_{n-1})\}$ of assertions, and an integer d.

<u>Question</u> : Is there a sequence $i_1, \ldots, i_t$ of indices such that

1. Each i_j is in $\{0, 1, \ldots, n-1\}$, but the i_j need not be distinct or collectively exhaustive of $\{0, 1, \ldots, n-1\}$,
2. $(0, \text{POLICY}, R) \in (f_{i_t}, s_{i_t}) \circ \cdots \circ (f_{i_1}, s_{i_1})(\{(\Lambda, \Lambda, R)\})$, where R is the action string corresponding to request r, and
3. The computation of $(f_{i_t}, s_{i_t}) \circ \cdots \circ (f_{i_1}, s_{i_1})(\{(\Lambda, \Lambda, R)\})$ runs in (total) time $O(N^d)$?

Monotonic Proof of Compliance (MPOC):

<u>Input</u> : A request r, a set $\{(f_0, \text{POLICY}), (f_1, s_1), \ldots, (f_{n-1}, s_{n-1})\}$ of assertions, and integers l and c.

<u>Promise</u> : Each assertion (f_i, s_i) is monotonic and runs in time $O(N^c)$.

<u>Question</u> : Is there a sequence $i_1, \ldots, i_t$ of indices such that

1. Each i_j is in $\{0, 1, \ldots, n-1\}$, but the i_j need not be distinct or collectively exhaustive of $\{0, 1, \ldots, n-1\}$,
2. $t \leq l$, and
3. $(0, \text{POLICY}, R) \in (f_{i_t}, s_{i_t}) \circ \cdots \circ (f_{i_1}, s_{i_1})(\{(\Lambda, \Lambda, R)\})$, where R is the action string corresponding to request r?

Each version of POC can be defined using "agglomeration" $(f_2, s_2) \star (f_1, s_1)$ instead of composition $(f_2, s_2) \circ (f_1, s_1)$. The result of applying the sequence of assertions $(f_{i_1}, s_{i_1}), \ldots, (f_{i_t}, s_{i_t})$ agglomeratively to an acceptance set S_0 is defined inductively as follows: $S_1 \equiv (f_{i_1}, s_{i_1})(S_0) \cup S_0$ and, for $2 \leq j \leq t$, $S_j \equiv (f_{i_j}, s_{i_j})(S_{j-1}) \cup S_{j-1}$. Thus, for any acceptance set A, $A \subseteq (f_{i_t}, s_{i_t}) \star \cdots \star (f_{i_1}, s_{i_1})(A)$. The agglomerative versions of the decision problems are identical to the versions already given, except that the acceptance condition is "$(0, \text{POLICY}, R) \in (f_{i_t}, s_{i_t}) \star \cdots \star (f_{i_1}, s_{i_1})(\{(\Lambda, \Lambda, R)\})$?" We refer to "agglomerative POC," "agglomerative MPOC," etc., when we mean the version defined in terms of $\star$ instead of $\circ$.

A trust management system that defines "proof of compliance" in terms of agglomeration makes it impossible for an assertion to "undo" an approval that it or any other assertion has already given to an action string during the course of constructing a proof. This definition of proof makes sense if it is important for the trust management system to guard against a rogue credential-issuer's ability to thwart legitimate proofs. Note that the question of whether the compliance checker combines assertions using agglomeration or composition is separate from the question of whether the assertions themselves are monotonic.

In proving that certain POC variants, while decidable, are computationally intractable, we use the fact that the Bounded Post Correspondence Problem is NP-complete [6, Problem SR11].

Bounded Post Correspondence (BPCP):

Input : A finite alphabet Σ, two sequences $a = (a_1, a_2, \ldots, a_n)$ and $b = \overline{(b_1, b_2, \ldots, b_n)}$ of strings from Σ^*, and a positive integer $K \leq n$.

Question : Is there a sequence $i_1, i_2, \ldots, i_k$ of $k \leq K$ (not necessarily distinct) positive integers, each between 1 and n, such that the two strings $a_{i_1} a_{i_2} \cdots a_{i_k}$ and $b_{i_1} b_{i_2} \cdots b_{i_k}$ are identical?

Theorem 1. The Locally Bounded Proof of Compliance promise problem is in NPP and is NP-hard.

Proof. LBPOC is clearly in NPP, because the obvious nondeterministic polynomial-time procedure works on all instances that satisfy the promise: Guess a sequence $i_1, \ldots, i_t$ of indices, simulate the assertions (f_{i_j}, s_{i_j}) in the order specified by the sequence, and accept if and only if the acceptance record $(0, \text{POLICY}, R)$ is in the final acceptance set.

We now give a reduction from BPCP to LBPOC all of whose target instances satisfy the promise; this shows that LBPOC is NP-hard. Let $(\Sigma, (a_1, \ldots, a_q), (b_1, \ldots, b_q), K)$ be a BPCP instance. In the corresponding LBPOC instance, the request r and equivalent action string R do not play a significant role and can be taken to be σ, for any fixed $\sigma \in \Sigma$. Similarly, the only value of s_i that matters is $s_0 = \text{POLICY}$; we can put $s_i = \sigma$, for all $i \neq 0$. The number of assertions is $n = q + 1$. For $1 \leq i \leq q$, assertion (f_i, σ) produces action strings of the form (a_i, b_i, e), where a_i and b_i are identical to the strings in the BPCP instance, and e is a positive integer. (The integer e is only needed because the inputs and outputs of assertions are unordered sets, rather than ordered lists.) Specifically, when fed acceptance set S as input, (f_i, σ) outputs $S \cup \{(i, \sigma, (a_i, b_i, |S|))\}$. Let $c = 2$, $l = K$, and $m = K$. The parameter s, which should be an upper bound on the size of an acceptance record produced by the assertions in the LBPOC instance, can be taken to be $2(\log_2(q+1) + \log_2 |\Sigma| + \max_{1 \leq i \leq q}(|a_i| + |b_i|) + \log_2 K)$.

The policy assertion (f_0, POLICY) behaves as follows on input S.

- If S is not of the form $\{(\Lambda, \Lambda, R), (j_1, \sigma, (a_{j_1}, b_{j_1}, e_1)), \ldots, (j_t, \sigma, (a_{j_t}, b_{j_t}, e_t))\}$, for some $1 \leq t \leq l$, output the empty set.
- Sort $\{(\Lambda, \Lambda, R), (j_1, \sigma, (a_{j_1}, b_{j_1}, e_1)), \ldots, (j_t, \sigma, (a_{j_t}, b_{j_t}, e_t))\}$ into increasing order with respect to the e_j's. Let $i_1, \ldots, i_t$ be the resulting sorted sequence of first coordinates of acceptance records.
- If $a_{i_1} \cdots a_{i_t} = b_{i_1} \cdots b_{i_t}$, then output $\{(0, \text{POLICY}, R)\}$. Else output the empty set.

This reduction shows that LBPOC is NP-hard, because $(\Sigma, (a_1, \ldots, a_q), (b_1, \ldots, b_q), K)$ is a yes-instance of BPCP if and only if $(r, (f_0, \text{POLICY}), \ldots, (f_{n-1}, \sigma), c, l, m, s)$ is a yes-instance of LBPOC. The parameter c is set to two so that (f_0, POLICY) has (more than enough) time to sort. The other assertions run in linear time. $\square$

Theorem 2. The Globally Bounded Proof of Compliance problem is NP-complete.

Proof. It is clear that GBPOC is in NP, because a nondeterministic machine can guess a sequence of assertions and then simulate them in polynomial time to verify that conditions 1 through 3 are met.

The reduction given in the proof of Theorem 1 can be modified to yield a reduction from BPCP to GBPOC. In an LBPOC instance, each assertion can output an acceptance set of size at most ms. The total number of assertions run is at most l, and thus the size of the input to any assertion is at most lms. The running time of any assertion is thus at most $\alpha \cdot (lms)^2$, for some constant $\alpha > 0$, and the total running time of the entire simulation is at most $\alpha \cdot l \cdot (lms)^2$. In the definition of GBPOC, N is defined to be the total length of the GBPOC instance. To get a reduction from BPCP to GBPOC, choose d so that $N^d \geq \alpha \cdot l \cdot (lms)^2$. □

Theorem 3. The Monotonic Proof of Compliance promise problem is NP-hard. It remains NP-hard if the requirement that t be bounded by l is omitted.

Proof. Consider the following assertion (f_a, s_a): If the input set contains action strings encoding i for all i, $1 \leq i \leq 2^{b^2}$, then output the union of the acceptance records in the input set and a set of acceptance records with action strings encoding $2^{b^2} + 1, \ldots, 2^{(b+1)^2}$, assertion number a, and source-ID s_a. Otherwise, just return the input set. This assertion is monotonic and runs in time polynomial *in the size of its input.*

An instance of BPCP of size n can be mapped in polynomial time to an instance of MPOC consisting of n assertions that produce no output, the assertion (f_a, s_a) described above that counts to $2^{(b+1)^2}$, the parameter $l = n$, and a monotonic policy assertion (f_0, POLICY) that solves the BPCP problem from scratch. The compliance checker solves the target instance by running (f_a, s_a) $n = l$ times, thereby producing $\Omega(2^{n^2})$ acceptance records. Because its input has size $\Omega(2^{n^2})$, the assertion (f_0, POLICY) has time $2^{c(n^2)}$ at its disposal, and this is sufficient to solve BPCP from scratch for some choice of the parameter c in the MPOC instance. Note that the size *of the MPOC instance* is linear in n.

Because the reduction just sets the parameter l to n, the problem becomes no easier if the parameter l is omitted.

Note that this reduction produces a language that is NP-hard but is not known to be in NP. It is not known whether this promise problem is in NPP. □

Corollary 1. The agglomerative versions of LBPOC, GBPOC, and MPOC are also NP-hard.

Proof. Essentially the same reductions from BPCP that work for the composition versions of these problems work for the agglomerative versions, too. In the agglomerative cases of LBPOC and GBPOC, the credential assertion (f_i, σ) can map input S to $\{(i, \sigma, (a_i, b_i, |S|))\}$ instead of $S \cup \{(i, \sigma, (a_i, b_i, |S|))\}$, because the compliance checker maintains the agglomeration. A similar, straightforward modification works for the hardness proof for MPOC. □

5.2 Polynomial-Time Algorithm

We now present the compliance-checking algorithm that is used in the current version of the PolicyMaker trust management system. We describe the special case of the POC problem that our algorithm is guaranteed to solve and, just as importantly, what the algorithm does when given a POC instance not of this special form. The promise that defines this special case includes some conditions that we have already discussed, namely monotonicity and bounds on the run-time of assertions and on the total size of acceptance sets that assertions can produce. For a working algorithm, however, we need to consider another condition, which we call "authenticity," that we could ignore when proving hardness results. An authentic assertion (f_i, s_i) only produces acceptance records of the form (i, s_i, R_{ij}), i.e., it does not "impersonate" another assertion by producing an acceptance record of the form $(i', s_{i'}, R_{i'j})$.

PolicyMaker constructs proofs in an agglomerative fashion, and hence we use $\star$ in the following problem statement. This variant of POC could be defined using $\circ$ as well, but the algorithm given in this section would *not* work for the $\circ$ version.

Locally Bounded, Monotonic, and Authentic Proof of Compliance (LBMAPOC):

Input : A request r, a set $\{(f_0, \text{POLICY}), (f_1, s_1), \ldots, (f_{n-1}, s_{n-1})\}$ of assertions, and integers c, m, and s.

Promise : Each assertion (f_i, s_i) is monotonic, authentic, and runs in time $O(N^c)$. On any input set that contains (Λ, Λ, R), where R is the action string corresponding to request r, for each (f_i, s_i) there is a set O_i of at most m action strings, such that (f_i, s_i) only produces output from O_i, and s is the maximum size of an acceptance record (i, s_i, R_{ij}), such that $R_{ij} \in O_i$.

Question : Is there a sequence $i_1, \ldots, i_t$ of indices such that each i_j is in $\{0, 1, \ldots, n-1\}$, but the i_j need not be distinct or collectively exhaustive of $\{0, 1, \ldots, n-1\}$, and $(0, \text{POLICY}, R) \in (f_{i_t}, s_{i_t}) \star \cdots \star (f_{i_1}, s_{i_1})(\{(\Lambda, \Lambda, R)\})$.

We present an algorithm called CCA_1, for "compliance-checking algorithm, version 1," to allow for the evolution of PolicyMaker, and for improved algorithms CCA_i, $i \geq 1$.

We call (f_i, s_i) "ill-formed" if it violates the promise. If CCA_1 discovers in the course of simulating it that (f_i, s_i) is ill-formed, CCA_1 ignores it for the remainder of the computation. Note that an assertion (f_i, s_i) may be undetectably ill-formed; for example, there may be sets $A \subseteq B$ such that $(f_i, s_i)(A) \not\subseteq (f_i, s_i)(B)$, but such that A and B do not arise in this run of the compliance checker. The CCA_1 algorithm checks for violations of the promise every time it simulates an assertion. We don't include pseudocode for these checks in the statement of CCA_1 displayed above, because it would not illustrate the basic structure of the algorithm; the predicate $IllFormed()$ is included in the main loop to indicate that the checks are done for each simulation.

Like the nondeterministic algorithms presented in Section 5.1, CCA_1 accepts if and only if the acceptance record $(0, \text{POLICY}, R)$ is produced when it simulates the input assertions. Unlike the previous algorithms, however, it cannot nondeterministically guess an order in which to do the simulation; it must have an algorithmic method of finding an order. CCA_1 must also ensure that, if a proper subset F of the input assertions contains a proof that r complies with POLICY and every $(f_i, s_i) \in F$ satisfies the promise, then the remaining assertions do not destroy all or part of the acceptance records produced by F during the simulation and thus destroy the proof, *even if these remaining assertions do not satisfy the promise*. CCA_1 achieves this by maintaining one set of approved acceptance records, from which no records are ever deleted (*i.e.*, by agglomerating), and by discarding assertions that it discovers are ill-formed.

Fig. 1. Pseudocode for Algorithm CCA_1

```
CCA₁(r, {(f₀, POLICY), (f₁, s₁), ..., (fₙ₋₁, sₙ₋₁)}, c, m, s):
    {
        S ← {(Λ, Λ, R)}
        I ← {}
        For j ← 1 to mn
        {
            For i ← n-1 to 0
            {
                If (fᵢ, sᵢ)∉ I, Then S' ← (fᵢ,sᵢ)(S)
                If IllFormed((fᵢ,sᵢ)), Then I ← I ∪ {(fᵢ,sᵢ)},
                    Else S ← S ∪ S'
            }
        }
        If (0, POLICY, R) ∈ S, Then Output(Accept),
            Else Output(Reject)
    }
```

Note that CCA_1 does mn iterations of the sequence $(f_{n-1}, s_{n-1}), \ldots, (f_1, s_1),$ (f_0, POLICY), for a total of mn^2 assertion-simulations. Recall that a set $F = \{(f_{j_1}, s_{j_1}), \ldots, (f_{j_t}, s_{j_t})\} \subseteq \{(f_0, \text{POLICY}), \ldots, (f_{n-1}, s_{n-1})\}$ "contains a proof that r complies with POLICY" if there is some sequence $k_1, \ldots, k_u$ of the indices $j_1, \ldots, j_t$, not necessarily distinct and not necessarily exhaustive of $j_1, \ldots, j_t$, such that $(0, \text{POLICY}, R) \in (f_{k_u}, s_{k_u}) \star \cdots \star (f_{k_1}, s_{k_1})(\{(\Lambda, \Lambda, R)\})$.

Theorem 4. Let $(r, \{(f_0, \text{POLICY}), (f_1, s_1), \ldots, (f_{n-1}, s_{n-1})\}, c, m, s)$ be an (agglomerative) LBMAPOC instance.

(1) Suppose that $F \subseteq \{(f_0, \text{POLICY}), (f_1, s_1), \ldots, (f_{n-1}, s_{n-1})\}$ contains a proof that r complies with POLICY and that every $(f_i, s_i) \in F$ satisfies the promise of LBMAPOC. Then CCA_1 accepts $(r, \{(f_0, \text{POLICY}), (f_1, s_1), \ldots, (f_{n-1}, s_{n-1})\}, c, m, s)$.

(2) If $\{(f_0, \text{POLICY}), (f_1, s_1), \ldots, (f_{n-1}, s_{n-1})\}$ does not contain a proof that r complies with POLICY, then CCA_1 rejects $(r, \{(f_0, \text{POLICY}), (f_1, s_1), \ldots, (f_{n-1}, s_{n-1})\}, c, m, s)$.

(3) CCA_1 runs in time $O(mn^2(nms)^c)$.

Proof. The only nontrivial claim is (1). Let $F = \{(f_{j_1}, s_{j_1}), \ldots, (f_{j_t}, s_{j_t})\}$ be a set that satisfies the hypothesis of (1). Each assertion in F is monotonic, and, as CCA_1 simulates assertions agglomeratively, it never deletes acceptance records that have already been produced but rather just adds new ones. Therefore, we may assume without loss of generality that F contains all of the well-formed assertions in $\{(f_0, \text{POLICY}), (f_1, s_1), \ldots, (f_{n-1}, s_{n-1})\}$.

Let $k_1, \ldots, k_u$ be a sequence of indices, each in $\{j_1, \ldots, j_t\}$, but not necessarily distinct and not necessarily exhaustive of $\{j_1, \ldots, j_t\}$, such that $(0, \text{POLICY}, R) \in (f_{k_u}, s_{k_u}) \star \cdots \star (f_{k_1}, s_{k_1})(\{(\varLambda, \varLambda, R)\})$. Assume without loss of generality that no sequence of length less than u has this property. Let $A_1, \ldots, A_u$ be the acceptance sets produced by applying $(f_{k_1}, s_{k_1}), \ldots, (f_{k_u}, s_{k_u})$. Because $k_1, \ldots, k_u$ is a shortest sequence that proves compliance using assertions in F, each set A_p must contain at least one action string that is not present in any of $A_1, \ldots, A_{p-1}$. Thus u iterations of $(f_0, \text{POLICY}) \star (f_1, s_1) \star \cdots \star (f_{n-1}, s_{n-1})$ would suffice for CCA_1: At some point in the first iteration, (f_{k_1}, s_{k_1}) would be run, and, because CCA_1 adds but never deletes acceptance records, A_1 or some superset of A_1 would be produced. At some point during the second iteration, (f_{k_2}, s_{k_2}) would be run, and because A_1 would be contained in its input, A_2 or some superset of A_2 would be produced. And so forth.

Each $(f_{j_h}, s_{j_h}) \in F$ satisfies the local boundedness promise and thus produces at most m distinct action strings in any computation that begins with $\{(\varLambda, \varLambda, R)\}$, regardless of the behavior of other assertions, even ill-formed ones. Because $|F| = t \leq n$, at most mn distinct action strings could ever be produced by assertions in F, and at most mn sets A_p can be produced if each is to contain a record that is not contained in any set that comes earlier in the sequence. Thus, $u \leq mn$, and mn iterations of $(f_0, \text{POLICY}) \star (f_1, s_1) \star \cdots \star (f_{n-1}, s_{n-1})$ suffice. $\square$

Note that cases (1) and (2) do not cover all possible inputs to CCA_1. There may be a subset F of the input assertions that does contain a proof that r complies with POLICY but that contains one or more ill-formed assertions. If CCA_1 does not detect that any of these assertions is ill-formed, because their ill-formedness is only exhibited on acceptance sets that do not occur in this computation, then CCA_1 will accept the input. If it does detect ill-formedness, then, as specified here, CCA_1 may or may not accept the input, perhaps depending on whether the record $(0, \text{POLICY}, R)$ has already been produced at the time of detection. CCA_1 could be modified so that it restarts every time ill-formedness is detected, after discarding the ill-formed assertion so that it is not used in the new computation. It is not clear whether this modification would be worth the performance penalty. The point is simply that CCA_1 offers no guarantees about what it does when it is fed a policy that trusts, directly or indirectly, a source of ill-formed assertions, except that it will terminate in time $O(mn^2(nms)^c)$. It is the responsibility of the policy author to know which sources to trust and to modify the policy if some trusted sources are discovered to be issuing ill-formed assertions.

6 Discussion

6.1 The PolicyMaker Notion of Proof

We have shown in this paper that the PolicyMaker system uses a notion of "proof that a request complies with a policy" that is amenable to definition and analysis. However, the choice of this notion of proof is still a subjective one, and there is no way to show definitively that it is *the* right notion of proof. We now briefly discuss three nontrivial design decisions that went into this choice.

A policy and credential set that are input to the compliance checker can be regarded as a "distributed policy" with which the request may or may not comply – when the local policy asserts that it trusts a credential issuer to authorize certain types of requests, it delegates part of its policy-writing responsibility to that credential issuer. The job of the compliance checker is to have the executable assertions in this distributed policy cooperate to produce a proof, and this cooperation requires a mechanism for "inter-assertion communication" of intermediate results. For simplicity, we chose to have assertions communicate just by outputting acceptance records that can be input to other assertions. More sophisticated interactions, such as allowing assertions to call each other as subroutines, might be useful but would require a more complex execution environment than the one PolicyMaker provides. An open question for future work on trust management is the trade-off between the cost of building and analyzing such an execution environment and the potential power to be gained by using more sophisticated interactions to construct proofs of compliance. Preliminary work along those lines can be found in [3].

The choice of this simple communication mechanism implies that an important part of constructing a proof of compliance is choosing an order in which to execute assertions. PolicyMaker assigns the responsibility of choosing this order to the compliance checker and not, for example, to the calling application. Although the compliance checker's job could be made easier by requiring the calling application to give it the correct order as an input, such a requirement would not be consistent with PolicyMaker's overall goals, some of which are discussed in Section 2 above. Applications should be able to use credentials issued by diverse and far-flung sources, without having to make assumptions about the order in which these credentials expect to communicate via acceptance records. In an extreme case, the issuing sources will not be aware of each others' existence, and no such assumptions by the calling application would be valid; the compliance checker has to have a way to proceed even in this case.

Although the most general version of the POC problem allows assertions to be arbitrary functions, the computationally tractable version that is analyzed in Section 5.2 and implemented in PolicyMaker is guaranteed to be correct only when all assertions are monotonic. In particular, correctness is guaranteed only for monotonic *policy* assertions, and this excludes certain types of policies that are used in practice, most notably those that make explicit use of "negative credentials" such as revocation lists. Although it is a limitation, the monotonicity requirement has certain advantages. One of them is that, although the compliance checker may not handle all potentially desireable policies, it is at least analyzable and provably correct on a well-defined class of policies. Furthermore, the requirements of many non-monotonic policies can often be achieved by monotonic policies. For example, the effect of requiring that an entity *not* occur on a revocation list can also be achieved by requiring that it present a "certificate of non-revocation"; the choice between these two approaches involves trade-offs among the (system-wide) costs of the two kinds of credentials and the benefits of a standard compliance checker with provable properties. Finally, restriction to monotonic assertions encourages a conservative, prudent approach to security: In order to perform a potentially dangerous action, a user must present an adequate set of affirmative credentials; no potentially dangerous action is allowed "by default," simply because of the absence of negative credentials.

Thus, we believe that the notion of proof now implemented in PolicyMaker is quite widely applicable. However, the question of how to handle non-monotonic policies in a general-purpose trust management system is an important one for future research.

6.2 A Trade-off Between Expressiveness and Verifiability

We have formulated the POC problem in a way that allows assertions to be as expressive as possible. As a result, well-formedness promises such as monotonicity and boundedness, while formal and precise, cannot in general be verified. Each assertion that conditionally trusts an assertion source for application-specific expertise (such as suitability for a loan) must also trust that source only to write bounded and monotonic assertions *and* only to trust other similar sources of assertions. The resulting notion of soundness is that if there is no proof from a set of trusted, well-formed assertions, then CCA_1 will not accept the input.

Full expressiveness, however, is just one goal of a trust management system. Another goal is the clear separation of the trust relationships of assertions from programming details. To some extent, these goals are at odds — the compliance checker cannot be expected to perform verifications on fully general programs, and thus the assertion writers must worry about some programming details.

We note that one can require monotonic assertions actually to be written as AND-OR circuits and bounded assertions to "declare" the finite set from which they will produce output. A compliance-checking algorithm could then easily detect the ill-formed assertions and discard them. This would free assertion writers of the burden of deciding when another writer is trusted to write bounded and monotonic code, just as requiring assertions to be written in a safe (and therefore restricted) language frees the assertion writer from worrying about certain application-independent programming details. This verifiability comes at a price; listing a finite output set is relatively inexpensive, but there are monotonic functions that require exponentially bigger circuits to express over a basis of AND and OR than they require over a basis of AND, OR, and NOT [11]. In some applications it may be cheaper, on average, to write assertions that are verifiably bounded and monotonic than to determine the set of sources trusted (even indirectly) by a given assertion and to judge whether they are trusted to be monotonic and bounded.

We mention another possibility for the compliance checker that gives both expressiveness and verification tools, although only at a possible performance penalty. Another possible approach that we have not yet explored is for the compliance checker to make available to assertions reading acceptance records the original code of the assertions that produced those records. A conservative policy then, before trusting assertions (f_1, s_1) and (f_2, s_2), could require and check that f_1 and f_2 be *verifiably* monotonic and bounded *and* that f_1 and f_2 each include specific standard code to check all assertions whose acceptance records (f_1, s_1) and (f_2, s_2) wish to trust. A complex monotonic assertion that needs to be written compactly using NOT gates can, if desired, still be used with the modified compliance algorithm.

References

1. M. Blaze, J. Feigenbaum, and J. Lacy, *Decentralized Trust Management*, in Proceedings of the Symposium on Security and Privacy, IEEE Computer Society Press, Los Alamitos, 1996, pp. 164–173.
2. M. Blaze, J. Feigenbaum, P. Resnick, and M. Strauss, *Managing Trust in an Information-Labeling System*, European Transactions on Telecommunications, 8 (1997), pp. 491–501. (Special issue of selected papers from the 1996 Amalfi Conference on Secure Communication in Networks.)
3. Y.-H. Chu, J. Feigenbaum, B. LaMacchia, P. Resnick, and M. Strauss, REFEREE: *Trust Management for Web Applications*, World Wide Web Journal, 2 (1997), pp. 127–139. (Reprinted from Proceedings of the 6th International World Wide Web Conference, World Wide Web Consortium, Cambridge, 1997, pp. 227–238.)
4. D. Denning, **Cryptography and Data Security**, Addison-Wesley, Reading, 1982.
5. S. Even, A. Selman, and Y. Yacobi, *The Complexity of Promise Problems with Applications to Public-Key Cryptography*, Information and Control, 61 (1984), pp. 159–174.
6. M. Garey and D. Johnson, **Computers and Intractability: A Guide to the Theory of NP-Completeness**, Freeman, San Fancisco, 1979.
7. M. A. Harrison, W. L. Ruzzo, and J. D. Ullman, *Protection in Operating Systems*, Communications of the ACM, 19 (1976), pp. 461–471.
8. A. K. Jones, R. J. Lipton, and L. Snyder, *A Linear Time Algorithm for Deciding Security*, in Proceedings of the Symposium on Foundations of Computer Science, IEEE Computer Society Press, Los Alamitos, 1976, pp. 33-41.
9. J. Lacy, D. P. Maher, and J. H. Snyder, *Music on the Internet and the Intellectual Property Protection Problem*, in Proceedings of the International Symposium on Industrial Electronics, IEEE Press, New York, 1997, pp. SS77–83.

10. R. Levien, L. McCarthy, and M. Blaze, *Transparent Internet E-mail Security*, http://www.cs.umass.edu/~lmccarth/crypto/papers/email.ps
11. E. Tardos, *The Gap Between Monotone and Non-monotone Circuit Complexity is Exponential*, Combinatorica, 8 (1988), pp. 141–142.
12. T. Y. C. Woo and S. S. Lam, *Authorization in Distributed Systems: A New Approach*, Journal of Computer Security, 2 (1993), pp. 107–36.

An Efficient Fair Off-Line Electronic Cash System with Extensions to Checks and Wallets with Observers

Aymeric de Solages and Jacques Traoré

France Télécom - Branche Dévéloppement
Centre National d'Etudes des Télécommunications
42, rue des Coutures, BP 6243
14066 Caen Cedex, France
{aymeric.desolages, jacques.traore}@cnet.francetelecom.fr

Abstract. In this paper, we present a privacy-protecting off-line electronic cash system which is *fair*, that is, the transactions are (potentially) traceable by a trusted authority but anonymous otherwise. Our scheme, based on a modification of Brands'restrictive blind signature scheme [2], is significantly more efficient than that of [11], while offering the same functionalities (*off-line* trusted authority, *direct* identification of the owner[1] of a coin when the tracing of a user from his coin is performed by the trusted authority). Furthermore, we show how to extend our system to wallets with *observers* [9] and to electronic *checks* [1, 2, 15]. These two extensions are more efficient than previous ones [2, 6]. The first extension is featured by a high computational efficiency and low storage requirements for observers. The second extension provides checks which are more efficiently computed than checks in [2] (twice as fast) and which also require less memory for their storage (half as much).

1 Introduction

Current cashless payment systems such as credit card payment systems provide little or no protection of the users' privacy. Indeed, in these systems, the banks could easily observe who pays which amount to whom and when.

At Crypto'82, D. Chaum [7] introduced a new cryptographic tool, the blind signature scheme, which has made it possible to design anonymous (privacy-protecting) prepaid payment systems [2, 3, 8]. A blind signature scheme is a cryptographic protocol involving two entities: a sender and a signer. This protocol allows the sender to choose a message and obtain a digital signature of this message from the signer without revealing anything about the contents of the message to the signer. Moreover, the signer cannot link later on (i.e. after the signature has been

---

[1] By owner of a coin, we mean in fact the person who has withdrawn the coin.

revealed to the public) a given message-signature pair to the corresponding execution of the blind signature protocol.

Recent anonymous prepaid electronic payment systems [2, 3, 8], based on the blind signature technique, 'emulate' physical cash. In these systems, the users withdraw electronic coins which consist of numbers, generated by users, and *blindly* signed by an electronic money issuer (a bank). Each signature represents a given amount. These coins are then spent (released) in shops which can authenticate them by using the public signature key of the bank. In these systems it is impossible to link a withdrawal of an electronic coin to a payment made with this coin (perfect anonymity).

Unfortunately, these perfect anonymous payment systems could be abused for unlawful and criminal activities, such as money laundering and *perfect* blackmailing [21]. For these reasons, it has been argued that perfect anonymity is certainly not the suitable level of privacy that an electronic payment system must offer to its users. Future electronic cash systems should be provided with incomplete or conditional anonymity.

A step in this direction has recently been made by several researchers. In [19], Stadler et al. proposed a new type of blind signature scheme called *fair Blind Signature Scheme* (*fair BSS* in short), that can replace ordinary BSS within anonymous payment systems. In a fair BSS, the signer can, with the help of a single (or several) trusted authority (ies) (who is (are) given some extra information), either link a message-signature pair to the corresponding execution of the signing protocol or extract the content of a message from its *blind* form. By replacing *ordinary* blind signature schemes by *fair* blind signature schemes in electronic payment systems, the bank and anyone else would still be unable to link a withdrawal to the payment made with the withdrawn coin. However, if abuse is suspected, the trusted authority could help the bank in auditing a particular account or to finding out the author's identity in one particular transaction. In this way, privacy of honest users would be preserved and embezzlement by criminals prevented. Unfortunately the schemes of Stadler et al. are inefficient. Moreover, one of their schemes has been recently broken by one of the authors of this paper [20].

In [4], Brickell, Gemmell and Kravitz proposed an anonymous off-line electronic cash scheme, based on Brands' system [3], which is fair, insofar as the transactions are (potentially) traceable by proper trusted authorities but anonymous otherwise. In this scheme, the trusted authorities are *on-line*, that is, they are involved[1] in every withdrawal so that they are able to revoke (if requested) the user's anonymity.

Recently, Camenisch, Maurer and Stadler proposed a more efficient fair off-line electronic cash system [5]. Moreover, in their scheme, the trusted authorities are *off-line*, that is, they need not be involved in either the withdrawal protocol or the payment protocol in order to be able to revoke the user's anonymity. In [6], Camenish et al. showed how to extend their basic fair cash system [5] to wallets with observers.

---

[1] In fact, the trusted authority can pre-compute his involvement in the withdrawal.

In [14], Frankel, Tsiounis and Yung achieved similar results to [5], but with a stronger model of fair cash: in [14], the trusted authority finds directly the identity of the owner of a specific coin, whereas in [5] the trusted authority performs a search in a large database (the withdrawal database).

In [11], Davida et al. improved the efficiency of [14].

In this paper, we propose an efficient fair off-line electronic cash system. Our scheme, based on a modification of Brands'restrictive blind signature scheme [3], is significantly more efficient than that of [11], while offering the same functionalities (*off-line* trusted authority, *direct* identification of the owner of a coin when the tracing of a user from his coin is performed by the trusted authority).

Moreover, we show how to extend our system to wallets with *observers* [9] and to electronic *checks* [1, 2, 15]. These two extensions are significantly more efficient than previous ones [1, 6].

Organization of the paper: In section 2, we explain some notations and introduce our assumptions and the background of the key techniques that will be useful in the sequel. In section 3, our generic fair cash system is described, followed by a discussion on its security. We also compare the efficiency of our system with the system of [11]. In section 4, we show how to extend our generic fair cash system to the setting of wallets with observers. Then, we examine the security of this extension and compare its efficiency with [6]. In section 5, we show how our system can be extended to handle electronic checks. In section 6, we conclude this paper and introduce some open problems.

In the following sections, we describe a generic fair off-line payment system. In the simplified model of off-line electronic cash system that we use, three types of parties are involved: the customers (or 'users'), the shops and a bank. Three possible transactions may occur between them: the withdrawal (by a user from the bank), the payment (by a user to a shop), and the deposit (by a shop to the bank). In the withdrawal protocol, the user withdraws electronic coins from the bank while his account is being debited. In the payment protocol, the user pays the shop with the coins he has withdrawn. In the deposit protocol, the shop deposits the coins it has received to the bank and the shop's account is credited.

Our scheme is an anonymous payment system, however the customers' anonymity may be revoked by a proper trusted authority. The customers' anonymity can be revoked in two different ways:

- *coin tracing:* the bank provides the trusted authority with the data of withdrawals of a (suspect) user and asks for the information that allows it to determine the corresponding deposits (or payments).

- *owner tracing:* the bank provides the trusted authority with data of a (suspect) payment (in fact the deposit) and asks for the identity of the customer who has withdrawn the money used in this (suspect) payment.

2 Notations, Assumptions and Basic Tools

The security of our schemes is based on assumptions about the difficulty of solving certain problems. In this section, we define these assumptions and problems, explain our notations and introduce the background of the key techniques that will be useful in the sequel.

The symbol $\parallel$ will denote the concatenation of two strings.

The symbol ε will denote the empty string.

The notation ' $x \in_R E$ ' means that x is chosen uniformly at random from the set E.

The notation ' $x \overset{?}{=} y$ ', used in a protocol, means that the party must check whether x is equal to y. It is assumed that if the verification fails, the protocol stops.

H will denote a collision-resistant hash function.

2.1 The Representation Problem in a Group of Prime Order

For convenience, we use in this paper, as a group of prime order, the cyclic subgroup G_q of order q of Z_p^*, where q and p are two large primes such that $q/p-1$.

The representation problem in G_q is the following:

Given as inputs a k-tuple $\left(g_1, g_2, ..., g_k\right)$ *of distinct generators of* G_q, *the problem is to find a tuple* $\left(x_1, x_2, ..., x_k\right)$, *with* $x_i \in Z_q$ *for all* $1 \leq i \leq k$ *such that*

$$h = \prod_{i=1}^{k} g_i^{x_i} .$$

$\left(x_1, x_2, ..., x_k\right)$ *is called a representation of h with respect to* $\left(g_1, g_2, ..., g_k\right)$.

Remark. For $h = 1$, there is a *trivial* representation namely $(0,0,...,0)$. It is believed to be difficult to solve the representation problem for randomly chosen inputs. In fact, the hardness of finding a representation for random elements is based on the difficulty in computing discrete logarithms in G_q (for more details, we refer interested readers to [2]). A consequence of the difficulty in solving the representation problem is that only one representation of a (non random) element h, with respect to a random tuple of generators, can be known (see [2] for more details).

2.2 The Decision-Diffie-Hellman Problem

The Decision-Diffie-Hellman problem is defined as follows: given as inputs g_1, g_2, g_3 and g_4 four elements of G_q, decide whether $\log_{g_4} g_3 = \log_{g_4} g_1 \times \log_{g_4} g_2$. In other words, decide whether $\log_{g_2} g_3 = \log_{g_4} g_1$. For randomly chosen inputs, the Decision-Diffie-Hellman problem is assumed to be difficult to solve.

2.3 Proofs of Knowledge

In this section, we define some well-known cryptographic primitives closely related to the above supposedly hard problems.

In the sequel, we will need a proof of knowledge of a representation and a proof of equality of two discrete logarithms. As proof of knowledge of a representation, we are inspired by a proof due to T. Okamoto [16]. For the proof of equality of two discrete logarithms, we use the proof described in [9].

Definition 1 (*Proof$_{REP}$*) A (message-dependent) proof of knowledge of a representation of h with respect to $(g_1, g_2, ..., g_k)$ is the $k+1$-tuple $(c, r_1, r_2, ..., r_k) = Proof_{REP}(M, g_1, g_2, ..., g_k, h)$, where M is a message associated to the proof[1], and $c = H(M \parallel g_1 \parallel g_2 \parallel .... \parallel g_k \parallel h \parallel g_1^{r_1} g_2^{r_2} \cdots g_k^{r_k} h^c)$.

The prover who knows the representation $(x_1, x_2, ..., x_k)$ of h with respect to $(g_1, g_2, ..., g_k)$ can construct such a proof.

For this purpose, he chooses k random numbers $(a_1, a_2, ..., a_k) \in_R Z_q^{*k}$ and computes $c = H(M \parallel g_1 \parallel g_2 \parallel .... \parallel g_k \parallel h \parallel g_1^{a_1} g_2^{a_2} \cdots g_k^{a_k})$. Then, he computes $r_i = a_i - c\, x_i \bmod q$ for $1 \leq i \leq k$. To verify such a proof, the verifier checks whether c is equal to $H(M \parallel g_1 \parallel g_2 \parallel .... \parallel g_k \parallel h \parallel g_1^{r_1} g_2^{r_2} \cdots g_k^{r_k} h^c)$.

Note: According to the definition of [13], Proof$_{REP}$ is not a proof of knowledge. However, it is assumed that this proof does not leak any information about the representation that the prover knows.

Definition 2 (*Proof$_{LOGEQ}$*) A (message-dependent) proof of equality of the discrete logarithm of h with respect to g and of h' with respect to g' is a tuple $(c, r) = Proof_{LOGEQ}(M, g, h, g', h')$ where, as before, M is a (possibly empty) message associated to the proof, and $c = H(M \parallel g \parallel h \parallel g' \parallel h' \parallel g^r h^c \parallel g'^r h'^c)$.

This proof can be obtained, if and only if the prover knows the discrete logarithms $\log_g h$ and $\log_{g'} h'$ and if these values are equal. To construct the proof, the prover chooses $a \in_R Z_q$ and computes $c = H(M \parallel g \parallel h \parallel g' \parallel h' \parallel g^a \parallel g'^a)$ and $r = a - c\, x \bmod q$ (where x denotes $\log_g h$ and also $\log_{g'} h'$). To verify such a proof, the verifier checks whether c is equal to $H(M \parallel g \parallel h \parallel g' \parallel h' \parallel g^r h^c \parallel g'^r h'^c)$.

---

[1] Since the proof involves the message M, it is called *message-dependent*. This message may be the empty string ε.

Note: It is assumed that this proof does not leak any information about x.

For some purposes it is more efficient to merge both above defined proofs, which leads to the following definition:

Definition 3 (**Proof**$_{REP+LOGEQ}$) A (message-dependent) proof of knowledge of a representation of h with respect to $(g_1, g_2, ..., g_k)$, which also proves that the exponent of g_1 in this representation is equal to $\log_{g_1'} h'$ is a $k+1$-tuple $(c, r_1, r_2, ..., r_k) = Proof_{REP+LOGEQ}(M, g_1, g_2, ..., g_k, h, g_1', h')$, where c is equal to $H(M \parallel g_1 \parallel g_2 \parallel ... \parallel g_k \parallel h \parallel g_1' \parallel h' \parallel g_1^{r_1} g_2^{r_2} \cdots g_k^{r_k} h^c \parallel g_1'^{r_1} h'^c)$.

The prover who knows the representation $(x_1, x_2, ..., x_k)$ of h with respect to $(g_1, g_2, ..., g_k)$ and $\log_{g_1'} h' = x_1$ can construct such a proof. For this purpose, he chooses k random numbers $(a_1, a_2, ..., a_k) \in_R Z_q^{*k}$ and computes $c = H(M \parallel g_1 \parallel g_2 \parallel ... \parallel g_k \parallel h \parallel g_1' \parallel h' \parallel g_1^{a_1} g_2^{a_2} \cdots g_k^{a_k} \parallel g_1'^{a_1})$. Then he computes $r_i = a_i - c\, x_i \bmod q$ for $1 \le i \le k$. The verifier of this proof checks whether c is equal to $H(M \parallel g_1 \parallel g_2 \parallel ... \parallel g_k \parallel h \parallel g_1' \parallel h' \parallel g_1^{r_1} g_2^{r_2} \cdots g_k^{r_k} h^c \parallel g_1'^{r_1} h'^c)$.

2.4 The Basic Signature Scheme

In our system, the withdrawn coins are signed by the bank using the signature scheme presented in [9]. We now briefly describe this scheme.

The Parameters. Before the scheme can be used, the following parameters must be generated:

1. p and q are two large primes such that $q/p-1$.
2. g is a generator of G_q.
3. $x \in Z_q^*$ is the signer's secret key, and (p, q, g, h), where $h = g^x$, is the signer's public key.
4. $m \in G_q$ is the message to be signed, and $M \in \{0,1\}^*$ is another (possibly empty) message associated to the signature, for which it is called *message-dependent*.

The Scheme. The message-dependent signature $Sig(m)$ on m consists of $z = m^x$ along with a proof that $\log_g h = \log_m z$.

So, we have $Sig(m) = (\, z, Proof_{LOGEQ}(M, g, h, m, z)\,) = (z, c, r)$.

The verifier of such a signature checks whether c is equal to $H(M \parallel g \parallel h \parallel m \parallel z \parallel g^r h^c \parallel m^r z^c)$.

Note: In the sequel, we will deliberately omit the fixed values g and h in the computation of c. For a discussion of the security of this scheme, we refer interested readers to [9].

The Blind Signature Scheme. The signature scheme described in the previous section can be transformed into a blind signature scheme using Ohta-Okamoto's techniques [17]. To get a blind signature on the message $m \in G_q$, one chooses a random $s \in Z_q^*$ and asks the signer to sign $m_0 = m\, g^s$ (the input of the protocol). Let $z_0 = m_0^x$. The signer then proves that $\log_g h = \log_{m_0} z_0$, as described in figure 1 below.

We will denote this protocol *BlindSig(M, m_0)*. The following two propositions from [9] show that *BlindSig* is really a blind signature scheme.

Proposition 1 (correctness). If both parties follow the protocol, then *Sig(m)* will be a correct signature on m.

Proposition 2 (blindness). The signer will get no information about m and *Sig(m)*, if the verifier follows the protocol.

The security of our fair electronic cash relies on some assumptions about *BlindSig*. Let us formulate these assumptions.

Assumption 1 (unforgeability). Several executions of *BlindSig* will not help a verifier to create more valid message-signature pairs than expected (i.e., from l, sequential or parallel, executions of *BlindSig* with the signer, the verifier cannot create more than l valid message-signature pairs). Furthermore, by executing *BlindSig*, the verifier obtains no useful information about the signer's secret key.

Assumption 2 (blinding restrictions). On input m_0 to *BlindSig*, the verifier can obtain a valid blind signature on a message $m \in G_q$ (if and) only if he knows a representation of m with respect to (m_0, g) [1].

It is not hard to prove (using the same technique as in *BlindSig*) that on input $m_0 \in G_q$ to *BlindSig*, the verifier can choose a tuple $(\alpha, \beta) \in_R Z_q$ and obtain a blind signature on $m = g^\alpha m_0^\beta$.

Any way of obtaining a valid signature on a message m, for which the verifier does not know the representation with respect to (m_0, g), would provide a new method for blinding this kind of signatures.

In our fair cash scheme which uses *BlindSig* as a subprotocol, we will further 'restrict' the blinding manipulations that the user can do. More precisely, we will 'constraint' the user to choose a tuple (α, β) with $\beta = 1$.

[1] The security of Brands' electronic cash system [3] is based on the same assumption.

Signer		**Verifier**

$$\text{choose} \quad s \in_R Z_q^*$$

$$\text{compute} \quad m_0 = m \, g^s$$

$$\xleftarrow{\qquad m_0 \qquad}$$

$$\text{choose} \quad \omega \in_R Z_q^*$$

$$\text{compute} \quad z_0 = m_0^x$$

$$A_0 = g^\omega$$

$$B_0 = m_0^\omega$$

$$\xrightarrow{\quad z_0, A_0, B_0 \quad}$$

$$\text{choose} \quad u, v \in_R Z_q^*$$

$$\text{compute} \quad A = A_0^u \, g^v$$

$$B = B_0^u \, m_0^v \big/ A^s$$

$$z = z_0 \big/ h^s$$

$$c = H(M, m, z, A, B)$$

$$c_0 = c/u \bmod q$$

$$\xleftarrow{\qquad c_0 \qquad}$$

$$\text{compute} \quad r_0 = \omega - c_0 x \bmod q$$

$$\xrightarrow{\qquad r_0 \qquad}$$

$$\text{verify} \quad A_0 \overset{?}{=} g^{r_0} \, h^{c_0}$$

$$B_0 \overset{?}{=} m_0^{r_0} \, z_0^{c_0}$$

$$\text{compute} \quad r = u \, r_0 + v \bmod q$$

$$Sig(m) = (z, c, r)$$

Figure 1 : The blind signature protocol $BlindSig(M, m_0)$

Note: From the mere Chaum and Pedersen signature protocol of [9], we obtain the blinding of the *BlindSig* protocol as follows:

From $\begin{cases} A_0 = g^{r_0} \, h^{c_0} \\ B_0 = m_0^{r_0} \, z_0^{c_0} \end{cases}$, we first blind (r_0, c_0) with (u, v) and obtain

$\begin{cases} A_0' = A_0^u \, g^v = g^r \, h^c \\ B_0' = B_0^u \, m_0^v = m_0^r \, z_0^c \end{cases}$, where $\begin{cases} r = u \, r_0 + v \\ c = u \, c_0 \end{cases}$. Then we blind (m_0, z_0) with (α, β), which leads to $\begin{cases} A = A_0' = g^r\, h^c \\ B = A_0'^{\alpha} B_0'^{\beta} = m^r\, z^c \end{cases}$, where $\begin{cases} m = g^{\alpha} m_0^{\beta} \\ z = h^{\alpha} z_0^{\beta} \end{cases}$. We finally put $\begin{cases} \alpha = -s \\ \beta = 1 \end{cases}$,

which corresponds to the required blinding restriction $m_0 = m\, g^s$. Note that the *BlindSig* protocol does not enforce $\beta = 1$, but this property will be verified when the signature is presented, so the verifier must set $\beta = 1$ in order to get a valid signature. The actual calculation is performed in reverse order, as shown in the *BlindSig* protocol.

3 A Generic Fair Electronic Cash System

3.1 The Setup of the System

The Parameters. For the sake of simplicity, we assume that there is only one coin denomination in the system (extension to multiple denominations is easy).
Two large primes p and q such that $q/p-1$ are generated. Let G_q be the unique subgroup of Z_p^* of order q.

The Trusted Authority. We assume that there is only one trusted authority T (extension to several trustees is easy).

1. T chooses two secret values x_T and y_T of Z_q^*, and a public value $g_T \in G_q$.

2. T publishes g_T, $h_{CT} = g_T^{x_T^{-1}}$ and $h_{OT} = g_T^{y_T^{-1}}$.

The Bank. Before issuing coins, the bank has to make publicly known some parameters.

1. First, B generates at random her secret key $x \in Z_q^*$.

2. B generates the three generators g, g_1, g_2 of G_q (it is assumed that no representation of either of these elements with respect to the others is known), and publishes the corresponding public values $h = g^x$ (the bank's public key), $h_1 = g_1^x$, and $h_2 = g_2^x$.

3. B publishes $h_T = g_T^x$.

4. B finally determines a collision-free hash function H that maps $\{0,1\}^*$ to Z_{2^k}, where k is an appropriate security parameter.

Opening an Account (performed for each new user U). When a user U opens an account at the bank B, he generates at random his secret key $x_u \in Z_q^*$ and computes $Id_U = g_1^{x_u}$ (U 's account number).

Then, U must prove to B that he knows the representation of Id_U with respect to g_1. For this purpose, U computes a $Proof_{REP}(\varepsilon, g_1, Id_U)$ (or uses Schnorr's identification scheme [18]) and sends this proof to B. B verifies this proof and if the verification is successful, stores Id_U in the new user's entry of the account database. U and B then independently compute $P_U = h_1^{x_u} = (Id_U)^x$.

3.2 The Withdrawal Protocol

Before the user U and the bank B begin the protocol, U must authenticate itself to B, so that B is sure that U is the owner of the account Id_U. This can be done by any (fast) standard authentication protocol.

The withdrawal consists of two phases: the coin tracing phase and the coin withdrawal phase. During the coin tracing phase, the user gives the bank the information that will enable the trusted authority to recognize the withdrawn coin after it has been spent. In the coin withdrawal phase, the user executes *BlindSig* with the bank in order to obtain a blind signature on his coin.

Step 1 - The Coin Tracing Protocol. Roughly, the user generates a 'verifiable' El-Gamal encryption [12], computed with T's public key, of the value that will be used to blind the input of *BlindSig*. By verifiable we mean that the user gives a proof to the bank that he has really encrypted this value (without revealing it).

In the sequel, we will put $F = g_T\, g$.

1. U chooses $s \in_R Z_q$, computes $G = F^s = g_T^s\, g^s$ and the *'cointrace'* $ct = h_{CT}^s$ [1].

    U generates $Proof(ct) = Proof_{LOGEQ}(r_a, F, G, h_{CT}, ct)$ in order to convince B that $\log_F G$ and $\log_{h_{CT}} ct$ are equal. The message r_a is provided for linking the withdrawal to the prior authentication and represents for instance the last user response of the authentication protocol.

    U sends ct, G, and $Proof(ct)$ to B.

2. The bank verifies this proof and if the verification holds, stores ct in the user's entry of the withdrawal database for possible later anonymity revocation.

---

[1] g^s will blind the input of *BlindSig*, while g_T^s computationally blinds this blind factor.

The tuple (ct, G) can be seen as an El-Gamal encryption, computed with T's public key (h_{CT}, g_T), of the blind factor $Bf = g^s$.

Step 2 - The Withdrawal of a Coin

1. Both the user and the bank prepare the execution of the *Blindsig* protocol by computing independently the blinded coin $Blindcoin = Id_U \times g_2 \times G$, where B has got G from step 1. Note that $Blindcoin = coin \times g^s$, where $coin = Id_U \times g_2 \times g_T^s$ is the message to be (blindly) signed. As we will see later on (section 3.3), the value g_2 is used to *restrict* the blind manipulations that the user can do (see also the discussion about assumption 2). Note also that U need not get z_0 (see figure 1) from B in order to compute $z = coin^x = P_U\ h_2\ h_T^s$.

2. The bank and the user execute a *message-dependent BlindSig* protocol *BlindSig(M, Blindcoin)*, where the message $M = ot\ \|\ D\ \|\ E$ inserted by U (and disclosed during the payment protocol) is intended to both assure *owner-tracing* (thanks to the '*ownertrace*' $ot = h_{OT}^s$) and prevent future *double-spending* of the coin (thanks to $D = g_1^a\ g_T^b$ and $E = h_{OT}^b$ where $(a,b) \in_R Z_q^{*2}$ are chosen by U).

So at the end of *BlindSig*, U obtains $Sig(coin) = (\ z,\ Proof_{LOGEQ}(M, g, h, coin, z)\ )$, and the bank debits the real money counterpart of the withdrawn coin from U's account.

3.3   The Payment Protocol

We assume that the shop S is known under Id_S (its account number for example), and define 't' to be the payment (date and) time. During the payment protocol, the user U sends the coin signed by the bank to the shop, along with a proof of knowledge of the representation of $C = coin/g_2 = g_1^{x_u}\ g_T^s$ with respect to (g_1, g_T). This proof also provides the shop with the information (ot) that will enable the trusted authority to possibly trace him. The message $msg = (\ Id_S\ \|\ t\ )$ is inserted in this proof in order to detect theft (by another shop) and replay (that is, multiple spending by the user, as explained in 3.5) of the coin.

1. U uses the commitments D and E to generate :
   $Proof(ot) = Proof_{REP+LOGEQ}(msg, g_T, g_1, C, h_{OT}, ot)$.
   More precisely, $Proof(ot) = (c, r_1, r_2)$, where:
   · $c = H(msg\ \|\ g_T\ \|\ g_1\ \|\ C\ \|\ h_{OT}\ \|\ ot\ \|\ D\ \|\ E)$
   · $r_1 = b - c\ s$ mod q and $r_2 = a - c\ x_u$ mod q, with (a, b) from the withdrawal (see section 3.2 Step 2).
   U sends M, *coin*, *Sig* (*coin*) and *Proof*(*ot*) to the shop.

2. S verifies the signature and the proof and, if the verification holds, accepts the payment.

Roughly speaking, U generates a 'verifiable' El-Gamal encryption of Id_U, computed with T's public key (h_{OT}, g_T).

3.4   The Deposit Protocol

To be credited the value of this coin, the shop sends the transcript of the execution of the payment protocol to the bank, which verifies, exactly as the shop did, that the coin (*coin*) bears the bank's signature and that the other responses are correct.

3.5   The Tracing Mechanisms

Double-Spenders Tracing (without having recourse to T). If the user U spends the same coin twice, either in two different shops S and S' (in which case $Id_S \neq Id_{S'}$), or in the same shop but at two different times t and t', the messages *msg* and *msg'* associated to these payments will always be different, and so will be the values c and c' with high probability. After the deposit of both payment transcripts, the bank will be able to detect the double spending of the coin (thanks to *coin*) *and* to retrieve the double spender's identity, that is x_u, and therefore U's account number ($Id_U = g_1^{x_u}$).   Indeed,   from   ($c = H(msg \| g_T \| g_1 \| C \| h_{OT} \| ot \| D \| E)$, $r_2 = a - c\,x_u$ mod q) received   during   the   one   deposit   and ($c' = H(msg' \| g_T \| g_1 \| C \| h_{OT} \| ot \| D \| E)$, $r_2' = a - c'\,x_u$ mod q) received during the other, the bank can compute $x_u = \dfrac{r_2' - r_2}{c - c'}$ mod q.

Coin Tracing. The coin tracing mechanism allows the trusted authority to compute the information needed to recognize the money after it has been spent.

Given the transcript of the execution of the withdrawal protocol (in fact ct), the trusted authority can compute $g_T^s = (ct)^{x_T}$ and then $coin = Id_U\, g_2\, g_T^s$ (so, the coin is traceable).

Owner Tracing. The owner tracing mechanism allows the trusted authority to find the identity of the person (in fact the account number) who has withdrawn a specific coin.

Given the execution transcript of the payment protocol (in fact *coin* and ot), the trusted authority can retrieve U's account number: $Id_U = (coin/g_2)/(ot)^{y_T}$.

3.6   The Security of the Scheme

Let us analyze, informally speaking, the security of our scheme.

Correctness. If U and B behave correctly, then U will obtain a valid signature of *coin* (correctness of the protocol *BlindSig*, see Proposition 1). Moreover, if U behaves correctly, then he knows s and x_u and will be able to generate the two valid proofs *Proof*(*ct*) and *Proof*(*ot*) (see Definition 2 and 3). So, S will accept the payment.

Security for B (unforgeability). We refer to the first assumption about *BlindSig*, which says that it is hard to forge a signature of our basic signature scheme even after several sequential or parallel executions of *BlindSig*. Moreover, in the withdrawal protocol the bank executes only *BlindSig*, so the withdrawal protocol does not leak more useful information about the bank's secret key than *BlindSig*.

So, it seems difficult to get more distinct coins than the ones that have been withdrawn.

Anonymity. Let us now explain why our system provides anonymity to the users[1].

From proposition 2 we know that *BlindSig* is a perfect blind signature scheme, that is, the signer's *view*[2] of *BlindSig* and the verifier's output of *BlindSig* (the message-signature pair) are unlinkable.

So, in our cash system only the extra parts of *BlindSig* (namely, $G = F^s$, $ct = h_{CT}^s$, and $ot = h_{OT}^s$) could help bank to link its view of the withdrawal protocol to the coin obtained (and spent) by the user. As the signer B knows neither $\log_{g_T} h_{OT}$ nor $\log_{g_T} h_{CT}$, these extra parts are computationally unlinkable (see the Decision-Diffie-Hellman problem section 2.2).

Moreover, *Proof*(*ct*) and *Proof*(*ot*) leak no information that seems useful for establishing a link between a withdrawal and a payment.

Security for T. We explain why it is infeasible for a user to get a valid coin, which, if spent, would not allow T to trace him (i.e. it is impossible to 'bypass' the tracing mechanisms):

1. The proof *Proof*(*ct*) guarantees that the input of *BlindSig* in the withdrawal protocol (*Blindcoin*) is of the form: $g_1^{x_u} g_2 g_T^s g^s$ with $s \in Z_q$.

2. According to Assumption 2, on input *Blindcoin* to *BlindSig*, *Sig*(*coin*) is a valid (blind) signature on *coin*, only if the user knows a representation $(\alpha, \beta) \in Z_q$ of

---

[1] which can only be computational in fair cash system (as proved in [14]).
[2] A view consists of the complete list of data seen during the execution of a protocol.

coin with respect to $(g, Blindcoin)$. So *coin* is necessarily of the form $coin = g^{\alpha} g_1^{\beta x_u} g_2^{\beta} g_T^{\beta s} g^{\beta s}$.

3. The proof *Proof* (ot) guarantees that the user knows a representation $(\gamma, \delta) \in Z_q$ of $coin/g_2$ with respect to (g_1, g_T). So, *coin* is also of the form: $coin = g_1^{\gamma} g_2 g_T^{\delta}$.

Since the user knows at most only one representation of *coin* with respect to (g_1, g_2, g, g_T) (see the remark in section 2.1), this implies that $\begin{cases} \alpha = -s \\ \beta = 1 \end{cases}$ (as set in the end of section 2.4) and $\begin{cases} \gamma = x_u \bmod q \\ \delta = s \bmod q \end{cases}$.

As *Proof* (ct) guarantees that $s = \log_{h_{CT}} ct$ and *Proof* (ot) guarantees that $\delta = \log_{h_{OT}} ot$, and since these values are necessarily equal, this implies that the coin tracing and the owner tracing are possible.

Efficiency. Let us now briefly compare the efficiency of our scheme with that of [11]. Roughly, in the payment protocol of [11], the user and the shop perform each 11 more exponentiations than in our system. In the deposit protocol of [11], the bank performs on the order of 9 more exponentiations than in our system. The withdrawal protocol of [11] is about as efficient as ours.

4   Extension to Wallet with Observer

In our basic fair off-line cash system, the multiple spending of coins can only be detected but not prevented. In [9], Chaum and Pedersen introduced the concept of 'electronic wallet with observer' as a way to offer prior restraint of multiple spending in off-line anonymous electronic cash systems, without compromising the untraceability of payments.

An observer is a tamper-resistant device, issued by the bank (so, not necessarily trusted by the user), and inserted into the payment device of the user. Transactions can only be executed with the cooperation of the observer, which will only cooperate in spending each coin once. The protocols involving an observer are constructed in such a way that the observer cannot 'leak' (subliminal) information that would compromise the privacy of the transaction made by the user. Moreover, the transactions remain untraceable even if it is possible to analyze the information collected by the observer when it was involved (except if the observer has an internal clock).

It is possible in observer-based systems, to use a double-spender tracing mechanism (like in our generic cash system), which will serve in this case as a second level of protection useful in case the tamper-resistance of an observer has been broken (for a thorough discussion about wallet with observers, see [9, 10]).

In this section, we describe how to extend our generic fair cash system to the setting of a wallet with observers. In this extension, a double-spender tracing mechanism is incorporated and the owner tracing provides a link to the account of the user.

4.1 The Setup of the System

The setup of the system is the same as in the generic fair cash system.

Opening an Account. U generates at random his secret key $x_u \in Z_q^*$, computes $Id_U = g_1^{x_u}$ and transmits Id_U to B.

Then, U proves (using, for example, Schnorr's identification scheme) to B that he knows the representation of Id_U with respect to g_1. B verifies this proof and if the verification is successful, stores Id_U in the new user's entry of the account database.

Then the bank B supplies U with an observer O. O holds in its memory a secret key $x_o \in_R Z_q^*$ which is unknown to U (each observer has its own secret key). Let us denote $Id_O = g_1^{x_o}$ and $P_O = Id_O^x$. B computes $Id_U' = Id_O \, Id_U$ and $P_U' = Id_U'^x$, and transmits these values to U. Id_U' will designate U's account number (it should be noted that U does not know $\log_{g_1} Id_U' = x_o + x_u$). We will put $x_u' = \log_{g_1} Id_U'$.

The Withdrawal Protocol. The withdrawal protocol is very similar to the withdrawal protocol of the generic fair cash system, except that (x_u, Id_U) is replaced by (x_u', Id_U') and that the user and the observer 'jointly' compute the commitment D (see section 3.2.2). More precisely, D is computed as follows:

1. O chooses $\omega \in_R Z_q^*$ and computes the commitment $A = g_1^\omega$. O sends A to U. O then stores A in its list of active commitments (i.e. not yet used in a payment).

2. U chooses $(u,v,b) \in_R Z_q^{*3}$ and computes $D = A^u \, g_1^v \, g_T^b$. As in section 3.2, we have $D = g_1^a \, g_T^b$, where here $a = u \, \omega + v$.

The Payment Protocol. The payment protocol is very similar to the payment protocol of the generic fair cash system, except that the user and the observer jointly generate the proof $Proof(ot)$ (see section 3.3). Indeed, in order to prevent multiple spending, the participation of O is somehow needed.

More precisely, *Proof* (*ot*) is generated as follows (we use the same notations as in section 3.3):

1. U computes $c = H(msg \parallel g_T \parallel g_1 \parallel C \parallel h_{OT} \parallel ot \parallel D \parallel E)$ and $c_0 = c/u \bmod q$.

   Then U sends c_0 to O and asks O to prove his knowledge of $\log_{g_1} Id_O$ [1] using A.

2. O verifies that A is on its list of active commitments and if so computes $r_0 = \omega - c_0 \, x_o \bmod q$. O then sends r_0 to U and erases A from its list of active commitments.

3. U computes $r_1 = b - c \, s \bmod q$ and $r_2 = u \, r_0 + v - c \, x_u \bmod q$ (also equal to $a - cx'_u$) and sends *Proof* (*ot*) to the shop, where
   $Proof\,(ot) = (c, r_1, r_2) = Proof_{REP+LOGEQ}(msg, g_T, g_1, C, h_{OT}, ot)$.

4. The shop verifies the signature and the proof (as in the generic fair cash system) and if the verification holds, accepts the payment.

The deposit protocol is exactly the same as in the generic fair cash system.

The tracing mechanisms follow immediately from those of the generic fair cash system. It should be noted that contrarily to the scheme of [6], the owner tracing in our scheme yields the account number of the user Id'_U and not only a link to the withdrawal database.

Security of this Extension. If we view O and U as one party, then this extension does not differ from the generic fair cash system. Consequently, the discussion concerning the security for B, the security for T and the correctness of the generic fair cash system, also applies to this extension.

Under our assumptions, it can be shown that the withdrawn coin (*coin*) is necessarily of the form: $coin = g_1^{x'_u} \, g_2 \, g_T^s$ with $s \in Z_q$.

In order to be able to pay the shop with this coin, the user must know a representation of $coin/g_2$ with respect to (g_1, g_T). Since the user does not know by himself x'_u (recall that $x'_u = x_o + x_u \bmod q$), he cannot spend this coin without the cooperation of O [2].

---

[1] For this purpose O and U will perform the Schnorr's identification protocol [18]. In fact, the protocol that they will execute, referred to as *BlindSchnorr* in the sequel, is a blind issuing protocol for Schnorr signatures [16].

[2] We implicitly assume that the tamper-resistance of O has not been broken. In this extension, O executes only *BlindSchnorr*. So, we also assume that it is hard to forge a Schnorr-like signature (even after several sequential or parallel executions of *BlindSchnorr*) and that U obtains no useful information about O's secret key by executing *BlindSchnorr* with O.

As the user blinds all the values sent by O (recall that the observer proves that he knows $\log_{g_1} Id_O$ in a blind manner), the observer cannot compromise the privacy of the transaction made by U (even if the bank can obtain the observer, for maintenance purposes for example, and analyze its contents).

Efficiency of this Extension. Let us now briefly compare the efficiency of our extension with that of [6]. Roughly, in [6] the observer performs 9 times more computations than in our system, while the global workload of the other entities is roughly the same in the two systems.

Note: we can reduce (by a factor 2) the computations of U and S in the payment protocol, if we only require a link to the withdrawal database for the owner tracing.

5 Extension to Checks

A drawback of off-line coins based-systems (fair or not) is that they are not practical (in terms of computation, communication and storage requirements) when amounts to be paid require several coins. Moreover, for privacy reasons, anonymous off-line electronic coins schemes do not provide means to give change in a payment transaction. This implies that a user may have enough money to perform a transaction but be unable to pay because he has not the correct change.

A more convenient means of payment is the electronic check. An electronic check can be used for any amount up to a maximum value and then returned to the bank for a refund of the unspent part (so, an extra protocol, the *refund protocol* is needed). In this section, we describe how to extend our generic fair cash system to a fair electronic check system.

5.1 The Setup

For the sake of simplicity, in our description the owner tracing provides only a link to the transcript of the withdrawal of the check (see section 5.5). We will make the following modifications:

1. The trustee T, unlike 3.1, chooses $x_T, y_T \in_R Z_q$, and publishes $G_{CT} = g^{x_T^{-1}}$ and $G_{OT} = G_{CT}^{y_T^{-1}}$.

2. The bank B, in addition to 3.1, makes publicly known $(d_1, d_2, \ldots, d_k)$ a k-tuple of randomly chosen generators of G_q, and a defined amount of money associated to each of these generators; in our description, we assume that the bank assigns a value of $2^{i-1}\$$ to d_i. B also publishes the k values $D_i = d_i^x$, for $1 \le i \le k$.

5.2 The Withdrawal of a Fair Check

1. To withdraw a (fair) check that can be spent up to $2^k - 1$ \$, U generates k random values $(a_1, a_2, ..., a_k) \in_R Z_q^{*k}$, called the *payment terms*, and $s \in_R Z_q^*$, and computes $G = F^s \prod_{i=1}^{k} d_i^{a_i}$.

   U generates $Proof(ct) = Proof_{REP+LOGEQ}(r_a, F, d_1, d_2, ..., d_k, G, G_{CT}, ct)$, where $ct = G_{CT}^s$, and r_a was defined in 3.2, and sends G, ct, and $Proof(ct)$ to B.

2. The bank verifies this proof and, if the verification holds, stores (G, ct) in the user's entry of the cheque database (otherwise stops the protocol).

3. Both the user and the bank prepare the execution of the *BlindSig* protocol by computing independently $Blindcheck = Id_U \times g_2 \times G^1$. Note that

   $Blindcheck = check \times g^s$, where $check = Id_U \; g_2 \; g_T^s \prod_{i=1}^{k} d_i^{a_i}$ is the message to be (blindly) signed. Note also that U need not get z_0 (see figure 1) from B to compute $z = check^x = P_U \; h_2 \; h_T^s \prod_{i=1}^{k} D_i^{a_i}$

4. U and B then execute the *BlindSig(M, Blindcheck)* in order for U to get the (blind) signature $Sig(check) = (z, Proof_{LOGEQ}(M, g, h, check, z))$, where $M = D \| E \| ot$ is intended to detect multiple spending of the check. To compute the commitments D and E, and the *ownertrace* ot, the user U chooses $(b_1, b_2, ..., b_k, a, b) \in_R Z_q^{*(k+2)}$, and puts $D = d_1^{b_1} \; d_2^{b_2} \cdots d_k^{b_k} \; g_1^a \; g_T^b$, $E = G_{OT}^b$, and $ot = G_{OT}^s$. Finally, the bank debits $2^k - 1$ \$ from U's account.

5.3 The Payment Protocol

Let K be the subset $\{1, \cdots, k\}$ of N. Suppose the user wishes to spend in the shop S a certain amount of money $\sum_{j \in J} 2^{j-1}$, where $J \subset K$.

1. U reveals to S the values $check$, $Sig(check)$, $(a_j)_{j \in J}$ and $(b_j)_{j \in J}$.

2. U proves to S, using the commitments $D / \prod_{j \in J} d_j^{b_j}$ and E, that he knows a representation of $C = (check/g_2) / \prod_{j \in J} d_j^{a_j}$ with respect to $(g_T, g_1, (d_i)_{i \in K \setminus J})$, and

---

[1] In fact, the factor Id_U is only necessary if a direct owner tracing is required (see section 5.5 for more details).

that the exponent of g_T in this representation is equal to $\log_{G_{or}} ot$. Doing so, U proves that he is the owner of *check* and gives the shop some useful information that will enable the trusted authority to trace him.

3. S verifies the signature *Sig(check)* and the proof of knowledge, and if the verifications hold, accepts the payment.

5.4 The Deposit and Refund Protocols

1. S sends the transcript of the execution of the payment protocol to the bank B, who (after verifying its correctness) stores the a_j for $j \in J$ on a list, that we will call the *refund list*.

When U wishes to get a refund of the unspent part $\sum_{i \in K \backslash J} 2^{i-1}$ of the check,

2. U sends the unspent payment terms $(a_i)_{i \in K \backslash J}$ to the bank, along with G and a proof of knowledge of a representation of $G / \prod_{i \in K \backslash J} d_i^{a_i}$ with respect to $(F, (d_j)_{j \in J})$.

3. The bank B verifies that the user's entry in the cheque database holds G, and also that the a_i for $i \in K \backslash J$ are not already on the refund list. Then B verifies the proof, and if the verification holds, B refunds the user the corresponding amount of money, erases G from the cheque database, and stores the a_i for $i \in K \backslash J$ on the refund list.

The refund list maintained by B prevents the refunding of spent payment terms, and also the spending of (already) refunded payment terms. After the deposit of a check, the user is excluded not only if he spent the check twice, but also if he had already got a refund of some spent payment terms.

5.5 Tracing Mechanisms, Security, Efficiency

The double-spender tracing follows immediately from that of the generic fair cash system. The check tracing mechanism consists for T in computing $check = Blindcheck / ct^{x_T}$, and, as said in section 5.1, to simplify our description the owner tracing mechanism provides only a link to the withdrawal database: that is, with ot, T can compute $ct = ot^{y_T}$, which was stored during the withdrawal of this check in the user's entry of the cheque database, and therefore T and B can retrieve U's identity.

The proof of correctness of this extension as well as the other security requirements follow immediately from those of the generic fair cash system.

The fair check system described here is more efficient than the *basic* (not fair) check system of Brands [2]. Indeed, our system provides checks which are more efficiently computed (twice as fast as checks in [2]) and which also require less memory for their storage (half as much).

6   Conclusion and Open Problems

We have proposed an efficient discrete logarithm based fair payment system that is more efficient than that of [11]. Our system supports extensions to wallets with observers and electronic checks which are more efficient than previous ones [2, 6].

The security of the proposed schemes relies on (trustworthy) assumptions about the blind signature scheme that we use. It would be interesting to prove these assumptions.

It is an open problem to find an efficient (avoiding in particular the cut and choose technique) fair payment system based on the factorization problem.

Acknowledgments

We would like to thank Marc Girault and the anonymous referees for their useful comments.

References

1. B. den Boer, D. Chaum, E. van Heyst, S. Mjolsnes and A. Steenbeek, Efficient Off-Line Electronic Checks, *Proceedings of* EUROCRYPT'89, Lecture Notes in Computer Science, Vol 434, Springer-Verlag, pp. 294-301.
2. S. Brands, An Efficient Off-Line Electronic Cash System based on the Representation Problem, Technical Report CS-R9323, CWI, April 1993.
3. S. Brands, Untraceable Off-Line Cash in Wallets with Observers, *Proceedings of* CRYPTO'93, Lecture Notes in Computer Science, Vol 773, Springer-Verlag, pp. 302-318.
4. E. Brickell, P. Gemmel and D. Kravitz, Trustee-Based Tracing Extensions to Anonymous Cash and the Making of Anonymous Change, *Proceedings of* the 6th Annual Symposium on Discrete Algorithm, pp. 457-466, Jan 1995.
5. J. Camenisch, U. Maurer and M. Stadler, Digital Payment Systems with Passive Anonymity-Revoking Trustees, *Proceedings of* ESORICS'96, Lecture Notes in Computer Science, Vol 1146, Springer-Verlag, pp. 33-43.
6. J. Camenisch, U. Maurer and M. Stadler, Digital Payment Systems with Passive Anonymity-Revoking Trustees, Journal of Computer Security, volume 5, number 1, IOS Press, 1997.
7. D. Chaum, Blind Signatures for Untraceable Payments, *Proceedings of* CRYPTO'82, Plenum Press, 1983, pp. 199-203.

8. D. Chaum, A. Fiat and M. Naor, Untraceable Electronic Cash, *Proceedings of* CRYPTO'88, Lecture Notes in Computer Science, Vol 403, Springer-Verlag, pp. 319-327.

9. D. Chaum and T. Pedersen, Wallet Databases with Observers, *Proceedings of* CRYPTO'92, Lecture Notes in Computer Science, Vol 740, Springer-Verlag, pp. 89-105.

10. R. Cramer and T. Pedersen, Improved Privacy in Wallets with Observers, *Proceedings of* EUROCRYPT'93, Lecture Notes in Computer Science, Vol 765, Springer-Verlag, pp. 329-343.

11. G. Davida, Y. Frankel, Y. Tsiounis and M. Yung, Anonymity Control in E-Cash Systems, Financial Cryptography'97, Anguilla, British West Indies, February 24-27.

12. T. ElGamal, A Public Key Cryptosystem and a Signature Scheme Based on Discrete Logarithms, *Proceedings of* CRYPTO'84, Lecture Notes in Computer Science, Vol 196, Springer-Verlag, pp. 10-18.

13. U. Feige, A. Fiat and A. Shamir, Zero Knowledge Proofs of Identity, Journal of Cryptology, 1 (2), pp. 77-94, 1988.

14. Y. Frankel, Y. Tsiounis and M. Yung, Indirect Discourse Proofs: Achieving Fair Off-Line Electronic Cash, *Proceedings of* ASIACRYPT'96, Lecture Notes in Computer Science, Vol 1163, Springer-Verlag, pp. 286-300.

15. R. Hirschfeld, Making Electronic Refunds Safer, *Proceedings of* CRYPTO'92, Lecture Notes in Computer Science, Vol 740, Springer-Verlag, pp. 106-112.

16. T. Okamoto, Provably Secure and Practical Identification Schemes and Corresponding Signature Schemes, *Proceedings of* CRYPTO'92, Lecture Notes in Computer Science, Vol 740, Springer-Verlag, pp. 31-53.

17. T. Okamoto and K. Ohta, Divertible Zero-Knowledge Interactive Proofs and Commutative Random Self-Reducibility, *Proceedings of* EUROCRYPT'89, Lecture Notes in Computer Science, Vol 434, Springer-Verlag, pp. 481-496.

18. C.P. Schnorr, Efficient Signature Generation by Smart Cards, Journal of Cryptology, 4(3), pp. 161-174, 1991.

19. M. Stadler, J.M. Piveteau and J. Camenisch, Fair Blind Signatures, *Proceedings of* EUROCRYPT'95, Lecture Notes in Computer Science, Vol 921, Springer-Verlag, pp. 209-219.

20. J. Traoré, Making Unfair a 'Fair' Blind Signature Scheme, *Proceedings of* ICICS'97, Lecture Notes in Computer Science, Vol 1334, Springer-Verlag, pp. 386-397.

21. S. von Solms and D. Naccache, On Blind Signatures and Perfect Crimes, Computer & Security, 11, 1992, pp. 581-583.

A More Efficient Untraceable E-Cash System with Partially Blind Signatures Based on the Discrete Logarithm Problem

Shingo MIYAZAKI   and   Kouichi SAKURAI*

Dept. of Computer Science, Kyushu Univ.
Hakozaki, Higashi-ku, Fukuoka, 812-8581, JAPAN.
{shingo,sakurai}@csce.kyushu-u.ac.jp

Abstract. We propose a new untraceable electronic money system based on the discrete logarithm problem. Our system improves the efficiency of Yacobi's E-money system by making the applied blind signature *partial*. We compare our system to the previous e-money systems which use the ElGamal-type scheme in their tracing a double-spender.
We also remark a double-registration problem on a digital cash system, recently presented in [Nguyen-Mu-Varadharajan, in Information Security Workshop'97], based on the blind Nyberg-Rueppel signature.

1   Introduction

Electronic cash systems, which use the conventional blind signature schemes [Cha83, CPS94], require many public keys corresponding to the face-values of coins [Bra94, Bra95a, CFN88, Cha83, Scho95, Yac94]. Partially blind signatures introduced in [AF96] makes such systems efficient by decreasing the number of public keys.

The original paper [AF96] preented a RSA-based partially blind signature, and suggested how to apply it to an electronic cash system. Then, discrete-log. based partially blind signature protocols were developed in [AC97, MAS97]. However, no exact application of these partial blind protocols to electronic cash system is investigated. So, this paper further explores the power of partially blind signatures in electronic money systems.

We first discuss an applicability of the partially blind to the Yacobi's un-traceable E-money system [Yac94], which uses the ElGamal signature scheme, for making efficient. However, a direct adaptation of the partially blind signatures is shown to require additional cryptographic assumptions on zero-knowledge protocols, which play the central role in the Yacobi's original system.

Then, instead of using zero-knowledge protocols, we utilize the idea of the secret key certificate by Brands [Bra95a] for revising the Yacobi's system [Yac94], then apply a partially blind signature. Thus, our proposed e-money system checks the key certificates at the stage of payment, whereas the Yacobi's system [Yac94] does this in withdrawing.

---

* A part of this work is done while visiting in Columbia University, Computer Science Dept.

Alice   Nancy

$$(y_1 = g^{x_1}, y_2 = g^{x_2})$$

$$k \in_R Z_q^*$$

$$\alpha, \beta \in_R Z_q^* \quad \xleftarrow{\tilde{R}} \quad \tilde{R} = g^k \pmod{p}$$

$$r = m\tilde{R}^\alpha (y_1^I y_2)^\beta$$

$$\tilde{r} = \alpha^{-1} r \pmod{q} \quad \xrightarrow{\tilde{r}}$$

$$\tilde{s} = \frac{k + \tilde{r}}{x_1 I + x_2} \pmod{q}$$

$$\xleftarrow{\tilde{s}}$$

$$s = \alpha\tilde{s} + \beta \pmod{q}$$

Fig. 1. The partially blind signature scheme [MAS97]

We compare our proposed system to the previous e-money systems [Yac94, Bra94, Scho95, NMV97] that use the discrete-logarithm based scheme in their tracing a double-spender.

Another contribution of this paper is to remark a problem on digital cash system based on the blind Nyberg-Rueppel signature [NMV97]. Nguyen et al. [NMV97] considered the security of their proposed scheme (anonymity, untraceability, double spending detection), However, we show that the double registration by a user's (or by multiple users' conspiring) is possible in this scheme [NMV97] (Appendix).

2 The Partially Blind Signature Scheme

The partially blind signature [AF96] is a signature on message (m, I), where m is blinded part for the signer in the protocols and I is the common information between the message sender and the signer. Unlike the conventional blind signature scheme, in partial blind signature protocols, the signer signs the blinded part m under the common information I.

We review the partially blind signature protocols for Nyberg-Rueppel signature scheme proposed in [MAS97]. The technique used in this scheme is similar to a reduced restrictive blind signature scheme as used in [Bra95a, Scho95]. Using this technique based on the discrete logarithm problem, Abe and Camenisch [AC97] presented the partially blind signature scheme based on Schnorr signature. Miyazaki, Abe and Sakurai [MAS97] proposed the partially blind signature schemes based on DSS, in addition to the scheme for Message Recovery Signature described here.

A signature on a message (m, I) with respect to the public key (y_1, y_2), where $y_1 = g^{x_1} \pmod{p}$ and $y_2 = g^{x_2} \pmod{p}$, is a pair (r, s) satisfying

$$m = rg^r(y_1^I y_2)^{-s} \pmod{p}.$$

Here, the first part m can be any string while the second part I must be $I \in Z_q^*$. Such a signature can be generated by the signer, who knows both secret key x_1 and x_2 corresponding to the public key y_1 and y_2 respectively, and computed by choosing a random integer $k \in Z_q^*$ and computing

$$r = mg^k \pmod{p} \quad \text{and} \quad s = \frac{k+r}{x_1 I + x_2} \pmod{q}.$$

It can easily be verified that the resulting pair (r, s) is actually a valid signature on (m, I). The below reviews the protocols of partially blind signature scheme proposed in [MAS97].

Step 1 The signer *Nancy* selects randomly an integer $k \in Z_q^*$, and computes $\tilde{R} = g^k \pmod{p}$. Then, *Nancy* sends $\tilde{R}$ to *Alice*.

Step 2 *Alice* generates respectively random integers $\alpha, \beta \in Z_q^*$, and computes $r = m\tilde{R}^\alpha (y_1^I y_2)^\beta \pmod{p}$. Then, *Alice* computes $\tilde{r} = \alpha^{-1} r \pmod{q}$, and sends $\tilde{r}$ to *Nancy*.

Step 3 *Nancy* computes $\tilde{s} = (k + \tilde{r})/(x_1 I + x_2)^{-1} \pmod{q}$ with her secret key (x_1, x_2), sends $\tilde{s}$ to *Alice*.

Step 4 *Alice* verifies that $1 \le r \le (p - 1)$; if not, then rejects the signature. *Alice* computes $s = \alpha\tilde{s} + \beta \pmod{q}$ to obtain *Nancy's* signature (r, s). *Alice* verifies the validity of her signature by computing the verification formula satisfying $rg^r (y_1^I y_2)^{-s} = m$.

The equations below shows that the protocol is sound;

$$rg^r (y_1^I y_2)^{-s} = mg^{r - \alpha\tilde{r}} \pmod{p} = m \pmod{p}.$$

Throughout this paper, let $Sig_A^{(I)}[m]$ be the A's signature on the message (m, I) obtained as the result of the partially blind protocol, where m is the message that should be blinded and I is the common information between the message sender and the signer.

3 The Yacobi's e-money and Discussed Problems

3.1 Reviewing Yacobi's System

The Yacobi's system [Yac94] uses a protocol for tracing double spenders like the technique used in [Bra94]; if two different messages are signed by the same user using the ElGamal signature scheme, with high probability the secret key of the signer can be efficiently computed. So, the double spender is traced, because the secret key includes the user's ID, We review basic protocols in the system as follows;

At first, User i generates randomly $R_i \in \{0, 1\}^l$ (in practice $l = 200$ is currently sufficient), and creates the secret key $S_i = (I_i, R_i)$, where I_i is the user's name(ID). Then, she computes her public key $P_i \equiv g^{S_i} \pmod{p}$. Here, (e_C, N_C) is the CA's RSA public key and (e_B, N_B) is the Bank's one. Let γ be integer, $30 < \gamma < 50$, and 0^γ denotes a run of γ 0's.

299

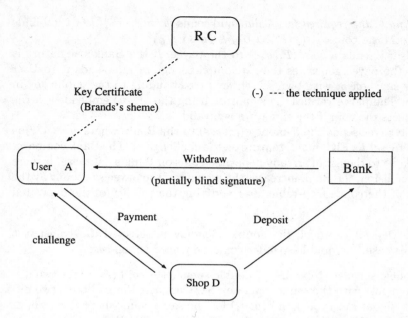

Fig. 2. The structure of our system and the technique applied

Initial-certificate: This operation takes place between a user and CA. User i selects randomly a integer $x \in Z^*_{N_C}$, and computes $z \equiv x^{e_C} f(P_i, 0^\gamma)$ (mod N_C) and sends z to CA with own ID, I_i. Next, User i proves to CA in Zero-Knowledge that S_i includes I_i. Precisely, the following predicate is proven to CA in zero-knowledge.

Predicate :

Given: z, g, p, N_C, e_C, I_i,
$(\exists x, P_i, R_i, S_i)[\; z \equiv_{N_C} x^{e_C} f(P_i, 0^\gamma);\; P_i \equiv_{N_C} g^{S_i};\; S_i = (I_i, R_i)]$

If CA verifies the proof of this predicate positively, CA computes z^{d_C} (mod N_C) and sends it to User i. User i multiplies it by x^{-1} (mod p) to obtain the unblinded certificate $Cert(i) \equiv (f(P_i, 0^\gamma))^{d_C}$ (mod N_C).

Withdrawal: User i computes $u \equiv g^r$ (mod p), where $gcd(r, p-1) = 1$. User i sends a candidate blinded coin $w \equiv x^{e_B} f(P_i, u, 0^\gamma)$ (mod N_B) to the Bank. Then, User i proves to the Bank in Zero-Knowledge that P_i is properly constructed. More precisely, the following predicate is proven to Bank.

Predicate :

Given: w, g, p, N_B, e_B, I_i,
$(\exists x, P_i, R_i, S_i, u)[\; w \equiv_{N_B} x^{e_B} f(P_i, u, 0^\gamma);\; P_i \equiv_{N_B} g^{S_i};\; S_i = (I_i, R_i)]$

After the Bank verifies the zero-knowledge proof on this predicate, the Bank computes $w^{d_B} \equiv x(f(P_i, u, 0^\gamma))^{d_B}$ (mod N_B) with the secret exponent *cor-*

responding to the required face-value, and sends w to User i. User i unblinds it to obtain the coin $c \equiv (f(P_i), u, 0^\gamma)^{d_B} \pmod{N_B}$.

Payment: User i sends a coin (P_i, u, c) to the payee. If the Bank's signature is correct, the payee generates the random challenge m and sends it to User i. User i signs on m with own secret key corresponding to the public key in the coin. The payee verifies the signature using the (P_i, u) embedded in the coin, rejects the coin if the signature is invalid.

Deposit: The payee sends the E-money (m, c, s) to the Bank, where $s = (u, v)$ is the payer User i's ElGamal signature on the challenge m. The Bank compares the (m, c, s) to the list of already deposited coins on Bank's database. If there is not a collision, the Bank increases the amount of the payee's account by the amount of the coin's face-value after verifying the validity of the deposited coin.

Now, in the Deposit protocol, the double-spending is detected if a collision is found. In this case, the double-spender could be traced as follows;

Tracing a double-spender: Now, User i double-spends the coin (P_i, u) for two distinct payments with the same secret key S_i. Then, the Bank obtains two different i's signatures (u, v_1) and (u, v_2) for the same coin, where $S_i u + r v_1 \equiv m_1 \pmod{(p-1)}$ and $S_i u + r v_2 \equiv m_2 \pmod{(p-1)}$. Hence, the relation $r(v_1 - v_2) \equiv (m_1 - m_2) \pmod{(p-1)}$ holds. So, if $gcd(v_1 - v_2, p-1) = 1$, then the Bank knowing the challenges m_1, m_2 can find r. Or, if $gcd(v, p-1) = 1$ then S_i can be computed. Finally, the Bank traces the double spender i by the I_i embedded in the S_i.

3.2 The drawbacks to be improved

The Yacobi's system has two problems: one is the complexity of the withdrawing protocol based on zero knowledge proofs and the other is the potential drawback of the e-money systems by using the conventional blind signature in the withdrawing protocol. The latter problem is to be necessary to prepare so many public keys corresponding to the face-values of coins in such systems.

Here, we discuss the direct adaptation of the partially blind signatures to the Yacobi's system. If this strategy is successful, then the resulted system would be more efficient by reducing the number of the pairs of the public and secret keys.

Now, User i performs the process of the initial-certificate same as the original Yacobi's system does. More precisely, the User must prove the existence of the parameters (a, P_i, u, S_i, R_i) satisfying below, giving (g, p, N_b, e_b, I_i, z) to the Bank via zero knowledge.

$$\begin{cases} z = a^{e_b} f(P_i, u, 0^\gamma) \pmod{N_b} \\ P_i = g^{S_i} \pmod{p} \\ S_i = (I_i, R_i) \end{cases}$$

Subsequently, the E-money is withdrawn through the protocol with the partially blind signature scheme on the agreed information I. Here, we use the scheme for

$$\text{User } A \qquad\qquad\qquad \text{Registration Center}$$
$$(P_A = g^{S_{A0}} h_1^{S_{A1}}) \qquad\qquad (h_0 = g^{S_{R0}}, h_1 = g^{S_{R1}})$$

$$w \in_R Z_q$$
$$a = g^w \ (\bmod\ p)$$

$$\xleftarrow{\quad a \quad}$$

$$\alpha, \beta \in_R Z_q$$
$$r = H(g^\alpha (h_0 h_1^{S_{i1}})^\beta a \ (\bmod\ p))$$
$$\tilde{r} = r + \beta \ (\bmod\ q)$$

$$\xrightarrow{\quad \tilde{r} \quad}$$

$$\tilde{s} = \tilde{r}(S_{R0} + S_{R1} S_{A1}) + w \ (\bmod\ q)$$

$$\xleftarrow{\quad \tilde{s} \quad}$$

$$a \stackrel{?}{=} g^{\tilde{s}} (h_0 h_1^{S_{i1}})^{-\tilde{r}} \ (\bmod\ p)$$
$$s = \tilde{s} + r S_{i0} + \alpha \ (\bmod\ q)$$

Fig. 3. Key Certificate issuing protocol

the Nyberg-Rueppel signature described in Section 2. In this case, User i must prove the Bank the following predicate via zero knowledge, where α, β, I, y_1, y_2 and $\tilde{R}$ correspond to those in Figure 1, respectively.

Predicate :
  Given: $I_i, \tilde{R}, \tilde{r}, p, q, y_1, y_2, I,$
  $(\exists r, \alpha, \beta, P_i, R_i, S_i, u)$

$$[\ r \equiv_p f(P_i, u, 0^\gamma) \tilde{R}^\alpha (y_1^I y_2)^\beta;$$
$$\tilde{r} \equiv_q \alpha^{-1} r; P_i \equiv_p g^{S_i}; S_i = (I_i, R_i)]$$

Here, this predicate is based on the (partially) blind signature for the Nyberg-Rueppel signature. It differs from the Yacobi's predicate based on the blind signature for RSA (the former is actually more complicated than the latter). So, the former requires additional assumption that the users could prove the predicate based on the discrete logarithm problem in zero-knowledge. A practical problem is that we do not have any practical solution to such a zero-knowledge proof than the theoretical method [GMW86] of reducing the predicate to NP-complete languages.

4 Our Proposed System

We describe our proposed system.

4.1 Registration

Brands presented the scheme issuing the secret key certificate [Bra95b] and proposed the E-money system [Bra95a] using this technique In our system, User obtains the certificate of the own key through the Brands's scheme. The system parameter consist of a large prime p, a prime factor q, and a generator g in Z_p^* of order q. Here, let (S_{A0}, S_{A1}) be the User A's secret key and (S_{R0}, S_{R1}) be the Registration Center(RC)'s secret key. Also, the part S_{A1} of User A's secret key (S_{A0}, S_{A1}) denotes the ID of User A and the common information between User A and Registration Center. Blinding own public key $P_A = g^{S_{A0}} h_1^{S_{A1}} \pmod{p}$ and the certificate (r, s), User A obtains the key certificate issued from Registration Center. Now, the public keys of Registration Center are $h_0 = g^{S_{R0}}$ and $h_1 = g^{S_{R1}} \pmod{p}$.

Our certificate issuing protocol between User A and Registration Center is the followings.

Step.1 Registration Center selects a random integer $w \in Z_q$ and computes $a = g^w \pmod{p}$. Registration Center sends a to User A.

Step.2 User A chooses random integers $\alpha, \beta \in Z_q$ and computes $r = H(g^\alpha (h_0 h_1^{S_{A1}})^\beta a \pmod{p})$ and $\tilde{r} = r + \beta \pmod{q}$. User A sends $\tilde{r}$ to Registration Center.

Step.3 Registration Center computes $\tilde{s} = \tilde{r}(S_{R0} + S_{R1} S_{A1}) + w \pmod{q}$ with own secret key (S_{R0}, S_{R1}) and sends $\tilde{s}$ to User A.

Step.4 After User A verifies the signature satisfying $a = g^{\tilde{s}} (h_0 h_1^{S_{A1}})^{-\tilde{r}} \pmod{p})$, computes $s = \tilde{s} + r S_{A0} + \alpha$.

The verification formula for the certificate of User A's key is $H(g^s (h_0 P_A)^{-r}) = r$. We prove the soundness of the verification formula below.

$$g^s (h_0 P_A)^{-r} = g^{\beta(S_{R0} + S_{R1} S_{A1}) + w + \alpha} \pmod{p}$$
$$= g^\alpha (h_0 h_1^{S_{A1}})^\beta a \pmod{p}$$

Remark: Bank itself may play the role of Registration Center.

4.2 Withdrawal

User A withdraws the E-money from his account as follows. Bank reserves own secret key (x_1, x_2) and the corresponding to public keys; $y_1 = g^{x_1}$ and $y_2 = g^{x_2} \pmod{p}$.

Step 1 User A generates random integers $k_0, k_1 \in Z_q^*$ and computes $t = g^{k_0} h_1^{k_1} \pmod{p}$. Then, User A requests the Bank's signature on the message (m, I) through the partially blind signature protocols, where $m = (P_A \| t)$ is the blind part for Bank and I is the common information between User A and Bank including the amount of the withdrawing money and date.

Step 2 Bank, after deducting the amount of the money withdrawn from User A's account, sends the signature on (m, I) through the partially blind signature protocols.

Step 3 *User A* verifies the Bank's signature $Sig_B^{(I)}[m]$ on the money.

Remark: In step 1, User A should check if there is no candidate in the agreed information I, which destroys the anonymity of E-money.

4.3 Payment

User A makes a payment to *Shop D* as follows.

Step 1 User A sends $(Sig_B^{(I)}[m], m)$ and the certificate (r, s) of own key to *Shop D*.

Step 2 *Shop D* verifies the Bank's signature on the money and the certificate (r, s) of User A's key. If the validness of them are accepted, *Shop D* generates the challenge M and sends it to User A.

Step 3 User A signs on the challenge M with own secret key (S_{A0}, S_{A1}) and sends the signature (t, u, v) satisfying the following equations;

$$u = h(M)k_0 + S_{A0}t \pmod{q}$$
$$v = h(M)k_1 + S_{A1}t \pmod{q}.$$

Step 4 *Shop D* verifies User A's signature on challenge M with the following formula;

$$g^u h_1^v = t^{h(M)} P_A^t \pmod{p}.$$

4.4 Deposit

In Deposit protocol, *Shop D* sends the E-money $((Sig_B^{(I)}[m], m), (r, s), (t, u, v, M))$ to Bank. At the begin, Bank verifies the signature $(Sig_B^{(I)}[m], m)$ on the money, then, compares $(Sig_B^{(I)}[m], m)$ to the list of already deposited money on the database. If the deposited money $(Sig_B^{(I)}[m], m)$ is the first visit to Bank's database, Bank adds $(Sig_B^{(I)}[m], m)$ to the list linking the money to *Shop D* after increasing the amount of *Shop D*'s account by the amount indicated in I.

4.5 Tracing a Double-Spender

In Deposit, if Bank discovers the corresponding money with deposited *Coin* on the database, Bank performs the tracing the double-spender as follows, original idea of which is proposed by Franklin and Yung [FY93]. Like Yacobi's way, from the part of the double-spent money

$$v_1 = h(M_1)k_1 + S_{A1}t \pmod{q}$$
$$v_2 = h(M_2)k_1 + S_{A1}t \pmod{q},$$

Bank computes $v_1 - v_2 = (h(M_1) - h(M_2))k_1 \pmod{q}$ to obtain k_1. Finally, Bank computes the secret key S_{A1} corresponding to the User's ID, and detects the double-spender.

References	Public key	Secret key	Key Certificates	Tools
Yacobi [Yac94]	Open	User (only)	In Withdraw	ZK protocol & RSA
Brands [Bra95a]	Blind	User (Bank partially)	Nowhere	Tamper-resistant device Schnorr signature
Schoenmakers [Scho95]	Blind	Bank/User	Nowhere	Schnorr signature
Nguyen et al. [NMV97]	Blind	User(only)	Nowhere	Nyberg-Rueppel signature
Our scheme	Open	User (Bank partially)	In Payment	Schnorr signature Partially blind signature

Fig. 4. Comparison to other systems

5 Comparison to the Previous e-money Systems

We depicts the comparison to related works [Yac94, Bra95a, Scho95, NMV97] in Figure 5, in which Bank uses the similar technique for tracing a double-spender.

5.1 Anonymity from public-keys

In Yacobi's [Yac94] and our system, the payer must show his own public key to payee in the payment protocol. Namely, in our system (also in Yacobi's), all e-money spent with the same user's public key P_A is linkable.

On the other hand, in [Bra95a, Scho95], the payer's public key is blinded by a random number at the payment. Then, the deposited money does not include any payer's footstep.

Thus, the systems presented in [Bra95a, Scho95, NMV97] achieves higher *anonymity* than ours (and Yacobi's).

5.2 Security vs. Efficiency

In [Yac94, NMV97] the user preserves only his own secret key including his ID. On the other hand, in [Scho95] Bank must conserve the user's secret key in addition to own secret key issuing much money. In terms of the dispersion of secret data, the former schemes are superior to the latter for their *security against the attack to user's secret keys*. However, the former have the lack of efficiency, because the user must prove the validity of the secret key, in which ID is embedded, by using a zero knowledge protocol.

In [Bra95a] and ours, Registration Center (maybe Bank) preserves the user's ID, which is only a part of the user's secret key, and embeds the ID in the issuing money or the user's key certificate. Hence, in such systems, the user can prove the validity of his own key without zero knowledge protocols (*efficiency*).

Even if a user's partial secret key stored in Bank is stolen, the thief cannot withdraw e-money from the user's account, because the thief cannot know the user's other secret key. For achieving this property, Brands [Bra95a] assumes the use of a tamper-resister device, while in our system the verification of the key certificate in the payment protocol performs the function. Note that, if the Brands's system [Bra95a] is implemented without the tamper-resister device, the secret data would be centralized to Bank as Schoenmaker's system [Scho95].

Therefore, such systems achieve higher *security against the compromise of the user's secret key* than one proposed in [Scho95] because of the distributions of secret data. We should remark that, in Brands's scheme [Bra95a], the withdrawn E-money is the certificate not of the user's fixed public key but of the blinded temporary public key. device.

5.3 Attacks

The scheme proposed by Nguyen at al. [NMV97] appears to withstand parallel attacks remarked by Schoenmakers [Scho95]. However, another attack proposed by Chan at al. [CFMT96] is applicable to the system, if the registration has no process of the verification that the public key of the user should be constructed in the correct manner (See Appendix).

Furthermore, at the first step of the withdrawal protocol, Bank constructs the commitment using the user's public key as a generator. This makes the application of the partially blind signature scheme to the system [NMV97] difficult.

5.4 Number of required keys for coins

Due to the partially blind signature scheme, only our system has no need for the keys corresponding to the face-values of coins (*efficiency*) and allows users to make flexible payments by embedding various information (e.g. amount of money, date, valid period and so on) in the agreed information I. Actually, how many keys are cut down in our improved system by applying the partially blind signature scheme? The number of keys required in the system with the conventional blind signature scheme depend on the number of kinds of the agreed information. Suppose that the issuing *Time* and *Amount* of money are set as the agreed information, where *Time* consists of 12 months $\{January, February, ..., December\}$ and *Amount* has 5 kinds of the amount $\{\$1, \$5, \$10\,\$20, \$50\}$. In this case, the system with conventional blind signature scheme needs $12 \times 5 = 60$ key-pairs to represent the validity of the money such as the $20 issued in a January. So, the more the number of kinds of the agreed information are set, the more the number of keys required are. On the other hand, our system with the partially blind signature scheme can deal with such a case by using only two fixed key-pairs. The more various information are set, the more efficient our system are getting compared with the previous systems.

6 Conclusion

We proposed a discrete-log based untraceable electronic money system with a partially blind signature protocol, discussed the advantage of our system over the previous systems.

However, it is hard for Yacobi's system [Yac94] and ours to achieve e-money's transferability, because there is a troublesome case that Bank cannot detect a double-spender. So, making our e-money transferable is a challenging open problem.

Acknowledgments

The authors would like to thank to U. Mauer and M. Abe for giving the first author a chance of presenting the primitive version of the proposed scheme in ETH-Zurich. The authors are also grateful to J. Camenish for remarking the connection of the authors' primitive scheme to Brands' work on secret-key certificates. The second author wish to thank Zvi Galil and Moti Yung for their hospitality while his visiting Columbia Univ. Computer Science Dept.

References

[AC97] M. Abe, J. Camenisch, *"Partially Blind Signature Schemes,"* Proceedings of the 1997 Symposium on Cryptography and Information Security, SCIS97-33D, 1997.

[AF96] M. Abe, E. Fujisaki, *"How to Date Blind Signatures,"* Advances in Cryptology – ASACRYPT '96, LNCS 1163, pp. 244-251, 1996.

[Bra94] S. Brands, *"Untraceable off-line cash in wallet with observers,"* In Advances in Cryptology – CRYPTO '93, LNCS 773, pp. 302-318, 1994.

[Bra95a] S. Brands, *"Off-Line Electronic Cash Based on Secret-KeyCertificates,"* Proceedings of the Second International Symposium of Latin American Theoretical Informatics, 1995.
http://www.cwi.nl/cwi/publications/CS-R9506.ps.Z

[Bra95b] S. Brands, *"Restrictive Binding of Secret-Key Certificates,"* Advances in Cryptology – EUROCRYPT '95, LNCS 921, pp.231-247, 1995.

[CFMT96] A. Chan, Y. Frankel, P. MacKenzie, Y. Tsiounis, *"Mis-representation of Identities in E-cash Schemes and how to Prevent it,"* Advances in Cryptology – ASIACRYPT '96, LNCS 1163, pp. 276-285, 1996.

[CFN88] D. Chaum, A. Fiat, M. Naor, *"Untraceable Electronic Cash,"* In Advances in Cryptology – CRYPTO '88, pp. 319-327, 1988.

[Cha83] D. Chaum, *"Blind Signature for Untraceable Payments,"* In Advances in Cryptology – CRYPTO '82, pp. 199-203, 1983.

[CPS94] J. Camenisch, J. M. Piveteau, M. StadlerœB!œ(B *"Blind Signatures Based on the Discrete Logarithm Problem,"* Advances in Cryptology – EUROCRYPT '94, LNCS 950, pp. 428-432, 1994.

[ElG84] T. ElGamal, *"A public key cryptosystem and a signature scheme based on discrete logarithms,"* IEEE Transactions on Information Theory, pp. 469-472, 1985.

[FY93] M. K. Franklin, M. Yung *"Secure and Efficient Off-line Digital Money,"* Proceedings of ICALP '93, 1993.

[GMW86] O. Goldreich, S. Micali, A. Wigderson, *"Proofs that yield nothing but their validity and a methodology of cryptographic protocol design,"* Proceedings of IEEE FOCS '86, p.174-187, 1986.

[HMP94a] P. Horster, M. Michels, H. Petersen, *"Meta-ElGamal signature schemes,"* Proceedings of 2nd ACM CCS manuscript, pp. 96-107, 1994.

[HMP94b] P. Horster, M. Michels, H. Petersen, *"Meta Message Recovery and Meta Blind signature schemes based on the discrete logarithm problem and their applications,"* Advances in Cryptology – ASIACRYPT '94, LNCS 917, pp. 224-237, 1994.

[MAS97] S. Miyazaki, M. Abe, K. Sakurai, *"Partially Blind Signature Schemes for the DSS and for a Discrete Log. based Message Recovery Signature,"* Proceedings of the 1997 Korea-Japan Joint Workshop on Information Security and Cryptology, pp. 217-226, 1997.

[NIST] NIST FIPS PUB XX, Digital Signature Standard(DSS), National Institute of Standards and Technology, U.S. Department of Commerce, DRAFT, 1993.

[NMV97] K. Q. Nguyen, Y. Mu, V. Varadharajan, *A new digital cash scheme based on blind Nyberg-Rueppel digital signature,"* Pre-Proceedings of 1997 Information Security Workshop, pp. 219-226, 1997.

[NR93] K. Nyberg, R. A. Rueppel, *"A new signature scheme based on the DSA giving message recovery,"* Proceedings of 1st ACM CCS manuscript, 1993.

[PS96] D. Pointcheval, J. Stern, *"Provably Secure Blind Signature Schemes,"* Advances in Cryptology – ASIACRYPT '96, LNCS 1163, pp. 252-265, 1996.

[Sch91] C. P. Schnorr, *"Efficient signature generation by smart cards,"* Journal of Cryptology, pp. 161-174, 1991.

[Scho95] B. Schoenmakers, *"An efficient electronic payment system with standing parallel attacks,"* Technical report, CWI, 1995.
http://www.cwi.nl/ftp/CWIreports/AA/CSR9522.ps.Z

[Yac94] Y. Yacobi, *"Efficient electronic money,"* Advances in Cryptology – ASIACRYPT '94, LNCS 917, pp. 153-163, 1994.

A The Double-Registration Problem on Nguyn-Mu-Varadharajan's Digicash Scheme

In the system [NMV97], Bank chooses two random integers w_1, w_2 and computes $g_1 = g^{w_1} \bmod p, g_2 = g^{w_2} \bmod p$, where (p, q, g) are public informations satisfying that $g^q = 1 \bmod p$. Then, Bank computes $h_1 = g_1^x \bmod p, h_2 = g_2^x \bmod p$ with his secret key x. (g_1, g_2, h_1, h_2) are made public. The user has own secret key u and public key $w = g_1 g_2^u \bmod p$. Bank registers u with the database as the user's identity, then sends the certificate $w = v^x \bmod p$ to the user. The user makes withdrawals and payments with (v, u, w). In case the E-money has been double-spent in the system, Bank derives u from the partial informations of the E-money double-spent and computes the User's identity v finally. We tried to apply the partially blind signature scheme to the this system[NMV97], but found out that this system has a vulnerability to the attack as follows.

User A, who has (v_A, u_A, w_A), might obtain the another keys and certificate (v_B, u_B, w_B) by the double-registration or conspiring with the other(User B). Then, User A can generate the unauthorized keys and certificate $(\tilde{v}, \tilde{u}, \tilde{w})$ by himself from the distinct components, (v_A, u_A, w_A) (v_B, u_B, w_B), as follows.

$$\tilde{u} = (u_A + u_B)2^{-1} \pmod{q}$$
$$\tilde{v} = (v_A v_B)^{2^{-1}} \pmod{p}$$
$$= (g_1^2 g_2^{u_A + u_B})^{2^{-1}} \pmod{p}$$
$$= g_1 g_2^{(u_A + u_B)2^{-1}} \pmod{p}$$

$$= g_1 g_2^{\tilde{u}} \pmod{p}$$

$$\tilde{w} = (w_A w_B)^{2^{-1}} \pmod{p}$$

$$= ((g_1 g_2^{u_A})^x (g_1 g_2^{u_B})^x)^{2^{-1}} \pmod{p}$$

$$= (g_1 g_2^{(u_A + u_B) 2^{-1}})^x \pmod{p}$$

$$= \tilde{v}^x \pmod{p}$$

Here, User A withdraws the E-money with $(\tilde{v}, \tilde{u}, \tilde{w})$ and makes payments with this E-money and the generated identity $\tilde{u}$ in order to double-spend it without trouble.

Cryptanalysis of SPEED

(Extended Abstract)

Chris Hall[1], John Kelsey[1], Bruce Schneier[1], and David Wagner[2]

[1] Counterpane Systems
101 E. Minnehaha Pkwy
Minneapolis, MN 55419
(612) 823-1098
{hall,kelsey,schneier}@counterpane.com
[2] U.C. at Berkeley
Soda Hall
Berkeley, CA 94720-1776
daw@cs.berkeley.edu

Abstract. The cipher family SPEED (and an associated hashing mode) was recently proposed in *Financial Cryptography '97*. In cryptanalyzing the cipher we found several troubling potential weaknesses. Next, we were able to efficiently break the SPEED hashing mode using differential related-key techniques. Finally, we examined differential attacks against the 48-round version of SPEED. These results raise some significant questions about the security of the SPEED design.

1 Introduction

In *Financial Cryptography '97*, Zheng proposed a new family of block ciphers, called SPEED [1]. One specifies a particular SPEED cipher by choosing parameters such as the block size and number of rounds; the variations are otherwise alike in their key schedule and round structure. Under the hood, SPEED is built out of an unbalanced Feistel network. Zheng also proposed a hash function based on running a SPEED block cipher in a slightly modified Davies-Meyer mode.

One of the main contributions of the SPEED design is its prominent use of carefully chosen Boolean functions which can be shown to have very good non-linearity, as well as other desirable theoretical properties. One might therefore hope that SPEED rests on a solid theoretical foundation in cryptographic Boolean function theory. Nonetheless, we have found serious weaknesses in the cipher; many lead to practical attacks on SPEED.

In examining the cipher there appears to be an obvious 1-bit differential attack which works with probability 2^{-50} against the 48-round version of the cipher. However, our analysis indicates that this attack may in fact fail to work. A future paper will address the strength of SPEED against differential cryptanalysis in greater detail.

Despite our difficulties with the differential attack, we succeeded in finding collisions for the SPEED hash function. For the 128-bit hash with 32 rounds, we found the following collision (in base-16):

$$M = \text{21EA FE8E 1637 19F7 22D2 8CCB} \quad M' = \text{21EA FE8E 1637 19F7 22D2 8CCB}$$

M =	21EA FE8E 1637 19F7 22D2 8CCB	M' =	21EA FE8E 1637 19F7 22D2 8CCB
	3724 3437 B00F 7607 3C91 3710		3724 3437 B00F 7607 3C91 3710
	2B69 C9C9 58FB 0823 AEC2 CD05		2B69 C9C9 58FB 0823 AEC2 CD05
	FD80 14E6 B11E 43C0 5767 76F7		FDC0 14E6 B11E 4380 5767 76F7
	FF07 17EC FCBA 224E 9627 A16A		FF07 17EC 7CBA 224E 9627 216A
	8D6E 83A9		8D6E 83A9

This leads to the following values when hashing (in base-16):

$$D_0 = \text{0000 0000 0000 0000 0000 0000 0000 0000}$$
$$D_1 = \text{90DA 7F34 46FA A373 B048 11F7 F8D9 BB3D}$$
$$D_2 - D_1 = \text{9781 9517 B5CC A046 D0F1 3719 ED9B A0B6}$$

We also found the following collision for the 128-bit hash with 48 rounds (in base-16):

M =	3725 6571 48D5 CF52 DAE1 4065	M' =	3725 6571 48D5 CF52 DAE1 4065
	7115 11A0 E3C5 9428 7BFD 18CB		7115 11A0 E3C5 9428 7BFD 18CB
	EF79 82BB 1D7F 2F55 36F2 CD58		EF79 82BB 1D7F 2F55 38F2 CB58
	9058 FE57 D696 EA4C BD75 F7C9		9058 FC57 D896 EA4C BD75 F7C9
	1989 A048 39FB 9B76 9011 CAC0		1985 A04C 39FB 9B7A 900D CAC0
	65F6 EBC7		65F6 EBC7

This leads to the following values when hashing (in base-16):

$$D_0 = \text{0000 0000 0000 0000 0000 0000 0000 0000}$$
$$D_1 = \text{DA2B A119 A4F8 AA70 59ED 6FE4 188B 7969}$$
$$D_2 - D_1 = \text{CAB1 DA86 B6D3 1442 E05C A005 7B26 C432}$$

2 Conclusions

It is interesting to note that SPEED, though built using very strong component functions, doesn't appear to be terribly secure. The SPEED design apparently relied upon the high quality of the binary functions used, the fact that different functions were used at different points in the cipher, and the data-dependent rotations to provide resistance to cryptanalysis. Unfortunately, the most effective attacks aren't made much less powerful by any of these defenses.

Due to these weaknesses, we would recommend against using SPEED for high security applications. It's not clear whether or not someone could design a security cipher using the same sort of boolean function theory. Therefore the utility of these functions in cipher design is still an open avenue of research.

References

1. Y. Zheng, "The SPEED Cipher," in Proceedings of *Financial Cryptography '97*, Springer-Verlag.

Author Index

Springer
and the
environment

At Springer we firmly believe that an international science publisher has a special obligation to the environment, and our corporate policies consistently reflect this conviction.

We also expect our business partners – paper mills, printers, packaging manufacturers, etc. – to commit themselves to using materials and production processes that do not harm the environment. The paper in this book is made from low- or no-chlorine pulp and is acid free, in conformance with international standards for paper permanency.

Lecture Notes in Computer Science

For information about Vols. 1–1386

please contact your bookseller or Springer-Verlag

Vol. 1424: L. Polkowski, A. Skowron (Eds.), Rough Sets and Current Trends in Computing. Proceedings, 1998. XIII, 626 pages. 1998. (Subseries LNAI).

Vol. 1425: D. Hutchison, R. Schäfer (Eds.), Multimedia Applications, Services and Techniques – ECMAST'98. Proceedings, 1998. XVI, 532 pages. 1998.

Vol. 1427: A.J. Hu, M.Y. Vardi (Eds.), Computer Aided Verification. Proceedings, 1998. IX, 552 pages. 1998.

Vol. 1429: F. van der Linden (Ed.), Development and Evolution of Software Architectures for Product Families. Proceedings, 1998. IX, 258 pages. 1998.

Vol. 1430: S. Trigila, A. Mullery, M. Campolargo, H. Vanderstraeten, M. Mampaey (Eds.), Intelligence in Services and Networks: Technology for Ubiquitous Telecom Services. Proceedings, 1998. XII, 550 pages. 1998.

Vol. 1431: H. Imai, Y. Zheng (Eds.), Public Key Cryptography. Proceedings, 1998. XI, 263 pages. 1998.

Vol. 1432: S. Arnborg, L. Ivansson (Eds.), Algorithm Theory – SWAT '98. Proceedings, 1998. IX, 347 pages. 1998.

Vol. 1433: V. Honavar, G. Slutzki (Eds.), Grammatical Inference. Proceedings, 1998. X, 271 pages. 1998. (Subseries LNAI).

Vol. 1434: J.-C. Heudin (Ed.), Virtual Worlds. Proceedings, 1998. XII, 412 pages. 1998. (Subseries LNAI).

Vol. 1435: M. Klusch, G. Weiß (Eds.), Cooperative Information Agents II. Proceedings, 1998. IX, 307 pages. 1998. (Subseries LNAI).

Vol. 1436: D. Wood, S. Yu (Eds.), Automata Implementation. Proceedings, 1997. VIII, 253 pages. 1998.

Vol. 1437: S. Albayrak, F.J. Garijo (Eds.), Intelligent Agents for Telecommunication Applications. Proceedings, 1998. XII, 251 pages. 1998. (Subseries LNAI).

Vol. 1438: C. Boyd, E. Dawson (Eds.), Information Security and Privacy. Proceedings, 1998. XI, 423 pages. 1998.

Vol. 1439: B. Magnusson (Ed.), System Configuration Management. Proceedings, 1998. X, 207 pages. 1998.

Vol. 1441: W. Wobcke, M. Pagnucco, C. Zhang (Eds.), Agents and Multi-Agent Systems. Proceedings, 1997. XII, 241 pages. 1998. (Subseries LNAI).

Vol. 1442: A. Fiat. G.J. Woeginger (Eds.), Online Algorithms. XVIII, 436 pages. 1998.

Vol. 1443: K.G. Larsen, S. Skyum, G. Winskel (Eds.), Automata, Languages and Programming. Proceedings, 1998. XVI, 932 pages. 1998.

Vol. 1444: K. Jansen, J. Rolim (Eds.), Approximation Algorithms for Combinatorial Optimization. Proceedings, 1998. VIII, 201 pages. 1998.

Vol. 1445: E. Jul (Ed.), ECOOP'98 – Object-Oriented Programming. Proceedings, 1998. XII, 635 pages. 1998.

Vol. 1446: D. Page (Ed.), Inductive Logic Programming. Proceedings, 1998. VIII, 301 pages. 1998. (Subseries LNAI).

Vol. 1447: V.W. Porto, N. Saravanan, D. Waagen, A.E. Eiben (Eds.), Evolutionary Programming VII. Proceedings, 1998. XVI, 840 pages. 1998.

Vol. 1448: M. Farach-Colton (Ed.), Combinatorial Pattern Matching. Proceedings, 1998. VIII, 251 pages. 1998.

Vol. 1449: W.-L. Hsu, M.-Y. Kao (Eds.), Computing and Combinatorics. Proceedings, 1998. XII, 372 pages. 1998.

Vol. 1450: L. Brim, F. Gruska, J. Zlatuška (Eds.), Mathematical Foundations of Computer Science 1998. Proceedings, 1998. XVII, 846 pages. 1998.

Vol. 1451: A. Amin, D. Dori, P. Pudil, H. Freeman (Eds.), Advances in Pattern Recognition. Proceedings, 1998. XXI, 1048 pages. 1998.

Vol. 1452: B.P. Goettl, H.M. Halff, C.L. Redfield, V.J. Shute (Eds.), Intelligent Tutoring Systems. Proceedings, 1998. XIX, 629 pages. 1998.

Vol. 1453: M.-L. Mugnier, M. Chein (Eds.), Conceptual Structures: Theory, Tools and Applications. Proceedings, 1998. XIII, 439 pages. (Subseries LNAI).

Vol. 1454: I. Smith (Ed.), Artificial Intelligence in Structural Engineering. XI, 497 pages. 1998. (Subseries LNAI).

Vol. 1456: A. Drogoul, M. Tambe, T. Fukuda (Eds.), Collective Robotics. Proceedings, 1998. VII, 161 pages. 1998. (Subseries LNAI).

Vol. 1457: A. Ferreira, J. Rolim, H. Simon, S.-H. Teng (Eds.), Solving Irregularly Structured Problems in Prallel. Proceedings, 1998. X, 408 pages. 1998.

Vol. 1458: V.O. Mittal, H.A. Yanco, J. Aronis, R-. Simpson (Eds.), Assistive Technology in Artificial Intelligence. X, 273 pages. 1998. (Subseries LNAI).

Vol. 1459: D.G. Feitelson, L. Rudolph (Eds.), Job Scheduling Strategies for Parallel Processing. Proceedings, 1998. VII, 257 pages. 1998.

Vol. 1460: G. Quirchmayr, E. Schweighofer, T.J.M. Bench-Capon (Eds.), Database and Expert Systems Applications. Proceedings, 1998. XVI, 905 pages. 1998.

Vol. 1461: G. Bilardi, G.F. Italiano, A. Pietracaprina, G. Pucci (Eds.), Algorithms – ESA'98. Proceedings, 1998. XII, 516 pages. 1998.

Vol. 1462: H. Krawczyk (Ed.), Advances in Cryptology - CRYPTO '98. Proceedings, 1998. XII, 519 pages. 1998.

Vol. 1464: H.H.S. Ip, A.W.M. Smeulders (Eds.), Multimedia Information Analysis and Retrieval. Proceedings, 1998. VIII, 264 pages. 1998.

Vol. 1465: R. Hirschfeld (Ed.), Financial Cryptography. Proceedings, 1998. VIII, 311 pages. 1998.

Vol. 1466: D. Sangiorgi, R. de Simone (Eds.), CONCUR'98: Concurrency Theory. Proceedings, 1998. XI, 657 pages. 1998.

Vol. 1467: C. Clack, K. Hammond, T. Davie (Eds.), Implementation of Functional Languages. Proceedings, 1997. X, 375 pages. 1998.

Vol. 1469: R. Puigjaner, N.N. Savino, B. Serra (Eds.), Computer Performance Evaluation. Proceedings, 1998. XIII, 376 pages. 1998.

Vol. 1473: X. Leroy, A. Ohori (Eds.), Types in Compilation. Proceedings, 1998. VIII, 299 pages. 1998.

Vol. 1475: W. Litwin, T. Morzy, G. Vossen (Eds.), Advances in Databases and Information Systems. Proceedings, 1998. XIV, 369 pages. 1998.

Vol. 1482: R.W. Hartenstein, A. Keevallik (Eds.), Field-Programmable Logic and Applications. Proceedings, 1998. XI, 533 pages. 1998.